OFFICIAL

BLUE BOOK OF UNITED STATES COINS ®

# 1983 HANDBOOK OF UNITED STATES COINS

*With Premium List*

*By* R. S. YEOMAN

★

*FORTIETH EDITION*

*Edited by Kenneth Bressett*

**Containing mint records and prices paid by dealers for all U.S. coins from 1616 to the present time, including Colonials, Regular Issues, Commemoratives, Territorials, Gold, Proof Sets, and Mint Sets. Information on collecting coins—how coins are produced—mints and mint marks—grading of coins—location of mint marks—preserving and cleaning coins—starting a collection—history of mints and interesting descriptions of all U.S. copper, nickel, silver and gold coins. Fully illustrated.**

**Whitman Coin Products**



9050-83 ISBN: 0-307-01983-7 Printed in U.S.A.

# *Important Notice*

## THIS BOOK IS *NOT A RETAIL PRICE LIST*

*Premium prices are the average amount dealers will pay for coins (according to condition) if required for their stock.*

**(See page 11)**

Current *retail* valuations of all U.S. coins are listed in Whitman's A GUIDE BOOK OF UNITED STATES COINS by R. S. Yeoman, Western Publishing Company, Inc., Racine, Wisconsin ($5.95)

Brief guides to grading are placed before each major coin type in this book. For those readers who desire more detailed descriptions of all coin grades, we recommend OFFICIAL A.N.A. GRADING STANDARDS FOR UNITED STATES COINS, Western Publishing Company, Inc., Racine, Wisconsin ($6.95).

# *Foreword*

Since 1941, annually revised editions of this Handbook have aided thousands of people who have coins to sell or are actively engaged in collecting United States coins. The popular coin folder method of collecting by date has created ever-changing premium values, based on the supply and demand of each date and mint. Through its panel of contributors the Handbook has, over the years, reported these changing values. It also serves as a source of general numismatic information to all levels of interest in the hobby.

The premium list gives representative prices paid by dealers for various United States coins. These are averages of prices assembled from many widely separated sources. On some issues slight differences in price among dealers may result from proximity to the various mints or heavily populated centers. Other factors, such as local supply and demand or dealers' stock conditions, may also tend to cause deviations from the prices listed. While many coins bring no premium when circulated, they usually bring premium prices in Uncirculated and Proof condition.

*The publisher of this book does not deal in coins; therefore, the values shown here are not offers to purchase (or sell) but are included only as general information.*

## IF YOU HAVE COINS TO SELL

The publishers are not engaged in the rare coin business; however, the chances are that the dealer from whom you purchased this book is engaged in the buying and selling of rare coins—contact him first. In the event that you purchased this book from a source other than a numismatic establishment, consult your local telephone directory for the names of coin dealers (they will be found sometimes under the heading of "Stamp and Coin Dealers"). If you live in a city or town that does not have any coin dealers, it is suggested that you obtain a copy of one of the trade publications in order to obtain the names and addresses of many of the country's leading dealers.

Several popular magazines and papers are devoted to coin collecting:

COINage Magazine
17337 Ventura Boulevard
Encino, California 91316

Hobbies Magazine
1006 S. Michigan Ave.
Chicago, Ill. 60605
(Has a coin section)

Coins Magazine
Iola, Wisconsin 54990

Numismatic News Weekly
Iola, Wisconsin 54990

Coin World
P.O. Box 150
Sidney, Ohio 45367

The Numismatist
P.O. Box 2366
Colorado Springs, Colorado 80901
(Published monthly by American Numismatic Assn.)

# CONTRIBUTORS

Lee F. Hewitt, the former editor and publisher of the NUMISMATIC SCRAPBOOK MAGAZINE, was an early contributor, having supplied many of the historical references and explanations which appear throughout this book.

Charles E. Green gave valuable counsel when the first edition of the HANDBOOK was undertaken. He supplied most of the mint data and was a regular contributor to each revised edition until his death in 1955.

# CONTRIBUTORS TO THE FORTIETH EDITION

Dolores Toll — *Coordinating Editor*

Kamal M. Ahwash
Kamal M. Ahwash, Ltd.
P.O. Box 422
Media, PA 19063

Burl Armstrong
B & M Coins
802 Avenue G, Suite 3
Fort Madison, IA 52627

Michael Aron
Michael Aron Coin Auctions
P.O. Box 33166
Granada Hills, CA 91344

Richard August
Box 2
Ashton, RI 02864

Richard A. Bagg
Bowers and Ruddy Galleries
P.O. Box 2745
Boston, MA 02208

Robert F. Batchelder
Robert F. Batchelder Company
1 West Butler Avenue
Ambler, PA 19002

Gerald L. Bauman
Manfra, Tordella & Brookes, Inc.
59 West 49th Street
New York, NY 10112

Lee J. Bellisario
Bellisario, Inc.
30 Chestnut Street
Boston, MA 02108

Philip E. Benedetti
Pickwick Coin Gallery
P.O. Box 7, Saugatuck Station
Westport, CT 06880

Jed Berman
Neil S. Berman
First Federal Coin Corporation
18 East 48th Street
New York, NY 10017

George H. Blenker
Lincoln Yellow, Inc.
Box 56
Blenker, WI 54415

Q. David Bowers
Bowers and Ruddy Galleries
5525 Wilshire Blvd.
Los Angeles, CA 90036

Phil Bressett
Viking Coin & Currency
1210 N. Green Bay Rd.
Racine, WI 53406

Hy Brown
Hy Brown, Inc.
P.O. Box 111
Painesville, OH 44077

Judy Cahn
Bowers and Ruddy Galleries, Inc.
5525 Wilshire Boulevard
Los Angeles, CA 90036

Bill Causey
American Gold & Silver Corp.
985 West Foothill Blvd.
Claremont, CA 91711

J. H. Cline
Cline's Rare Coins
4421 Salem Avenue
Dayton, OH 45416

Jerry Cohen
Coin Gallery
344 North Beverly Drive
Beverly Hills, CA 90210

Kurt Eckstein

Chuck Furjanic
P.O. Box 8739
Pittsburgh, PA 15221

Dorothy Gershenson
Dorothy Gershenson, Inc.
P.O. Box 395
Bala Cynwyd, PA 19004

Harry M. Gittelson

Ira M. Goldberg
Lawrence S. Goldberg
Superior Stamp & Coin Co., Inc.
9301 Wilshire Blvd.
Beverly Hills, CA 90210

Kenneth M. Goldman
Kenneth Goldman, Inc.
P.O. Box 1477
Boston, MA 02104

David Hall

David Hendrickson
Leon Hendrickson
Silver Towne
P.O. Box 424
Winchester, IN 47394

C. Edward Hipps
Ed Hipps' Gallery
9100 North Central Expressway, #143
Dallas, TX 75231

Ed Hipps, Jr.
Ed Hipps' Gallery
624 Levittown Center
Levittown, PA 19055

Ron Howard
Kagin's Numismatic Investments
4 Embarcadero, Suite 2800
San Francisco, CA 94111

John Hunter
Silver Towne
P.O. Box 424
Winchester, IN 47394

Robert H. Jacobs
Jake's Marketplace, Inc.
2955 North Central Avenue
Chicago, IL 60634

Floyd O. Janney
Universal Numismatics Corp.
P.O. Box 469
Richland Center, WI 53581

James J. Jelinski
Essex Numismatics, Inc.
Eight Cannon Road
Wilton, CT 06897

A. M. Kagin
Donald Kagin
1000 Insurance Exchange Bldg.
Des Moines, IA 50309

Paul Kagin

David W. Karp
James, Inc.
P.O. Box 18088
Louisville, KY 40218

Stanley Kesselman

Mike Kliman
Numismatic Enterprises
P.O. Box 365
South Laguna, CA 92677

Abner Kreisberg
Coin Gallery
344 North Beverly Drive
Beverly Hills, CA 90210

Ed. Leventhal
J. J. Teaparty
43 Bromfield
Boston, MA 02108

Stuart Levine
Kearsarge House Rare Coins, Inc.
104 Congress Street
Portsmouth, NH 03801

Dennis W. Loring

Robert T. McIntire
McIntire Rare Coins & Auctions
Camelot Inn (Arcade)
Markham & Springs Sts.
Little Rock, AR 72201

Bill Mertes
1206 North 11th Avenue
St. Cloud, MN 56301

Sylvia Novack
P.O. Box 729
San Bernardino, CA 92402

Sidney L. Nusbaum
St. Louis, MO

William P. Paul
American Heritage Minting, Inc.
Benjamin Fox Pavilion, Suite 510
Box 1008
Jenkintown, PA 19046

Joe Person
Joe Person & Co., Inc.
Bank of Florida Bldg., Suite 2
1101 Pasadena Avenue, South
St. Petersburg, FL 33707

Lewis Revels
Chattanooga Coin & Stamp
P.O. Box 80125
824 Chickamauga Avenue
Chattanooga, TN 37411

Maurice Rosen
Numismatic Counseling, Inc.
P.O. Box 231
East Meadow, NY 11554

Earl Schill
1764 City National Bank Building
Detroit, MI 48226

Robert R. Shaw

Maurice A. Storck, Sr.
P.O. Box 644
Portland, ME 04104-0644

Charles Surasky
Essex Numismatics, Inc.
Eight Cannon Road
Wilton, CT 06897

Gary L. Young
Gary L. Young, Numismatist
P.O. Box 9
Manton, CA 96059

# COLLECTING COINS

Numismatics or coin collecting is one of the world's oldest hobbies, dating back several centuries. Coin collecting in America did not develop to any extent until about 1840, as our pioneer forefathers were too busy carving a country out of wilderness to afford the luxury of a hobby. The discontinuance of the large-sized cent in 1857 caused many persons to attempt to accumulate a complete set of the pieces while they were still in circulation. One of the first groups of collectors to band together for the study of numismatics was the Numismatic and Antiquarian Society of Philadelphia, organized on January 1, 1858. Lack of an economical method to house a collection held the number of devotees of coin collecting to a few thousand until the Whitman Publishing Company and other manufacturers placed the low-priced coin boards and folders on the market some years ago. Since that time the number of Americans collecting coins has increased many-fold.

## *The Production of Coins*

To collect coins intelligently it is necessary to have some knowledge of the manner in which our coins are produced. They are made in factories called "mints." The Mint of the United States was established at Philadelphia by a resolution of Congress dated April 2, 1792. The Act also provided for the coinage of gold eagles ($10), half-eagles and quarter-eagles, the silver dollar, half-dollar, quarter-dollar, dime (originally spelled "disme") and the half-disme or half-dime; the copper cent and half cent. According to the Treasury Department, the first coins struck were one-cent and half-cent pieces, in March of 1793 on a hand-operated press. Most numismatic authorities consider the half-disme of 1792 as the first United States coinage, quoting the words of George Washington as their authority. Washington, in his annual address, November 6, 1792, having said, "There has been a small beginning in the coining of the Half-Dimes, the want of small coins in circulation calling the first attention to them." In the new Philadelphia Mint are exhibited a number of implements, etc., from the original mint, and some coins discovered when the old building was wrecked. These coins included half-dismes, and the placard identifying them states that Washington furnished the silver and gave the coined pieces to his friends as souvenirs.

Prior to the adoption of the Constitution, the Continental Congress arranged for the issuance of copper coins under private contract. These are known as the "Fugio cents" from the design of the piece, which shows a sundial and the Latin word "fugio"—"I Fly" or, in connection with the sundial, "Time Flies." The ever appropriate motto. "Mind Your Business," is also on the coin.

In the manufacture of a given coin the first step is the cutting of the "die." Prior to the latter part of the nineteenth century dies for United States coins were "cut by hand." Briefly this method is as follows: The design having been determined, a drawing the exact size of the coin is made. A tracing is made from this drawing. A piece of steel is smoothed and coated with transfer wax, and the tracing impressed into the wax. The engraver then tools out the steel where the relief or raised effect is required. If the design is such that it can all be produced by cutting away steel, the die is hardened and ready for use. Some dies are not brought to a finished state, as some part of the design can perhaps be done better in relief. In that case, when all that can be accomplished to advantage in the die is completed, it is hardened, a soft-steel impression is taken from it, and the unfinished parts are then completed. This piece of steel is in turn hardened and, by a press, driven into another piece of soft-steel, thus making a die which, when hardened, is ready for the making of coins.

This hand method of cutting dies accounts for the many die varieties of early United States coins. Where the amount of coinage of a given year was large enough to wear out several dies, each new die placed in the coining press created another die variety of that year. The dies being cut by hand, no two were exactly alike in every detail, even though some of the major elements (head, wreath, etc.) were sunk into the die by individual master punches. Of the cents dated 1794, over sixty different die varieties have been discovered.

Hundreds of dies are now used by the mints of the United States each year, but they are all made from one master die, which is produced in the following manner:

After the design is settled upon, the plaster of paris or wax model is prepared several times the actual size of the coin. When this model is finished an electrotype (an exact duplicate in metal) is made and prepared for the reducing lathe. The reducing lathe is a machine, working on the principle of the pantograph, only in this case the one point traces or follows the form of the model while another and much smaller point in the form of a drill cuts away the steel and produces a reduced size die of the model. The die is finished and details are sharpened or worked over by an engraver with chisel and graver. The master die is used to make duplicates in soft-steel which are then hardened and ready for the coining press. To harden dies, they are placed in cast-iron boxes packed with carbon to exclude the air, and when heated to a bright red are cooled suddenly with water.

In the coinage operations the first step is to prepare the metal. The alloys used are: silver coins, 90% silver and 10% copper; five-cent pieces, 75% copper and 25% nickel; one-cent pieces, 95% copper and 5% zinc. (The 1943 cent consists of steel coated with zinc; and the five-cent piece 1942-1945 contains 35% silver, 56% copper and 9% manganese.) Under the Coinage Act of 1965, the composition of dimes, quarters and half dollars was changed to eliminate or reduce the silver content of these coins. The copper-nickel "clad" dimes, quarters, halves and dollars are composed of an outer layer of copper-nickel (75% copper and 25% nickel) bonded to an inner core of pure copper. The silver clad half dollar and dollar have an outer layer of 80% silver bonded to an inner core of 21% silver, with a total content of 40% silver.

Alloys are melted in crucibles and poured into molds to form ingots. The ingots are in the form of thin bars and vary in size according to the denomination of the coin. The width is sufficient to allow three or more coins to be cut from the strips.

The ingots are next put through rolling mills to reduce the thickness to required limits. The strips are then fed into cutting presses which cut circular blanks (planchets) of the approximate size of the finished coin. The blanks are run through annealing furnaces to soften them; next through tumbling barrels, rotating cyclinders containing cleaning solutions which clean and burnish the metal, and finally into centrifugal drying machines.

The blanks are next fed into a milling machine which produces the raised or upset rim. The blank is now ready for the coining press.

The blank is held firmly by a collar, as it is struck under heavy pressure varying from 40 tons for the one-cent pieces and dimes to 170 tons for silver dollars. Upper and lower dies impress the design on both sides of the coin. The pressure is sufficient to produce a raised surface level with that of the milled rim. The collar holding the blank for silver or clad coins is grooved. The pressure forces the metal into the grooves of the collar, producing the "reeding" on the finished coin.

## *How a Proof Coin Is Made*

Selected dies are inspected for perfection and are highly polished and cleaned. They are again wiped clean or polished after every 15 to 25 impressions and are replaced frequently to avoid imperfections from worn dies. Coinage blanks are polished and cleaned to assure high quality in striking. They are then hand fed into the coinage press one at a time, each blank receiving two blows from the dies to bring up sharp, high relief details. The coinage operation is done at slow speed with extra pressure. Finished proofs are individually inspected and are handled by gloves or tongs. They also receive a final inspection by packers before being sonically sealed in special plastic cases.

Certain coins, including Lincoln cents, Buffalo nickels, Quarter Eagles, Half Eagles, Eagles and Double Eagles, between the years 1908 and 1916 were made with a matte or sandblast surface. Matte proofs have a dull frosted surface which is produced by special treatment after striking.

## *Mints and Mint Marks*

In addition to the Philadelphia Mint, the U.S. Government has from time to time established branch mints in various parts of the country. At the present time a branch mint operates in Denver. Starting in 1968, proof sets and some of the regular coins are produced at the San Francisco Assay Office. The Denver Mint has operated since 1906. A mint was operated at New Orleans from 1838 to 1861 and again from 1879 to 1909. Mints were also in service at Carson City, Nevada, from 1870 to 1893; at Charlotte, North Carolina, from 1838 to 1861; at Dahlonega, Georgia, from 1838 to 1861; and at San Francisco since 1854.

Coins struck at Philadelphia before 1979 (except 1942 to 1945 five-cent pieces) do not carry a mint mark. The mint mark is found only on coins struck at the branch mints. It is a small letter, usually found on the reverse side. The Lincoln cent is one exception to the rule. All coins minted after 1967 have the mint mark on the obverse. The letters to signify the various mints are as follows:

"C" for Charlotte, North Carolina (on gold coins only).
"CC" for Carson City, Nevada.
"D" for Dahlonega, Georgia (gold coins only, 1838 to 1861).
"D" For Denver, Colorado (from 1906 to date).
"O" for New Orleans, Louisiana.
"P" for Philadelphia, Pennsylvania.
"S" for San Francisco, California.

The mint mark is of utmost importance to collectors due to the fact that the coinage at the branch mints has usually been much smaller than at Philadelphia and many of the branch mint pieces are very scarce.

## DISTINGUISHING MARKS

The illustrations and explanations in this section will help the collector to identify certain well-known varieties.

HALF CENTS OF
1795-1796
SHOWING LOCATION OF
POLE TO CAP

The end of the staff or pole lies parallel with the line of the bust, which is pointed. The die-maker, probably through error, omitted the pole on some of the dies of 1795 and 1796.

Pole to Cap

No Pole to Cap

Stemless Wreath

Stems to Wreath

STEMLESS WREATH VARIETY OF HALF CENTS AND LARGE CENTS

Observe the reverse side for this variety. Illustrations at left show both stemless and stems to wreath types for each comparison—stemless wreath found on 1804, 1805, 1806, Half cents. 1797, 1802, 1803 Large cents.

1804 HALF CENT PROTRUDING
TONGUE OR SPIKED CHIN VARIETY

# DISTINGUISHING MARKS

Details showing differences in 1804 plain 4 and crosslet 4. Note serif on horizontal bar of figure 4 as shown at right.

Plain 4

Crosslet 4

THE 1856 FLYING EAGLE CENT

Collectors are advised to inspect any 1856 Flying Eagle cent carefully.

A few tests will aid in establishing genuineness of this cent, as follows:

THE DATE

The 6 in the date should be as illustrated. If the lower half is thick, it is probably an altered 1858. A magnifying glass will often reveal poor workmanship.

The figure 5 slants slightly to the right on a genuine 1856. The vertical bar points to the center of the ball just beneath. On the 1858, this bar points *outside* the ball. (Compare the two illustrations.)

THE LEGEND

The center of the O in OF is crude and almost squared on the genuine 1856, but on the large letter 1858 it is rounded.

The letters A and M in America are joined in both the 1856 and large letter 1858, but they join at a slight angle on the 1856, while the bottom of the letters form a smooth curve on the 1858 large letter cent.

1858 FLYING EAGLE CENT

Large Letters

Letters A and M in the word AMERICA are joined on the LARGE LETTER variety. They are separated on the SMALL LETTER variety.

Small Letters

1864 BRONZE INDIAN HEAD CENT WITH "L" ON RIBBON

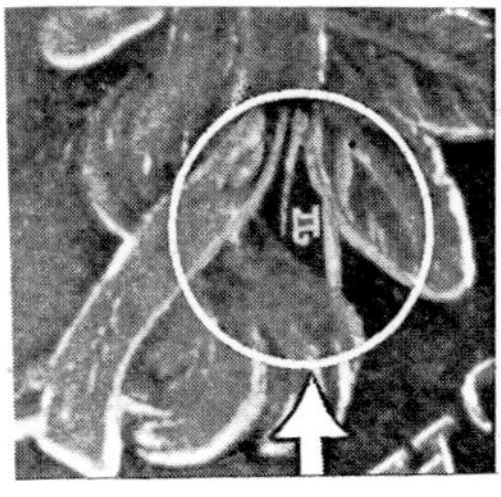

A small "L," the initial of the designer Longacre, was added to the Indian design late in 1864 and was continued through 1909. For coins in less than fine condition, this small letter will often be worn away. The point of the bust is rounded on the 1864 variety without "L"; pointed on the variety with "L." The initial must be visible, however, for the 1864 variety to bring the higher premium. If the coin is turned slightly so that the Indian faces the observer, the highlighted details will usually appear to better advantage.

# DISTINGUISHING MARKS

## LINCOLN CENTS SHOWING LOCATION OF INITIALS V D B

During 1909 initials appeared on reverse. Starting in 1918 they appear below the shoulder.

1918-S Quarter
8 Over 7
A variety of this kind is rarely found in coinage of the twentieth century.

1938D over S Nickel Variety

1942 Dime with 2 over 1

1955 Cent Error
"Doubled Die" Obverse

Large Date Cent
1960

Small Date Cent
1960

## CONDITION OF COINS

### *Essential elements of the A.N.A. grading system*

PROOF — A specially made coin distinguished by sharpness of detail and usually with a brilliant mirrorlike surface. Proof refers to the method of manufacture and is not a condition, but normally the term implies perfect mint state unless otherwise noted. See page 40 for details.

MINT STATE — The terms Mint State (MS) and Uncirculated (Unc.) are interchangeably used to describe coins showing no trace of wear. Such coins may vary to some degree because of blemishes, toning or slight imperfections as described in the following three subdivisions.

PERFECT UNCIRCULATED (MS-70) — Perfect new condition, showing no trace of wear. The finest quality possible, with no evidence of scratches, handling or contact with other coins. Very few regular issue coins are ever found in this condition.

CHOICE UNCIRCULATED (MS-65) — An above average Uncirculated coin which may be brilliant or lightly toned and has very few contact marks on the surface or rim. MS-67 or MS-63 indicates a slightly higher or lower grade of preservation.

UNCIRCULATED (MS-60) — Has no trace of wear but may show a number of contact marks, and surface may be spotted or lack some luster.

CHOICE ABOUT UNCIRCULATED (AU-55) — Barest evidence of light wear on only the highest points of the design. Most of the mint luster remains.

ABOUT UNCIRCULATED (AU-50) — Has traces of light wear on many of the high points. At least half of the mint luster is still present.

CHOICE EXTREMELY FINE (EF-45) — Light overall wear shows on highest points. All design details are very sharp. Some of the mint luster is evident.

EXTREMELY FINE (EF-40) — Design is lightly worn throughout, but all features are sharp and well defined. Traces of luster may show.

CHOICE VERY FINE (VF-30) — Light even wear on the surface and highest parts of the design. All lettering and major features are sharp.

VERY FINE (VF-20) — Shows moderate wear on high points of design. All major details are clear.

FINE (F-12) — Moderate to considerable even wear. Entire design is bold with overall pleasing appearance.

VERY GOOD (VG-8) — Well worn with main features clear and bold although rather flat.

GOOD (G-4) — Heavily worn with design visible but faint in areas. Many details are flat.

ABOUT GOOD (AG-3) — Very heavily worn with portions of lettering, date and legends worn smooth. The date may be barely readable.

IMPORTANT: Damaged coins, such as those which are bent, corroded, scratched, holed, nicked, stained, oxidized, or mutilated, are worth less than those without defects. *Flawless uncirculated coins are generally worth more than values quoted in this book.* Slightly worn coins which have been cleaned and conditioned to simulate uncirculated luster are worth considerably less than perfect pieces.

Manufacturing defects do not lessen value as much as other damage. Examples are: Colonial coins with planchet flaws and weakly struck designs; early silver and gold with weight adjustment "file marks" (parallel cuts made prior to striking); and proofs with "lint marks" (dust particles which mar the surface during striking).

Brief guides to grading are placed before each major coin type in this book. For those readers who desire more detailed descriptions of all coin grades, we recommend OFFICIAL A.N.A. GRADING STANDARDS FOR UNITED STATES COINS, by the American Numismatic Association.

## *Preserving and Cleaning Coins*

Most numismatists will tell you to "never clean a coin" and it is good advice! Cleaning coins will almost always reduce their value.

Some effort should be made to keep uncirculated and proof coins bright so they won't need cleaning. Tarnish on a coin is purely a chemical process caused by oxygen in the air acting on the metal or by chemicals with which the coin comes in contact. One of the commonest chemicals causing tarnish is sulphur; most paper, with the exception of specially manufactured "sulphur-free" kinds, contains sulphur due to the sulphuric acid that is used in paper manufacture. Therefore do not wrap coins in ordinary paper; also keep uncirculated and proof coins away from rubber bands (a rubber band placed on a silver coin for a few days will produce a black stripe on the coin where the band touched). The utmost in protection is obtained by storing the coin in an airtight box.

Many coins become marred by careless handling. Always hold the coin by the edge. The accompanying illustration shows the right and wrong way to handle numismatic specimens. It is a breach of numismatic etiquette to handle another collector's coin except by the edge, even if it is not an uncirculated or proof piece.

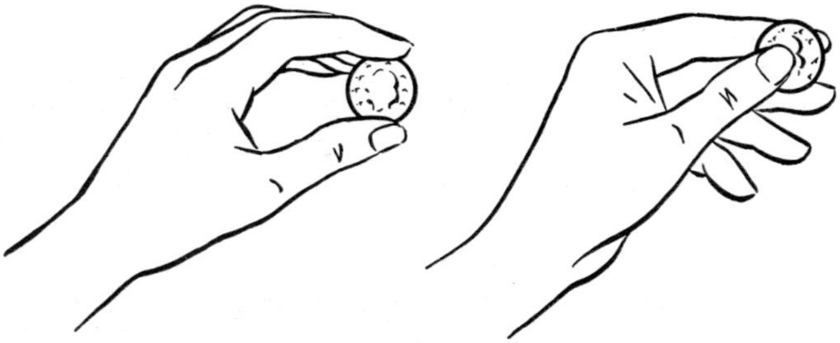

RIGHT WRONG

## *Starting a Collection*

One may start a collection of United States coins with very little expense by systematically assembling the various dates and mint marks of all the types and denominations that are now in general circulation. Whitman's coin folders make this possible.

With the exception of the price paid for the coin folder, collecting coins received in everyday business transactions entails no expense whatever; a Jefferson nickel taken out of circulation, for example, can always be spent for 5 cents if the occasion arrives. Filling an album or two out of circulation is probably the best method of determining whether coin collecting appeals to you. Not everyone can be a successful coin collector. It requires patience, intelligence of a high order, and a certain desire to know the meaning behind a lot of things that at first glance and to the ordinary mortal appear meaningless. You may not be cut out to be a collector but you'll never know until you look further into the subject, and if by the time an album or two of coins are collected you have no burning desire to acquire many more different coins, you will probably never be a collector. However, the chances are that you will be, because if you have read this far in this book it shows that you are interested in the subject.

Perfection is the goal of every endeavor and coin collecting is no exception. After an album has been filled with circulated specimens, the next step will be to replace them with coins in uncirculated condition, or perhaps to start collecting an obsolete series; in either case, it will be necessary to purchase some coins from dealers or other collectors. The most logical way to keep abreast with the market, or obtain the addresses of the country's leading dealers, is to subscribe to one or more of the trade publications (see page 3 for list of the coin publications). These magazines carry advertisements of various dealers listing coins for sale. Moreover, through this source the beginner may obtain price lists and catalogs from the dealers.

There are several good reference books available at reasonable prices which will be helpful to the collector who wishes to know more about U. S. coins and paper money. The GUIDEBOOK OF U. S. COINS (Red Book) is an expanded version of THE HANDBOOK. It lists retail values of all regular U. S. coins and also lists all coins of the U. S. Colonial period and private and territorial gold coins.

Most coin, book and hobby dealers can supply the following titles:

*Guide Book of U.S. Coins* — Yeoman
*Let's Collect Coins* — Bressett
*Prices for Buying and Selling U.S. Coins* — Bressett
*Official Grading Standards for U.S. Coins* — A.N.A.
*Common Sense Coin Investment* — Bowers
*Basics of Coin Grading* — Bressett

### *Join a Coin Club*

A beginner should join a "coin club" if he is fortunate enough to live in a city which has one. The association with more experienced collectors will be of great benefit. Practically all the larger cities have one or more clubs and they are being rapidly organized in the smaller towns. The publications mentioned on page 3 carry lists of coin clubs and special events such as coin shows and conventions.

## UNITED STATES PAPER MONEY

Paper money issued by the United States government is collected widely in this country. The first issue of "greenbacks" was made in 1861; paper money was not issued by our government for circulation prior to that date. Collectors of U.S. notes prefer them in crisp, new condition; but the old style large-sized notes even in worn condition are usually worth more than face value.

Before the issuance of the first U.S. government paper money, many banks throughout the country issued their own currency. These issues are commonly referred to as "broken bank notes" although that is somewhat of a misnomer as many of the banks did not "go broke" (a few are still in existence) and redeemed their paper money issues. There are thousands of varieties of these notes in existence, most of which are very common and worth from $1.00 to $3.00 each. Before and during the American Revolution the various individual states and the Continental Congress issued paper money. The common varieties of these Colonial notes are worth from $3.00 to $10.00; a few are quite rare.

# I. THE BRITISH COLONIES IN AMERICA

## SOMMER ISLANDS (Bermuda)

This coinage, the first struck for the English colonies in America, was issued about 1616. The coins were known as "Hogge Money" or "Hoggies."

The pieces were made of copper lightly silvered, in four denominations: shilling, sixpence, threepence and twopence, indicated by Roman numerals. The hog is the main device and appears on the obverse side of each. SOMMER ISLANDS is inscribed within beaded circles. The reverse shows a full-rigged galleon with the flag of St. George on each of four masts.

Shilling

| | Fair | Good | V. Good | Fine |
|---|---|---|---|---|
| Twopence | $500.00 | $1,000 | $1,750 | $4,000 |
| Threepence (V. Rare) | —— | —— | —— | —— |
| Sixpence | 350.00 | 700.00 | 1,500 | 3,500 |
| Shilling | 400.00 | 800.00 | 1,750 | 4,000 |

# MASSACHUSETTS

## "NEW ENGLAND" COINAGE (1652)

In 1652 the General Court of Massachusetts ordered the first metallic currency to be struck in the English Americas, the New England silver threepence, sixpence, and shilling. These coins were made from silver bullion procured principally from the West Indies. Joseph Jenks made the punches for the first coins at his Iron Works in Saugus, Massachusetts, close to Boston where the mint was located. John Hull was appointed mintmaster; his assistant was Robert Sanderson.

*Note: Early American coins are rare in conditions better than listed and valued much higher.*

NE Shilling (1652)

| | V. Good | Fine | V. Fine |
|---|---|---|---|
| NE Threepence *(2 known)* | —— | —— | —— |
| NE Sixpence *(7 known)* | —— | —— | $25,000 |
| NE Shilling | $2,000 | $5,000 | 9,000 |

# MASSACHUSETTS

## WILLOW TREE COINAGE (1653-1660)

The simplicity of the design on the N.E. coins invited counterfeiting and clipping of the edges. Therefore, they were soon replaced by the Willow, Oak and Pine Tree series. The Willow Tree coins were struck from 1653 to 1660, the Oak Trees 1660 to 1667, and the Pine Trees 1667 to 1682. All of them (with the exception of the Oak Tree twopence) bore the date 1652.

Many varieties of all of these coins exist. Values shown are for the most common types.

Sixpence

| | *Fair* | *Good* | *Fine* |
|---|---|---|---|
| Willow Tree Threepence 1652 *(3 known)*. | — | — | — |
| Willow Tree Sixpence 1652 . . . . . . . . . . . . . | — | — | — |
| Willow Tree Shilling 1652 . . . . . . . . . . . . . . | $1,500 | $3,500 | $6,500 |

## OAK TREE COINAGE (1660-1667)

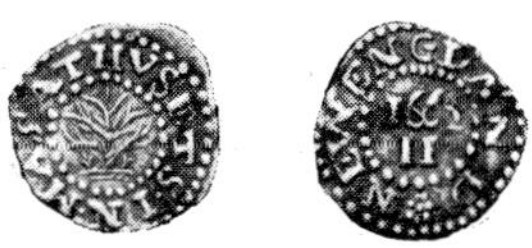

Twopence

Threepence

| | *Good* | *V. Good* | *Fine* | *V. Fine* |
|---|---|---|---|---|
| Oak Tree Twopence 1662. . . . . . . . . . . . . . . | $175.00 | $250.00 | $450.00 | $1,000 |
| Oak Tree Threepence 1652 . . . . . . . . . . . . . | 200.00 | 300.00 | 600.00 | 1,500 |
| Oak Tree Sixpence 1652. . . . . . . . . . . . . . . . | 200.00 | 300.00 | 600.00 | 1,600 |
| Oak Tree Shilling 1652. . . . . . . . . . . . . . . . . | 200.00 | 300.00 | 500.00 | 1,500 |

## PINE TREE COINAGE (1667-1682)

The first pine tree coins were minted on the same size planchets as the Oak Tree pieces. Subsequent issues of the shilling were narrower and thicker to conform to the size of English coins.

Shilling,
Large Planchet
(1667-1674)

# MASSACHUSETTS
## PINE TREE COINAGE (1667-1682)

Shilling,
Small Planchet
(1675-1682)

| | *Good* | *V. Good* | *Fine* | *V. Fine* |
|---|---|---|---|---|
| Pine Tree Threepence 1652 .................. | $100.00 | $200.00 | $300.00 | $500.00 |
| Pine Tree Sixpence 1652 .................. | 150.00 | 225.00 | 350.00 | 600.00 |
| Pine Tree Shilling, large planchet 1652 ....... | 150.00 | 225.00 | 400.00 | 700.00 |
| Pine Tree Shilling, small planchet 1652 ....... | 150.00 | 225.00 | 350.00 | 600.00 |

# MARYLAND

In 1658 Cecil Calvert, the "Lord Proprietor of Maryland," had coinage struck in England for use in Maryland.

There were four denominations: shillings, sixpence, and fourpence (groat) in silver, and a copper penny (denarium). The silver coins have the bust of Lord Baltimore on the obverse, and the Baltimore family Arms with the denomination in Roman numerals on the reverse.

Lord Baltimore Shilling

Fourpence (groat)

| | *Fair* | *Good* | *Fine* | *V. Fine* |
|---|---|---|---|---|
| Penny (Copper) (Ex. Rare) ............ | —— | —— | —— | —— |
| Fourpence ........................... | $175.00 | $450.00 | $1,800 | $3,500 |
| Sixpence ............................ | 175.00 | 400.00 | 1,000 | 2,000 |
| Shilling ............................ | 200.00 | 500.00 | 2,000 | 4,000 |

# NEW JERSEY
## ST. PATRICK OR MARK NEWBY COINAGE

Mark Newby, who came to America from Dublin, Ireland, in November 1681, brought copper pieces believed by numismatists to have been struck in England c. 1650. These are called St. Patrick Halfpence.

The coin received wide currency in the New Jersey Province, having been authorized to pass as legal tender by the General Assembly in May 1682.

The smaller piece, known as a farthing, was never authorized for circulation in the Colonies.

# NEW JERSEY

St. Patrick Farthing

| | V. Good | Fine | V. Fine |
|---|---|---|---|
| St. Patrick "Farthing" | $35.00 | $75.00 | $250.00 |
| St. Patrick "Halfpenny" | 50.00 | 100.00 | 250.00 |

# II. COINAGE AUTHORIZED BY ROYAL PATENT

## AMERICAN PLANTATIONS TOKEN

These tokens struck in nearly pure tin were the first authorized coinage for the British colonies in America. They were made under a franchise granted in 1688 to John Holt.

| | Fine | E. Fine | Unc. |
|---|---|---|---|
| (1688) James II Plantation Token farthing, 1/24 PART REAL — Tin | $100.00 | $200.00 | $800.00 |

# COINAGE OF WILLIAM WOOD

## ROSA AMERICANA COINS

William Wood, an Englishman, obtained a patent from George I to make tokens for Ireland and the American Colonies.

The Rosa Americana pieces were issued in three denominations, halfpenny, penny and twopence, and were intended for use in America.

Penny

# ROSA AMERICANA

| | V. Good | Fine | V. Fine | E. Fine |
|---|---|---|---|---|
| Twopence (no date) | $25.00 | $80.00 | $175.00 | $275.00 |
| 1722 Halfpenny DEI GRATIS REX UTILE DULCI | 20.00 | 60.00 | 90.00 | 175.00 |
| 1722 Penny | 18.00 | 50.00 | 85.00 | 150.00 |
| 1722 Twopence | 50.00 | 90.00 | 125.00 | 200.00 |

| | | | | |
|---|---|---|---|---|
| 1723 Halfpenny | 20.00 | 70.00 | 100.00 | 185.00 |

| | | | | |
|---|---|---|---|---|
| 1723 Penny | 20.00 | 60.00 | 90.00 | 150.00 |
| 1723 Twopence (illustrated) | 50.00 | 90.00 | 125.00 | 250.00 |

# WOOD'S HIBERNIA COINAGE

The type intended for Ireland had a seated figure with a harp on the reverse side and the word HIBERNIA. Denominations struck were halfpenny and farthing with dates 1722, 1723 and 1724. Hibernia coins were unpopular in Ireland, so many of them were sent to the American colonies.

1722 Hibernia Halfpenny

First Type

Second Type

| | V. Good | V. Fine | E. Fine |
|---|---|---|---|
| 1722 Farthing (2nd type) | | $125.00 | $250.00 |
| 1722 Halfpenny (1st or 2nd type) | $10.00 | 35.00 | 95.00 |

# WOOD'S HIBERNIA COINAGE

1723 Hibernia Farthing

1724 Hibernia Halfpenny

| | *V. Good* | *V. Fine* | *E. Fine* |
|---|---|---|---|
| 1723 Farthing . . . . . . . . . . | $7.00 | $20.00 | $80.00 |
| 1723 Halfpenny . . . . . . . . . . | 7.00 | 18.00 | 75.00 |
| 1724 Farthing . . . . . . . . . . | 18.00 | 35.00 | 100.00 |
| 1724 Halfpenny . . . . . . . . . . | 15.00 | 22.00 | 90.00 |

## VIRGINIA HALFPENNY

In 1773 coinage of a copper halfpenny was authorized for Virginia by the English Crown. The style is similar to the regular English coinage. These pieces were never popular, but did circulate by necessity.

| | *V. Good* | *V. Fine* | *Unc.* |
|---|---|---|---|
| 1773 Halfpenny . . . . . . . . . . | $10.00 | $25.00 | $250.00 |

# III. EARLY AMERICAN TOKENS

### *Struck in America or England for use by American Merchants*

## LONDON ELEPHANT TOKENS

Struck c. 1664-1666 during the reign of Charles II, the London Token, an early historian states, was produced during the great plague raging in London. The legend on this piece relates directly to that crisis. It has also been stated that the London

# LONDON ELEPHANT TOKENS

Token was to have been current in Tangier, Africa, but was never used in that locality. No date appears on this token.

It is unlikely that many ever circulated in America. They are associated with the 1694 pieces through use of a common obverse die.

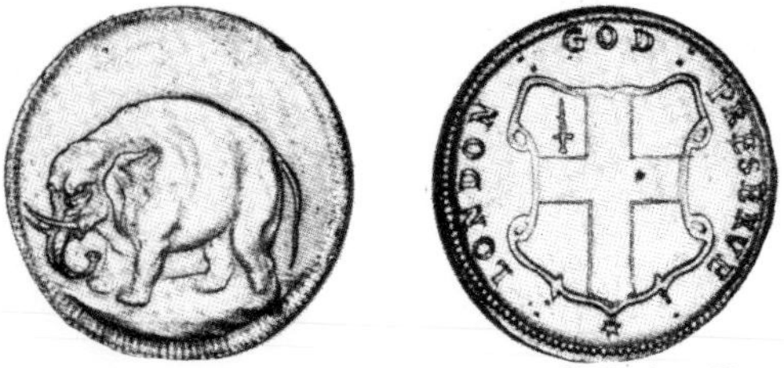


| | V. Good | Fine | V. Fine | E. Fine |
|---|---|---|---|---|
| (1664) Halfpenny GOD PRESERVE LONDON (Thick or thin planchet) | $30.00 | $50.00 | $100.00 | $250.00 |

# CAROLINA AND NEW ENGLAND ELEPHANT TOKENS

Although no law is known authorizing coinage for Carolina, very interesting pieces known as Elephant Tokens were made with the date 1694. These copper tokens were of halfpenny denomination. The reverse reads GOD PRESERVE CAROLINA AND THE LORDS PROPRIETERS. 1694.

The Carolina pieces were probably struck in England and perhaps intended only as tokens, or possibly as advertising to heighten interest in the Carolina Plantation.

Like the Carolina Tokens, the New England Elephant Tokens were believed to have been struck in England as a promotional piece to increase interest in the American Colonies.

| | V. Good | Fine |
|---|---|---|
| 1694 PROPRIETORS | $500.00 | $2,200 |

# NEW ENGLAND ELEPHANT TOKEN

| | V. Good | Fine |
|---|---|---|
| 1694 NEW ENGLAND | 5,000 | — |

# THE NEW YORKE TOKEN

Little is known about the origin of this token. The style of design and execution seem to be Dutch, and it is probable that the dies were prepared in Holland. There is no date on the piece which evidently belongs to the period between 1664, when the name New Yorke was first adopted, and 1710 after which it was rarely spelled that way.

UNDATED

| | V. Good | Fine |
|---|---|---|
| Brass ............ | $1,000 | $2,200 |

# GLOUCESTER TOKEN

This token appears to have been a private coinage by a merchant of Gloucester (county), Virginia. The only specimens known are struck in brass. The exact origin and use of these pieces is still unknown.

| | |
|---|---|
| 1714 Shilling Brass ........................................ | — |

# HIGLEY OR GRANBY COPPERS

The Higley coppers were never officially authorized. All the tokens were made of pure copper. There were seven obverse and four reverse dies. The first issue, in 1737, bore the legend THE VALUE OF THREEPENCE. After a time the quantity exceeded the local demand, and a protest arose against the value of the piece. The inscription was changed to VALUE ME AS YOU PLEASE.

| | Good | V. Good |
|---|---|---|
| 1737 THE • VALVE • OF • THREE • PENCE. — 3 Hammers — CONNECTICVT ........................ | $2,750 | $4,000 |
| 1737 THE • VALVE • OF • THREE • PENCE. — 3 Hammers — I • AM • GOOD • COPPER ................. | 3,000 | 4,200 |
| 1737 VALUE • ME • AS • YOU • PLEASE — 3 Hammers — I • AM • GOOD • COPPER ................. | 2,750 | 3,750 |
| (1737) VALUE • ME • AS • YOU • PLEASE — Broad Axe — J • CUT • MY • WAY • THROUGH ............ | 3,000 | 4,200 |
| 1739 VALUE • ME • AS • YOU • PLEASE — Broad Axe — J • CUT • MY • WAY • THROUGH ............ | 3,500 | 5,000 |

# HIBERNIA-VOCE POPULI

These coins, struck in the year 1760, were made in Dublin. Like other Irish tokens, some of these pieces found their way to Colonial America.

Farthing 1760

Halfpenny 1760

| | Good | V. Fine | E. Fine |
|---|---|---|---|
| 1760 Farthing .......................................... | $80.00 | $200.00 | $500.00 |
| 1760 Halfpenny.......................................... | 10.00 | 45.00 | 100.00 |

# PITT TOKENS

William Pitt is the subject of these pieces, probably intended as commemorative medalets. The halfpenny served as currency during a shortage of regular coinage.

1766 Farthing .................... $1,000

1766 Halfpenny........ (illustrated)

| V. Good | Fine | E. Fine |
|---|---|---|
| $75.00 | $150.00 | $400.00 |

# RHODE ISLAND SHIP MEDAL

Although this medal has a Dutch inscription, the spelling and design indicate an English or Anglo-American origin. The satirical theme depicts the retreat from Rhode Island by Continental troops. Specimens are known in brass, copper, tin and pewter.

1778-1779
Rhode Island
Ship Medal

| V. Fine | E. Fine |
|---|---|
| $200.00 | $400.00 |

# J. CHALMERS — Annapolis, Maryland

John Chalmers, a goldsmith, struck a series of silver tokens at Annapolis in 1783. The shortage of change and the refusal of the people to use underweight coins prompted the issuance of these pieces.

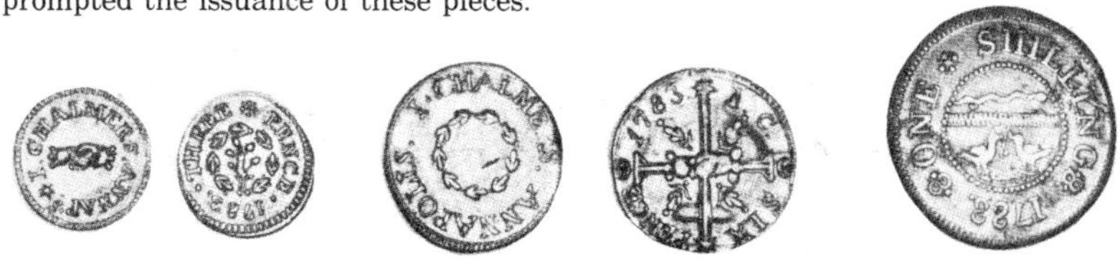

| | V. Good | V. Fine |
|---|---|---|
| 1783 Threepence | $200.00 | $700.00 |
| 1783 Sixpence | 250.00 | 900.00 |
| 1783 Shilling (Rev. illustrated) | 200.00 | 800.00 |

# IV. THE FRENCH COLONIES

None of the coins of the French regime is strictly American. They were all general issues for the French colonies of the New World. The copper of 1717 to 1722 was authorized by edicts of 1716 and 1721 for use in New France, Louisiana, and the French West Indies.

## COPPER SOU OR NINE DENIERS

| | V. Good | Fine |
|---|---|---|
| 1721-B (Rouen) | $30.00 | $70.00 |
| 1721-H (La Rochelle) | 20.00 | 35.00 |
| 1722-H | 15.00 | 30.00 |

## FRENCH COLONIES IN GENERAL

Coined for use in the French colonies and only unofficially circulated in Louisiana along with other foreign coins and tokens. Most were counterstamped RF (République Française) for use in the West Indies.

| | V. Good | V. Fine | E. Fine |
|---|---|---|---|
| 1767 French Colonies, Sou | $15.00 | $40.00 | $100.00 |
| 1767 French Colonies, Sou. Counterstamped RF | 10.00 | 35.00 | 80.00 |

# V. SPECULATIVE ISSUES, TOKENS & PATTERNS

## THE CONTINENTAL DOLLAR

The Continental Dollars were probably a pattern issue only and never reached general circulation. It was the first silver dollar size coin ever proposed for the United States. The coins were probably struck in Philadelphia.

| | Good | Fine | E. Fine | Unc. |
|---|---|---|---|---|
| 1776 CURENCY — Pewter .................... | $500.00 | $1,750 | $2,500 | $6,000 |
| 1776 CURENCY — Silver .................... | | | | 25,000 |
| 1776 CURRENCY — Pewter .................. | 600.00 | 2,000 | 3,000 | 7,000 |
| 1776 CURRENCY — Pewter, EG FECIT above date | 500.00 | 1,800 | 2,750 | 6,500 |

## NOVA CONSTELLATIO COPPERS

The Nova Constellatio pieces were struck supposedly by order of Gouverneur Morris. Evidence indicates that they were all struck in Birmingham and imported for American circulation as a private business venture.

1783
"CONSTELLATIO"
Pointed Rays

| | |
|---|---|
| V. Good ........... | $10.00 |
| Fine............... | 25.00 |
| V. Fine............ | 50.00 |
| Ex. Fine........... | 200.00 |

1783
"CONSTELATIO"
Blunt Rays

| | |
|---|---|
| V. Good ........... | $10.00 |
| Fine............... | 25.00 |
| V. Fine............ | 60.00 |
| Ex. Fine........... | 215.00 |

# NOVA CONSTELLATIO COPPERS

1785
"CONSTELATIO"
Blunt Rays

| | |
|---|---|
| V. Good . . . . . . . . . . . | $12.00 |
| Fine. . . . . . . . . . . . . . . | 35.00 |
| V. Fine . . . . . . . . . . . . | 75.00 |
| Ex. Fine . . . . . . . . . . . | 225.00 |

1785
"CONSTELLATIO"
Pointed Rays

| | |
|---|---|
| V. Good . . . . . . . . . . . | $10.00 |
| Fine. . . . . . . . . . . . . . . | 25.00 |
| V. Fine . . . . . . . . . . . . | 50.00 |
| Ex. Fine . . . . . . . . . . . | 200.00 |

# IMMUNE COLUMBIA PIECES

These are considered experimental or pattern pieces. No laws describing them are known.

1785 Copper, Star reverse. . . . $10,000

1785
George III Obverse

| | |
|---|---|
| Good. . . . . . . . . . . . . . . . . . . . . . . . . | $800.00 |
| Fine . . . . . . . . . . . . . . . . . . . . . . . . . | 2,500 |

1785
Vermon Auctori Obverse

| | |
|---|---|
| Good. . . . . . . . . . . . . . . . . . . . . . . . . | $750.00 |
| Fine . . . . . . . . . . . . . . . . . . . . . . . . . | 2,000 |

1787
IMMUNIS COLUMBIA
Eagle Reverse

| | |
|---|---|
| V. Good. . . . . . . . . . . . | $100.00 |
| Fine . . . . . . . . . . . . . . . | 200.00 |
| V. Fine . . . . . . . . . . . . | 500.00 |
| Ex. Fine . . . . . . . . . . . | 1,500 |

# CONFEDERATIO COPPERS

The Confederatio Coppers are experimental or pattern pieces. This will explain why the die with the CONFEDERATIO legend was combined with other designs such as bust of George Washington, Libertas et Justitia of 1785, Immunis Columbia of 1786, the New York "Excelsiors," Inimica Tyrannis Americana and others. There were in all thirteen dies struck in fourteen combinations.

There are two types of the Confederatio reverse. In one instance the stars are contained in a small circle; in the other larger stars are in a larger circle.

Typical Obverse

Small Circle Reverse

Large Circle Reverse

| | Fine |
|---|---|
| 1785 Stars in small circle — various obverses | $5,000 |
| 1785 Stars in large circle — various obverses | 5,000 |

# SPECULATIVE PATTERNS

1786 IMMUNIS COLUMBIA

Eagle Reverse

Shield Reverse

| | |
|---|---|
| 1786 IMMUNIS COLUMBIA, eagle rev | $9,000 |
| 1786 IMMUNIS COLUMBIA, shield rev | 6,000 |
| 1786 (No date) Washington obv | 20,000 |
| 1786 Eagle obverse | 12,000 |
| 1786 Washington obverse, eagle reverse (Unique) | —— |

# VI. COINAGE OF THE STATES

## NEW HAMPSHIRE

New Hampshire was the first of the states to consider the subject of coinage following the Declaration of Independence.

# NEW HAMPSHIRE

William Moulton was empowered to make a limited quantity of coins of pure copper authorized by the State House of Representatives in 1776.

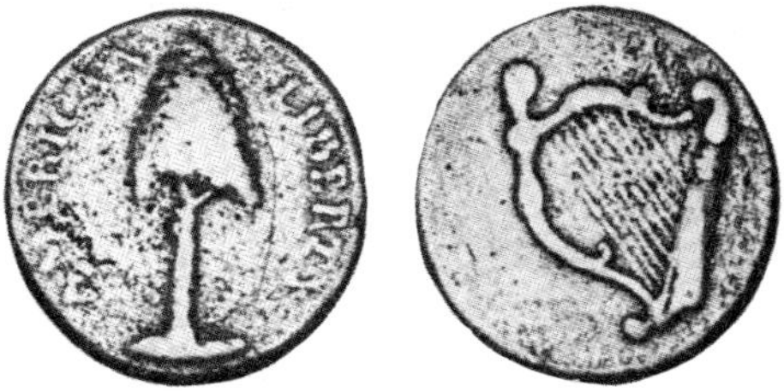

| | *V. Good* |
|---|---|
| 1776 New Hampshire copper | $6,000 |

# MASSACHUSETTS

The coinage of Massachusetts copper cents and half cents in 1787 and 1788 was under the direction of Joshua Witherle. These were the first coins bearing the denomination Cent as established by Congress. Many varieties exist, the most valuable being that with arrows in the eagle's right talon.

| 1787 Half Cent | |
|---|---|
| Good | $15.00 |
| Fine | 30.00 |
| V. Fine | 60.00 |
| Ex. Fine | 175.00 |

| | *Good* | *Fine* | *V. Fine* | *E. Fine* |
|---|---|---|---|---|
| 1787 Cent, arrows in left talon (illustrated) | $12.00 | $25.00 | $60.00 | $175.00 |
| 1787 Cent, arrows in right talon | — | 2,200 | — | — |

| 1788 Half Cent | |
|---|---|
| Good | $15.00 |
| Fine | 30.00 |
| Very Fine | 65.00 |
| Ex. Fine | 200.00 |

# MASSACHUSETTS

| 1788 Cent | |
|---|---|
| Good | $12.00 |
| Fine | 25.00 |
| V. Fine | 60.00 |
| Ex. Fine | 175.00 |

# CONNECTICUT

Authority for establishing a mint near New Haven was granted by the State to Samuel Bishop, Joseph Hopkins, James Hillhouse and John Goodrich in 1785.

| 1785 Copper Bust Facing Right | |
|---|---|
| Good | $15.00 |
| V. Good | 20.00 |
| Fine | 40.00 |
| V. Fine | 100.00 |

| 1785 Copper Bust Facing Left | |
|---|---|
| Good | $50.00 |
| V. Good | 65.00 |
| Fine | 125.00 |
| V. Fine | 200.00 |

| | *Good* | *V.G.* | *Fine* | *V. Fine* |
|---|---|---|---|---|
| 1786 Bust facing right | $20.00 | $30.00 | $55.00 | $125.00 |
| 1787 Mailed bust facing right | 30.00 | 50.00 | 100.00 | 300.00 |

# CONNECTICUT

| | Good | V.G. | Fine | V. Fine |
|---|---|---|---|---|
| 1786 Mailed bust facing left .................. | $12.00 | $18.00 | $35.00 | $85.00 |
| 1787 Mailed bust facing left .................. | 8.00 | 15.00 | 25.00 | 70.00 |

| | | | | |
|---|---|---|---|---|
| 1787 Draped bust facing left.................. | 7.00 | 12.00 | 18.00 | 50.00 |

| | | | | |
|---|---|---|---|---|
| 1788 Mailed bust facing right................. | 10.00 | 18.00 | 40.00 | 100.00 |

| | | | | |
|---|---|---|---|---|
| 1788 Mailed bust facing left .................. | 10.00 | 15.00 | 35.00 | 85.00 |

# CONNECTICUT

| | Good | V.G. | Fine | V. Fine |
|---|---|---|---|---|
| 1788 Draped bust facing left.................... | $10.00 | $15.00 | $35.00 | $85.00 |

# NEW YORK

## THE BRASHER DOUBLOON

Perhaps the most famous pieces coined before the establishment of the U.S. Mint at Philadelphia were those produced by a well-known goldsmith and jeweler, Ephraim Brasher.

Brasher produced a gold piece weighing about 408 grains, approximately equal in value to a Spanish doubloon (about $16.00).

The punch-mark EB appears in either of two positions as illustrated. This mark is found on some foreign gold coins as well, and probably was so used by Brasher as evidence of his testing of their value.

| | |
|---|---|
| 1787 Doubloon, punch on breast. Gold (Unique)................................ | — |
| 1787 Doubloon, punch on wing. Gold........................................ | — |

## COPPER COINAGE

No coinage was authorized for New York following the Revolutionary War although several propositions were considered. The only coinage laws passed were those regulating coins already in use.

1786
NON VI VIRTUTE VICI

| | |
|---|---|
| Good .......... | $1,000 |
| Fine........... | 2,000 |
| V. Fine ........ | 4,000 |

# NEW YORK

| | Good | Fine | V. Fine |
|---|---|---|---|
| 1787 EXCELSIOR copper, eagle on globe facing right | $300.00 | $600.00 | $3,000 |
| 1787 EXCELSIOR copper, eagle on globe facing left | 250.00 | 600.00 | 3,000 |

1787 George Clinton

| | |
|---|---|
| Good | $1,500 |
| Fine | 3,500 |
| V. Fine | 10,000 |

1787
Indian and N.Y. Arms

| | |
|---|---|
| Good | $1,250 |
| Fine | 2,750 |
| V. Fine | 5,000 |

1787
Indian and Eagle
on Globe

| | |
|---|---|
| Good | $1,500 |
| Fine | 3,500 |
| V. Fine | 6,000 |

# NEW YORK
## THE NOVA EBORACS

1787
NOVA EBORAC
Reverse Seated
Figure Facing Right

| | |
|---|---|
| Fair | $10.00 |
| Good | 25.00 |
| Fine | 75.00 |
| V. Fine | 250.00 |

1787
NOVA EBORAC
Reverse Seated
Figure Facing Left

| | |
|---|---|
| Fair | $8.00 |
| Good | 15.00 |
| Fine | 60.00 |
| V. Fine | 175.00 |

# NEW JERSEY

On June 1, 1786, the New Jersey Colonial legislature granted to Thomas Goadsby, Albion Cox and Walter Mould authority to coin some three million coppers, not later than June 1788, on condition that they delivered to the Treasurer of the State, "one-tenth part of the full sum they shall strike and coin," in quarterly installments. These coppers were to pass current at 15 to the shilling.

Narrow Shield

Wide Shield

| | *Good* | *Fine* | *V. Fine* |
|---|---|---|---|
| 1786 Narrow shield | $10.00 | $25.00 | $55.00 |
| 1786 Wide shield | 12.00 | 30.00 | 75.00 |

# NEW JERSEY

Small Planchet

| | Good | Fine | V. Fine |
|---|---|---|---|
| 1787 Small planchet.................................. | $10.00 | $25.00 | $55.00 |
| 1787 Large planchet .................................. | 10.00 | 25.00 | 55.00 |

| | Good | Fine | V. Fine |
|---|---|---|---|
| 1788 Horse's head facing right........................ | 10.00 | 22.00 | 50.00 |
| 1788 Horse's head facing left ......................... | 40.00 | 150.00 | 225.00 |

# VERMONT

Reuben Harmon, Jr., of Rupert, Vermont, was granted permission to coin copper pieces for a period of two years beginning July 1, 1785. The well-known Vermont plow coppers were first produced in that year. The franchise was extended for eight years in 1786.

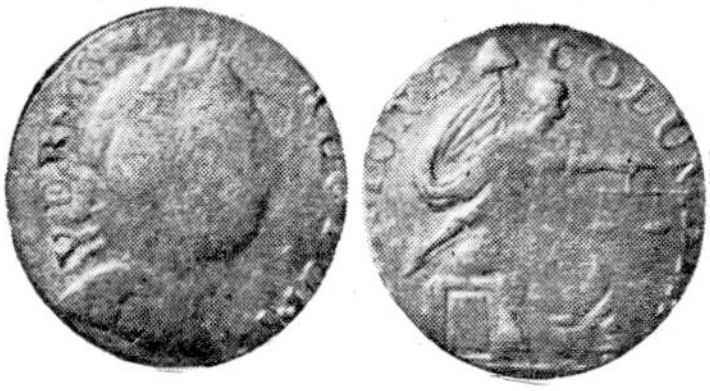

| | Good | Fine |
|---|---|---|
| 1785 IMMUNE COLUMBIA ..... | $750.00 | $2,000 |

| | Good | Fine |
|---|---|---|
| 1785 Plow type .. | $60.00 | $175.00 |
| 1786 Plow type .. | 40.00 | 150.00 |

| | Good | Fine |
|---|---|---|
| 1786 Baby head | $70.00 | $300.00 |

| | Good | Fine |
|---|---|---|
| 1786 Bust left . . . | $30.00 | $200.00 |
| 1787 Bust left . . . | 350.00 | 700.00 |

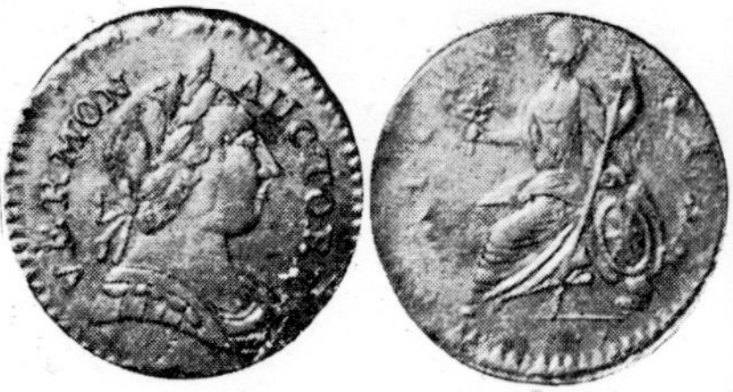

| | Good | Fine |
|---|---|---|
| 1787 BRITANNIA. . | $22.00 | $75.00 |

1787 Bust right. . $25.00 $85.00

1788 Bust right. . $25.00 $85.00

1788 GEORGIVS III REX* . . . . . . . . $60.00 $200.00

*This piece should not be confused with the common English halfpence with similar design and reverse legend BRITANNIA.

# VII. PRIVATE TOKENS AFTER CONFEDERATION

## NORTH AMERICAN TOKEN

This piece was struck in Dublin, Ireland. The obverse shows the seated figure of Hibernia facing left.

Copper or Brass

| | V. Good | Fine | V. Fine |
|---|---|---|---|
| 1781 . . . | $7.00 | $15.00 | $30.00 |

## THE BAR "CENT"

The Bar "Cent" is undated and of uncertain origin. It has thirteen parallel and unconnected bars on one side. On the other side is the large roman letter USA monogram. The design was supposedly copied from a Continental button.

| | V. Good | Fine | V. Fine | E. Fine |
|---|---|---|---|---|
| Undated (about 1785) Bar "Cent" ............. | $75.00 | $100.00 | $200.00 | $500.00 |

## AUCTORI PLEBIS TOKEN

This token is sometimes included with the coins of Connecticut as it greatly resembles issues of that state. It was struck in England by an unknown maker, possibly for use in America.

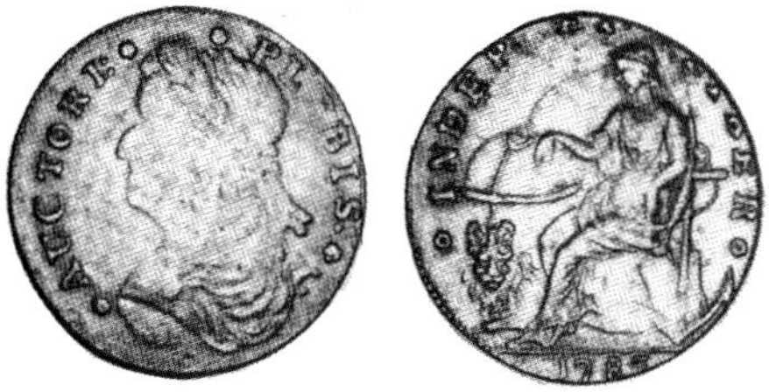

| 1787 AUCTORI PLEBIS | |
|---|---|
| Good ............. | $15.00 |
| V. Good .......... | 25.00 |
| Fine............... | 50.00 |
| V. Fine........... | 90.00 |

## THE MOTT TOKEN

This was one of the first tradesman's tokens issued in America. Manufactured in England, they were issued by Messrs. Mott of New York in 1789.

| | V. Good | Fine | V. Fine | E. Fine |
|---|---|---|---|---|
| 1789 Mott Token............................ | $30.00 | $50.00 | $100.00 | $200.00 |

# STANDISH BARRY, BALTIMORE, MARYLAND

Standish Barry, a Baltimore silversmith, circulated a silver threepence in 1790. The tokens were believed to have been an advertising venture at a time when small change was scarce.

| | *Fine* | *V. Fine* |
|---|---|---|
| 1790 Threepence | $1,000 | $3,500 |

# KENTUCKY TOKEN

These tokens were struck in England about 1792-94. Each star in the triangle represents a state, identified by its initial letter. These pieces are usually called Kentucky Cents because the letter K (for Kentucky) happens to be at the top.

| | *V. Good* | *V. Fine* | *E. Fine* | *Unc.* |
|---|---|---|---|---|
| Cent (1792-94) | $20.00 | $50.00 | $75.00 | $450.00 |

# FRANKLIN PRESS

This piece is an English tradesmans' token but, being associated with Benjamin Franklin, has accordingly been included in American collections.

| | | | | |
|---|---|---|---|---|
| 1794 Franklin Press Token | 18.00 | 50.00 | 75.00 | 350.00 |

# TALBOT, ALLUM & LEE CENTS

Talbot, Allum & Lee, engaged in the India trade and located in New York, placed a large quantity of English-made coppers in circulation during 1794 and 1795. ONE CENT appears on the 1794 issue.

| 1794 Cent with NEW YORK | |
|---|---|
| V. Good | $15.00 |
| V. Fine | 35.00 |
| Unc. | 350.00 |

| 1794 Cent Without NEW YORK | |
|---|---|
| V. Good | 50.00 |
| V. Fine | 200.00 |
| Unc. | 700.00 |

| 1795 Cent | |
|---|---|
| V. Good | $14.00 |
| V. Fine | 35.00 |
| E. Fine | 75.00 |
| Unc. | 300.00 |

# VIII. WASHINGTON PIECES

An interesting series of coins and tokens dated from 1783 to 1795 bear the portrait of George Washington. The likenesses in most instances were faithfully reproduced and were designed to honor Washington. Many of these pieces were of English origin and made later than the dates indicate.

| | *Fine* | *V. Fine* | *E. Fine* |
|---|---|---|---|
| 1783 Large military bust | $15.00 | $30.00 | $85.00 |

| | | | |
|---|---|---|---|
| 1783 Draped bust | 15.00 | 30.00 | 85.00 |

# WASHINGTON PIECES

UNITY STATES

| | |
|---|---|
| V. Good | $15.00 |
| V. Fine | 45.00 |
| Ex. Fine | 100.00 |

Undated
Double Head
Cent

| | |
|---|---|
| Fine | $20.00 |
| V. Fine | 40.00 |
| Ex. Fine | 100.00 |

| | *Fine* | *E. Fine* | *Unc.* |
|---|---|---|---|
| 1791 Cent, small eagle | $55.00 | $150.00 | $450.00 |
| 1791 Cent, large eagle | 55.00 | 150.00 | 450.00 |

1791 Liverpool
Halfpenny
Lettered Edge

| | |
|---|---|
| Fine | $225.00 |
| Ex. Fine | 500.00 |
| Unc. | 1,000 |

1792 Eagle with Stars

| | |
|---|---|
| Copper | —— |
| Silver | —— |
| Gold | —— |

# WASHINGTON PIECES

(1792) Undated Cent
"WASHINGTON BORN VIRGINIA"

1792 Cent
"WASHINGTON PRESIDENT"

| | *Fine* |
|---|---|
| Copper | $1,000 |

| | *Fine* |
|---|---|
| Plain edge | $2,500 |

| | *V. Good* | *Fine* |
|---|---|---|
| 1792 Small eagle. Copper | $1,000 | $2,000 |

1793 Ship
Halfpenny

| | |
|---|---|
| Fine | $50.00 |
| V. Fine | 75.00 |
| Ex. Fine | 150.00 |

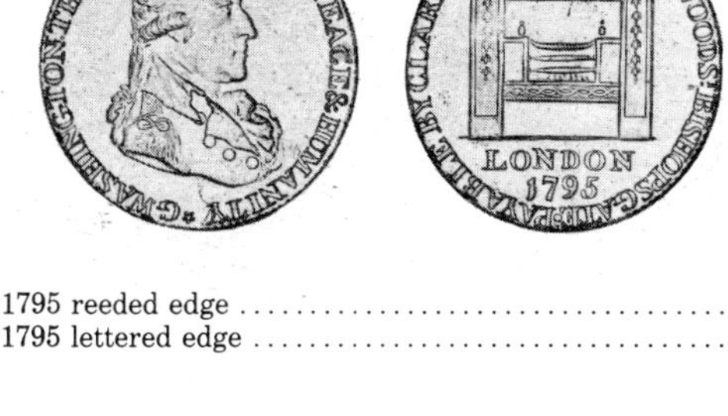


1795 Halfpenny
Grate Token

| | *V. Fine* | *E. Fine* | *Unc.* |
|---|---|---|---|
| 1795 reeded edge | $30.00 | $65.00 | $200.00 |
| 1795 lettered edge | 125.00 | 250.00 | 550.00 |

# WASHINGTON PIECES

Liberty and Security Halfpenny

| | Fine | V. Fine | E. Fine |
|---|---|---|---|
| 1795 Halfpenny, plain edge | $30.00 | $50.00 | $125.00 |
| 1795 Halfpenny, lettered edge | 20.00 | 40.00 | 100.00 |

Liberty and Security Penny

| | |
|---|---|
| Fine | $60.00 |
| V. Fine | 100.00 |
| Ex. Fine | 170.00 |
| Unc. | 900.00 |

# SUCCESS MEDALS

| | Fine | V. Fine | E. Fine |
|---|---|---|---|
| SUCCESS medal, large. Plain or reeded edge | $50.00 | $100.00 | $150.00 |
| SUCCESS medal, small. Plain or reeded edge | 50.00 | 100.00 | 175.00 |

# NORTH WALES HALFPENNY

| | Good | Fine |
|---|---|---|
| 1795 NORTH WALES Halfpenny | $30.00 | $75.00 |

# IX. THE FUGIO CENTS

The first coins issued by authority of the United States were the "Fugio" cents.
The legends have been credited to Benjamin Franklin by many, and the coin, as a consequence, has been referred to as the Franklin Cent.

1787 WITH CLUB RAYS

| | *V. Good* | *Fine* | *V. Fine* |
|---|---|---|---|
| Club Rays. Rounded ends . . . . . . . . . . . . . . . . . . . . . . . . . . . . | $50.00 | $75.00 | $200.00 |

1787 WITH POINTED RAYS

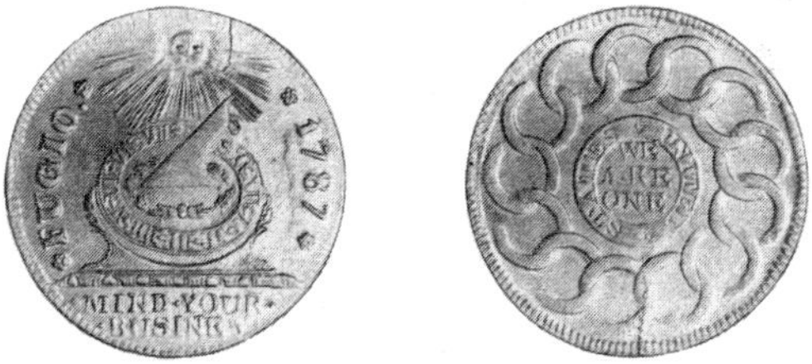


| | *V.G.* | *Fine* | *V.F.* | *E.F.* | *Unc.* |
|---|---|---|---|---|---|
| STATES UNITED at sides of circle (illustrated) | $30.00 | $50.00 | $90.00 | $150.00 | $650.00 |
| UNITED STATES at sides of circle . . . . . . . . . . | 30.00 | 50.00 | 90.00 | 150.00 | 650.00 |

# MODERN PROOF COINS

Proof coins can usually be distinguished by their sharpness of detail, high wire edge, and extremely brilliant, mirrorlike surface. All proofs are originally sold by the mint at a premium.

Proof coins were not struck during 1943-1949 or 1965-67. Sets from 1936 through 1972 include the cent, nickel, dime, quarter and half; from 1973 through 1981 the dollar was also included.

**Figures in parentheses represent the total number of full sets minted.**

| | | | |
|---|---|---|---|
| 1936 (3,837) | $3,200 | 1961 (3,028,244) | $8.50 |
| 1937 (5,542) | 2,250 | 1962 (3,218,019) | 8.50 |
| 1938 (8,045) | 1,000 | 1963 (3,075,645) | 8.50 |
| 1939 (8,795) | 900.00 | 1964 (3,950,762) | 7.50 |
| 1940 (11,246) | 800.00 | 1968S (3,041,506) | 4.00 |
| 1941 (15,287) | 725.00 | 1969S (2,934,631) | 4.00 |
| 1942 both nickels (21,120) | 900.00 | 1970S (2,632,810) | 9.00 |
| 1942 one nickel (21,120) | 725.00 | 1971S (3,220,733) | 3.75 |
| 1950 (51,386) | 350.00 | 1972S (3,260,996) | 3.75 |
| 1951 (57,500) | 210.00 | 1973S (2,760,339) | 6.00 |
| 1952 (81,980) | 125.00 | 1974S (2,612,568) | 6.00 |
| 1953 (128,800) | 80.00 | 1975S (2,845,450) | 10.00 |
| 1954 (233,300) | 55.00 | 1976S (4,149,730) | 6.00 |
| 1955 (378,200) | 45.00 | 1976S 3-pc. set (3,295,714)† | 13.00 |
| 1956 (669,384) | 20.00 | 1977S (3,251,152) | 5.00 |
| 1957 (1,247,952 | 13.00 | 1978S (3,127,781) | 8.50 |
| 1958 (875,652) | 17.00 | 1979S filled S (3,677,175) | 14.00 |
| 1959 (1,149,291) | 14.00 | 1979S clear S (3,677,175) | 75.00 |
| 1960 (1,691,602 both kinds) | | 1980S (3,554,806) | 8.00 |
| with lg. date 1c | 11.00 | 1981S (4,063,083) | 9.00 |
| 1960 with sm. date 1c | 22.00 | 1982S | 11.00 |

# UNCIRCULATED MINT SETS

Official Mint Sets are specially packaged by the government for sale to collectors. They contain uncirculated specimens of each year's coins for every denomination issued from each mint. Unlike the proof sets, these are normal coins intended for circulation and are not minted with any special consideration for quality.

| | | | |
|---|---|---|---|
| 1947 P-D-S | $485.00 | 1965 *(2,360,000) | $3.00 |
| 1948 P-D-S | 160.00 | 1966 *(2,261,583) | 3.25 |
| 1949 P-D-S | 650.00 | 1967 *(1,863,344) | 8.00 |
| 1951 P-D-S (8,654) | 300.00 | 1968 P-D-S (2,105,128) | 2.00 |
| 1952 P-D-S (11,499) | 175.00 | 1969 P-D-S (1,817,392) | 2.25 |
| 1953 P-D-S (15,538) | 145.00 | 1970 P-D-S (2,038,134) | 25.00 |
| 1954 P-D-S (25,599) | 75.00 | 1971 P-D-S (2,193,396) | 2.00 |
| 1955 P-D-S (49,656) | 40.00 | 1972 P-D-S (2,750,000) | 2.00 |
| 1956 P-D (45,475) | 30.00 | 1973 P-D-S (1,767,691) | 15.00 |
| 1957 P-D (34,324) | 45.00 | 1974 P-D-S (1,975,981) | 3.85 |
| 1958 P-D (50,314) | 38.00 | 1975 P-D-S (1,921,488) | 4.00 |
| 1959 P-D (187,000) | 15.00 | 1976 3 pieces (3,400,000)† | 8.00 |
| 1960 P-D Lg. Date (260,485) | 10.00 | 1976 P-D (1,892,513) | 4.00 |
| 1960 P-D Sm. Date (260,485) | 11.00 | 1977 P-D (2,006,869) | 4.00 |
| 1961 P-D (223,704) | 9.50 | 1978 P-D (2,162,609) | 4.50 |
| 1962 P-D (385,285) | 9.00 | 1979 P-D (2,526,000) | 4.00 |
| 1963 P-D (606,612) | 9.00 | 1980 P-D-S (2,813,118) | 5.00 |
| 1964 P-D (1,008,108) | 8.50 | 1981 P-D-S | 12.00 |

*Special Mint Sets †Estimated

# UNITED STATES REGULAR ISSUES

## HALF CENTS — 1793-1857

The half cent was authorized to be coined April 2, 1792. Originally the weight was to have been 132 grains, but this was changed to 104 grains by the Act of January 14, 1793, before coinage commenced. The weight was again changed to 84 grains January 26, 1796 by presidential proclamation in conformity with the Act of March 3, 1795. Coinage was discontinued by the Act of February 21, 1857. All were coined at the Philadelphia Mint.

### LIBERTY CAP TYPE 1793-1797

**AG-3 ABOUT GOOD**—*Clear enough to identify.*
**G-4 GOOD**—*Outline of bust clear, no details. Date readable. Reverse lettering incomplete.*
**VG-8 VERY GOOD**—*Some hair details. Reverse lettering complete.*
**F-12 FINE**—*Most of hair detail shows. Leaves worn but all visible.*
**VF-20 VERY FINE**—*Hair near ear and forehead worn, other areas distinct. Some details in leaves show.*
**EF-40 EXTREMELY FINE**—*Light wear on highest parts of head and wreath.*

Head Facing Left 1793

| | *Quan. Minted* | *AG-3* | *G-4* | *VG-8* | *F-12* | *VF-20* | *EF-40* |
|---|---|---|---|---|---|---|---|
| 1793 .................... | 35,334 | $275.00 | $750.00 | $1,000 | $1,500 | $2,000 | $4,500 |

Head Facing Right 1794-1797

| | | | | | | | |
|---|---|---|---|---|---|---|---|
| 1794 .................... | 81,600 | 50.00 | 100.00 | 150.00 | 250.00 | 500.00 | 900.00 |

Pole to Cap

Punctuated Date

No Pole to Cap

| | *Quan. Minted* | *AG-3* | *G-4* | *VG-8* | *F-12* | *VF-20* | *EF-40* |
|---|---|---|---|---|---|---|---|
| 1795 Lettered edge, with pole........... | 25,600 | $40.00 | $90.00 | $130.00 | $235.00 | $450.00 | $800.00 |
| 1795 Lettered edge, punctuated date | | 40.00 | 90.00 | 130.00 | 235.00 | 450.00 | 800.00 |

# HALF CENTS

| | Quan. Minted | AG-3 | G-4 | VG-8 | F-12 | VF-20 | EF-40 |
|---|---|---|---|---|---|---|---|
| 1795 Plain edge, punctuated date | 109,000 | $40.00 | $90.00 | $130.00 | $235.00 | $450.00 | $800.00 |
| 1795 Pl. edge, no pole | | 40.00 | 90.00 | 130.00 | 235.00 | 450.00 | 800.00 |
| 1796 With pole .......... | 5,090 | 600.00 | 1,200 | 2,000 | 3,500 | 6,000 | —— |
| 1796 No pole ............ | 1,390 | 900.00 | 2,300 | 3,750 | 6,500 | 11,000 | |

1797 Plain Edge

1797, 1 above 1, Plain Edge

| | Quan. Minted | AG-3 | G-4 | VG-8 | F-12 | VF-20 | EF-40 |
|---|---|---|---|---|---|---|---|
| 1797 All kinds ............... | 119,215 | | | | | | |
| 1797 Lettered edge.................. | | 90.00 | 175.00 | 275.00 | 600.00 | 1,200 | 2,000 |
| 1797 Plain edge.................... | | 30.00 | 75.00 | 125.00 | 200.00 | 400.00 | 750.00 |
| 1797, 1 above 1, plain edge .......... | | 30.00 | 75.00 | 125.00 | 200.00 | 400.00 | 750.00 |

## DRAPED BUST TYPE 1800-1808

**AG-3 ABOUT GOOD**—*Clear enough to identify.*
**G-4 GOOD**—*Bust outline clear, few details, date readable. Reverse lettering worn and incomplete.*
**VG-8 VERY GOOD**—*Some drapery shows. Date and legends complete.*
**F-12 FINE**—*Shoulder drapery and hair over brow worn smooth.*
**VF-20 VERY FINE**—*Only slight wear in above areas. Slight wear on reverse.*
**EF-40 EXTREMELY FINE**—*Light wear on highest parts of head and wreath.*

| | Quan. Minted | AG-3 | G-4 | VG-8 | F-12 | VF-20 | EF-40 |
|---|---|---|---|---|---|---|---|
| 1800 ........................ | 211,530 | 6.50 | 12.00 | 18.00 | 25.00 | 40.00 | 100.00 |
| 1802, 2 over 0 ................ | 14,366 | 40.00 | 85.00 | 150.00 | 350.00 | 700.00 | 1,500 |
| 1803 ........................ | 97,900 | 7.00 | 14.00 | 19.00 | 25.00 | 45.00 | 120.00 |

Plain 4

Crosslet 4

Stemless Wreath

Stems to Wreath

| | Quan. Minted | AG-3 | G-4 | VG-8 | F-12 | VF-20 | EF-40 |
|---|---|---|---|---|---|---|---|
| 1804 Plain 4, stems ....... | 1,055,312 | 6.50 | 12.00 | 18.00 | 25.00 | 45.00 | 120.00 |
| 1804 Pl. 4, stemless ....... | | 6.00 | 11.00 | 17.00 | 20.00 | 40.00 | 85.00 |
| 1804 Cr. 4, stems .......... | | 6.00 | 11.00 | 17.00 | 20.00 | 40.00 | 85.00 |
| 1804 Cr. 4, stemless ....... | | 6.00 | 11.00 | 17.00 | 20.00 | 40.00 | 85.00 |

# HALF CENTS

1804 "Spiked Chin" Variety

Small 5

Large 5

| | *Quan. Minted* | *AG-3* | *G-4* | *VG-8* | *F-12* | *VF-20* | *EF-40* |
|---|---|---|---|---|---|---|---|
| 1804 "Spiked chin" | Inc. above | $8.00 | $15.00 | $20.00 | $30.00 | $50.00 | $150.00 |
| 1805 Sm. 5, stemless | | 6.00 | 11.00 | 17.00 | 20.00 | 40.00 | 75.00 |
| 1805 Small 5, stems | 814,464 | 20.00 | 45.00 | 75.00 | 180.00 | 350.00 | 650.00 |
| 1805 Large 5, stems | | 16.00 | 11.00 | 17.00 | 20.00 | 40.00 | 75.00 |

Small 6

Large 6

1808, 8 over 7

Normal Date

| | *Quan. Minted* | *AG-3* | *G-4* | *VG-8* | *F-12* | *VF-20* | *EF-40* |
|---|---|---|---|---|---|---|---|
| 1806 Small 6, stems | | 9.00 | 20.00 | 35.00 | 75.00 | 115.00 | 200.00 |
| 1806 Sm. 6, stemless | 356,000 | 6.00 | 11.00 | 17.00 | 20.00 | 40.00 | 85.00 |
| 1806 Large 6, stems | | 6.00 | 11.00 | 17.00 | 20.00 | 40.00 | 85.00 |
| 1807 | 476,000 | 6.00 | 11.00 | 17.00 | 20.00 | 40.00 | 85.00 |
| 1808, 8 over 7 | 400,000 | 18.00 | 35.00 | 45.00 | 90.00 | 180.00 | 250.00 |
| 1808 Normal date | | 6.50 | 12.00 | 18.00 | 22.00 | 45.00 | 100.00 |

## CLASSIC HEAD TYPE 1809-1836

**G-4GOOD**—*LIBERTY only partly visible on hair band. Lettering, date, stars, worn but visible.*
**VG-8 VERY GOOD**—*LIBERTY entirely visible on hair band. Lower curls worn.*
**F-12 FINE**—*Only part wear on LIBERTY and hair at top worn in spots.*
**VF-20 VERY FINE**—*Lettering clear-cut. Hair only slightly worn.*
**EF-40 EXTREMELY FINE**—*Light wear on highest points of hair and leaves.*
**MS-60 UNCIRCULATED**—*Typical brown to red surface. No trace of wear.*

*Brilliant or red uncirculated coins are worth more than prices shown. Spotted, cleaned or discolored pieces are worth less.*

| | *Quan. Minted* | *G-4* | *VG-8* | *F-12* | *VF-20* | *EF-40* | *MS-60* |
|---|---|---|---|---|---|---|---|
| 1809 | 1,154,572 | $7.00 | $14.00 | $17.00 | $27.00 | $45.00 | $270.00 |
| 1810 | 215,000 | 14.00 | 17.00 | 27.00 | 45.00 | 80.00 | 600.00 |
| 1811 | 63,140 | 33.00 | 55.00 | 90.00 | 200.00 | 400.00 | 1,100 |
| 1825 | 63,000 | 12.00 | 15.00 | 20.00 | 28.00 | 40.00 | 250.00 |
| 1826 | 234,000 | 6.50 | 12.00 | 16.00 | 20.00 | 35.00 | 250.00 |

# HALF CENTS

13 Stars

12 Stars

| | Quan. Minted | VG-8 | F-12 | VF-20 | EF-40 | MS-60 | Proof-63 |
|---|---|---|---|---|---|---|---|
| 1828, 13 Stars | 606,000 | $6.50 | $12.00 | $16.00 | $20.00 | $35.00 | $250.00 |
| 1828, 12 Stars | | 7.00 | 13.00 | 17.00 | 25.00 | 40.00 | 300.00 |
| 1829 | 487,000 | 6.50 | 12.00 | 16.00 | 20.00 | 35.00 | 250.00 |
| 1831 (Beware of altered date) | 2,200 | | | | | 1,700 | 4,000 |
| 1832 | 154,000 | 10.00 | 15.00 | 20.00 | 30.00 | 225.00 | 1,800 |
| 1833 | 120,000 | 10.00 | 15.00 | 20.00 | 30.00 | 225.00 | 1,800 |
| 1834 | 141,000 | 10.00 | 15.00 | 20.00 | 30.00 | 225.00 | 1,800 |
| 1835 | 398,000 | 10.00 | 15.00 | 20.00 | 30.00 | 225.00 | 1,800 |
| 1836 | | | | | | | 3,000 |

## BRAIDED HAIR TYPE 1840-1857

| | Proof-63 | | Proof-63 |
|---|---|---|---|
| 1840 Original | $1,750 | 1845 Original | $2,700 |
| 1840 Restrike | 1,700 | 1845 Restrike | 1,900 |
| 1841 Original | 1,750 | 1846 Original | 1,900 |
| 1841 Restrike | 1,800 | 1846 Restrike | 1,800 |
| 1842 Original | 2,000 | 1847 Original | 1,800 |
| 1842 Restrike | 1,750 | 1847 Restrike | 1,800 |
| 1843 Original | 1,800 | 1848 Original | 1,800 |
| 1843 Restrike | 1,800 | 1848 Restrike | 1,800 |
| 1844 Original | 2,700 | 1849 Original. Small date | 1,850 |
| 1844 Restrike | 1,800 | 1849 Restrike. Small date | 1,850 |

*Brilliant or red uncirculated coins are worth more than prices shown. Spotted, cleaned or discolored pieces are worth less.*

**VG-8 VERY GOOD**—*Beads uniformly distinct. Hairlines show in spots.*
**F-12 FINE**—*Hairlines above ear worn. Beads sharp.*
**VF-20 VERY FINE**—*Lowest curl shows wear, hair otherwise distinct.*
**EF-40 EXTREMELY FINE**—*Light wear on highest points of hair and leaves.*
**MS-60 UNCIRCULATED**—*No trace of wear, light blemishes.*

Small Date

Large Date

| | Quan. Minted | VG-8 | F-12 | VF-20 | EF-40 | MS-60 | Proof-63 |
|---|---|---|---|---|---|---|---|
| 1849 Large date | 39,864 | $13.00 | $17.00 | $25.00 | $40.00 | $225.00 | — |
| 1850 | 39,812 | 13.00 | 17.00 | 25.00 | 40.00 | 225.00 | — |
| 1851 | 147,672 | 12.00 | 16.00 | 22.00 | 35.00 | 200.00 | — |
| 1852 | | | | | | | $1,900 |
| 1853 | 129,694 | 12.00 | 16.00 | 22.00 | 35.00 | 200.00 | |
| 1854 | 55,358 | 12.00 | 16.00 | 22.00 | 35.00 | 200.00 | 1,900 |
| 1855 | 56,500 | 12.00 | 16.00 | 22.00 | 35.00 | 200.00 | 1,900 |
| 1856 | 40,430 | 12.00 | 16.00 | 23.00 | 37.00 | 200.00 | 1,900 |
| 1857 | 35,180 | 13.00 | 17.00 | 25.00 | 40.00 | 225.00 | 1,900 |

# LARGE CENTS — 1793-1857

Cents and half cents were the first coins struck under the authority of the United States Government. Coinage began in 1793 with laws specifying that the cent should weigh exactly twice as much as the half cent. Large cents were coined every year from 1793 to 1857 with the exception of 1815, when a lack of copper prevented production. All were coined at the Philadelphia Mint. Varieties listed are those most significant to collectors. Numerous other die varieties may be found because each of the early dies was individually made.

## FLOWING HAIR, CHAIN TYPE REVERSE 1793

**AG-3 ABOUT GOOD**—*Date and devices clear enough to identify.*
**G-4 GOOD**—*Lettering worn but readable. Bust has no detail.*
**VG-8 VERY GOOD**—*Date and lettering distinct, some details of head visible.*
**F-12 FINE**—*About half of hair, etc. details show.*
**VF-20 VERY FINE**—*Ear visible. Most of details can be seen.*
**EF-40 EXTREMELY FINE**—*Highest points of hair and back of temple show wear.*

Obverse

AMERI. Reverse

AMERICA Reverse

| | *Quan. Minted* | *AG-3* | *G-4* | *VG-8* | *F-12* | *VF-20* | *EF-40* |
|---|---|---|---|---|---|---|---|
| 1793 Chain | 36,103 | | | | | | |
| 1793 AMERI. in legend | | $250.00 | $850.00 | $1,250 | $2,500 | $4,500 | $10,000 |
| 1793 AMERICA | | 225.00 | 800.00 | 1,100 | 2,250 | 4,000 | 9,000 |

## FLOWING HAIR, WREATH TYPE REVERSE 1793

Wreath Type

Strawberry Leaf Var.,

| | *Quan. Minted* | *AG-3* | *G-4* | *VG-8* | *F-12* | *VF-20* | *EF-40* |
|---|---|---|---|---|---|---|---|
| 1793 Wreath | 63,353 | | | | | | |
| 1793 Vine/bars edge | | $125.00 | $400.00 | $600.00 | $1,100 | $2,000 | $4,500 |
| 1793 Lettered Edge | | 150.00 | 450.00 | 650.00 | 1,200 | 2,100 | 5,000 |
| 1793 Strawberry leaf | | | | (4 known) | | | |

# LARGE CENTS
## LIBERTY CAP TYPE 1793-1796

1793 Vine and Bar edge
Chain and Wreath Type Only

Lettered edge 1793-1795
ONE HUNDRED FOR A DOLLAR

Beaded Border, 1793 Only

**1793-1794**

"Head of 1793"
Head is in high
rounded relief

**1794 Only**

"Head of 1794"
Well defined hair,
hook on lowest curl

**1794-1796**

"Head of 1795"
Head in low relief,
no hook on lowest curl

| | *Quan. Minted* | *AG-3* | *G-4* | *VG-8* | *F-12* | *VF-20* | *EF-40* |
|---|---|---|---|---|---|---|---|
| 1793 Lib. Cap........ | 11,056 | $250.00 | $550.00 | $900.00 | $1,500 | $3,500 | $8,000 |
| 1794 All kinds...... | 918,521 | | | | | | |
| 1794 "Head of 1793"....... | | 70.00 | 110.00 | 200.00 | 550.00 | 1,200 | 3,500 |
| 1794 "Head of 1794"....... | | 20.00 | 50.00 | 80.00 | 135.00 | 350.00 | 850.00 |
| 1794 "Head of 1795"....... | | 20.00 | 50.00 | 80.00 | 135.00 | 350.00 | 850.00 |
| 1795 Ltd. ed. ......... | 37,000 | 20.00 | 50.00 | 90.00 | 150.00 | 370.00 | 900.00 |
| 1795 Plain ed. ....... | 501,500 | 15.00 | 40.00 | 65.00 | 110.00 | 250.00 | 500.00 |
| 1796 Lib. Cap....... | 109,825 | 20.00 | 50.00 | 80.00 | 135.00 | 250.00 | 650.00 |

## DRAPED BUST TYPE 1796-1807

**AG-3 ABOUT GOOD**—*Clear enough to identify.*
**G-4 GOOD**—*Lettering worn, but clear; date clear. Bust lacks details.*
**VG-8 VERY GOOD**—*Drapery partly visible. Less wear in date and lettering.*
**F-12 FINE**—*Hair over brow is smooth, some details showing in other parts of hair.*
**VF-20 VERY FINE**—*Hairlines slightly worn. Hair over brow better defined.*
**EF-40 EXTREMELY FINE**—*Hair above forehead and left of eye outlined and detailed. Only slight wear on olive leaves.*

# LARGE CENTS

LIHERTY error

Gripped or Milled Edge

Stems

Stemless

| | Quan. Minted | AG-3 | G-4 | VG-8 | F-12 | VF-20 | EF-40 |
|---|---|---|---|---|---|---|---|
| 1796 Dr. Bust. | 363,375 | $16.00 | $32.00 | $50.00 | $100.00 | $250.00 | $600.00 |
| 1796 LIHERTY error | | 20.00 | 40.00 | 80.00 | 150.00 | 300.00 | 800.00 |
| 1797 All kinds | 897,510 | | | | | | |
| 1797 Gr. edge, '96 rev | | 10.00 | 16.00 | 35.00 | 65.00 | 150.00 | 300.00 |
| 1797 Pl. edge, '96 rev | | 10.00 | 16.00 | 35.00 | 70.00 | 160.00 | 350.00 |
| 1797, '97 rev., Stems | | 7.00 | 14.00 | 20.00 | 40.00 | 100.00 | 250.00 |
| 1797, '97 rev., Stemless | | 15.00 | 25.00 | 50.00 | 100.00 | 180.00 | 450.00 |

1798, 8 over 7

1799, 9 over 8

1800 over 1798

1800, 80 over 79

| | Quan. Minted | AG-3 | G-4 | VG-8 | F-12 | VF-20 | EF-40 |
|---|---|---|---|---|---|---|---|
| 1798 All kinds | 1,841,745 | | | | | | |
| 1798, 8 over 7 | | 10.00 | 18.00 | 40.00 | 100.00 | 200.00 | 500.00 |
| 1798 | | 6.00 | 12.00 | 18.00 | 40.00 | 80.00 | 200.00 |
| 1799, 9 over 8 | * | 150.00 | 300.00 | 500.00 | 1,300 | 3,000 | — |
| 1799 Nor. date | 42,540 | 125.00 | 225.00 | 450.00 | 1,200 | 2,750 | — |
| 1800 All kds. | 2,822,175 | | | | | | |
| 1800 over 1798 | | 5.00 | 10.00 | 17.00 | 30.00 | 80.00 | 250.00 |
| 1800, 80 over 79 | | 4.00 | 9.00 | 15.00 | 27.00 | 75.00 | 180.00 |
| 1800 Normal date | | 4.00 | 9.00 | 15.00 | 27.00 | 75.00 | 180.00 |

*Mintage for 1799, 9 over 8 variety is included with the 1798 figure.

Fraction 1/000

Corrected Fraction

1801 Reverse, 3 Errors

| | Quan. Minted | AG-3 | G-4 | VG-8 | F-12 | VF-20 | EF-40 |
|---|---|---|---|---|---|---|---|
| 1801 All kds. | 1,362,837 | | | | | | |
| 1801 Normal rev. | | 4.00 | 9.00 | 15.00 | 27.00 | 75.00 | 180.00 |
| 1801, 3 errors: 1/000, one stem & IINITED | | 10.00 | 20.00 | 40.00 | 100.00 | 200.00 | 600.00 |
| 1801 Fraction 1/000 | | 5.00 | 10.00 | 20.00 | 45.00 | 100.00 | 250.00 |
| 1801, 1/100 over 1/000 | | 5.00 | 10.00 | 20.00 | 50.00 | 110.00 | 275.00 |
| 1802 All kds. | 3,435,100 | | | | | | |
| 1802 Normal rev. | | 4.00 | 8.00 | 14.00 | 25.00 | 70.00 | 150.00 |
| 1802 Fraction 1/000 | | 5.00 | 10.00 | 20.00 | 30.00 | 80.00 | 200.00 |
| 1802 Stemless wreath | | 4.00 | 9.00 | 15.00 | 27.00 | 70.00 | 175.00 |

1803 Sm. Date, Blunt 1

1803 Large Date, Pointed 1

Small Fraction

Large Fraction

| | Quan. Minted | AG-3 | G-4 | VG-8 | F-12 | VF-20 | EF-40 |
|---|---|---|---|---|---|---|---|
| 1803 All kds. | 3,131,691 | | | | | | |
| 1803 Sm. dt., sm. fract. | | $4.00 | $8.00 | $14.00 | $25.00 | $70.00 | $150.00 |
| 1803 Sm. dt., lg. fract. | | 4.00 | 8.00 | 14.00 | 25.00 | 70.00 | 150.00 |
| 1803 Lg. dt., sm. fract. | | 85.00 | 125.00 | 250.00 | 550.00 | 1,500 | |
| 1803 Lg. dt., lg. fract. | | 13.00 | 20.00 | 50.00 | 100.00 | 170.00 | 500.00 |
| 1803, 1/100 over 1/000 | | 5.00 | 10.00 | 20.00 | 40.00 | 100.00 | 300.00 |
| 1803 Stemless wreath | | 4.50 | 9.00 | 18.00 | 35.00 | 100.00 | 250.00 |

**1804 With Broken Dies (see arrows)**

All genuine 1804 Cents have a crosslet 4 in the date and a large fraction. The 0 in the date is in line with the O in OF on the reverse of the coin.

| | Quan. Minted | AG-3 | G-4 | VG-8 | F-12 | VF-20 | EF-40 |
|---|---|---|---|---|---|---|---|
| 1804 | 96,500 | 85.00 | 150.00 | 285.00 | 450.00 | 900.00 | 2,500 |
| 1805 | 941,116 | 4.00 | 8.00 | 14.00 | 25.00 | 70.00 | 150.00 |
| 1806 | 348,000 | 5.00 | 10.00 | 21.00 | 50.00 | 100.00 | 285.00 |

Sm. 1807, 7 over 6, blunt 1

Lg. 1807, 7 over 6, pointed 1

| | Quan. Minted | AG-3 | G-4 | VG-8 | F-12 | VF-20 | EF-40 |
|---|---|---|---|---|---|---|---|
| 1807 All kinds | 829,221 | | | | | | |
| 1807 Small 7 over 6 | | 60.00 | 125.00 | 230.00 | 450.00 | 1,000 | —— |
| 1807 Large 7 over 6 | | 4.00 | 8.00 | 14.00 | 25.00 | 70.00 | 175.00 |
| 1807 Small fraction | | 4.00 | 10.00 | 18.00 | 30.00 | 85.00 | 275.00 |
| 1807 Large fraction | | 4.00 | 8.00 | 14.00 | 25.00 | 70.00 | 175.00 |

## CLASSIC HEAD TYPE 1808-1814

**AG-3 ABOUT GOOD**—*Details clear enough to identify.*

**G-4 GOOD**—*Legends, stars, date worn, but plain.*

**VG-8 VERY GOOD**—*LIBERTY all readable. Ear shows. Details worn but plain.*

**F-12 FINE**—*Hair on forehead and before ear nearly smooth. Ear and hair under ear sharp.*

**VF-20 VERY FINE**—*All hairlines show some detail. Leaves on rev. show slight wear.*

**EF-40 EXTREMELY FINE**—*All hairlines sharp. Very slight wear on high points.*

# LARGE CENTS

| | Quan. Minted | AG-3 | G-4 | VG-8 | F-12 | VF-20 | EF-40 |
|---|---|---|---|---|---|---|---|
| 1808 | 1,007,000 | $6.00 | $14.00 | $25.00 | $40.00 | $100.00 | $325.00 |
| 1809 | 222,867 | 16.00 | 30.00 | 60.00 | 110.00 | 270.00 | 600.00 |

1810, 10 over 09

1810 Normal Date

1811, last 1 over 0

1811 Normal Date

| | Quan. Minted | AG-3 | G-4 | VG-8 | F-12 | VF-20 | EF-40 |
|---|---|---|---|---|---|---|---|
| 1810 All kds. | 1,458,500 | | | | | | |
| 1810, 10 over 09 | | 6.00 | 11.00 | 20.00 | 35.00 | 100.00 | 300.00 |
| 1810 Normal date | | 6.00 | 11.00 | 20.00 | 35.00 | 100.00 | 300.00 |
| 1811 All kds. | 218,025 | | | | | | |
| 1811 Last 1 over 0 | | 12.00 | 20.00 | 35.00 | 85.00 | 175.00 | 450.00 |
| 1811 Normal date | | 10.00 | 18.00 | 32.00 | 80.00 | 150.00 | 400.00 |
| 1812 | 1,075,500 | 6.00 | 11.00 | 20.00 | 35.00 | 100.00 | 300.00 |
| 1813 | 418,000 | 7.00 | 15.00 | 28.00 | 60.00 | 130.00 | 350.00 |
| 1814 | 357,830 | 6.00 | 11.00 | 20.00 | 35.00 | 100.00 | 310.00 |

## CORONET TYPE 1816-1857

**G-4 GOOD**—*Head details partly visible. Even wear in date and legends.*
**VG-8 VERY GOOD**—*LIBERTY, date, stars, legends clear. Part of hair cord visible.*
**F-12 FINE**—*All hairlines show. Hair cords show uniformly.*
**VF-20 VERY FINE**—*Hair cords only slightly worn. Hairlines only partly worn, all well defined.*
**EF-40 EXTREMELY FINE**—*Both hair cords stand out sharply. All hairlines sharp.*
**MS-60 UNCIRCULATED**—*Typical brown to red surface. No trace of wear.*

13 Stars

15 Stars

*Brilliant or red uncirculated coins are worth more than prices shown. Spotted, cleaned or discolored pieces are worth less.*

| | Quan. Minted | G-4 | VG-8 | F-12 | VF-20 | EF-40 | MS-60 |
|---|---|---|---|---|---|---|---|
| 1816 | 2,820,982 | $3.75 | $4.50 | $7.00 | $12.00 | $32.00 | $185.00 |
| 1817, 13 stars | 3,948,400 | 3.75 | 4.50 | 6.00 | 10.00 | 32.00 | 185.00 |
| 1817, 15 stars | | 4.00 | 5.00 | 8.00 | 15.00 | 40.00 | 225.00 |
| 1818 | 3,167,000 | 3.75 | 4.50 | 6.00 | 10.00 | 32.00 | 185.00 |

# LARGE CENTS

1819, 9 over 8

1820, 20 over 19

| | Quan. Minted | G-4 | VG-8 | F-12 | VF-20 | EF-40 | MS-60 |
|---|---|---|---|---|---|---|---|
| 1819, 9 over 8 | 2,671,000 | $4.00 | $5.00 | $8.00 | $11.00 | $35.00 | $200.00 |
| 1819 | | 3.75 | 4.50 | 6.00 | 10.00 | 32.00 | 185.00 |
| 1820, 20 over 19 | | 4.00 | 5.00 | 8.00 | 14.00 | 35.00 | 200.00 |
| 1820 | 4,407,550 | 3.75 | 4.50 | 6.00 | 10.00 | 30.00 | 185.00 |
| 1821 | 389,000 | 5.00 | 10.00 | 18.00 | 40.00 | 100.00 | 650.00 |
| 1822 | 2,072,339 | 3.75 | 4.50 | 6.00 | 10.00 | 35.00 | 200.00 |

1823, 3 over 2

1824, 4 over 2

1826, 6 over 5

| | Quan. Minted | G-4 | VG-8 | F-12 | VF-20 | EF-40 | MS-60 |
|---|---|---|---|---|---|---|---|
| 1823, 3 over 2 | Included with 1824 | 12.00 | 16.00 | 30.00 | 75.00 | 200.00 | — |
| 1823 Normal date | | 13.00 | 20.00 | 35.00 | 80.00 | 300.00 | — |
| 1824, 4 over 2 | 1,262,000 | 4.50 | 6.00 | 13.00 | 35.00 | 100.00 | — |
| 1824 Normal date | | 4.00 | 5.00 | 8.00 | 17.00 | 45.00 | 300.00 |
| 1825 | 1,461,100 | 3.75 | 4.50 | 7.00 | 15.00 | 35.00 | 200.00 |
| 1826, 6 over 5 | 1,517,425 | 5.00 | 9.00 | 14.00 | 30.00 | 75.00 | 275.00 |
| 1826 Normal date | | 3.75 | 4.50 | 6.00 | 10.00 | 30.00 | 185.00 |
| 1827 | 2,357,732 | 3.75 | 4.50 | 6.00 | 10.00 | 30.00 | 185.00 |

This date size appears on cents before 1828.

This date size appears on cents after 1828.

| | Quan. Minted | G-4 | VG-8 | F-12 | VF-20 | EF-40 | MS-60 |
|---|---|---|---|---|---|---|---|
| 1828 Lg. nar. date | 2,260,624 | 3.75 | 4.50 | 6.00 | 10.00 | 30.00 | 200.00 |
| 1828 Sm. wide date | | 4.00 | 5.00 | 8.00 | 15.00 | 35.00 | 225.00 |
| 1829 | 1,414,500 | 3.75 | 4.50 | 6.00 | 10.00 | 30.00 | 185.00 |
| 1830 | 1,711,500 | 3.75 | 4.50 | 6.00 | 10.00 | 30.00 | 185.00 |
| 1831 | 3,359,260 | 3.50 | 4.25 | 5.50 | 8.00 | 27.00 | 185.00 |
| 1832 | 2,362,000 | 3.50 | 4.25 | 5.50 | 8.00 | 27.00 | 185.00 |
| 1833 | 2,739,000 | 3.50 | 4.25 | 5.50 | 8.00 | 27.00 | 185.00 |
| 1834 | 1,855,100 | 3.50 | 4.25 | 5.50 | 10.00 | 30.00 | 225.00 |
| 1835 | 3,878,400 | 4.00 | 5.00 | 7.00 | 12.00 | 30.00 | 200.00 |
| 1836 | 2,111,000 | 3.50 | 4.25 | 5.50 | 9.00 | 27.00 | 185.00 |

# LARGE CENTS

**G-4 GOOD**—*Considerably worn. LIBERTY readable.*
**VG-8 VERY GOOD**—*Hairlines smooth but visible, outline of ear clearly defined.*
**F-12 FINE**—*Hairlines at top of head and behind ear worn but visible. Braid over brow plain, ear clear.*
**VF-20 VERY FINE**—*All details more sharp. Hair over brow shows only slight wear.*
**EF-40 EXTREMELY FINE**—*Hair above ear detailed, but slightly worn.*
**MS-60 UNCIRCULATED**—*Typical brown to red surface. No trace of wear.*

1839 over 1836

*Brilliant or red uncirculated coins are worth more than prices shown. Spotted, cleaned or discolored pieces are worth less.*

| | *Quan. Minted* | *G-4* | *VG-8* | *F-12* | *VF-20* | *EF-40* | *MS-60* |
|---|---|---|---|---|---|---|---|
| 1837 | 5,558,300 | $3.75 | $4.50 | $6.00 | $10.00 | $30.00 | $200.00 |
| 1838 | 6,370,200 | 3.50 | 4.25 | 5.50 | 8.00 | 27.00 | 185.00 |
| 1839 | 3,128,661 | 3.50 | 5.00 | 6.00 | 10.00 | 30.00 | 200.00 |
| 1839, 9 over 6 | | 35.00 | 60.00 | 125.00 | 200.00 | 650.00 | —— |
| 1840 | 2,462,700 | 3.00 | 4.00 | 5.00 | 8.00 | 25.00 | 185.00 |
| 1841 | 1,597,367 | 3.00 | 4.00 | 5.00 | 8.00 | 25.00 | 185.00 |
| 1842 | 2,383,390 | 3.00 | 4.00 | 5.00 | 8.00 | 25.00 | 175.00 |

"Head of 1840"
Petite Head
1839-1843

"Head of 1844"
Mature Head
1843-1857

Small Letters

Large Letters

| | | | | | | | |
|---|---|---|---|---|---|---|---|
| 1843 Petite, sm. let. | 2,425,342 | 3.00 | 4.00 | 5.00 | 8.00 | 25.00 | 175.00 |
| 1843 Petite, lg. let. | | 5.00 | 8.00 | 12.00 | 25.00 | 45.00 | 300.00 |
| 1843 Mature, lg. let. | | 3.50 | 5.00 | 8.00 | 14.00 | 30.00 | 175.00 |
| 1844 Normal date | 2,398,752 | 3.00 | 4.00 | 5.00 | 8.00 | 25.00 | 175.00 |
| 1844 over 81 (error-photo page 54) | | 4.00 | 5.00 | 9.00 | 17.00 | 60.00 | 325.00 |
| 1845 | 3,894,804 | 2.75 | 3.75 | 4.75 | 7.00 | 22.00 | 165.00 |
| 1846 | 4,120,800 | 3.00 | 4.00 | 5.00 | 8.00 | 25.00 | 175.00 |
| 1847 | 6,183,669 | 2.75 | 3.75 | 4.75 | 7.00 | 22.00 | 165.00 |
| 1847, 7 over "sm." 7 | | 4.00 | 5.00 | 9.00 | 15.00 | 35.00 | 200.00 |

# LARGE CENTS

| | Quan. Minted | G-4 | VG-8 | F-12 | VF-20 | EF-40 | MS-60 |
|---|---|---|---|---|---|---|---|
| 1848 | 6,415,799 | $2.75 | $3.75 | $4.75 | $7.00 | $22.00 | $165.00 |
| 1849 | 4,178,500 | 2.75 | 3.75 | 4.75 | 7.00 | 22.00 | 165.00 |
| 1850 | 4,426,844 | 2.75 | 2.75 | 4.75 | 7.00 | 22.00 | 165.00 |

1844, 44 over 81

1851, 51 over 81

1847, 7 over "Small" 7

*Brilliant or red uncirculated coins are worth more than prices shown. Spotted, cleaned or discolored pieces are worth less.*

| | Quan. Minted | G-4 | VG-8 | F-12 | VF-20 | EF-40 | MS-60 |
|---|---|---|---|---|---|---|---|
| 1851 Normal date | 9,889,707 (both) | 2.75 | 3.75 | 4.75 | 7.00 | 22.00 | 165.00 |
| 1851 over 81 (error) | | 4.00 | 5.00 | 8.00 | 17.00 | 30.00 | 200.00 |
| 1852 | 5,063,094 | 2.75 | 3.75 | 4.75 | 7.00 | 22.00 | 165.00 |
| 1853 | 6,641,131 | 2.75 | 3.75 | 4.75 | 7.00 | 22.00 | 165.00 |
| 1854 | 4,236,156 | 2.75 | 3.75 | 4.75 | 7.00 | 22.00 | 165.00 |

1855 Upright 5's

1855 Slanting 5's

1855 Knob on ear

| | Quan. Minted | G-4 | VG-8 | F-12 | VF-20 | EF-40 | MS-60 |
|---|---|---|---|---|---|---|---|
| 1855 All kinds | 1,574,829 | | | | | | |
| 1855 Upright 5's | | 2.75 | 3.75 | 4.75 | 7.00 | 22.00 | 165.00 |
| 1855 Slanting 5's | | 2.75 | 3.75 | 4.75 | 7.00 | 22.00 | 165.00 |
| 1855 Slanting 5's, knob on ear | | 3.00 | 4.00 | 5.50 | 12.00 | 27.00 | 185.00 |
| 1856 Upright 5 | 2,690,463 (both) | 2.75 | 3.75 | 4.75 | 7.00 | 22.00 | 165.00 |
| 1856 Slanting 5 | | 2.75 | 3.75 | 4.75 | 7.00 | 22.00 | 165.00 |

1857 Large Date

1857 Small Date

| | Quan. Minted | G-4 | VG-8 | F-12 | VF-20 | EF-40 | MS-60 |
|---|---|---|---|---|---|---|---|
| 1857 Large date | 333,456 (both) | 9.00 | 13.00 | 19.00 | 24.00 | 26.00 | 200.00 |
| 1857 Small date | | 10.00 | 15.00 | 22.00 | 26.00 | 30.00 | 225.00 |

# SMALL CENTS — 1856 to Date

## FLYING EAGLE TYPE 1856-1858

The Act of February 21, 1857 provided for the coinage of the small cent. The 1856 Eagle cent was not an authorized mint issue, as the law governing the new size coin was enacted after the date of issue. It is believed that about 1,000 of these pieces were struck. They are properly referred to as patterns.

**G-4 GOOD**—*All details worn, but readable.*
**VG-8 VERY GOOD**—*Feather details and eye of eagle are evident but worn.*
**F-12 FINE**—*Eagle head details and feather tips sharp.*
**VF-20 VERY FINE**—*Feathers in right wing and tail show considerable detail.*
**EF-40 EXTREMELY FINE**—*Slight wear, all details sharp.*
**MS-60 UNCIRCULATED**—*No trace of wear. Light blemishes.*

1858, 8 over 7

1856-1858 Large Letters

1858 Small Letters

*Brilliant uncirculated and proof coins are worth more than prices shown. Spotted, cleaned or discolored pieces are worth less.*

| | *Quan. Minted* |
|---|---|
| 1856 | est. *1,000* |
| 1857 | 17,450,000 |
| 1858 Lg. letters (*80*) / 1858 Sm. letters (*200*) | 24,600,000 |

| | *G-4* | *VG-8* | *F-12* | *VF-20* | *EF-40* | *MS-60* | *Proof-60* |
|---|---|---|---|---|---|---|---|
| 1856 | $500.00 | $700.00 | $850.00 | $1,000 | $1,400 | $1,700 | $1,800 |
| 1857 | 4.50 | 6.00 | 9.00 | 16.00 | 40.00 | 185.00 | 1,200 |
| 1858 Lg. let. | 4.50 | 6.00 | 9.00 | 16.00 | 40.00 | 185.00 | 1,200 |
| 1858, 8 over 7 | | | 60.00 | 125.00 | 250.00 | 500.00 | |
| 1858 Sm let. | 4.50 | 6.00 | 9.00 | 16.00 | 40.00 | 185.00 | 1,200 |

# SMALL CENTS

## INDIAN HEAD TYPE 1859-1909

The small cent was redesigned in 1859, and a representation of an Indian girl was adopted as the obverse device. The 1859 reverse was also changed to represent a laurel wreath. In 1860 the reverse was modified to display an oak wreath with a small shield at the top. From 1859 to 1863 cents were struck in copper-nickel. In 1864 the composition was changed to bronze, although copper-nickel cents were also struck during that year.

# SMALL CENTS

**G-4 GOOD**—*No LIBERTY visible.*
**VG-8 VERY GOOD**—*At least three letters of LIBERTY readable on head band.*
**F-12 FINE**—*LIBERTY completely visible.*
**VF-20 VERY FINE**—*Slight but even wear on LIBERTY.*
**EF-40 EXTREMELY FINE**—*LIBERTY sharp. All other details sharp. Only slight wear on ribbon end.*
**MS-60 UNCIRCULATED**—*No trace of wear. Light blemishes.*

Without Shield at Top of Wreath
1859 Only

With Shield on Reverse
1860 to 1909

*Brilliant uncirculated and proof coins are worth more than prices shown. Spotted, cleaned or discolored pieces are worth less.*

### Copper-nickel, Laurel Wreath Reverse 1859

| | *Quan. Minted* | *G-4* | *VG-8* | *F-12* | *VF-20* | *EF-40* | *MS-60* | *Proof-63* |
|---|---|---|---|---|---|---|---|---|
| 1859 . . . . . . . . . *(800)* | 36,400,000 | $2.50 | $3.00 | $5.00 | $12.00 | $35.00 | $200.00 | $650.00 |

### Copper-nickel, Oak Wreath with Shield Reverse 1860-1864

| | | | | | | | | |
|---|---|---|---|---|---|---|---|---|
| 1860 . . . . . . . *(1,000)* | 20,566,000 | 2.50 | 3.00 | 4.00 | 7.00 | 15.00 | 100.00 | 550.00 |
| 1861 . . . . . . . *(1,000)* | 10,100,000 | 5.00 | 7.00 | 10.00 | 17.00 | 25.00 | 150.00 | 575.00 |
| 1862 . . . . . . . . . *(550)* | 28,075,000 | 1.75 | 2.00 | 3.00 | 5.00 | 10.00 | 85.00 | 475.00 |
| 1863 . . . . . . . . . *(460)* | 49,840,000 | 1.75 | 2.00 | 3.00 | 5.00 | 10.00 | 85.00 | 475.00 |
| 1864 . . . . . . . . . *(370)* | 13,740,000 | 4.00 | 5.00 | 7.00 | 10.00 | 15.00 | 95.00 | 550.00 |

### Bronze 1864-1909

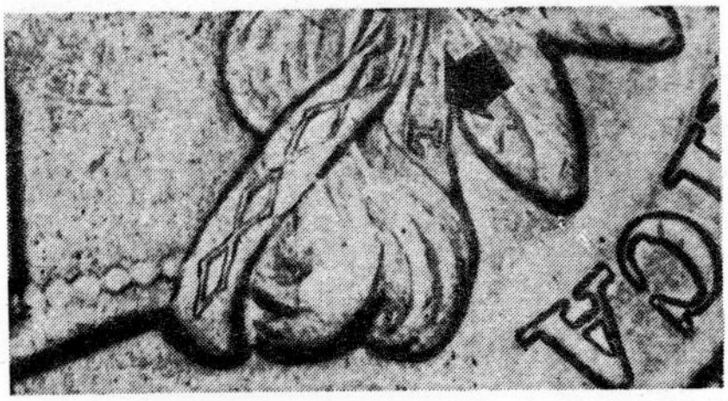

1864 Indian Head Cent with "L"

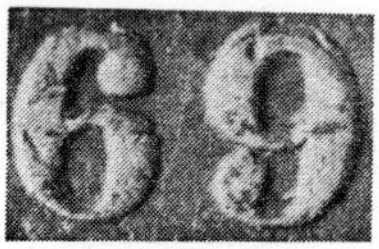


1869, 9 over 8

| | *Quan. Minted* | *G-4* | *VG-8* | *F-12* | *VF-20* | *EF-40* | *MS-60* | *Proof-63* |
|---|---|---|---|---|---|---|---|---|
| 1864 | | | | | | | | |
| All kinds . . . . . . . . . . | 39,233,714 | | | | | | | |
| 1864 No L. . . . . . . . . . . . . . . . . *(150)* | | $2.00 | $3.00 | $5.00 | $10.00 | $15.00 | $40.00 | $550.00 |
| 1864 L must show . . . . . . . . . *(20)* | | 17.00 | 22.00 | 35.00 | 60.00 | 85.00 | 230.00 | — |
| 1865 . . . . . . . . . *(500)* | 35,429,286 | 2.00 | 2.50 | 4.50 | 9.00 | 15.00 | 35.00 | 275.00 |
| 1866 . . . . . . . . . *(725)* | 9,826,500 | 13.00 | 15.00 | 22.00 | 35.00 | 50.00 | 115.00 | 275.00 |
| 1867 . . . . . . . . . *(625)* | 9,821,000 | 13.00 | 15.00 | 22.00 | 35.00 | 50.00 | 115.00 | 275.00 |
| 1868 . . . . . . . . . *(600)* | 10,266,500 | 13.00 | 15.00 | 22.00 | 35.00 | 50.00 | 115.00 | 275.00 |
| 1869 over 8 . . } *(600)* | 6,420,000 | 65.00 | 85.00 | 150.00 | 250.00 | 350.00 | 700.00 | — |
| 1869 . . . . . . . . } | | 18.00 | 25.00 | 45.00 | 65.00 | 100.00 | 250.00 | 375.00 |

# SMALL CENTS

*Brilliant or red uncirculated coins are worth more than prices shown. Spotted, cleaned or discolored pieces are worth less.*

| | *Quan. Minted* | *G-4* | *VG-8* | *F-12* | *VF-20* | *EF-40* | *MS-60* | *Proof-63* |
|---|---|---|---|---|---|---|---|---|
| 1870 ....... *(1,000)* | 5,275,000 | $16.00 | $20.00 | $35.00 | $50.00 | $75.00 | $160.00 | $275.00 |
| 1871 ......... *(960)* | 3,929,500 | 20.00 | 25.00 | 50.00 | 70.00 | 95.00 | 200.00 | 325.00 |
| 1872 ......... *(950)* | 4,042,000 | 30.00 | 35.00 | 55.00 | 85.00 | 120.00 | 280.00 | 350.00 |
| 1873 ....... *(1,100)* | 11,676,500 | 5.50 | 6.50 | 11.00 | 18.00 | 35.00 | 75.00 | 225.00 |
| 1874 ......... *(700)* | 14,187,500 | 5.50 | 6.50 | 11.00 | 17.00 | 32.00 | 70.00 | 200.00 |
| 1875 ......... *(700)* | 13,528,000 | 5.50 | 6.50 | 11.00 | 17.00 | 32.00 | 70.00 | 200.00 |
| 1876 ....... *(1,150)* | 7,944,000 | 10.00 | 12.00 | 16.00 | 25.00 | 40.00 | 85.00 | 200.00 |
| 1877 ......... *(510)* | 852,500 | 175.00 | 200.00 | 260.00 | 400.00 | 650.00 | 1,100 | 1,400 |
| 1878 ....... (2,350) | 5,799,850 | 10.00 | 12.00 | 16.00 | 30.00 | 45.00 | 90.00 | 185.00 |
| 1879 ....... (3,200) | 16,231,200 | 2.00 | 2.25 | 3.50 | 7.00 | 12.00 | 40.00 | 175.00 |
| 1880 ....... (3,955) | 38,964,955 | .60 | 1.00 | 1.75 | 2.75 | 7.00 | 27.00 | 170.00 |
| 1881 ....... (3,575) | 39,211,575 | .60 | 1.00 | 1.75 | 2.75 | 7.00 | 27.00 | 170.00 |
| 1882 ....... (3,100) | 38,581,100 | .60 | 1.00 | 1.75 | 2.75 | 7.00 | 27.00 | 170.00 |
| 1883 ....... (6,609) | 45,598,109 | .60 | 1.00 | 1.75 | 2.75 | 7.00 | 27.00 | 170.00 |
| 1884 ....... (3,942) | 23,261,742 | .75 | 1.25 | 2.25 | 5.00 | 9.00 | 35.00 | 180.00 |
| 1885 ....... (3,790) | 11,765,384 | 2.00 | 2.75 | 5.00 | 9.00 | 16.00 | 45.00 | 195.00 |
| 1886 ....... (4,290) | 17,654,290 | .60 | 1.25 | 3.25 | 5.50 | 10.00 | 40.00 | 170.00 |
| 1887 ....... (2,960) | 45,226,483 | .50 | .60 | .90 | 1.75 | 5.50 | 25.00 | 170.00 |
| 1888 ....... (4,582) | 37,494,414 | .50 | .60 | .90 | 1.75 | 5.50 | 25.00 | 170.00 |
| 1889 ....... (3,336) | 48,869,361 | .50 | .60 | .90 | 1.75 | 5.50 | 25.00 | 160.00 |
| 1890 ....... (2,740) | 57,182,854 | .50 | .60 | .90 | 1.75 | 5.50 | 25.00 | 160.00 |
| 1891 ....... (2,350) | 47,072,350 | .50 | .60 | .90 | 1.75 | 5.50 | 25.00 | 160.00 |
| 1892 ....... (2,745) | 37,649,832 | .50 | .60 | .90 | 1.75 | 5.50 | 25.00 | 160.00 |
| 1893 ....... (2,195) | 46,642,195 | .50 | .60 | .90 | 1.75 | 5.50 | 25.00 | 160.00 |
| 1894 ....... (2,632) | 16,752,132 | .75 | 1.25 | 2.75 | 5.00 | 9.00 | 30.00 | 170.00 |
| 1895 ....... (2,062) | 38,343,636 | .35 | .50 | .75 | 1.25 | 4.50 | 23.00 | 160.00 |
| 1896 ....... (1,862) | 39,057,293 | .35 | .50 | .75 | 1.25 | 4.50 | 23.00 | 160.00 |
| 1897 ....... (1,938) | 50,466,330 | .35 | .50 | .75 | 1.25 | 4.50 | 23.00 | 160.00 |
| 1898 ....... (1,795) | 49,823,079 | .35 | .50 | .75 | 1.25 | 4.50 | 23.00 | 140.00 |
| 1899 ....... (2,031) | 53,600,031 | .35 | .50 | .75 | 1.25 | 4.50 | 23.00 | 140.00 |
| 1900 ....... (2,262) | 66,833,764 | .30 | .40 | .60 | .85 | 3.50 | 20.00 | 130.00 |
| 1901 ....... (1,985) | 79,611,143 | .30 | .40 | .60 | .85 | 3.50 | 20.00 | 130.00 |
| 1902 ....... (2,018) | 87,376,722 | .30 | .40 | .60 | .85 | 3.50 | 20.00 | 130.00 |
| 1903 ....... (1,790) | 85,094,493 | .30 | .40 | .60 | .85 | 3.50 | 20.00 | 130.00 |
| 1904 ....... (1,817) | 61,328,015 | .30 | .40 | .60 | .85 | 3.50 | 20.00 | 130.00 |
| 1905 ....... (2,152) | 80,719,163 | .30 | .40 | .60 | .85 | 3.50 | 20.00 | 130.00 |
| 1906 ....... (1,725) | 96,022,255 | .30 | .40 | .60 | .85 | 3.50 | 20.00 | 130.00 |
| 1907 ....... (1,475) | 108,138,618 | .30 | .40 | .60 | .85 | 3.50 | 20.00 | 130.00 |

Location of mint mark S on reverse of Indian cent (1908 and 1909 only).

| | | | | | | | | |
|---|---|---|---|---|---|---|---|---|
| 1908 ....... (1,620) | 32,327,987 | .30 | .40 | .60 | .85 | 3.50 | 20.00 | 140.00 |
| 1908S ................ | 1,115,000 | 15.00 | 16.00 | 18.00 | 23.00 | 35.00 | 110.00 | |
| 1909 ....... (2,175) | 14,370,645 | .50 | .65 | .80 | 1.50 | 5.00 | 23.00 | 150.00 |
| 1909S .................. | 309,000 | 70.00 | 80.00 | 100.00 | 125.00 | 150.00 | 275.00 | |

# SMALL CENTS

## LINCOLN TYPE, WHEAT EARS REVERSE 1909-1958

Victor D. Brenner designed this cent which was issued to commemorate the hundredth anniversary of Lincoln's birth. The designer's initials VDB appear on the reverse of a limited quantity of cents of 1909. Later in the year they were removed from the dies but restored in 1918 as very small incuse letters beneath the shoulder. The Lincoln type was the first cent to have the motto IN GOD WE TRUST.

**G-4 GOOD**—*Date worn but apparent. Lines in wheat ears missing. Full rims.*
**VG-8 VERY GOOD**—*Half of lines show in upper wheat ears.*
**F-12 FINE**—*Wheat lines worn but visible.*
**VF-20 VERY FINE**—*Cheek and jaw bones worn but separated. No worn spots on wheat ears.*
**EF-40 EXTREMELY FINE**—*Slight wear. All details sharp.*
**MS-60 UNCIRCULATED**—*No trace of wear. Light blemishes or discoloration.*
**MS-63 SELECT UNCIRCULATED**—*No trace of wear. Slight blemishes.*
**MS-65 CHOICE UNCIRCULATED**—*No trace of wear. Barely noticeable blemishes.*

Location of mint mark S or D on obverse of Lincoln cent.

### Bronze 1909-1942

Location of designer's initials V.D.B. on 1909 only.

No V.D.B. on reverse 1909-1958.

*Brilliant uncirculated coins are worth more than prices shown. Spotted, cleaned, or discolored pieces are worth less.*

| | *Quan. Minted* | *G-4* | *VG-8* | *F-12* | *VF-20* | *EF-40* | *MS-60* |
|---|---|---|---|---|---|---|---|
| 1909 V.D.B. | 27,995,000 | $1.00 | $1.25 | $1.50 | $2.00 | $2.50 | $7.00 |
| 1909 V.D.B. Matte proof | (420) | | | | | | 450.00 |
| 1909S, V.D.B. | 484,000 | 165.00 | 180.00 | 200.00 | 225.00 | 275.00 | 375.00 |
| 1909 | 72,702,618 | .15 | .20 | .25 | .40 | .75 | 6.00 |
| 1909 Matte proof | (2,198) | | | | | | 90.00 |
| 1909S | 1,825,000 | 28.00 | 30.00 | 32.00 | 40.00 | 65.00 | 125.00 |
| 1910 | 146,801,218 | .05 | .08 | .10 | .20 | .50 | 7.00 |
| 1910 Matte proof | (2,405) | | | | | | 90.00 |
| 1910S | 6,045,000 | 4.00 | 4.50 | 5.00 | 6.00 | 10.00 | 50.00 |
| 1911 | 101,177,787 | .05 | .08 | .15 | .40 | .75 | 8.00 |
| 1911 Matte proof | (1,733) | | | | | | 90.00 |
| 1911D | 12,672,000 | 2.50 | 2.75 | 3.25 | 6.00 | 12.00 | 55.00 |
| 1911S | 4,026,000 | 8.00 | 8.50 | 9.00 | 12.00 | 18.00 | 60.00 |
| 1912 | 68,153,060 | .05 | .10 | .40 | 1.00 | 1.75 | 10.00 |
| 1912 Matte proof | (2,145) | | | | | | 90.00 |
| 1912D | 10,411,000 | 2.50 | 2.75 | 3.50 | 6.00 | 15.00 | 60.00 |
| 1912S | 4,431,000 | 6.00 | 7.00 | 8.00 | 9.00 | 15.00 | 60.00 |
| 1913 | 76,532,352 | .05 | .10 | .30 | .75 | 1.25 | 10.00 |
| 1913 Matte proof | (2,848) | | | | | | 90.00 |
| 1913D | 15,804,000 | 1.00 | 1.25 | 1.75 | 3.00 | 8.00 | 40.00 |

# SMALL CENTS

*Brilliant uncirculated coins before 1934 are worth more than prices shown. Spotted, cleaned or discolored pieces are worth less*

| | *Quan. Minted* | *G-4* | *VG-8* | *F-12* | *VF-20* | *EF-40* | *MS-60* |
|---|---|---|---|---|---|---|---|
| 1913S | 6,101,000 | $4.00 | $5.00 | $5.50 | $6.00 | $10.00 | $50.00 |
| 1914 | 75,238,432 | .05 | .10 | .30 | .75 | 3.00 | 30.00 |
| 1914 Matte proof | (1,365) | | | | | | 160.00 |
| 1914D* | 1,193,000 | 50.00 | 55.00 | 65.00 | 100.00 | 225.00 | 500.00 |
| 1914S | 4,137,000 | 5.50 | 6.00 | 6.50 | 8.00 | 16.00 | 75.00 |
| 1915 | 29,092,120 | .30 | .50 | 1.25 | 3.00 | 14.00 | 50.00 |
| 1915 Matte proof | (1,150) | | | | | | 160.00 |
| 1915D | 22,050,000 | .20 | .40 | .65 | 1.50 | 4.00 | 25.00 |
| 1915S | 4,833,000 | 5.00 | 5.50 | 6.00 | 7.00 | 12.00 | 50.00 |
| 1916 | 131,833,677 | .03 | .05 | .10 | .20 | .80 | 5.00 |
| 1916 Matte proof | (1,050) | | | | | | 185.00 |
| 1916D | 35,956,000 | .08 | .13 | .40 | 1.00 | 2.50 | 20.00 |
| 1916S | 22,510,000 | .30 | .40 | .75 | 1.25 | 3.50 | 30.00 |
| 1917 | 196,429,785 | .03 | .05 | .10 | .20 | .50 | 6.00 |
| 1917D | 55,120,000 | .08 | .13 | .35 | .80 | 2.50 | 30.00 |
| 1917S | 32,620,000 | .08 | .13 | .35 | .80 | 2.50 | 35.00 |

Designer's initials restored starting 1918.

| | *Quan. Minted* | *G-4* | *VG-8* | *F-12* | *VF-20* | *EF-40* | *MS-60* |
|---|---|---|---|---|---|---|---|
| 1918 | 288,104,634 | .03 | .05 | .10 | .20 | .75 | 5.00 |
| 1918D | 47,830,000 | .08 | .13 | .35 | .80 | 2.50 | 30.00 |
| 1918S | 34,680,000 | .08 | .13 | .35 | .80 | 2.50 | 35.00 |
| 1919 | 392,021,000 | .02 | .03 | .05 | .15 | .50 | 4.00 |
| 1919D | 57,154,000 | .04 | .06 | .10 | .30 | 1.00 | 25.00 |
| 1919S | 139,760,000 | .04 | .06 | .10 | .25 | .50 | 15.00 |
| 1920 | 310,165,000 | .02 | .03 | .05 | .15 | .50 | 4.00 |
| 1920D | 49,280,000 | .04 | .06 | .10 | .30 | 1.00 | 28.00 |
| 1920S | 46,220,000 | .04 | .06 | .10 | .30 | 1.25 | 32.00 |
| 1921 | 39,157,000 | .05 | .08 | .15 | .35 | 1.50 | 20.00 |
| 1921S | 15,274,000 | .35 | .45 | .70 | 1.25 | 6.00 | 75.00 |
| 1922D | 7,160,000 | 3.00 | 3.75 | 4.50 | 6.00 | 10.00 | 40.00 |
| 1922 Plain† | | 140.00 | 160.00 | 200.00 | 325.00 | 500.00 | 1,900 |
| 1923 | 74,723,000 | .02 | .03 | .05 | .15 | .50 | 4.00 |
| 1923S | 8,700,000 | .75 | .85 | 1.25 | 2.00 | 6.00 | 90.00 |
| 1924 | 75,178,000 | .02 | .03 | .05 | .15 | .75 | 8.00 |
| 1924D | 2,520,000 | 6.50 | 7.00 | 8.00 | 11.00 | 15.00 | 100.00 |
| 1924S | 11,696,000 | .35 | .45 | .70 | 1.00 | 1.75 | 50.00 |
| 1925 | 139,949,000 | .02 | .03 | .05 | .15 | .45 | 3.00 |
| 1925D | 22,580,000 | .04 | .06 | .10 | .30 | 1.50 | 20.00 |
| 1925S | 26,380,000 | .04 | .06 | .10 | .25 | 1.25 | 25.00 |
| 1926 | 157,088,000 | .02 | .03 | .05 | .15 | .45 | 3.00 |
| 1926D | 28,020,000 | .04 | .06 | .10 | .25 | 1.50 | 20.00 |
| 1926S | 4,550,000 | 1.50 | 1.75 | 2.25 | 2.75 | 4.00 | 35.00 |
| 1927 | 144,440,000 | .02 | .03 | .05 | .15 | .45 | 3.00 |
| 1927D | 27,170,000 | .04 | .06 | .10 | .25 | .85 | 11.00 |
| 1927S | 14,276,000 | .25 | .30 | .50 | .75 | 1.25 | 30.00 |
| 1928 | 134,116,000 | .02 | .03 | .05 | .15 | .45 | 3.00 |
| 1928D | 31,170,000 | .04 | .06 | .10 | .25 | .75 | 8.00 |
| 1928S | 17,266,000 | .06 | .10 | .25 | .50 | 1.00 | 22.00 |

*Beware of altered date or mint mark. No VDB on shoulder of genuine 1914D cent.
†The 1922 without D caused by defective die. Beware removed mint mark.

# SMALL CENTS

| | Quan. Minted | G-4 | VG-8 | F-12 | VF-20 | EF-40 | MS-60 |
|---|---|---|---|---|---|---|---|
| 1929 | 185,262,000 | $.02 | $.03 | $.05 | $.15 | $.25 | $2.50 |
| 1929D | 41,730,000 | .04 | .06 | .10 | .25 | .60 | 7.00 |
| 1929S | 50,148,000 | .03 | .05 | .10 | .15 | .40 | 3.00 |
| 1930 | 157,415,000 | .02 | .03 | .05 | .15 | .25 | 2.50 |
| 1930D | 40,100,000 | .04 | .06 | .10 | .25 | .60 | 5.00 |
| 1930S | 24,286,000 | .03 | .05 | .10 | .15 | .40 | 2.50 |
| 1931 | 19,396,000 | .15 | .20 | .30 | .40 | .60 | 6.00 |
| 1931D | 4,480,000 | 1.50 | 1.75 | 2.00 | 2.50 | 4.00 | 25.00 |
| 1931S | 866,000 | 20.00 | 22.00 | 24.00 | 26.00 | 30.00 | 40.00 |
| 1932 | 9,062,000 | .70 | .80 | 1.00 | 1.15 | 1.75 | 8.00 |
| 1932D | 10,500,000 | .25 | .35 | .40 | .50 | .75 | 6.00 |
| 1933 | 14,360,000 | .25 | .35 | .45 | .60 | 1.00 | 7.50 |
| 1933D | 6,200,000 | .80 | 1.00 | 1.20 | 1.50 | 1.75 | 9.00 |

| | Quan. Minted | G-4 | VG-8 | F-12 | VF-20 | EF-40 | MS-60 | MS-65 |
|---|---|---|---|---|---|---|---|---|
| 1934 | 219,080,000 | .02 | .02 | .02 | .03 | .10 | 1.00 | 2.00 |
| 1934D | 28,446,000 | .04 | .06 | .08 | .10 | .25 | 7.50 | 15.00 |
| 1935 | 245,388,000 | .02 | .02 | .02 | .03 | .06 | .75 | 1.50 |
| 1935D | 47,000,000 | .02 | .02 | .02 | .03 | .10 | 1.00 | 2.00 |
| 1935S | 38,702,000 | .02 | .03 | .03 | .04 | .08 | 3.00 | 8.00 |
| 1936 | 309,637,569 | .02 | .02 | .02 | .03 | .06 | .60 | 1.25 |
| 1936 Proof-63 | (5,569) | | | | | | | 100.00 |
| 1936D | 40,620,000 | .02 | .02 | .02 | .03 | .08 | 1.00 | 2.00 |
| 1936S | 29,130,000 | .03 | .03 | .03 | .04 | .10 | 1.00 | 2.00 |
| 1937 | 309,179,320 | .02 | .02 | .02 | .03 | .05 | .60 | 1.25 |
| 1937 Proof-63 | (9,320) | | | | | | | 30.00 |
| 1937D | 50,430,000 | .02 | .02 | .02 | .03 | .06 | .50 | 1.00 |
| 1937S | 34,500,000 | .03 | .03 | .03 | .04 | .06 | .50 | 1.00 |
| 1938 | 156,696,734 | .02 | .02 | .02 | .03 | .05 | .60 | 1.25 |
| 1938 Proof-63 | (14,784) | | | | | | | 20.00 |
| 1938D | 20,010,000 | .02 | .03 | .04 | .06 | .15 | 1.00 | 2.00 |
| 1938S | 15,180,000 | .06 | .08 | .10 | .12 | .15 | 2.00 | |

| | Quan. Minted | G-4 | VG-8 | F-12 | VF-20 | EF-40 | MS-65 | Proof-63 |
|---|---|---|---|---|---|---|---|---|
| 1939 ... (13,520) | 316,479,520 | .02 | .02 | .02 | .03 | .05 | .75 | 20.00 |
| 1939D | 15,160,000 | .06 | .08 | .10 | .12 | .15 | 3.00 | |
| 1939S | 52,070,000 | .03 | .03 | .03 | .04 | .10 | 1.25 | |
| 1940 ... (15,872) | 586,825,872 | .02 | .02 | .02 | .02 | .03 | .40 | 15.00 |
| 1940D | 81,390,000 | .02 | .02 | .02 | .02 | .03 | 1.00 | |
| 1940S | 112,940,000 | .04 | .02 | .02 | .03 | .04 | 1.00 | |
| 1941 ... (21,100) | 887,039,100 | .02 | .02 | .02 | .02 | .03 | .60 | 15.00 |
| 1941D | 128,700,000 | .02 | .02 | .02 | .02 | .03 | 2.00 | |
| 1941S | 92,360,000 | .02 | .02 | .02 | .03 | .04 | 2.75 | |
| 1942 ... (32,600) | 657,828,600 | .02 | .02 | .02 | .02 | .03 | .30 | 15.00 |
| 1942D | 206,698,000 | .02 | .02 | .02 | .02 | .03 | .30 | |
| 1942S | 85,590,000 | .02 | .02 | .02 | .03 | .05 | 2.25 | |

## Zinc-coated Steel 1943 Only

No bronze cents were officially issued in 1943, although a few were struck in error. The steel cents of 1943 will be attracted to a magnet while bronze cents will not. A few of the 1944 cents were likewise struck on steel planchets.

| | | F-12 | VF-20 | EF-40 | MS-65 |
|---|---|---|---|---|---|
| 1943 | 684,628,670 | .03 | .03 | .08 | .65 |
| 1943D | 217,660,000 | .03 | .04 | .10 | 1.10 |
| 1943S | 191,550,000 | .04 | .05 | .15 | 2.50 |

# SMALL CENTS

## Bronze Resumed 1944-1958

1944D, D over S

| | Quan. Minted | VF-20 | EF-40 | MS-65 | Proof-65 |
|---|---|---|---|---|---|
| 1944 | 1,435,400,000 | $.02 | $.02 | $.25 | |
| 1944D | 430,578,000 | .02 | .02 | .30 | |
| 1944D, D over S (varieties) | | 35.00 | 45.00 | *125.00 | |
| 1944S | 282,760,000 | .02 | .03 | .25 | |
| 1945 | 1,040,515,000 | .02 | .02 | .10 | |
| 1945D | 266,268,000 | .02 | .02 | .20 | |
| 1945S | 181,770,000 | .02 | .03 | .20 | |
| 1946 | 991,655,000 | .02 | .02 | .10 | |
| 1946D | 315,690,000 | .02 | .02 | .15 | |
| 1946S | 198,100,000 | .02 | .03 | .20 | |
| 1947 | 190,555,000 | .02 | .02 | .15 | |
| 1947D | 194,750,000 | .02 | .02 | .15 | |
| 1947S | 99,000,000 | .02 | .03 | .25 | |
| 1948 | 317,570,000 | .02 | .02 | .20 | |
| 1948D | 172,637,500 | .02 | .02 | .20 | |
| 1948S | 81,735,000 | .02 | .03 | .35 | |
| 1949 | 217,775,000 | .02 | .02 | .40 | |
| 1949D | 153,132,500 | .02 | .02 | .30 | |
| 1949S | 64,290,000 | .03 | .05 | 1.00 | |
| 1950 (51,386) | 272,686,386 | .02 | .02 | .75 | $30.00 |
| 1950D | 334,950,000 | .02 | .02 | .20 | |
| 1950S | 118,505,000 | .02 | .03 | .40 | |
| 1951 (57,500) | 284,633,500 | .02 | .02 | .65 | 18.00 |
| 1951D | 625,355,000 | .02 | .02 | .25 | |
| 1951S | 136,010,000 | .02 | .03 | .85 | |
| 1952 (81,980) | 186,856,980 | .02 | .02 | .30 | 10.00 |
| 1952D | 746,130,000 | .02 | .02 | .20 | |
| 1952S | 137,800,004 | .02 | .03 | .35 | |
| 1953 (128,800) | 256,883,800 | .02 | .20 | 6.00 | |
| 1953D | 700,515,000 | .02 | .02 | .10 | |
| 1953S | 181,835,000 | .02 | .03 | .15 | |
| 1954 (233,300) | 71,873,350 | .03 | .05 | .25 | 5.00 |
| 1954D | 251,552,500 | .02 | .02 | .10 | |
| 1954S | 96,190,000 | .02 | .03 | .10 | |

*Value is for MS-60 uncirculated.

1955 Doubled Die Error

Enlarged Detail of 1972 Doubled Die Error

1969S Doubled Die Error

# SMALL CENTS

| | | Quan. Minted | VF-20 | EF-40 | MS-65 | Proof-65 |
|---|---|---|---|---|---|---|
| 1955 Doubled die obv | | | $225.00 | $250.00 | $*1,600 | |
| 1955 | (378,200) | 330,958,200 | .02 | .02 | .10 | 3.00 |
| 1955D | | 563,257,500 | .02 | .02 | .08 | |
| 1955S | | 44,610,000 | .10 | .15 | .25 | |
| 1956 | (669,384) | 421,414,384 | .02 | .02 | .05 | 1.50 |
| 1956D | | 1,098,201,100 | .02 | .02 | .05 | |
| 1957 | (1,247,952) | 283,787,952 | .02 | .02 | .05 | 1.00 |
| 1957D | | 1,051,342,000 | .02 | .02 | .04 | |
| 1958 | (875,652) | 253,400,652 | .02 | .02 | .05 | 1.00 |
| 1958D | | 800,953,300 | .02 | .02 | .04 | |

*Value for MS-60 Uncirculated is $400.00; MS-63 is $700.00

## LINCOLN TYPE, MEMORIAL REVERSE 1959 TO DATE

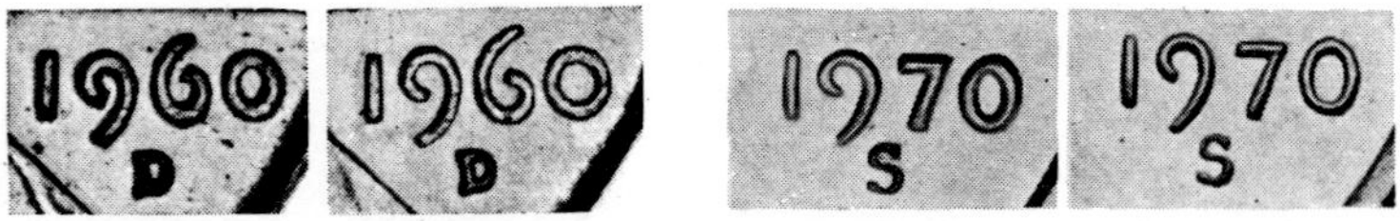

Small Date — Large Date — Small Date, Numbers aligned at top — Large Date, Low 7 in date

| | | Quan. Minted | MS-65 | Proof-65 |
|---|---|---|---|---|
| 1959 | (1,149,291) | 610,864,291 | $.01 | $.75 |
| 1959D | | 1,279,760,000 | .01 | |
| 1960 Large date | | | .01 | .50 |
| 1960 Sm. date | (1,691,602) | 588,096,602 | 1.25 | 10.00 |
| 1960D Large date | | 1,580,884,000 | .01 | |
| 1960D Small date | | | .02 | |
| 1961 | (3,028,244) | 756,373,244 | .01 | .40 |
| 1961D | | 1,753,266,700 | .01 | |

| | Quan. Minted | MS-65 | Proof-65 |
|---|---|---|---|
| 1962 (3,218,019) | 609,263,019 | $.01 | $.40 |
| 1962D | 1,793,148,400 | .01 | |
| 1963 (3,075,645) | 757,185,645 | .01 | .40 |
| 1963D | 1,774,020,400 | .01 | |
| 1964 (3,950,762) | 2,652,525,762 | .01 | .40 |
| 1964D | 3,799,071,500 | .01 | |
| 1965 | 1,497,224,900 | .01 | |
| 1966 | 2,188,147,783 | .02 | |
| 1967 | 3,048,667,100 | .02 | |
| 1968 | 1,707,880,970 | .03 | |
| 1968D | 2,886,269,600 | .01 | |
| 1968S (3,041,506) | 261,311,510 | .02 | .40 |
| 1969 | 1,136,910,000 | .15 | |
| 1969D | 4,002,832,200 | .02 | |
| 1969S (2,934,631) | 547,309,631 | .02 | .40 |
| 1969S Doubled die obv | | — | |
| 1970 | 1,898,315,000 | .10 | |
| 1970D | 2,891,438,900 | .01 | |
| 1970S (2,632,810) | 693,192,814 | | |
| 1970S Sm. date | | 4.00 | 45.00 |
| 1970S Lg. date (low 7) | | $.02 | $.40 |
| 1971 | 1,919,490,000 | .08 | |
| 1971D | 2,911,045,600 | .05 | |
| 1971S (3,220,733) | 528,354,192 | .08 | .40 |
| 1972 Doubled die obv | | 225.00 | |
| 1972 | 2,933,255,000 | .02 | |
| 1972D | 2,665,071,400 | .03 | |
| 1972S (3,260,996) | 380,200,104 | .01 | .40 |
| 1973 | 3,728,245,000 | .01 | |
| 1973D | 3,549,576,588 | .01 | |
| 1973S (2,760,339) | 319,937,634 | .02 | .40 |
| 1974 | 4,232,140,523 | .01 | |
| 1974D | 4,235,098,000 | .01 | |
| 1974S (2,612,568) | 412,039,228 | .03 | .40 |
| 1975 | 5,451,476,142 | .01 | |
| 1975D | 4,505,275,300 | .02 | |
| 1975S Proof | (2,845,450) | | 5.00 |
| 1976 | 4,674,292,426 | .01 | |
| 1976D | 4,221,592,455 | .02 | |
| 1976S Proof | (4,149,730) | | 1.50 |
| 1977 | 4,469,930,000 | .01 | |
| 1977D | 4,194,062,300 | .01 | |

## SMALL CENTS

| | Quan. Minted | MS-65 | Proof-65 |
|---|---|---|---|
| 1977S Proof | (3,251,152) | | $1.50 |
| 1978 | 5,558,605,000 | $.02 | |
| 1978D | 4,280,233,400 | .02 | |
| 1978S Proof | (3,127,781) | | 1.75 |
| 1979 | 6,018,515,000 | .01 | |
| 1979D | 4,139,357,254 | .01 | |
| 1979S Proof | (3,677,175) | | |
| Filled S | | | 2.00 |
| Clear S | | | 4.00 |

| | Quan. Minted | MS-65 | Proof-65 |
|---|---|---|---|
| 1980 | 7,414,705,000 | $.01 | |
| 1980D | 5,140,098,660 | .01 | |
| 1980S Proof | (3,554,806) | | $1.35 |
| 1981 | 7,491,750,000 | .01 | |
| 1981D | 5,373,235,677 | .01 | |
| 1981S Proof | (4,063,083) | | 2.50 |
| 1982 | | .01 | |
| 1982D | | .01 | |
| 1982S Proof | | | 2.50 |

## TWO-CENT PIECES — 1864-1873

The Act of April 22, 1864, which changed the weight and composition of the cent, included a provision for the bronze two-cent piece. The weight was specified as 96 grains, the alloy being the same as for the cent.

There are two varieties for the first year of issue, 1864: the small motto and the large motto. The differences are explained in the illustrations below.

1864 Small Motto

1864 Large Motto

On the obverse the D in GOD is narrow on the large motto. The stem to the leaf shows plainly on the small motto variety.

**G-4 GOOD**—*At least IN GOD visible.*

**F-12 FINE**—*Complete motto visible. WE weak.*

**EF-40 EXTREMELY FINE**—*WE is bold.*

**MS-60 UNCIRCULATED**—*No trace of wear. Light blemishes.*

**MS-63 SELECT UNCIRCULATED**—*No trace of wear. Nice color, few blemishes.*

*Brilliant red choice uncirculated and proof coins are worth more than prices shown. Spotted, cleaned or discolored pieces are worth less.*

| | Quan. Minted | G-4 | F-12 | EF-40 | MS-60 | MS-63 | Proof-63 |
|---|---|---|---|---|---|---|---|
| 1864 Sm. motto | 19,847,500 | $25.00 | $40.00 | $85.00 | $250.00 | $650.00 | —— |
| 1864 Lg. motto | | 3.00 | 5.00 | 18.00 | 120.00 | 310.00 | $700.00 |
| 1865 | 13,640,000 | 3.00 | 5.00 | 18.00 | 120.00 | 310.00 | 675.00 |
| 1866 | 3,177,000 | 3.00 | 5.00 | 18.00 | 120.00 | 310.00 | 650.00 |
| 1867 | 2,938,750 | 3.00 | 5.00 | 18.00 | 120.00 | 310.00 | 650.00 |
| 1868 | 2,803,750 | 3.00 | 5.00 | 18.00 | 120.00 | 310.00 | 650.00 |
| 1869, 9 over 8 | 1,546,500 | 50.00 | 100.00 | 350.00 | | | |
| 1869 | | 3.25 | 6.00 | 19.00 | 150.00 | 325.00 | 700.00 |
| 1870 | 861,250 | 4.00 | 7.00 | 20.00 | 175.00 | 350.00 | 750.00 |
| 1871 | 721,250 | 4.50 | 8.00 | 22.00 | 200.00 | 400.00 | 825.00 |
| 1872 | 65,000 | 22.00 | 40.00 | 125.00 | 400.00 | 750.00 | 1,000 |
| 1873 Proofs only (Est. 1,100) | | | | | | | 1,300 |

# SILVER THREE-CENT PIECES 1851-1873

This smallest of United States silver coins was authorized by Congress March 3, 1851. The first three-cent silver pieces had no lines bordering the six-pointed star. From 1854 through 1858 there were three lines, while issues of the last fifteen years show only two lines. Issues from 1854 through 1873 have an olive sprig over the III and a bundle of three arrows beneath.

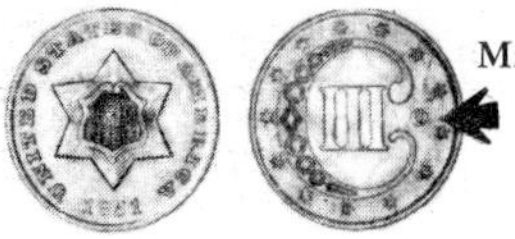

Mint Mark O

**G-4 GOOD**—*Star worn smooth. Legend and date readable.*
**VG-8 VERY GOOD**—*Outline of shield defined. Legend and date clear.*
**F-12 FINE**—*Only star points worn smooth.*
**VF-20 VERY FINE**—*Only partial wear on star ridges.*
**EF-40 EXTREMELY FINE**—*Ridges on star points show.*
**MS-60 UNCIRCULATED**—*No trace of wear. Light blemishes.*

*Well struck specimens command higher prices.*

| | *Quan. Minted* | *G-4* | *VG-8* | *F-12* | *VF-20* | *EF-40* | *MS-60* | *Proof-63* |
|---|---|---|---|---|---|---|---|---|
| No outline around star. | | | | | | | | |
| 1851 | 5,447,440 | $4.50 | $6.00 | $8.00 | $13.00 | $25.00 | $180.00 | — |
| 1851O | 720,000 | 6.00 | 9.00 | 14.00 | 24.00 | 40.00 | 275.00 | |
| 1852 | 18,663,500 | 4.00 | 5.00 | 7.00 | 12.00 | 25.00 | 180.00 | — |
| 1853 | 11,400,000 | 4.00 | 5.00 | 7.00 | 12.00 | 25.00 | 180.00 | |

| | *Quan. Minted* | *G-4* | *VG-8* | *F-12* | *VF-20* | *EF-40* | *MS-60* | *Proof-63* |
|---|---|---|---|---|---|---|---|---|
| Three outlines to star, large date. | | | | | | | | |
| 1854 | 671,000 | 7.00 | 8.00 | 11.00 | 20.00 | 42.00 | 290.00 | — |
| 1855 | 139,000 | 8.00 | 10.00 | 18.00 | 25.00 | 70.00 | 400.00 | $1,900 |
| 1856 | 1,458,000 | 6.00 | 7.50 | 10.00 | 18.00 | 40.00 | 290.00 | 1,800 |
| 1857 | 1,042,000 | 6.00 | 7.50 | 10.00 | 18.00 | 40.00 | 290.00 | 1,800 |
| 1858 | 1,604,000 | 6.00 | 7.50 | 10.00 | 18.00 | 40.00 | 290.00 | 1,200 |
| Two outlines to star, small date. | | | | | | | | |
| 1859 (800) | 365,000 | 6.00 | 7.00 | 10.00 | 17.00 | 30.00 | 180.00 | 650.00 |
| 1860 (1,000) | 287,000 | 6.00 | 7.00 | 10.00 | 17.00 | 30.00 | 180.00 | 650.00 |
| 1861 (1,000) | 498,000 | 6.00 | 7.00 | 10.00 | 17.00 | 30.00 | 180.00 | 650.00 |
| 1862, 2 over 1 | 343,550 | 8.00 | 10.00 | 18.00 | 27.00 | 55.00 | 200.00 | |
| 1862 (550) | | 6.00 | 7.00 | 10.00 | 17.00 | 30.00 | 180.00 | 650.00 |
| 1863 (460) | 21,460 | | | | | | 285.00 | 700.00 |
| 1864 (470) | 12,470 | | | | | | 325.00 | 700.00 |
| 1865 (500) | 8,500 | | | | | | 350.00 | 700.00 |
| 1866 (725) | 22,725 | | | | | | 350.00 | 700.00 |
| 1867 (625) | 4,625 | | | | | | 350.00 | 700.00 |
| 1868 (600) | 4,100 | | | | | | 350.00 | 700.00 |
| 1869 (600) | 5,100 | | | | | | 350.00 | 700.00 |
| 1870 (1,000) | 4,000 | | | | | | 350.00 | 700.00 |
| 1871 (960) | 4,360 | | | | | | 350.00 | 700.00 |
| 1872 (950) | 1,950 | | | | | | 350.00 | 700.00 |
| 1873 (600) | 600 | | | | | | | 800.00 |

# THREE-CENT PIECES (NICKEL)

## ISSUED 1865-1889

The three-cent pieces struck in nickel composition were designed to replace the silver three cent coins. Composition is 75% copper and 25% nickel. All were coined at Philadelphia and have plain edges.

**G-4 GOOD**—*Date and legends complete though worn. III smooth.*

**VG-8 VERY GOOD**—*III is half worn. Rims complete.*

**F-12 FINE**—*Hair curls well defined.*

**EF-40 EXTREMELY FINE**—*Slight, even wear.*

**MS-60 UNCIRCULATED**—*No trace of wear. Light blemishes.*

*Brilliant choice uncirculated and proof coins are worth more than prices shown. Spotted, cleaned or discolored pieces are worth less.*

| | | *Quan. Minted* | *G-4* | *VG-8* | *F-12* | *EF-40* | *MS-60* | *Proof-63* |
|---|---|---|---|---|---|---|---|---|
| 1865 | | 11,382,000 | $2.50 | $3.00 | $4.00 | $8.00 | $80.00 | $400.00 |
| 1866 | | 4,801,000 | 2.50 | 3.00 | 4.00 | 8.00 | 80.00 | 250.00 |
| 1867 | | 3,915,000 | 2.50 | 3.00 | 4.00 | 8.00 | 80.00 | 200.00 |
| 1868 | | 3,252,000 | 2.50 | 3.00 | 4.00 | 8.00 | 80.00 | 200.00 |
| 1869 | | 1,604,000 | 2.50 | 3.00 | 4.00 | 8.00 | 80.00 | 200.00 |
| 1870 | | 1,335,000 | 3.00 | 4.00 | 5.00 | 9.00 | 80.00 | 200.00 |
| 1871 | | 604,000 | 3.00 | 4.00 | 5.00 | 9.00 | 85.00 | 200.00 |
| 1872 | | 862,000 | 3.00 | 4.00 | 5.00 | 9.00 | 85.00 | 200.00 |
| 1873 | (1,100) | 1,173,000 | 3.00 | 4.00 | 5.00 | 9.00 | 80.00 | 200.00 |
| 1874 | | 790,000 | 3.50 | 4.50 | 5.50 | 10.00 | 85.00 | 200.00 |
| 1875 | | 228,000 | 5.00 | 6.00 | 7.00 | 14.00 | 90.00 | 200.00 |
| 1876 | | 162,000 | 5.00 | 6.00 | 7.00 | 14.00 | 100.00 | 200.00 |
| 1877 (Proofs only) | | | | | | | | 600.00 |
| 1878 | (2,350) | 2,350 | | | | | | 450.00 |
| 1879 | (3,200) | 41,200 | 17.00 | 20.00 | 24.00 | 32.50 | 200.00 | 200.00 |
| 1880 | (3,955) | 24,955 | 20.00 | 22.00 | 27.00 | 40.00 | 200.00 | 200.00 |
| 1881 | (3,575) | 1,080,575 | 2.50 | 3.00 | 4.00 | 8.00 | 80.00 | 200.00 |
| 1882 | (3,100) | 25,300 | 18.00 | 20.00 | 25.00 | 35.00 | 200.00 | 300.00 |
| 1883 | (6,609) | 10,609 | 24.00 | 27.00 | 35.00 | 70.00 | 225.00 | 350.00 |
| 1884 | (3,942) | 5,642 | 26.00 | 30.00 | 40.00 | 75.00 | 275.00 | 375.00 |
| 1885 | (3,790) | 4,790 | 28.00 | 35.00 | 45.00 | 85.00 | 275.00 | 400.00 |
| 1886 | (4,290) | 4,290 | | | | | | 500.00 |
| 1887, 7 over 6 | | | | | | | | 500.00 |
| 1887 All kinds | (2,960) | 7,961 | 26.00 | 30.00 | 35.00 | 70.00 | 275.00 | 450.00 |
| 1888 | (4,582) | 41,083 | 16.00 | 20.00 | 25.00 | 32.00 | 200.00 | 200.00 |
| 1889 | (3,436) | 21,561 | 16.00 | 20.00 | 25.00 | 32.00 | 200.00 | 200.00 |

# NICKEL FIVE-CENT PIECES — 1866 to Date

## SHIELD TYPE 1866-1883

The shield type nickel was made possible by the Act of May 16, 1866. Its weight was set at 77-16/100 grains with the same composition as the nickel three-cent piece which was authorized in 1865.

Rays Between Stars 1866-1867

**G-4 GOOD**—*All letters in motto readable.*

**VG-8 VERY GOOD**—*Motto stands out clearly. Rims worn slightly but even. Part of shield lines visible.*

**F-12 FINE**—*Half of each olive leaf is smooth.*

**EF-40 EXTREMELY FINE**—*Leaf tips show slight wear. Cross over shield slightly worn.*

**MS-60 UNCIRCULATED**—*No trace of wear. Light blemishes.*

# NICKEL FIVE-CENT PIECES

*Brilliant choice uncirculated and proof coins are worth more than prices shown. Spotted, cleaned or discolored pieces are worth less.*

| | *Quan. Minted* | *G-4* | *VG-8* | *F-12* | *EF-40* | *MS-60* | *Proof-63* |
|---|---|---|---|---|---|---|---|
| 1866 Rays | 14,742,500 | $6.00 | $7.50 | $12.00 | $40.00 | $250.00 | $1,000 |
| 1867 Rays | 2,019,000 | 7.00 | 9.00 | 15.00 | 45.00 | 270.00 | 4,000 |

Without Rays 1867-1883

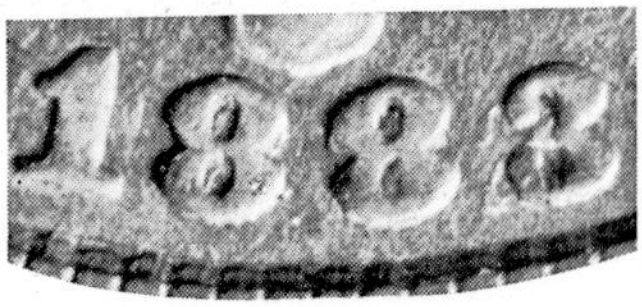

Typical example of 1883, 3 over 2. Other varieties exist.

| | *Quan. Minted* | *G-4* | *VG-8* | *F-12* | *EF-40* | *MS-60* | *Proof-63* |
|---|---|---|---|---|---|---|---|
| 1867 No rays | 28,890,500 | 4.00 | 5.00 | 6.00 | 15.00 | 100.00 | 400.00 |
| 1868 | 28,817,000 | 4.00 | 5.00 | 6.00 | 15.00 | 100.00 | 400.00 |
| 1869 | 16,395,000 | 4.00 | 5.00 | 6.00 | 15.00 | 100.00 | 400.00 |
| 1870 | 4,806,000 | 4.00 | 5.00 | 6.00 | 16.00 | 110.00 | 400.00 |
| 1871 | 561,000 | 15.00 | 20.00 | 27.00 | 50.00 | 170.00 | 500.00 |
| 1872 | 6,036,000 | 4.00 | 5.00 | 6.00 | 16.00 | 100.00 | 400.00 |
| 1873 Closed 3 (1,100) | 436,050 | 4.00 | 5.00 | 6.00 | 16.00 | 110.00 | 400.00 |
| 1873 Open 3 | 4,113,950 | 4.00 | 5.00 | 6.00 | 16.00 | 110.00 | |
| 1874 | 3,538,000 | 5.00 | 6.00 | 7.00 | 16.00 | 110.00 | 400.00 |
| 1875 | 2,097,000 | 6.00 | 7.00 | 10.00 | 20.00 | 120.00 | 400.00 |
| 1876 | 2,530,000 | 6.00 | 7.00 | 10.00 | 20.00 | 110.00 | 400.00 |
| 1877 Est. Issued (500) | 500 | | | | | | 1,300 |
| 1878 (2,350) | 2,350 | | | | | | 725.00 |
| 1879 (3,200) | 29,100 | 85.00 | 100.00 | 150.00 | 175.00 | 300.00 | 600.00 |
| 1880 (3,955) | 19,955 | 100.00 | 125.00 | 150.00 | 200.00 | 325.00 | 600.00 |
| 1881 (3,575) | 72,375 | 60.00 | 85.00 | 125.00 | 175.00 | 300.00 | 600.00 |
| 1882 (3,100) | 11,476,000 | 4.00 | 5.00 | 6.00 | 15.00 | 100.00 | 400.00 |
| 1883 (5,419) | 1,456,919 | 4.00 | 5.00 | 6.00 | 15.00 | 100.00 | 400.00 |
| 1883, 3 over 2 | | | 12.00 | 20.00 | 50.00 | 250.00 | |

## LIBERTY HEAD TYPE 1883-1913

In 1883 the design was changed to the familiar "Liberty head." This type first appeared without the word CENTS on the coin, merely a large letter "V." These "centless" coins were goldplated and passed for five dollars. Later in that year the word CENTS was added.

### Without CENTS 1883 Only

**G-4 GOOD**—*No details in head. LIBERTY obliterated.*
**VG-8 VERY GOOD**—*At least 3 letters in LIBERTY readable.*
**F-12 FINE**—*All letters in LIBERTY show.*
**VF-20 VERY FINE**—*LIBERTY bold, including letter I.*
**EF-40 EXTREMELY FINE**—*LIBERTY sharp. Corn grains at bottom of wreath show, on reverse.*
**MS-60 UNCIRCULATED**—*No trace of wear. Light blemishes.*

| | *Quan. Minted* | *G-4* | *VG-8* | *F-12* | *VF-20* | *EF-40* | *MS-60* | *Proof-63* |
|---|---|---|---|---|---|---|---|---|
| 1883 without CENTS (5,219) | 5,479,519 | $1.00 | $1.50 | $2.00 | $3.00 | $4.00 | $30.00 | $425.00 |

# NICKEL FIVE-CENT PIECES

## With CENTS 1883-1913

Location of mint mark

*Brilliant choice uncirculated and proof coins are worth more than prices shown. Spotted, cleaned or discolored pieces are worth less.*

| | Quan. Minted | G-4 | VG-8 | F-12 | VF-20 | EF-40 | MS-60 | Proof-63 |
|---|---|---|---|---|---|---|---|---|
| 1883 with CENTS ....... (6,783) | 16,032,983 | $2.00 | $3.00 | $5.00 | $10.00 | $15.00 | $100.00 | $300.00 |
| 1884 ....... (3,942) | 11,273,942 | 2.50 | 3.50 | 5.50 | 11.00 | 16.00 | 110.00 | 300.00 |
| 1885 ....... (3,790) | 1,476,490 | 175.00 | 200.00 | 300.00 | 400.00 | 500.00 | 850.00 | 1,000 |
| 1886 ....... (4,290) | 3,330,290 | 25.00 | 30.00 | 40.00 | 60.00 | 125.00 | 300.00 | 700.00 |
| 1887 ....... (2,960) | 15,263,652 | 1.50 | 2.00 | 5.00 | 8.00 | 15.00 | 100.00 | 285.00 |
| 1888 ....... (4,582) | 10,720,483 | 2.50 | 4.00 | 6.00 | 12.00 | 18.00 | 110.00 | 285.00 |
| 1889 ....... (3,336) | 15,881,361 | 1.50 | 2.00 | 4.00 | 8.00 | 15.00 | 100.00 | 285.00 |
| 1890 ....... (2,740) | 16,259,272 | 1.50 | 2.00 | 4.00 | 8.00 | 15.00 | 110.00 | 285.00 |
| 1891 ....... (2,350) | 16,834,350 | 1.50 | 2.00 | 4.00 | 8.00 | 15.00 | 100.00 | 285.00 |
| 1892 ....... (2,745) | 11,699,642 | 1.50 | 2.00 | 4.00 | 8.00 | 15.00 | 100.00 | 285.00 |
| 1893 ....... (2,195) | 13,370,195 | 1.50 | 2.00 | 4.00 | 8.00 | 15.00 | 100.00 | 285.00 |
| 1894 ....... (2,632) | 5,413,132 | 2.00 | 3.00 | 6.00 | 12.00 | 19.00 | 120.00 | 285.00 |
| 1895 ....... (2,062) | 9,979,884 | 1.25 | 2.00 | 4.00 | 7.00 | 13.00 | 80.00 | 285.00 |
| 1896 ....... (1,862) | 8,842,920 | 1.50 | 2.00 | 5.00 | 8.00 | 15.00 | 80.00 | 285.00 |
| 1897 ....... (1,938) | 20,428,735 | .40 | .50 | 1.50 | 3.00 | 10.00 | 75.00 | 285.00 |
| 1898 ....... (1,795) | 12,532,087 | .40 | .50 | 1.50 | 3.00 | 10.00 | 75.00 | 285.00 |
| 1899 ....... (2,031) | 26,029,031 | .40 | .50 | 1.50 | 3.00 | 10.00 | 75.00 | 285.00 |
| 1900 ....... (2,262) | 27,255,995 | .25 | .40 | .80 | 2.50 | 9.00 | 70.00 | 275.00 |
| 1901 ....... (1,985) | 26,480,213 | .25 | .40 | .80 | 2.50 | 9.00 | 70.00 | 275.00 |
| 1902 ....... (2,018) | 31,489,579 | .25 | .40 | .80 | 2.50 | 9.00 | 70.00 | 275.00 |
| 1903 ....... (1,790) | 28,006,725 | .25 | .40 | .80 | 2.50 | 9.00 | 70.00 | 275.00 |
| 1904 ....... (1,817) | 21,404,984 | .25 | .40 | .80 | 2.50 | 9.00 | 70.00 | 275.00 |
| 1905 ....... (2,152) | 29,827,276 | .25 | .40 | .80 | 2.50 | 9.00 | 70.00 | 275.00 |
| 1906 ....... (1,725) | 38,613,725 | .25 | .40 | .80 | 2.50 | 9.00 | 70.00 | 275.00 |
| 1907 ....... (1,475) | 39,214,800 | .25 | .40 | .80 | 2.50 | 9.00 | 70.00 | 275.00 |
| 1908 ....... (1,620) | 22,686,177 | .25 | .40 | .80 | 2.50 | 9.00 | 70.00 | 275.00 |
| 1909 ....... (4,763) | 11,590,526 | .25 | .40 | .80 | 3.00 | 10.00 | 70.00 | 275.00 |
| 1910 ....... (2,405) | 30,169,353 | .25 | .40 | .80 | 2.50 | 9.00 | 70.00 | 275.00 |
| 1911 ....... (1,733) | 39,559,372 | .25 | .40 | .80 | 2.50 | 9.00 | 70.00 | 275.00 |
| 1912 ....... (2,145) | 26,236,714 | .25 | .40 | .80 | 2.50 | 9.00 | 70.00 | 275.00 |
| 1912D ................ | 8,474,000 | .40 | .50 | 1.50 | 5.00 | 22.00 | 175.00 | |
| 1912S .................. | 238,000 | 22.00 | 27.00 | 35.00 | 80.00 | 150.00 | 375.00 | |
| 1913 Liberty Head (5 known) ......................................................... | | | | | | | | —— |

## INDIAN HEAD or BUFFALO TYPE 1913-1938

The Buffalo nickel was designed by James E. Fraser, whose initial F is below the date. He modeled the bison after Black Diamond in the New York Zoological Gardens. The three Indians used in the portrait were Irontail, Two Moons, and John Big Tree.

# NICKEL FIVE-CENT PIECES

## Variety 1 — FIVE CENTS on Raised Ground

**G-4 GOOD**—*Legends and date readable. Horn worn off.*
**VG-8 VERY GOOD**—*Half horn shows.*
**F-12 FINE**—*Three-quarters of horn shows. Obv. rim intact.*
**VF-20 VERY FINE**—*Full horn shows. Indian's cheekbone worn.*
**EF-40 EXTREMELY FINE**—*Full horn. Slight wear on Indian's hair ribbon.*
**MS-60 UNCIRCULATED**—*No trace of wear. Light blemishes.*

*Brilliant choice uncirculated coins are worth more than prices shown. Spotted, cleaned or discolored pieces are worth less.*

| | *Quan. Minted* | *G-4* | *VG-8* | *F-12* | *VF-20* | *EF-40* | *MS-60* | *Matte Proof-63* |
|---|---|---|---|---|---|---|---|---|
| 1913 Var. 1. (1,520) | 30,993,520 | $1.25 | $2.00 | $2.50 | $3.00 | $7.50 | $25.00 | $1,200 |
| 1913D Var. 1 ......... | 5,337,000 | 2.50 | 3.00 | 3.50 | 6.00 | 12.00 | 60.00 | |
| 1913S Var. 1 ......... | 2,105,000 | 5.50 | 6.50 | 9.00 | 11.00 | 25.00 | 100.00 | |

## Variety 2 — FIVE CENTS Recessed

Mint mark below FIVE CENTS

1916 Doubled Die Obverse

1918D, 8 over 7

| | *Quan. Minted* | *G-4* | *VG-8* | *F-12* | *VF-20* | *EF-40* | *MS-60* | *Matte Proof-63* |
|---|---|---|---|---|---|---|---|---|
| 1913 Var. 2. (1,514) | 29,858,700 | 1.50 | 2.25 | 3.00 | 3.75 | 6.00 | 28.00 | 600.00 |
| 1913D Var. 2 ......... | 4,156,000 | 25.00 | 28.00 | 33.00 | 40.00 | 50.00 | 165.00 | |
| 1913S Var. 2 ......... | 1,209,000 | 40.00 | 50.00 | 65.00 | 80.00 | 110.00 | 225.00 | |
| 1914 ....... (1,275) | 20,665,738 | 2.00 | 2.50 | 3.00 | 4.00 | 9.00 | 40.00 | 600.00 |
| 1914D................ | 3,912,000 | 17.00 | 20.00 | 25.00 | 40.00 | 70.00 | 225.00 | |
| 1914S................ | 3,470,000 | 2.00 | 3.00 | 5.00 | 8.00 | 22.00 | 100.00 | |
| 1915 ....... (1,050) | 20,987,270 | 1.00 | 1.25 | 2.00 | 3.00 | 7.00 | 40.00 | 600.00 |
| 1915D................ | 7,569,000 | 3.00 | 4.00 | 6.50 | 15.00 | 30.00 | 140.00 | |
| 1915S................ | 1,505,000 | 6.00 | 7.50 | 10.00 | 30.00 | 55.00 | 250.00 | |
| 1916 ......... (600) | 63,498,066 | .35 | .50 | .90 | 1.40 | 2.80 | 30.00 | 1,300 |
| 1916 Doubled die obv.......... | | 25.00 | 50.00 | 100.00 | 150.00 | 275.00 | 600.00 | |
| 1916D............... | 13,333,000 | 2.00 | 3.00 | 4.50 | 12.00 | 25.00 | 140.00 | |
| 1916S............... | 11,860,000 | 1.50 | 2.00 | 3.00 | 12.00 | 30.00 | 100.00 | |
| 1917 ................ | 51,424,019 | .30 | .40 | .75 | 1.00 | 5.00 | 25.00 | —— |
| 1917D................ | 9,910,000 | 2.50 | 3.00 | 6.00 | 15.00 | 50.00 | 200.00 | |
| 1917S................ | 4,193,000 | 2.00 | 2.50 | 5.00 | 20.00 | 40.00 | 210.00 | |
| 1918 ................ | 32,086,314 | .25 | .50 | 1.00 | 3.00 | 8.00 | 60.00 | |
| 1918D, 8 over 7 | } 8,362,000 | 360.00 | 440.00 | 625.00 | 900.00 | 1,900 | 6,500 | |
| 1918D............... | | 2.50 | 3.50 | 6.50 | 35.00 | 60.00 | 250.00 | |
| 1918S................ | 4,882,000 | 2.00 | 3.00 | 6.00 | 22.00 | 50.00 | 200.00 | |
| 1919 ................ | 60,868,000 | .20 | .30 | .55 | 1.00 | 4.00 | 35.00 | |
| 1919D†............... | 8,006,000 | 2.00 | 3.00 | 7.50 | 45.00 | 65.00 | 300.00 | |
| 1919S†............... | 7,521,000 | 1.50 | 2.00 | 4.00 | 30.00 | 50.00 | 175.00 | |

†Uncirculated pieces with full sharp details are worth considerably more.

# NICKEL FIVE-CENT PIECES

*Brilliant choice uncirculated coins are worth more than prices shown. Spotted, cleaned or discolored pieces are worth less.*

| | *Quan. Minted* | *G-4* | *VG-8* | *F-12* | *VF-20* | *EF-40* | *MS-60* |
|---|---|---|---|---|---|---|---|
| 1920 | 63,093,000 | $.20 | $.30 | $.55 | $1.00 | $4.00 | $35.00 |
| 1920D† | 9,418,000 | 2.00 | 2.50 | 5.00 | 35.00 | 60.00 | 300.00 |
| 1920S | 9,689,000 | .90 | 1.25 | 2.50 | 15.00 | 50.00 | 160.00 |
| 1921 | 10,663,000 | .25 | .50 | 1.00 | 3.00 | 10.00 | 75.00 |
| 1921S† | 1,557,000 | 7.50 | 10.00 | 20.00 | 50.00 | 140.00 | 450.00 |
| 1923 | 35,715,000 | .15 | .20 | .30 | .90 | 3.00 | 35.00 |
| 1923S† | 6,142,000 | 1.00 | 1.50 | 2.50 | 12.00 | 35.00 | 150.00 |
| 1924 | 21,620,000 | .15 | .20 | .30 | 1.00 | 4.50 | 50.00 |
| 1924D | 5,258,000 | 1.25 | 1.75 | 3.00 | 30.00 | 50.00 | 175.00 |
| 1924S | 1,437,000 | 2.00 | 3.00 | 7.50 | 65.00 | 150.00 | 550.00 |
| 1925 | 35,565,100 | .15 | .20 | .30 | 1.00 | 3.00 | 30.00 |
| 1925D† | 4,450,000 | 2.00 | 3.00 | 5.00 | 32.00 | 50.00 | 275.00 |
| 1925S | 6,256,000 | 1.00 | 1.50 | 3.00 | 12.00 | 30.00 | 200.00 |
| 1926 | 44,693,000 | .12 | .15 | .20 | .50 | 1.50 | 30.00 |
| 1926D† | 5,638,000 | 1.00 | 1.50 | 4.00 | 25.00 | 50.00 | 125.00 |
| 1926S | 970,000 | 2.00 | 3.00 | 7.00 | 35.00 | 125.00 | 450.00 |
| 1927 | 37,981,000 | .12 | .15 | .20 | .50 | 1.50 | 30.00 |
| 1927D | 5,730,000 | .40 | .85 | 1.00 | 6.00 | 22.00 | 75.00 |
| 1927S | 3,430,000 | .25 | .35 | .75 | 8.00 | 35.00 | 175.00 |
| 1928 | 23,411,000 | .12 | .15 | .20 | .50 | 1.50 | 30.00 |
| 1928D | 6,436,000 | .25 | .35 | .65 | 2.00 | 6.00 | 40.00 |
| 1928S | 6,936,000 | .20 | .30 | .50 | 1.00 | 4.50 | 60.00 |
| 1929 | 36,446,000 | .12 | .15 | .20 | .40 | 1.50 | 25.00 |
| 1929D | 8,370,000 | .25 | .40 | .60 | 1.75 | 6.00 | 40.00 |
| 1929S | 7,754,000 | .12 | .15 | .20 | .75 | 3.50 | 30.00 |
| 1930 | 22,849,000 | .12 | .15 | .20 | .50 | 1.75 | 27.50 |
| 1930S | 5,435,000 | .15 | .20 | .25 | .50 | 3.50 | 35.00 |
| 1931S | 1,200,000 | 1.50 | 1.75 | 2.00 | 2.50 | 5.00 | 37.50 |
| 1934 | 20,213,003 | .11 | .14 | .18 | .25 | 1.10 | 18.00 |
| 1934D | 7,480,000 | .11 | .14 | .18 | .25 | 2.00 | 27.50 |
| 1935 | 58,264,000 | .11 | .14 | .18 | .20 | .60 | 10.00 |
| 1935D | 12,092,000 | .11 | .14 | .18 | .30 | 1.10 | 25.00 |
| 1935S | 10,300,000 | .11 | .14 | .18 | .25 | .90 | 18.00 |
| 1936 | 119,001,420 | .11 | .14 | .18 | .20 | .50 | 9.00 |
| 1936 Proof-65 | (4,420) | | | | | | 650.00 |
| 1936D | 24,814,000 | .11 | .14 | .18 | .25 | .60 | 10.00 |
| 1936S | 14,930,000 | .11 | .14 | .18 | .25 | .60 | 12.50 |
| 1937 | 79,485,769 | .11 | .14 | .18 | .20 | .50 | 7.00 |
| 1937 Proof-65 | (5,769) | | | | | | 500.00 |
| 1937D | 17,826,000 | .11 | .14 | .18 | .25 | .60 | 9.00 |
| 1937D 3-Legged* | | 50.00 | 65.00 | 80.00 | 110.00 | 135.00 | 425.00 |
| 1937S | 5,635,000 | .11 | .14 | .18 | .25 | .60 | 10.00 |
| 1938D | 7,020,000 | .11 | .14 | .18 | .25 | .60 | 7.00 |
| 1938D, D over S | | | | 2.00 | 3.00 | 4.00 | 15.00 |

*Beware of removed leg.
†Uncirculated pieces with full sharp details are worth considerably more.

1937D "3-Legged" Variety

1938D, D over S

# NICKEL FIVE-CENT PIECES

## JEFFERSON TYPE 1938 to Date

This nickel was designed by Felix Schlag. He won an award of $1,000 in a competition with some 390 artists. It established the definite public approval of portrait and pictorial rather than symbolic devices on our coinage. On October 8, 1942, the wartime five-cent piece composed of copper (56%), silver (35%) and manganese (9%) was introduced to eliminate nickel, a critical war material. A larger mint mark was placed above the dome. Letter P (Philadelphia) was used for the first time, indicating the change of alloy. The designer's initials FS were added below the bust starting in 1966. Mint mark position was moved to the obverse starting in 1968.

**VG-8 VERY GOOD**—*Second porch pillar from right nearly gone, other three still visible but weak.*

**F-12 FINE**—*Cheekbone worn flat. Hairlines and eyebrow faint. Second pillar weak, especially at bottom.*

**VF-20 VERY FINE**—*Second pillar plain and complete on both sides.*

**EF-40 EXTREMELY FINE**—*Cheekbone, hairlines, eyebrow slightly worn but well defined. Base of triangle above pillars visible but weak.*

**MS-65 CHOICE UNCIRCULATED**—*No trace of wear. Barely noticeable blemishes.*

Mint mark located at right of building

Wartime Silver

*Uncirculated pieces with fully struck steps are valued higher.*

| | *Quan. Minted* | *VG-8* | *F-12* | *VF-20* | *EF-40* | *MS-65* | *Proof-65* |
|---|---|---|---|---|---|---|---|
| 1938 | (19,365) 19,515,365 | $.06 | $.08 | $.10 | $.20 | $1.00 | $37.50 |
| 1938D | 5,376,000 | .30 | .40 | .50 | .75 | 4.00 | |
| 1938S | 4,105,000 | .50 | .75 | 1.00 | 1.25 | 5.00 | |
| 1939 | (12,535) 120,627,535 | .06 | .08 | .10 | .20 | 1.00 | 40.00 |
| 1939D | 3,514,000 | 1.00 | 1.50 | 2.00 | 4.00 | 40.00 | |
| 1939S | 6,630,000 | .20 | .25 | .30 | 1.00 | 25.00 | |
| 1940 | (14,158) 176,499,158 | | | .05 | .08 | .50 | 32.00 |
| 1940D | 43,540,000 | | | .05 | .08 | 1.25 | |
| 1940S | 39,690,000 | | | .05 | .10 | 1.25 | |
| 1941 | (18,720) 203,283,720 | | | .05 | .08 | .40 | 25.00 |
| 1941D | 53,432,000 | | | .05 | .08 | 2.25 | |
| 1941S | 43,445,000 | | | .05 | .09 | 3.00 | |
| 1942 | (29,600) 49,818,600 | | | .05 | .08 | .90 | 22.50 |
| 1942D | 13,938,000 | .06 | .08 | .20 | .40 | 14.00 | |

### Wartime Silver Five-Cent Pieces 1942-1945

| | | | | | | | |
|---|---|---|---|---|---|---|---|
| 1942P | (27,600) 579,900,600 | *.20* | *.20* | *.25* | *.35* | 5.00 | 175.00 |
| 1942S | 32,900,000 | *.20* | *.20* | *.25* | *.35* | 4.00 | |
| 1943P, 3 over 2 | } 271,165,000 | | 20.00 | 30.00 | 60.00 | 300.00 | |
| 1943P | } | *.20* | *.20* | *.25* | *.35* | 2.00 | |
| 1943D | 15,294,000 | *.20* | *.20* | *.25* | *.35* | 2.25 | |
| 1943S | 104,060,000 | *.20* | *.20* | *.25* | *.35* | 2.50 | |
| 1944P | 119,150,000 | *.20* | *.20* | *.25* | *.35* | 2.00 | |
| 1944D | 32,309,000 | *.20* | *.20* | *.25* | *.35* | 4.00 | |
| 1944S | 21,640,000 | *.20* | *.20* | *.25* | *.35* | 3.00 | |
| 1945P | 119,408,100 | *.20* | *.20* | *.25* | *.35* | 2.50 | |
| 1945D | 37,158,000 | *.20* | *.20* | *.25* | *.35* | 2.00 | |
| 1945S | 58,939,000 | *.20* | *.20* | *.25* | *.35* | 1.50 | |

*Italic prices indicate unsettled values due to fluctuating bullion market. See Bullion Chart.*

# NICKEL FIVE-CENT PIECES

## Prewar composition and mint mark style resumed

| | | *Quan. Minted* | *VF-20* | *EF-40* | *MS-65* | *Proof-65* |
|---|---|---|---|---|---|---|
| 1946 | | 161,116,000 | $.05 | $.05 | $.25 | |
| 1946D | | 45,292,200 | .05 | .05 | .30 | |
| 1946S | | 13,560,000 | .05 | .06 | .30 | |
| 1947 | | 95,000,000 | .05 | .05 | .20 | |
| 1947D | | 37,822,000 | .05 | .05 | .30 | |
| 1947S | | 24,720,000 | .05 | .06 | .30 | |
| 1948 | | 89,348,000 | .05 | .05 | .25 | |
| 1948D | | 44,734,000 | .05 | .06 | .50 | |
| 1948S | | 11,300,000 | .05 | .06 | .40 | |
| 1949 | | 60,652,000 | .05 | .05 | .60 | |
| 1949D | | 36,498,000 | .05 | .05 | .45 | |
| 1949D, D over S | | | 15.00 | 25.00 | 150.00 | |
| 1949S | | 9,716,000 | .05 | .10 | .75 | |
| 1950 | (51,386) | 9,847,386 | .05 | .10 | .70 | $35.00 |
| 1950D | | 2,630,030 | 4.00 | 4.50 | 5.50 | |
| 1951 | (57,500) | 28,609,500 | .05 | .05 | .50 | 25.00 |
| 1951D | | 20,460,000 | .05 | .05 | .50 | |
| 1951S | | 7,776,000 | .05 | .10 | 1.10 | |
| 1952 | (81,980) | 64,069,980 | .05 | .05 | .30 | 15.00 |
| 1952D | | 30,638,000 | .05 | .05 | .85 | |
| 1952S | | 20,572,000 | .05 | .05 | .25 | |
| 1953 | (128,800) | 46,772,800 | .05 | .05 | .10 | 9.00 |
| 1953D | | 59,878,600 | .05 | .05 | .10 | |
| 1953S | | 19,210,900 | .05 | .05 | .20 | |
| 1954 | (233,300) | 47,917,350 | .05 | .05 | .10 | 7.00 |
| 1954D | | 117,183,060 | .05 | .05 | .10 | |
| 1954S | | 29,384,000 | .05 | .05 | .12 | |
| 1954S, S over D | | | 2.50 | 5.00 | 15.00 | |
| 1955 | (378,200) | 8,266,200 | .06 | .08 | .25 | 4.00 |
| 1955D | | 74,464,100 | .05 | .05 | .07 | |
| 1955D, D over S* | | | 3.00 | 5.00 | 25.00 | |

1943, 3 over 2

1954S, S over D

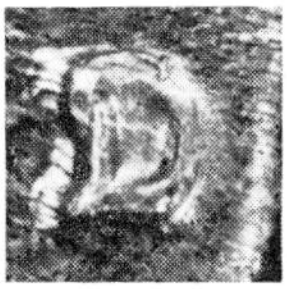

1955D, D over S*

| | | | | | | |
|---|---|---|---|---|---|---|
| 1956 | (669,384) | 35,885,384 | | .05 | .06 | 1.50 |
| 1956D | | 67,222,940 | | .05 | .06 | |
| 1957 | (1,247,952) | 39,655,952 | | .05 | .07 | 1.25 |
| 1957D | | 136,828,900 | | .05 | .07 | |
| 1958 | (875,652) | 17,963,652 | | .05 | .08 | 1.50 |
| 1958D | | 168,249,120 | | .05 | .06 | |
| 1959 | (1,149,291) | 28,397,291 | | .05 | .06 | .75 |
| 1959D | | 160,738,240 | | .05 | .05 | |
| 1960 | (1,691,602) | 57,107,602 | | .05 | .05 | .50 |
| 1960D | | 192,582,180 | | .05 | .05 | |
| 1961 | (3,028,144) | 76,668,244 | | .05 | .05 | .50 |
| 1961D | | 229,342,760 | | .05 | .05 | |
| 1962 | (3,218,019) | 100,602,019 | | .05 | .05 | .50 |
| 1962D | | 280,195,720 | | .05 | .07 | |
| 1963 | (3,075,645) | 178,851,645 | | .05 | .05 | .50 |

*Varieties exist.

# NICKEL FIVE-CENT PIECES

| | Quan. Minted | MS-65 | Proof |
|---|---|---|---|
| 1963D | 276,829,460 | $.05 | |
| 1964 (3,950,762) | 1,028,622,762 | .05 | $.50 |
| 1964D | 1,787,297,160 | .05 | |
| 1965 | 136,131,380 | .05 | |
| 1966 | 156,208,283 | .05 | |
| 1967 | 107,325,800 | .05 | |
| 1968D | 91,227,880 | .05 | |
| 1968S (3,041,506) | 103,437,510 | .05 | .25 |
| 1969D | 202,807,500 | .05 | |
| 1969S (2,934,631) | 123,009,631 | .05 | .25 |
| 1970D | 515,485,380 | .05 | |
| 1970S (2,632,810) | 241,464,814 | .05 | .35 |
| 1971 | 106,884,000 | .30 | |
| 1971D | 316,144,800 | .05 | |
| 1971S Proof | (3,220,733) | | .75 |
| 1972 | 202,036,000 | .05 | |
| 1972D | 351,694,600 | .05 | |
| 1972S Proof | (3,260,996) | | .75 |
| 1973 | 384,396,000 | .05 | |
| 1973D | 261,405,000 | .05 | |
| 1973S Proof | (2,760,339) | | .90 |
| 1974 | 601,752,000 | .05 | |
| 1974D | 277,373,000 | .07 | |
| 1974S Proof | (2,612,568) | | $1.25 |
| 1975 | 181,772,000 | $.06 | |
| 1975D | 401,875,300 | .07 | |
| 1975S Proof | (2,845,450) | | .75 |
| 1976 | 367,124,000 | .05 | |
| 1976D | 563,964,147 | .05 | |
| 1976S Proof | (4,149,730) | | .35 |
| 1977 | 585,376,000 | .05 | |
| 1977D | 297,313,422 | .07 | |
| 1977S Proof | (3,251,152) | | .35 |
| 1978 | 391,308,000 | .05 | |
| 1978D | 313,092,780 | .05 | |
| 1978S Proof | (3,127,781) | | .50 |
| 1979 | 463,188,000 | .05 | |
| 1979D | 325,867,672 | .05 | |
| 1979S Proof (3,677,175) Filled S | | | .65 |
| Clear S | | | 3.25 |
| 1980P | 593,004,000 | .05 | |
| 1980D | 502,323,448 | .05 | |
| 1980S Proof | (3,554,806) | | .35 |
| 1981P | 657,504,000 | .05 | |
| 1981D | 364,801,843 | .05 | |
| 1981S Proof | (4,063,083) | | .35 |
| 1982P | | .05 | |
| 1982D | | .05 | |
| 1982S Proof | | | .90 |

# HALF DIMES 1794-1873

The half dime types present the same general characteristics as larger United States silver coins. Authorized by the Act of April 2, 1792, they were not coined until February, 1795, although dated 1794. At first the weight was 20.8 grains, and fineness 892.4. By the Act of January 18, 1837, the weight was slightly reduced to 20 5/8 grains and the fineness changed to .900. Finally the weight was reduced to 19.2 grains by the Act of February 21, 1853.

## FLOWING HAIR TYPE 1794-1795

**AG-3 ABOUT GOOD**—*Details clear enough to identify.*
**G-5 GOOD**—*Eagle, wreath, bust outlined but lack details.*
**VG-8 VERY GOOD**—*Some details remain on face. All lettering readable.*
**F-12 FINE**—*Hair ends show. Hair at top smooth.*
**VF-20 VERY FINE**—*Hairlines at top show. Hair about ear defined.*
**EF-40 EXTREMELY FINE**—*Hair above forehead and at neck well defined but shows some wear.*
**MS-60 UNCIRCULATED**—*No trace of wear. Light blemishes.*

*Weakly struck uncirculated coins are worth less than values shown.*

| | Quan. Minted | AG-3 | G-4 | VG-8 | F-12 | VF-20 | EF-40 | MS-60 |
|---|---|---|---|---|---|---|---|---|
| 1794 | 86,416 (1794 and 1795) | $200.00 | $500.00 | $600.00 | $1,100 | $1,700 | $2,500 | $6,500 |
| 1795 | | 200.00 | 500.00 | 600.00 | 1,000 | 1,600 | 2,200 | 5,000 |

# HALF DIMES

## DRAPED BUST TYPE, SMALL EAGLE REVERSE 1796-1797

**AG-3 ABOUT GOOD**—*Details clear enough to identify.*
**G-4 GOOD**—*Date, stars, LIBERTY readable. Bust outlined but no details.*
**VG-8 VERY GOOD**—*Some details show.*
**F-12 FINE**—*Hair and drapery lines worn, but visible.*
**VF-20 VERY FINE**—*Only left of drapery indistinct.*
**EF-40 EXTREMELY FINE**—*All hairlines show details.*
**MS-60 UNCIRCULATED**—*No trace of wear. Light blemishes.*

| | *Quan. Minted* | *AG-3* | *G-4* | *VG-8* | *F-12* | *VF-20* | *EF-40* | *MS-60* |
|---|---|---|---|---|---|---|---|---|
| 1796, 6 over 5 | 10,230 | $225.00 | $450.00 | $675.00 | $1,100 | $1,900 | $2,600 | $7,000 |
| 1796 Nor. dt. | | 200.00 | 400.00 | 650.00 | 1,000 | 1,750 | 2,500 | 6,000 |
| 1796 LIKERTY | | 200.00 | 400.00 | 650.00 | 1,000 | 1,750 | 2,500 | 7,000 |
| 1797, 15 Stars | 44,527 | 175.00 | 375.00 | 500.00 | 900.00 | 1,500 | 2,200 | 6,000 |
| 1797, 16 stars | | 175.00 | 375.00 | 500.00 | 900.00 | 1,500 | 2,200 | 6,000 |
| 1797, 13 stars | | 175.00 | 375.00 | 500.00 | 900.00 | 1,500 | 2,200 | 6,000 |

## DRAPED BUST TYPE, HERALDIC EAGLE REVERSE 1800-1805

1800 LIBEKTY

| | | | | | | | | |
|---|---|---|---|---|---|---|---|---|
| 1800 | 24,000 | 135.00 | 350.00 | 450.00 | 650.00 | 1,100 | 1,800 | 5,250 |
| 1800 LIBEKTY | 16,000 | 135.00 | 350.00 | 450.00 | 650.00 | 1,100 | 1,800 | 5,500 |
| 1801 | 27,760 | 135.00 | 350.00 | 450.00 | 650.00 | 1,100 | 2,000 | 6,000 |
| 1802 | 3,060 | 1,200 | 2,250 | 3,500 | 6,000 | 10,000 | 17,000 | — |
| 1803 | 37,850 | 135.00 | 350.00 | 450.00 | 650.00 | 1,100 | 1,800 | 5,250 |
| 1805 | 15,600 | 150.00 | 375.00 | 475.00 | 700.00 | 1,250 | 2,200 | — |

## CAPPED BUST TYPE 1829-1837

**G-4 GOOD**—*Bust outlined, no detail. Date and legend readable.*
**VG-8 VERY GOOD**—*Complete legend and date plain. At least 3 letters of LIBERTY show clearly.*
**F-12 FINE**—*All letters in LIBERTY show.*
**VF-20 VERY FINE**—*Full rims. Ear and shoulder clasp show plainly.*
**EF-40 EXTREMELY FINE**—*Ear very distinct, eyebrow and hair well defined.*
**MS-60 UNCIRCULATED**—*No trace of wear. Light blemishes.*

| | *Quan. Minted* | *G-4* | *VG-8* | *F-12* | *VF-20* | *EF-40* | *MS-60* |
|---|---|---|---|---|---|---|---|
| 1829 | 1,230,000 | 9.00 | 12.00 | 14.00 | 25.00 | 65.00 | 400.00 |
| 1830 | 1,240,000 | 9.00 | 12.00 | 14.00 | 25.00 | 65.00 | 375.00 |
| 1831 | 1,242,700 | 9.00 | 12.00 | 14.00 | 25.00 | 65.00 | 375.00 |
| 1832 | 965,000 | 9.00 | 12.00 | 14.00 | 25.00 | 65.00 | 375.00 |
| 1833 | 1,370,000 | 9.00 | 12.00 | 14.00 | 25.00 | 65.00 | 375.00 |
| 1834 | 1,480,000 | 9.00 | 12.00 | 14.00 | 25.00 | 65.00 | 375.00 |
| 1835 | 2,760,000 | 9.00 | 12.00 | 14.00 | 25.00 | 65.00 | 375.00 |
| 1836 | 1,900,000 | 9.00 | 12.00 | 14.00 | 25.00 | 65.00 | 375.00 |
| 1837 Small 5c. | 871,000 | 13.00 | 22.00 | 30.00 | 50.00 | 110.00 | 675.00 |
| 1837 Large 5c | | 9.00 | 12.00 | 14.00 | 25.00 | 65.00 | 375.00 |

# HALF DIMES

## LIBERTY SEATED TYPE 1837-1873

### No Stars on Obverse 1837-1838

**G-4 GOOD**—*LIBERTY On shield smooth. Date and letters readable.*
**VG-8 VERY GOOD**—*At least 3 letters in LIBERTY are visible.*
**F-12 FINE**—*Entire LIBERTY visible, weak spots.*
**VF-20 VERY FINE**—*Entire LIBERTY strong and even.*
**EF-40 EXTREMELY FINE**—*LIBERTY and scroll edges distinct.*
**MS-60 UNCIRCULATED**—*No trace of wear. Light blemishes.*

| | *Quan. Minted* | *G-4* | *VG-8* | *F-12* | *VF-20* | *EF-40* | *MS-60* |
|---|---|---|---|---|---|---|---|
| 1837 | 1,405,000 | $15.00 | $20.00 | $27.50 | $47.50 | $125.00 | $450.00 |
| 1838O No stars | 70,000 | 27.50 | 40.00 | 55.00 | 95.00 | 200.00 | 2,700 |

### Stars on Obverse 1838-1853

From 1838 through 1859 mint mark is located above bow on reverse. Large, medium or small mint mark varieties occur for several dates.

| | | | | | | | |
|---|---|---|---|---|---|---|---|
| 1838 | 2,255,000 | 3.00 | 4.00 | 6.00 | 13.00 | 23.00 | 300.00 |
| 1839 | 1,069,150 | 3.00 | 4.00 | 6.00 | 13.00 | 23.00 | 280.00 |
| 1839O | 1,034,039 | 4.00 | 6.00 | 9.00 | 15.00 | 27.50 | 350.00 |
| 1840 | 1,344,085 | 3.00 | 4.00 | 6.00 | 12.00 | 22.00 | 300.00 |
| 1840O | 935,000 | 3.50 | 5.00 | 9.00 | 17.00 | 30.00 | 280.00 |
| 1841 | 1,150,000 | 3.00 | 4.00 | 6.00 | 11.00 | 22.00 | 200.00 |
| 1841O | 815,000 | 5.00 | 8.00 | 12.00 | 20.00 | 30.00 | 350.00 |
| 1842 | 815,000 | 3.00 | 4.00 | 6.00 | 11.00 | 22.00 | 200.00 |
| 1842O | 350,000 | 6.00 | 10.00 | 17.00 | 30.00 | 75.00 | —— |
| 1843 | 1,165,000 | 3.00 | 4.00 | 6.00 | 11.00 | 22.00 | 200.00 |
| 1844 | 430,000 | 3.00 | 4.00 | 6.00 | 11.00 | 22.00 | 200.00 |
| 1844O | 220,000 | 15.00 | 21.00 | 45.00 | 125.00 | 315.00 | —— |
| 1845 | 1,564,000 | 3.00 | 4.00 | 6.00 | 11.00 | 22.00 | 200.00 |
| 1846 | 27,000 | 55.00 | 70.00 | 100.00 | 175.00 | 350.00 | —— |
| 1847 | 1,274,000 | 3.00 | 4.00 | 6.00 | 11.00 | 22.00 | 200.00 |
| 1848 | 668,000 | 3.00 | 4.00 | 6.00 | 11.00 | 22.00 | 200.00 |
| 1848O | 600,000 | 5.00 | 10.00 | 13.00 | 25.00 | 35.00 | 325.00 |
| 1849, 9 over 6 | | 3.50 | 6.00 | 9.00 | 12.00 | 25.00 | 280.00 |
| 1849, 9 over 8 | 1,309,000 | 4.00 | 7.00 | 10.00 | 15.00 | 35.00 | 300.00 |
| 1849 Nor. date | | 3.00 | 4.00 | 6.00 | 11.00 | 22.00 | 200.00 |
| 1849O | 140,000 | 12.00 | 20.00 | 30.00 | 75.00 | 200.00 | —— |
| 1850 | 955,000 | 3.00 | 4.00 | 6.00 | 11.00 | 22.00 | 200.00 |
| 1850O | 690,000 | 5.00 | 10.00 | 13.00 | 20.00 | 35.00 | 375.00 |
| 1851 | 781,000 | 3.00 | 4.00 | 6.00 | 11.00 | 22.00 | 200.00 |
| 1851O | 860,000 | 5.00 | 8.00 | 12.00 | 20.00 | 35.00 | 325.00 |
| 1852 | 1,000,500 | 3.00 | 4.00 | 6.00 | 11.00 | 22.00 | 200.00 |
| 1852O | 260,000 | 11.00 | 16.00 | 25.00 | 45.00 | 90.00 | —— |
| 1853 No arrows | 135,000 | 6.00 | 12.00 | 18.00 | 25.00 | 50.00 | 325.00 |
| 1853O No arrows | 160,000 | 50.00 | 75.00 | 100.00 | 185.00 | 400.00 | —— |

### Arrows at Date 1853-1855

As on the dimes, quarters and halves, arrows were placed at the sides of the date for a short period starting in 1853 to denote reduction of weight.

| | Quan. Minted | G-4 | VG-8 | F-12 | VF-20 | EF-40 | MS-60 | Proof-60 |
|---|---|---|---|---|---|---|---|---|
| 1853 | 13,210,020 | $3.00 | $4.00 | $5.00 | $10.00 | $20.00 | $210.00 | |
| 1853O | 2,200,000 | 4.00 | 5.00 | 7.00 | 12.00 | 30.00 | 225.00 | |
| 1854 | 5,740,000 | 3.00 | 4.00 | 5.00 | 9.00 | 18.00 | 210.00 | |
| 1854O | 1,560,000 | 3.00 | 4.00 | 6.00 | 11.00 | 22.00 | 350.00 | |
| 1855 | 1,750,000 | 3.00 | 4.00 | 5.00 | 10.00 | 20.00 | 210.00 | $2,000 |
| 1855O | 600,000 | 4.00 | 7.00 | 10.00 | 17.00 | 40.00 | 400.00 | |

## No Arrows at Date 1856-1859

| | Quan. Minted | G-4 | VG-8 | F-12 | VF-20 | EF-40 | MS-60 | Proof-60 |
|---|---|---|---|---|---|---|---|---|
| 1856 | 4,880,000 | 3.00 | 4.00 | 5.00 | 10.00 | 17.00 | 200.00 | 800.00 |
| 1856O | 1,100,000 | 3.00 | 4.00 | 6.00 | 11.00 | 20.00 | 250.00 | |
| 1857 | 7,280,000 | 3.00 | 4.00 | 5.00 | 10.00 | 17.00 | 200.00 | 750.00 |
| 1857O | 1,380,000 | 3.00 | 4.00 | 6.00 | 11.00 | 20.00 | 250.00 | |

1858 over Inverted Date

| | Quan. Minted | G-4 | VG-8 | F-12 | VF-20 | EF-40 | MS-60 | Proof-60 |
|---|---|---|---|---|---|---|---|---|
| 1858 | } 3,500,000 | 3.00 | 4.00 | 5.00 | 10.00 | 17.00 | 200.00 | 700.00 |
| 1858 over inv. date | } | 9.00 | 15.00 | 30.00 | 60.00 | 115.00 | 300.00 | |
| 1858O | 1,660,000 | 3.00 | 4.00 | 6.00 | 11.00 | 20.00 | 250.00 | |
| 1859O | 560,000 | 5.00 | 8.00 | 12.00 | 20.00 | 30.00 | 275.00 | |
| 1859 | 340,000 | 5.00 | 8.00 | 12.00 | 20.00 | 30.00 | 225.00 | 700.00 |

## Legend on Obverse 1860-1873

| | Quan. Minted | G-4 | VG-8 | F-12 | VF-20 | EF-40 | MS-60 | Proof-60 |
|---|---|---|---|---|---|---|---|---|
| 1860 .... (1,000) | 799,000 | 3.00 | 4.00 | 5.00 | 8.00 | 15.00 | 185.00 | 300.00 |
| 1860O | 1,060,000 | 3.00 | 4.00 | 5.00 | 9.00 | 18.00 | 200.00 | |
| 1861 .... (1,000) | 3,361,000 | 3.00 | 4.00 | 5.00 | 7.00 | 14.00 | 175.00 | 285.00 |
| 1862 ..... (550) | 1,492,550 | 3.00 | 4.00 | 5.00 | 7.00 | 14.00 | 175.00 | 285.00 |
| 1863 ..... (460) | 18,460 | 30.00 | 40.00 | 50.00 | 75.00 | 115.00 | 300.00 | 350.00 |
| 1863S | 100,000 | 7.00 | 9.00 | 12.00 | 21.00 | 45.00 | 425.00 | |
| 1864 ..... (470) | 48,470 | 75.00 | 100.00 | 125.00 | 175.00 | 200.00 | 1,100 | 700.00 |
| 1864S | 90,000 | 10.00 | 15.00 | 22.00 | 30.00 | 60.00 | 800.00 | |
| 1865 ..... (500) | 13,500 | 30.00 | 40.00 | 60.00 | 90.00 | 125.00 | 300.00 | 325.00 |
| 1865S | 120,000 | 6.00 | 9.00 | 13.00 | 22.00 | 32.00 | 425.00 | |
| 1866 ..... (725) | 10,725 | 30.00 | 40.00 | 60.00 | 100.00 | 125.00 | 300.00 | 325.00 |
| 1866S | 120,000 | 6.00 | 9.00 | 12.00 | 21.00 | 30.00 | 400.00 | |
| 1867 ..... (625) | 8,625 | 60.00 | 75.00 | 100.00 | 125.00 | 200.00 | 450.00 | 325.00 |
| 1867S | 120,000 | 6.00 | 9.00 | 12.00 | 21.00 | 30.00 | 350.00 | |
| 1868 ..... (600) | 89,200 | 9.00 | 15.00 | 20.00 | 30.00 | 50.00 | 285.00 | 285.00 |
| 1868S | 280,000 | 4.00 | 6.00 | 7.00 | 10.00 | 19.00 | 210.00 | |
| 1869 ..... (600) | 208,600 | 4.00 | 5.00 | 6.00 | 9.00 | 15.00 | 200.00 | 285.00 |
| 1869S | 230,000 | 4.00 | 6.00 | 7.00 | 10.00 | 19.00 | 225.00 | |
| 1870 .... (1,000) | 536,000 | 3.00 | 4.00 | 5.00 | 8.00 | 15.00 | 175.00 | 285.00 |
| 1870S | Unique | | | | | | —— | |
| 1871 ..... (960) | 1,873,960 | 3.00 | 4.00 | 5.00 | 8.00 | 15.00 | 175.00 | 285.00 |
| 1871S | 161,000 | 7.00 | 9.00 | 15.00 | 35.00 | 45.00 | 350.00 | |
| 1872 ..... (950) | 2,947,950 | 3.00 | 4.00 | 5.00 | 8.00 | 15.00 | 175.00 | 285.00 |
| 1872S | 837,000 | 3.00 | 4.00 | 5.00 | 8.00 | 15.00 | 175.00 | |
| 1873 ..... (600) | 712,600 | 3.00 | 4.00 | 5.00 | 8.00 | 15.00 | 175.00 | 285.00 |
| 1873S | 324,000 | 3.00 | 4.00 | 5.00 | 8.00 | 15.00 | 200.00 | |

# DIMES — 1796 to Date

The designs of the dimes, first coined in 1796, follow closely those of the half dimes up through the Liberty seated type. The dimes in each instance weigh twice as much as the half dimes.

## DRAPED BUST TYPE, SMALL EAGLE REVERSE 1796-1797

**AG-3 ABOUT GOOD**—*Details clear enough to identify.*

**G-4 GOOD**—*Date readable. Bust outlined, but no detail.*

**VG-8 VERY GOOD**—*All but deepest drapery folds worn smooth. Hairlines nearly gone and curls lack detail.*

**F-12 FINE**—*All drapery lines visible. Hair partly worn.*

**VF-20 VERY FINE**—*Only left side of drapery is indistinct.*

**EF-40 EXTREMELY FINE**—*Hair well outlined and shows details.*

**MS-60 UNCIRCULATED**—*No trace of wear. Light blemishes.*

1797, 16 Stars

1797, 13 Stars

| | *Quan. Minted* | *AG-3* | *G-4* | *VG-8* | *F-12* | *VF-20* | *EF-40* | *MS-60* |
|---|---|---|---|---|---|---|---|---|
| 1796 | 22,135 | $300.00 | $650.00 | $900.00 | $1,300 | $2,100 | $3,500 | $6,000 |
| 1797 16 stars | 25,261 (both) | 250.00 | 600.00 | 850.00 | 1,250 | 1,850 | 2,750 | 5,500 |
| 1797 13 stars | | 250.00 | 600.00 | 850.00 | 1,250 | 1,850 | 2,750 | 5,500 |

## DRAPED BUST TYPE, HERALDIC EAGLE REVERSE 1798-1807

| | | *AG-3* | *G-4* | *VG-8* | *F-12* | *VF-20* | *EF-40* | *MS-60* |
|---|---|---|---|---|---|---|---|---|
| 1798 All kinds | 27,550 | | | | | | | |
| 1798 over 97, 16 stars on rev. | | 100.00 | 250.00 | 400.00 | 750.00 | 950.00 | 1,700 | 3,800 |
| 1798 over 97, 13 stars | | | | 500.00 | 850.00 | 1,500 | — | |
| 1798 | | 100.00 | 250.00 | 400.00 | 750.00 | 950.00 | 1,700 | 3,800 |
| 1800 | 21,760 | 100.00 | 250.00 | 400.00 | 700.00 | 900.00 | 1,600 | 3,500 |
| 1801 | 34,640 | 100.00 | 250.00 | 400.00 | 700.00 | 900.00 | 1,600 | 3,500 |
| 1802 | 10,975 | 100.00 | 250.00 | 400.00 | 700.00 | 900.00 | 1,600 | 3,500 |
| 1803 | 33,040 | 100.00 | 250.00 | 400.00 | 700.00 | 900.00 | 1,600 | 3,500 |
| 1804 | 8,265 | 200.00 | 425.00 | 700.00 | 1,000 | 1,500 | 2,500 | 4,500 |
| 1805 | 120,780 | 100.00 | 250.00 | 400.00 | 700.00 | 900.00 | 1,600 | 3,000 |
| 1807 | 165,000 | 100.00 | 250.00 | 400.00 | 700.00 | 900.00 | 1,600 | 3,000 |

## CAPPED BUST TYPE 1809-1837

**AG-3 ABOUT GOOD**—*Details clear enough to identify.*

**G-4 GOOD**—*Date, letters and stars discernible. Bust outlined, no details.*

**VG-8 VERY GOOD**—*Legends and date plain. Minimum of 3 letters in LIBERTY.*

**F-12 FINE**—*Full LIBERTY. Ear and shoulder clasp visible. Part of rim shows both sides.*

**VF-20 VERY FINE**—*LIBERTY distinct. Full rim. Ear and clasp plain and distinct.*

**EF-40 EXTREMELY FINE**—*LIBERTY sharp. Ear distinct. Hair above eye well defined.*

**MS-60 UNCIRCULATED**—*No trace of wear. Light blemishes.*

# DIMES

## Large Size 1809-1828

| | *Quan. Minted* | *AG-3* | *G-4* | *VG-8* | *F-12* | *VF-20* | *EF-40* | *MS-60* |
|---|---|---|---|---|---|---|---|---|
| 1809 | 51,065 | $25.00 | $40.00 | $70.00 | $95.00 | $150.00 | $275.00 | $2,200 |
| 1811 over 9 | 65,180 | 15.00 | 25.00 | 37.00 | 50.00 | 110.00 | 200.00 | 1,800 |

| | *Quan. Minted* | *G-4* | *VG-8* | *F-12* | *VF-20* | *EF-40* | *MS-60* |
|---|---|---|---|---|---|---|---|
| 1814 | 421,500 | $14.00 | $18.00 | $25.00 | $50.00 | $135.00 | $1,200 |
| 1820 | 942,587 | 12.00 | 14.00 | 20.00 | 45.00 | 125.00 | 1,100 |
| 1821 | 1,186,512 | 12.00 | 14.00 | 20.00 | 45.00 | 125.00 | 1,100 |
| 1822 | 100,000 | 32.00 | 45.00 | 100.00 | 200.00 | 325.00 | 1,800 |

1823, 3 over 2

1824, 4 over 2

1828 Large Date

1828 Small Date

| | *Quan. Minted* | *G-4* | *VG-8* | *F-12* | *VF-20* | *EF-40* | *MS-60* |
|---|---|---|---|---|---|---|---|
| 1824, 4 over 2 | 510,000 (1824, 4 over 2 and 1825) | 14.00 | 19.00 | 30.00 | 50.00 | 135.00 | 1,400 |
| 1825 | | 12.00 | 14.00 | 20.00 | 45.00 | 125.00 | 1,100 |
| 1827 | 1,215,000 | 9.00 | 12.00 | 18.00 | 38.00 | 125.00 | 1,100 |
| 1828 Both vars | 125,000 | | | | | | |
| 1828 Lg. date, curl base 2 | | 15.00 | 22.00 | 35.00 | 60.00 | 150.00 | 1,200 |

## Reduced Size 1828-1837

1829 Small 10c

Large 10c

1830, 30 over 29

| | *Quan. Minted* | *G-4* | *F-12* | *VF-20* | *EF-40* | *MS-60* |
|---|---|---|---|---|---|---|
| 1828 Small date, sq. base 2 | | $14.00 | $23.00 | $45.00 | $125.00 | $1,100 |
| 1829 Small 10c | 770,000 (1829, all varieties) | 7.00 | 13.00 | 22.00 | 100.00 | 800.00 |
| 1829 Medium 10c | | 7.00 | 13.00 | 20.00 | 100.00 | 700.00 |
| 1829 Large 10c | | 10.00 | 18.00 | 30.00 | 110.00 | 800.00 |
| 1830, 30 over 29 | 510,000 (1830, all varieties) | 25.00 | 50.00 | 100.00 | 200.00 | 1,000 |
| 1830 Large 10c | | 7.00 | 13.00 | 20.00 | 100.00 | 700.00 |
| 1830 Small 10c | | 7.00 | 13.00 | 20.00 | 100.00 | 700.00 |

# DIMES

| | Quan. Minted | G-4 | F-12 | VF-20 | EF-40 | MS-60 |
|---|---|---|---|---|---|---|
| 1831 | 771,350 | $7.00 | $13.00 | $20.00 | $100.00 | $700.00 |
| 1832 | 522,500 | 7.00 | 13.00 | 20.00 | 100.00 | 700.00 |
| 1833 | 485,000 | 7.00 | 13.00 | 20.00 | 100.00 | 700.00 |
| 1834 | 635,000 | 7.00 | 13.00 | 20.00 | 100.00 | 850.00 |
| 1835 | 1,410,000 | 7.00 | 13.00 | 20.00 | 100.00 | 700.00 |
| 1836 | 1,190,000 | 7.00 | 13.00 | 20.00 | 100.00 | 700.00 |
| 1837 | 359,500 | 7.00 | 13.00 | 20.00 | 100.00 | 700.00 |

## LIBERTY SEATED TYPE 1837-1891

### No Stars on Obverse 1837-1838

**G-4 GOOD**—*LIBERTY on shield smooth. Date and letters readable.*
**VG-8 VERY GOOD**—*At least 3 letters in LIBERTY are visible.*
**F-12 FINE**—*Entire LIBERTY visible, weak spots.*
**VF-20 VERY FINE**—*Entire LIBERTY strong and even.*
**EF-40 EXTREMELY FINE**—*LIBERTY and scroll edges distinct.*
**MS-60 UNCIRCULATED**—*No trace of wear. Light blemishes.*

No Drapery from Elbow
No Stars on Obverse

Mint marks on Liberty seated dimes are placed on the reverse, within or below the wreath.

| | | | | | | |
|---|---|---|---|---|---|---|
| 1837 | 682,500 | 14.00 | 27.00 | 65.00 | 150.00 | 700.00 |
| 1838O | 406,034 | 20.00 | 45.00 | 100.00 | 200.00 | 1,750 |

### Stars on Obverse 1838-1853

No Drapery from Elbow
Tilted Shield

1838 Small Stars

1838 Large Stars

| | | | | | | |
|---|---|---|---|---|---|---|
| 1838 Small stars | } | 7.00 | 16.00 | 27.00 | 50.00 | 600.00 |
| 1838 Large stars | } 1,992,500 | 4.00 | 6.00 | 10.00 | 25.00 | 300.00 |
| 1838 Partial drapery | } | 7.00 | 15.00 | 25.00 | 50.00 | 550.00 |
| 1839 | 1,053,115 | 3.00 | 5.00 | 9.00 | 25.00 | 300.00 |
| 1839O | 1,323,000 | 3.50 | 7.00 | 14.00 | 27.00 | 300.00 |
| 1840 | 981,500 | 3.00 | 5.00 | 9.00 | 20.00 | 300.00 |
| 1840O | 1,175,000 | 3.50 | 7.00 | 15.00 | 27.00 | 550.00 |

# DIMES

Drapery from Elbow
Upright Shield

| | Quan. Minted | G-4 | F-12 | VF-20 | EF-40 | MS-60 | Proof-60 |
|---|---|---|---|---|---|---|---|
| 1840 | 377,500 | $7.00 | $14.00 | $22.00 | $125.00 | — | |
| 1841 | 1,622,500 | 2.50 | 4.00 | 9.00 | 18.00 | $250.00 | |
| 1841O | 2,007,500 | 3.50 | 7.00 | 12.00 | 25.00 | 500.00 | |
| 1842 | 1,887,500 | 2.50 | 4.00 | 9.00 | 18.00 | 250.00 | |
| 1842O | 2,020,000 | 2.50 | 4.00 | 10.00 | 25.00 | — | |
| 1843 | 1,370,000 | 2.50 | 4.00 | 9.00 | 18.00 | 250.00 | |
| 1843O | 150,000 | 13.00 | 45.00 | 120.00 | 300.00 | — | |
| 1844 | 72,500 | 13.00 | 45.00 | 90.00 | 185.00 | 1,000 | |
| 1845 | 1,755,000 | 2.50 | 4.00 | 9.00 | 18.00 | 250.00 | |
| 1845O | 230,000 | 7.00 | 20.00 | 60.00 | 325.00 | — | |
| 1846 | 31,300 | 20.00 | 40.00 | 100.00 | 225.00 | — | |
| 1847 | 245,000 | 5.00 | 14.00 | 25.00 | 75.00 | 650.00 | |
| 1848 | 451,500 | 3.00 | 5.00 | 10.00 | 21.00 | 270.00 | |
| 1849 | 839,000 | 2.50 | 4.00 | 9.00 | 18.00 | 270.00 | |
| 1849O | 300,000 | 5.00 | 10.00 | 40.00 | 110.00 | — | |
| 1850 | 1,931,500 | 2.50 | 4.00 | 9.00 | 18.00 | 250.00 | |
| 1850O | 510,000 | 4.00 | 7.00 | 30.00 | 60.00 | 650.00 | |
| 1851 | 1,026,500 | 2.50 | 4.00 | 9.00 | 18.00 | 270.00 | |
| 1851O | 400,000 | 4.00 | 7.00 | 20.00 | 55.00 | 650.00 | |
| 1852 | 1,535,500 | 2.50 | 4.00 | 9.00 | 18.00 | 270.00 | |
| 1852O | 430,000 | 4.00 | 7.00 | 22.00 | 75.00 | 750.00 | |
| 1853 No arrows | 95,000 | 13.00 | 22.00 | 50.00 | 120.00 | 750.00 | |

## Arrows at Date 1853-1855

Arrows at Date

Small Date, Arrows Removed

| | Quan. Minted | G-4 | F-12 | VF-20 | EF-40 | MS-60 | Proof-60 |
|---|---|---|---|---|---|---|---|
| 1853 With arrows | 12,078,010 | 3.00 | 4.50 | 9.00 | 25.00 | 260.00 | |
| 1853O | 1,100,000 | 3.50 | 5.00 | 12.00 | 45.00 | 425.00 | |
| 1854 | 4,470,000 | 3.00 | 4.50 | 9.00 | 25.00 | 260.00 | |
| 1854O | 1,770,000 | 3.50 | 5.00 | 11.00 | 40.00 | 425.00 | |
| 1855 | 2,075,000 | 3.00 | 4.50 | 9.00 | 25.00 | 260.00 | $1,200 |

## No Arrows at Date 1856-1860

| | Quan. Minted | G-4 | F-12 | VF-20 | EF-40 | MS-60 | Proof-60 |
|---|---|---|---|---|---|---|---|
| 1856 Lg. date | 5,780,000 (Lg. and Sm. date combined) | 2.35 | 3.75 | 7.00 | 16.00 | 270.00 | 950.00 |
| 1856 Sm. date | | 2.35 | 3.75 | 7.00 | 16.00 | 250.00 | |
| 1856O | 1,180,000 | 2.35 | 3.75 | 9.00 | 20.00 | 270.00 | |
| 1856S | 70,000 | 18.00 | 40.00 | 90.00 | 200.00 | — | |
| 1857 | 5,580,000 | 2.25 | 3.50 | 7.00 | 15.00 | 250.00 | 900.00 |
| 1857O | 1,540,000 | 2.25 | 3.50 | 7.00 | 15.00 | 270.00 | |

# DIMES

| | | Quan. Minted | G-4 | F-12 | VF-20 | EF-40 | MS-60 | Proof-60 |
|---|---|---|---|---|---|---|---|---|
| 1858 | | 1,540,000 | $2.25 | $3.50 | $7.00 | $15.00 | $250.00 | $850.00 |
| 1858O | | 290,000 | 5.00 | 12.00 | 30.00 | 70.00 | 600.00 | |
| 1858S | | 60,000 | 15.00 | 35.00 | 80.00 | 175.00 | — | |
| 1859 | (800) | 430,000 | 2.50 | 4.00 | 10.00 | 25.00 | 250.00 | 800.00 |
| 1859O | | 480,000 | 2.50 | 4.00 | 15.00 | 30.00 | 270.00 | |
| 1859S | | 60,000 | 15.00 | 35.00 | 90.00 | 225.00 | 1,500 | |
| 1860S | | 140,000 | 5.00 | 15.00 | 40.00 | 90.00 | — | |

## Legend on Obverse 1860-1873

| | | Quan. Minted | G-4 | F-12 | VF-20 | EF-40 | MS-60 | Proof-60 |
|---|---|---|---|---|---|---|---|---|
| 1860 | (1,000) | 607,000 | 2.00 | 3.50 | 6.50 | 13.00 | 160.00 | 300.00 |
| 1860O | | 40,000 | 150.00 | 350.00 | 550.00 | 1,100 | — | |
| 1861 | (1,000) | 1,884,000 | 2.00 | 3.50 | 6.50 | 13.00 | 160.00 | 300.00 |
| 1861S | | 172,500 | 7.00 | 18.00 | 40.00 | 90.00 | 575.00 | |
| 1862 | (550) | 847,550 | 2.00 | 3.50 | 6.50 | 13.00 | 160.00 | 300.00 |
| 1862S | | 180,750 | 7.00 | 15.00 | 35.00 | 80.00 | 600.00 | |
| 1863 | (460) | 14,460 | 30.00 | 55.00 | 90.00 | 150.00 | 600.00 | 325.00 |
| 1863S | | 157,500 | 9.00 | 20.00 | 40.00 | 90.00 | 625.00 | |
| 1864 | (470) | 11,470 | 30.00 | 55.00 | 80.00 | 140.00 | 400.00 | 325.00 |
| 1864S | | 230,000 | 6.00 | 15.00 | 30.00 | 75.00 | 600.00 | |
| 1865 | (500) | 10,500 | 35.00 | 75.00 | 125.00 | 165.00 | 575.00 | 325.00 |
| 1865S | | 175,000 | 6.00 | 15.00 | 30.00 | 75.00 | 600.00 | |
| 1866 | (725) | 8,725 | 50.00 | 100.00 | 150.00 | 200.00 | 600.00 | 325.00 |
| 1866S | | 135,000 | 7.00 | 15.00 | 30.00 | 70.00 | 600.00 | |
| 1867 | (625) | 6,625 | 80.00 | 150.00 | 200.00 | 250.00 | 650.00 | 325.00 |
| 1867S | | 140,000 | 6.00 | 14.00 | 30.00 | 65.00 | 600.00 | |
| 1868 | (600) | 464,600 | 2.50 | 5.00 | 14.00 | 35.00 | 350.00 | 300.00 |
| 1868S | | 260,000 | 5.00 | 10.00 | 30.00 | 70.00 | 250.00 | |
| 1869 | (600) | 256,000 | 2.50 | 5.00 | 14.00 | 35.00 | 250.00 | 300.00 |
| 1869S | | 450,000 | 4.00 | 7.00 | 15.00 | 40.00 | 275.00 | |
| 1870 | (1,000) | 471,500 | 2.00 | 3.50 | 8.00 | 17.00 | 160.00 | 300.00 |
| 1870S | | 50,000 | 20.00 | 50.00 | 100.00 | 200.00 | 1,700 | |
| 1871 | (960) | 907,710 | 2.00 | 3.50 | 6.50 | 13.00 | 160.00 | 300.00 |
| 1871CC | | 20,100 | 130.00 | 350.00 | 550.00 | 1,100 | — | |
| 1871S | | 320,000 | 5.00 | 14.00 | 25.00 | 60.00 | 475.00 | |
| 1872 | (950) | 2,396,450 | 2.00 | 3.50 | 6.50 | 13.00 | 140.00 | 300.00 |
| 1872CC | | 35,480 | 70.00 | 190.00 | 275.00 | 550.00 | 1,850 | |
| 1872S | | 190,000 | 6.00 | 15.00 | 30.00 | 70.00 | 350.00 | |
| 1873 Closed 3 | (1,100) | 1,508,000 | 2.00 | 3.50 | 6.50 | 13.00 | 250.00 | 300.00 |
| 1873 Open 3 | | 60,000 | 10.00 | 20.00 | 40.00 | 90.00 | 275.00 | |
| 1873CC (Unique) | | 12,400 | | | | | — | |

## Arrows at Date 1873-1874

In 1873 the dime was increased in weight to 2.50 grams. Arrows at date in 1873 and 1874 indicate this change.

# DIMES

| | Quan. Minted | G-4 | F-12 | VF-20 | EF-40 | MS-60 | Proof-60 |
|---|---|---|---|---|---|---|---|
| 1873 | (800) 2,378,500 | $4.00 | $9.00 | $20.00 | $50.00 | $500.00 | $650.00 |
| 1873CC | 18,791 | 180.00 | 325.00 | 550.00 | 1,000 | — | |
| 1873S | 455,000 | 8.00 | 16.00 | 30.00 | 55.00 | 550.00 | |
| 1874 | (700) 2,940,000 | 4.00 | 9.00 | 20.00 | 50.00 | 500.00 | 650.00 |
| 1874CC | 10,817 | 250.00 | 600.00 | 1,000 | 1,450 | — | |
| 1874S | 240,000 | 9.00 | 20.00 | 40.00 | 70.00 | 575.00 | |

## No Arrows at Date 1875-1891

| | Quan. Minted | G-4 | F-12 | VF-20 | EF-40 | MS-60 | Proof-60 |
|---|---|---|---|---|---|---|---|
| 1875 | (700) 10,350,700 | 2.00 | 3.00 | 6.00 | 11.00 | 140.00 | 300.00 |
| 1875CC | 4,645,000 | 2.00 | 3.00 | 6.00 | 11.00 | 160.00 | |
| 1875S | 9,070,000 | 2.00 | 3.00 | 6.00 | 11.00 | 140.00 | |
| 1876 | (1,150) 11,461,150 | 2.00 | 3.00 | 6.00 | 11.00 | 140.00 | 300.00 |
| 1876CC | 8,270,000 | 2.00 | 3.00 | 6.00 | 11.00 | 150.00 | |
| 1876S | 10,420,000 | 2.00 | 3.00 | 6.00 | 11.00 | 140.00 | |
| 1877 | (510) 7,310,510 | 2.00 | 3.00 | 6.00 | 11.00 | 140.00 | 310.00 |
| 1877CC | 7,700,000 | 2.00 | 3.00 | 6.00 | 11.00 | 150.00 | |
| 1877S | 2,340,000 | 2.00 | 3.00 | 6.00 | 11.00 | 150.00 | |
| 1878 | (800) 1,678,000 | 2.00 | 3.00 | 6.00 | 11.00 | 140.00 | 300.00 |
| 1878CC | 200,000 | 9.00 | 25.00 | 35.00 | 50.00 | 375.00 | |
| 1879 | (1,100) 15,100 | 20.00 | 35.00 | 55.00 | 80.00 | 300.00 | 310.00 |
| 1880 | (1,355) 37,355 | 18.00 | 30.00 | 45.00 | 70.00 | 275.00 | 310.00 |
| 1881 | (975) 24,975 | 19.00 | 32.00 | 50.00 | 75.00 | 275.00 | 310.00 |
| 1882 | (1,100) 3,911,100 | 2.00 | 3.00 | 6.00 | 11.00 | 140.00 | 300.00 |
| 1883 | (1,039) 7,675,712 | 2.00 | 3.00 | 6.00 | 11.00 | 140.00 | 300.00 |
| 1884 | (875) 3,366,380 | 2.00 | 3.00 | 6.00 | 11.00 | 140.00 | 300.00 |
| 1884S | 564,969 | 5.00 | 10.00 | 20.00 | 30.00 | 250.00 | |
| 1885 | (930) 2,533,427 | 2.00 | 3.00 | 6.00 | 11.00 | 140.00 | 300.00 |
| 1885S | 43,690 | 45.00 | 85.00 | 135.00 | 225.00 | 1,000 | |
| 1886 | (886) 6,377,570 | 2.00 | 3.00 | 6.00 | 11.00 | 140.00 | 250.00 |
| 1886S | 206,524 | 5.00 | 10.00 | 18.00 | 25.00 | 250.00 | |
| 1887 | (710) 11,283,939 | 2.00 | 3.00 | 6.00 | 11.00 | 140.00 | 250.00 |
| 1887S | 4,454,450 | 2.00 | 3.00 | 6.00 | 11.00 | 140.00 | |
| 1888 | (832) 5,496,487 | 2.00 | 3.00 | 6.00 | 11.00 | 140.00 | 250.00 |
| 1888S | 1,720,000 | 2.00 | 3.00 | 6.00 | 11.00 | 150.00 | |
| 1889 | (711) 7,380,711 | 2.00 | 3.00 | 6.00 | 11.00 | 140.00 | 250.00 |
| 1889S | 972,678 | 5.00 | 10.00 | 22.00 | 45.00 | 250.00 | |
| 1890 | (590) 9,911,541 | 2.00 | 3.00 | 6.00 | 11.00 | 140.00 | 300.00 |
| 1890S | 1,423,076 | 2.00 | 4.00 | 7.00 | 12.00 | 150.00 | |
| 1891 | (600) 15,310,600 | 2.00 | 3.00 | 6.00 | 11.00 | 140.00 | 300.00 |
| 1891O | 4,540,000 | 2.00 | 3.00 | 6.00 | 18.00 | 160.00 | |
| 1891O O over S | | 13.00 | 40.00 | 75.00 | 150.00 | — | |
| 1891S | 3,196,116 | 2.00 | 3.00 | 6.00 | 13.00 | 140.00 | |

## BARBER or LIBERTY HEAD TYPE 1892-1916

This type was designed by Charles E. Barber, Chief Engraver of the Mint. His initial B is at the truncation of the neck. He also designed quarters and half dollars of the same period.

**G-4 GOOD**—*Date and letters plain. LIBERTY Is obliterated.*

**VG-8 VERY GOOD**—*At least 3 letters visible in LIBERTY.*

**F-12 FINE**—*All letters in LIBERTY visible, though some are weak.*

**VF-20 VERY FINE**—*All letters of LBERTY evenly plain.*

**EF-40 EXTREMELY FINE**—*All letters in LIBERTY are sharp, distinct. Headband edges are distinct.*

**MS-60 UNCIRCULATED**—*No trace of wear. Light blemishes.*

Mint mark location is on the reverse below the wreath.

# DIMES

| | Quan. Minted | G-4 | VG-8 | F-12 | VF-20 | EF-40 | MS-60 | Proof-63 |
|---|---|---|---|---|---|---|---|---|
| 1892 . . . . . . (1,245) | 12,121,245 | $1.00 | $1.50 | $3.00 | $4.00 | $9.00 | $125.00 | $400.00 |
| 1892O . . . . . . . . . . . . . . . | 3,841,700 | 2.25 | 3.00 | 4.00 | 6.00 | 14.00 | 150.00 | |
| 1892S . . . . . . . . . . . . . . . . . | 990,710 | 12.00 | 14.00 | 20.00 | 25.00 | 40.00 | 150.00 | |
| 1893, 3 over 2 . . } | (792) 3,340,792 | | | | —— | 75.00 | 200.00 | 500.00 |
| 1893 . . . . . . . . } | | 2.00 | 2.75 | 3.75 | 5.00 | 13.00 | 130.00 | 400.00 |
| 1893O . . . . . . . . . . . . . . . | 1,760,000 | 7.00 | 8.00 | 62.00 | 20.00 | 25.00 | 200.00 | |
| 1893S . . . . . . . . . . . . . . . | 2,491,401 | 3.00 | 4.00 | 6.00 | 11.00 | 18.00 | 150.00 | |
| 1894 . . . . . . . . (972) | 1,330,972 | 3.00 | 4.00 | 6.00 | 12.00 | 20.00 | 150.00 | 400.00 |
| 1894O . . . . . . . . . . . . . . . . . | 720,000 | 18.00 | 22.00 | 32.00 | 50.00 | 125.00 | 900.00 | |
| 1894S . . . . . . . . . . . . . . . . . . . . . . | 24 | | | | | | —— | |
| 1895 . . . . . . . . (880) | 690,880 | 30.00 | 35.00 | 45.00 | 65.00 | 100.00 | 500.00 | 400.00 |
| 1895O . . . . . . . . . . . . . . . . . | 440,000 | 90.00 | 100.00 | 120.00 | 170.00 | 250.00 | 800.00 | |
| 1895S . . . . . . . . . . . . . . . | 1,120,000 | 6.00 | 9.00 | 14.00 | 20.00 | 30.00 | 200.00 | |
| 1896 . . . . . . . . (762) | 2,000,762 | 2.00 | 3.00 | 5.00 | 9.00 | 18.00 | 130.00 | 400.00 |
| 1896O . . . . . . . . . . . . . . . . . | 610,000 | 20.00 | 25.00 | 30.00 | 40.00 | 70.00 | 500.00 | |
| 1896S . . . . . . . . . . . . . . . . . | 575,056 | 20.00 | 24.00 | 27.50 | 37.50 | 65.00 | 300.00 | |
| 1897 . . . . . . . . (731) | 10,869,264 | *.60* | *.60* | *.85* | 2.75 | 9.00 | 75.00 | 400.00 |
| 1897O . . . . . . . . . . . . . . . . . | 666,000 | 20.00 | 22.00 | 32.00 | 42.00 | 100.00 | 675.00 | |
| 1897S . . . . . . . . . . . . . . . | 1,342,844 | 3.00 | 4.00 | 8.00 | 15.00 | 30.00 | 200.00 | |
| 1898 . . . . . . . . (735) | 16,320,735 | *.60* | *.60* | *.85* | 2.75 | 9.00 | 75.00 | 400.00 |
| 1898O . . . . . . . . . . . . . . . | 2,130,000 | 1.00 | 2.00 | 4.00 | 10.00 | 25.00 | 250.00 | |
| 1898S . . . . . . . . . . . . . . . | 1,702,507 | 1.00 | 2.00 | 4.00 | 8.00 | 17.00 | 165.00 | |
| 1899 . . . . . . . . (846) | 19,580,846 | *.60* | *.60* | *.85* | 2.75 | 9.00 | 75.00 | 400.00 |
| 1899O . . . . . . . . . . . . . . . | 2,650,000 | 1.00 | 2.00 | 4.00 | 10.00 | 23.00 | 225.00 | |
| 1899S . . . . . . . . . . . . . . . | 1,867,493 | 1.00 | 2.00 | 4.00 | 7.00 | 12.00 | 140.00 | |
| 1900 . . . . . . . . (912) | 17,600,912 | *.60* | *.60* | *.85* | 2.75 | 9.00 | 75.00 | 400.00 |
| 1900O . . . . . . . . . . . . . . . | 2,010,000 | 2.00 | 3.00 | 5.00 | 12.00 | 22.00 | 250.00 | |
| 1900S . . . . . . . . . . . . . . . | 5,168,270 | 1.00 | 1.50 | 2.50 | 4.00 | 12.00 | 140.00 | |
| 1901 . . . . . . . . (813) | 18,860,478 | *.60* | *.60* | *.85* | 2.75 | 9.00 | 75.00 | 400.00 |
| 1901O . . . . . . . . . . . . . . . | 5,620,000 | 1.00 | 1.50 | 2.50 | 6.00 | 20.00 | 225.00 | |
| 1901S . . . . . . . . . . . . . . . . . | 593,022 | 20.00 | 24.00 | 40.00 | 60.00 | 120.00 | 800.00 | |
| 1902 . . . . . . . . (777) | 21,380,777 | *.60* | *.60* | *.85* | 2.75 | 9.00 | 75.00 | 400.00 |
| 1902O . . . . . . . . . . . . . . . | 4,500,000 | 1.00 | 1.50 | 2.50 | 4.00 | 14.00 | 185.00 | |
| 1902S . . . . . . . . . . . . . . . | 2,070,000 | 1.50 | 2.50 | 5.00 | 11.00 | 25.00 | 250.00 | |
| 1903 . . . . . . . . (755) | 19,500,755 | *.60* | *.60* | *.85* | 2.75 | 9.00 | 75.00 | 400.00 |
| 1903O . . . . . . . . . . . . . . . | 8,180,000 | 1.00 | 1.50 | 2.00 | 4.00 | 13.00 | 200.00 | |
| 1903S . . . . . . . . . . . . . . . . . | 613,300 | 15.00 | 18.00 | 26.00 | 40.00 | 70.00 | 650.00 | |
| 1904 . . . . . . . . (670) | 14,601,027 | *.60* | *.60* | *.85* | 2.75 | 9.00 | 75.00 | 400.00 |
| 1904S . . . . . . . . . . . . . . . . . | 800,000 | 10.00 | 14.00 | 20.00 | 36.00 | 65.00 | 650.00 | |
| 1905 . . . . . . . . (727) | 14,552,350 | *.60* | *.60* | *.85* | 2.75 | 9.00 | 75.00 | 400.00 |
| 1905O . . . . . . . . . . . . . . . | 3,400,000 | .90 | 1.50 | 3.00 | 6.00 | 12.00 | 175.00 | |
| 1905S . . . . . . . . . . . . . . . | 6,855,199 | .90 | 1.50 | 2.50 | 4.50 | 12.00 | 175.00 | |
| 1906 . . . . . . . . (675) | 19,958,406 | *.60* | *.60* | *.85* | 2.75 | 9.00 | 75.00 | 400.00 |
| 1906D . . . . . . . . . . . . . . . | 4,060,000 | .90 | 1.50 | 2.50 | 4.50 | 11.00 | 140.00 | |
| 1906O . . . . . . . . . . . . . . . | 2,610,000 | 1.00 | 2.00 | 4.00 | 7.00 | 15.00 | 160.00 | |
| 1906S . . . . . . . . . . . . . . . | 3,136,640 | .90 | 1.50 | 2.50 | 5.00 | 13.00 | 160.00 | |
| 1907 . . . . . . . . (575) | 22,220,575 | *.60* | *.60* | *.85* | 2.75 | 9.00 | 75.00 | 400.00 |
| 1907D . . . . . . . . . . . . . . . | 4,080,000 | .80 | 1.25 | 2.25 | 4.25 | 12.00 | 150.00 | |
| 1907O . . . . . . . . . . . . . . . | 5,058,000 | .80 | 1.25 | 2.25 | 4.25 | 12.00 | 135.00 | |
| 1907S . . . . . . . . . . . . . . . | 3,178,470 | 1.00 | 1.50 | 2.50 | 5.00 | 14.00 | 165.00 | |
| 1908 . . . . . . . . (545) | 10,600,545 | *.60* | *.60* | *.85* | 2.75 | 9.00 | 75.00 | 400.00 |
| 1908D . . . . . . . . . . . . . . . | 7,490,000 | .80 | 1.25 | 2.25 | 2.75 | 10.00 | 110.00 | |
| 1908O . . . . . . . . . . . . . . . | 1,789,000 | 1.00 | 1.75 | 4.00 | 9.00 | 18.00 | 175.00 | |
| 1908S . . . . . . . . . . . . . . . | 3,220,000 | .80 | 1.25 | 2.25 | 4.00 | 12.00 | 175.00 | |

*Italic prices indicate unsettled values due to fluctuating bullion market. See Bullion Chart.*

# DIMES

| | Quan. Minted | G-4 | VG-8 | F-12 | VF-20 | EF-40 | MS-60 | Proof-63 |
|---|---|---|---|---|---|---|---|---|
| 1909 . . . . . . . . (650) | 10,240,650 | *$.60* | *$.60* | *$.85* | $2.75 | $9.00 | $75.00 | $400.00 |
| 1909D . . . . . . . . . . . . . . . . . | 954,000 | 1.25 | 2.75 | 7.00 | 14.00 | 25.00 | 200.00 | |
| 1909O . . . . . . . . . . . . . . . | 2,287,000 | 1.00 | 1.50 | 3.00 | 7.00 | 15.00 | 150.00 | |
| 1909S . . . . . . . . . . . . . . . | 1,000,000 | 1.25 | 2.75 | 6.00 | 10.00 | 20.00 | 185.00 | |
| 1910 . . . . . . . . (551) | 11,520,551 | *.60* | *.60* | *.85* | 2.75 | 9.00 | 75.00 | 400.00 |
| 1910D . . . . . . . . . . . . . . . | 3,490,000 | .80 | 1.25 | 2.25 | 4.00 | 14.00 | 185.00 | |
| 1910S . . . . . . . . . . . . . . . | 1,240,000 | .80 | 1.25 | 3.25 | 7.00 | 14.00 | 150.00 | |
| 1911 . . . . . . . . (543) | 18,870,543 | *.60* | *.60* | *.85* | 2.75 | 9.00 | 75.00 | 400.00 |
| 1911D . . . . . . . . . . . . . . | 11,209,000 | *.60* | *.60* | *.85* | 2.75 | 9.00 | 75.00 | |
| 1911S . . . . . . . . . . . . . . . | 3,520,000 | .80 | 1.25 | 2.25 | 4.00 | 10.00 | 150.00 | |
| 1912 . . . . . . . . (700) | 19,350,000 | *.60* | *.60* | *.85* | 2.75 | 9.00 | 75.00 | 400.00 |
| 1912D . . . . . . . . . . . . . . | 11,760,000 | *.60* | *.60* | *.85* | 2.75 | 9.00 | 75.00 | |
| 1912S . . . . . . . . . . . . . . . | 3,420,000 | .80 | 1.25 | 2.25 | 4.00 | 10.00 | 150.00 | |
| 1913 . . . . . . . . (622) | 19,760,622 | *.60* | *.60* | *.85* | 2.75 | 9.00 | 75.00 | 400.00 |
| 1913S . . . . . . . . . . . . . . . . . | 510,000 | 3.00 | 5.00 | 12.00 | 25.00 | 50.00 | 300.00 | |
| 1914 . . . . . . . . (425) | 17,360,655 | *.60* | *.60* | *.85* | 2.75 | 9.00 | 75.00 | 400.00 |
| 1914D . . . . . . . . . . . . . . | 11,908,000 | *.60* | *.60* | *.85* | 2.75 | 9.00 | 75.00 | |
| 1914S . . . . . . . . . . . . . . . | 2,100,000 | .80 | 1.25 | 2.25 | 4.00 | 10.00 | 150.00 | |
| 1915 . . . . . . . . (450) | 5,620,450 | *.60* | *.60* | *.85* | 2.75 | 9.00 | 75.00 | 400.00 |
| 1915S . . . . . . . . . . . . . . . . . | 960,000 | .90 | 1.50 | 2.75 | 4.25 | 14.00 | 200.00 | |
| 1916 . . . . . . . . . . . . . . . | 18,490,000 | *.60* | *.60* | *.85* | 2.75 | 9.00 | 75.00 | |
| 1916S . . . . . . . . . . . . . . . | 5,820,000 | *.60* | *.60* | *.85* | 2.75 | 9.00 | 75.00 | |

## WINGED LIBERTY HEAD or "MERCURY" TYPE 1916-1945

Although this coin is commonly called the "Mercury Dime," the main device is in fact a representation of Liberty. The wings crowning her cap are intended to symbolize liberty of thought. The designer's monogram AW is right of neck.

Mint mark location is on reverse left of fasces.

**G-4 GOOD**—*Letters and date clear. Lines and bands in fasces are obliterated.*
**VG-8 VERY GOOD**—*One-half of sticks discernible in fasces.*
**F-12 FINE**—*All sticks in fasces are defined. Diagonal bands worn nearly flat.*
**VF-20 VERY FINE**—*The two crossing diagonal bands must show.*
**EF-40 EXTREMELY FINE**—*Diagonal bands show only slight wear. Braids and hair before ear show clearly.*
**MS-60 UNCIRCULATED**—*No trace of wear. Light blemishes.*
**MS-65—CHOICE UNCIRCULATED**—*No trace of wear. Barely noticeable blemishes.*

*Uncirculated values shown are for average pieces with minimum blemishes, those with sharp strikes and split bands on reverse are worth much more.*

| | Quan. Minted | G-4 | VG-8 | F-12 | VF-20 | EF-40 | MS-60 | Proof-65 |
|---|---|---|---|---|---|---|---|---|
| 1916 . . . . . . . . . . . . . . . | 22,180,080 | *$.50* | *$.50* | *$.50* | $1.50 | $2.50 | $14.00 | |
| 1916D . . . . . . . . . . . . . . . . . | 264,000 | 300.00 | 375.00 | 600.00 | 900.00 | 1,200 | 1,600 | |
| 1916S . . . . . . . . . . . . . . | 10,450,000 | *.50* | *.50* | *1.00* | 3.00 | 7.00 | 22.50 | |
| 1917 . . . . . . . . . . . . . . . | 55,230,000 | *.50* | *.50* | *.50* | 1.25 | 2.50 | 12.00 | |
| 1917D . . . . . . . . . . . . . . . | 9,402,000 | *.50* | *.50* | *1.00* | 5.00 | 12.50 | 55.00 | |
| 1917S . . . . . . . . . . . . . . | 27,330,000 | *.50* | *.50* | *.75* | 1.50 | 3.50 | 20.00 | |

*Italic prices indicate unsettled values due to fluctuating bullion market. See Bullion Chart.*

| | Quan. Minted | G-4 | VG-8 | F-12 | VF-20 | EF-40 | MS-60 | Proof-65 |
|---|---|---|---|---|---|---|---|---|
| 1918 | 26,680,000 | *$.50* | *$.50* | *$.50* | $3.00 | $8.00 | $30.00 | |
| 1918D | 22,674,800 | *.50* | *.50* | *.75* | 3.00 | 8.00 | 35.00 | |
| 1918S | 19,300,000 | *.50* | *.50* | *.75* | 2.00 | 5.00 | 30.00 | |
| 1919 | 35,740,000 | *.50* | *.50* | *.50* | 1.50 | 2.50 | 12.00 | |
| 1919D | 9,939,000 | *.50* | *.50* | *1.00* | 5.00 | 12.00 | 65.00 | |
| 1919S | 8,850,000 | *.50* | *.50* | *.75* | 4.50 | 10.00 | 75.00 | |
| 1920 | 59,030,000 | *.50* | *.50* | *.50* | 2.00 | 3.00 | 12.00 | |
| 1920D | 19,171,000 | *.50* | *.50* | *.75* | 3.00 | 8.00 | 45.00 | |
| 1920S | 13,820,000 | *.50* | *.50* | *.75* | 2.50 | 7.00 | 40.00 | |
| 1921 | 1,230,000 | 12.00 | 18.00 | 40.00 | 80.00 | 275.00 | 750.00 | |
| 1921D | 1,080,000 | 20.00 | 28.00 | 65.00 | 100.00 | 275.00 | 750.00 | |
| 1923 | 50,130,000 | *.50* | *.50* | *.50* | *1.00* | 1.75 | 12.00 | |
| 1923S | 6,440,000 | *.50* | *.50* | *.75* | 2.50 | 8.00 | 55.00 | |
| 1924 | 24,010,000 | *.50* | *.50* | *.50* | 1.25 | 3.00 | 22.50 | |
| 1924D | 6,810,000 | *.50* | *.50* | *1.00* | 2.50 | 7.00 | 60.00 | |
| 1924S | 7,120,000 | *.50* | *.50* | *1.00* | 2.25 | 6.00 | 60.00 | |
| 1925 | 25,610,000 | *.50* | *.50* | *.50* | 1.25 | 2.25 | 22.50 | |
| 1925D | 5,117,000 | 1.50 | 2.00 | 4.00 | 12.00 | 35.00 | 160.00 | |
| 1925S | 5,850,000 | *.50* | *.50* | *1.00* | 2.25 | 8.00 | 65.00 | |
| 1926 | 32,160,000 | *.50* | *.50* | *.50* | 1.25 | 2.00 | 12.00 | |
| 1926D | 6,828,000 | *.50* | *.50* | *.75* | 2.00 | 6.00 | 45.00 | |
| 1926S | 1,520,000 | 3.00 | 4.00 | 8.00 | 15.00 | 40.00 | 275.00 | |
| 1927 | 28,080,000 | *.50* | *.50* | *.50* | *1.00* | 1.75 | 12.00 | |
| 1927D | 4,812,000 | *.50* | *.50* | *1.00* | 5.00 | 12.00 | 120.00 | |
| 1927S | 4,770,000 | *.50* | *.50* | *.75* | 1.25 | 5.00 | 55.00 | |
| 1928 | 19,480,000 | *.50* | *.50* | *.50* | *1.00* | 1.75 | 12.00 | |
| 1928D | 4,161,000 | *.50* | *.50* | 1.75 | 5.00 | 11.00 | 75.00 | |
| 1928S | 7,400,000 | *.50* | *.50* | *.75* | 1.25 | 4.00 | 37.50 | |
| 1929 | 25,970,000 | *.50* | *.50* | *.50* | *1.00* | 1.50 | 8.00 | |
| 1929D | 5,034,000 | *.50* | *.50* | *.75* | 1.75 | 3.00 | 18.00 | |
| 1929S | 4,730,000 | *.50* | *.50* | *.75* | 1.25 | 2.00 | 27.50 | |
| 1930 | 6,770,000 | *.50* | *.50* | *.50* | *1.00* | 2.00 | 12.00 | |
| 1930S | 1,843,000 | *.75* | *1.00* | 1.25 | 1.50 | 3.00 | 40.00 | |
| 1931 | 3,150,000 | *.50* | *.50* | *.50* | 1.50 | 3.50 | 20.00 | |
| 1931D | 1,260,000 | 3.00 | 4.00 | 5.00 | 8.00 | 18.00 | 75.00 | |
| 1931S | 1,800,000 | *.75* | *1.00* | 1.50 | 2.00 | 4.00 | 40.00 | |
| 1934 | 24,080,000 | *.50* | *.50* | *.50* | *.50* | *.60* | 8.00 | |
| 1934D | 6,772,000 | *.50* | *.50* | *.50* | *.50* | *.60* | 25.00 | |
| 1935 | 58,830,000 | *.50* | *.50* | *.50* | *.50* | *.60* | 6.00 | |
| 1935D | 10,477,000 | *.50* | *.50* | *.50* | *.50* | *.60* | 30.00 | |
| 1935S | 15,840,000 | *.50* | *.50* | *.50* | *.50* | *.60* | 18.00 | |
| 1936 (4,130) | 87,504,130 | *.50* | *.50* | *.50* | *.50* | *.60* | 5.00 | $400.00 |
| 1936D | 16,132,000 | *.50* | *.50* | *.50* | *.50* | *.60* | 20.00 | |
| 1936S | 9,210,000 | *.50* | *.50* | *.50* | *.50* | *.60* | 12.00 | |
| 1937 (5,756) | 56,865,756 | *.50* | *.50* | *.50* | *.50* | *.60* | 5.00 | 275.00 |
| 1937D | 14,146,000 | *.50* | *.50* | *.50* | *.50* | *.60* | 18.00 | |
| 1937S | 9,740,000 | *.50* | *.50* | *.50* | *.50* | *.60* | 12.00 | |

| | Quan. Minted | VG-8 | F-12 | VF-20 | EF-40 | MS-60 | MS-65 | Proof-65 |
|---|---|---|---|---|---|---|---|---|
| 1938 (8,728) | 22,198,728 | *$.50* | *$.50* | *$.50* | *$.50* | $7.00 | $18.00 | $225.00 |
| 1938D | 5,537,000 | *.50* | *.50* | *.50* | *.50* | 18.00 | 50.00 | |
| 1938S | 8,090,000 | *.50* | *.50* | *.50* | *.50* | 10.00 | 20.00 | |
| 1939 (9,321) | 67,749,321 | *.50* | *.50* | *.50* | *.50* | 4.00 | 12.00 | 200.00 |
| 1939D | 24,394,000 | *.50* | *.50* | *.50* | *.50* | 4.00 | 12.00 | |
| 1939S | 10,540,000 | *.50* | *.50* | *.50* | *.50* | 12.00 | 28.00 | |

*Italic prices indicate unsettled values due to fluctuating bullion market. See Bullion Chart.*

| | Quan. Minted | VG-8 | F-12 | VF-20 | EF-40 | MS-60 | MS-65 | Proof-65 |
|---|---|---|---|---|---|---|---|---|
| 1940 . . . . . (11,827) | 65,361,827 | *$.50* | *$.50* | *$.50* | *$.50* | $2.00 | $6.00 | $175.00 |
| 1940D. . . . . . . . . . . . . . | 21,198,000 | *.50* | *.50* | *.50* | *.50* | 8.00 | 20.00 | |
| 1940S . . . . . . . . . . . . . . | 21,560,000 | *.50* | *.50* | *.50* | *.50* | 2.50 | 8.00 | |
| 1941 . . . . . (16,557) | 175,106,557 | *.50* | *.50* | *.50* | *.50* | 2.00 | 6.00 | 150.00 |
| 1941D. . . . . . . . . . . . . . | 45,634,000 | *.50* | *.50* | *.50* | *.50* | 5.00 | 10.00 | |
| 1941S . . . . . . . . . . . . . . | 43,090,000 | *.50* | *.50* | *.50* | *.50* | 3.00 | 8.00 | |

1942, 2 over 1

1942D, 2 over 1

| | Quan. Minted | VG-8 | F-12 | VF-20 | EF-40 | MS-60 | MS-65 | Proof-65 |
|---|---|---|---|---|---|---|---|---|
| 1942, 2 over 1 . . . | 205,432,329 | 140.00 | 150.00 | 160.00 | 175.00 | 600.00 | 1,500 | |
| 1942 . . . . . (22,329) | | *.50* | *.50* | *.50* | *.50* | 2.00 | 7.00 | 150.00 |
| 1942D, 2 over 1. . | 60,740,000 | 140.00 | 150.00 | 160.00 | 185.00 | 650.00 | 1,600 | |
| 1942D. . . . . . . . . . . | | *.50* | *.50* | *.50* | *.50* | 2.00 | 10.00 | |
| 1942S . . . . . . . . . . . . . . | 49,300,000 | *.50* | *.50* | *.50* | *.50* | 4.00 | 18.00 | |
| 1943 . . . . . . . . . . . . . . | 191,710,000 | *.50* | *.50* | *.50* | *.50* | 2.00 | 6.00 | |
| 1943D. . . . . . . . . . . . . . | 71,949,000 | *.50* | *.50* | *.50* | *.50* | 2.00 | 9.00 | |
| 1943S . . . . . . . . . . . . . . | 60,400,000 | *.50* | *.50* | *.50* | *.50* | 3.00 | 12.00 | |
| 1944 . . . . . . . . . . . . . . | 231,410,000 | *.50* | *.50* | *.50* | *.50* | 2.00 | 7.00 | |
| 1944D. . . . . . . . . . . . . . | 62,224,000 | *.50* | *.50* | *.50* | *.50* | 2.00 | 9.00 | |
| 1944S . . . . . . . . . . . . . . | 49,490,000 | *.50* | *.50* | *.50* | *.50* | 2.00 | 9.00 | |
| 1945 . . . . . . . . . . . . . . | 159,130,000 | *.50* | *.50* | *.50* | *.50* | 2.00 | 6.00 | |
| 1945D. . . . . . . . . . . . . . | 40,245,000 | *.50* | *.50* | *.50* | *.50* | 2.00 | 8.00 | |
| 1945S Normal S. . . . | 41,920,000 | *.50* | *.50* | *.50* | *.50* | 2.00 | 8.00 | |
| 1945S Micro S . . . . . . | | *.50* | *.50* | *.50* | *.50* | 5.00 | 16.00 | |

## ROOSEVELT TYPE 1946 to Date

John R. Sinnock (whose initials JS are at the truncation of the neck) designed this dime showing a portrait of Franklin D. Roosevelt. The design has heavier lettering and a more modernistic character than preceding types.

**VF-20 VERY FINE**—*Hair above ear slightly worn. All vertical lines on torch plain.*
**EF-40 EXTREMELY FINE**—*All lines of torch, flame and hair very plain.*
**MS-63 SELECT UNCIRCULATED**—*No trace of wear. Slight blemishes.*
**MS-65 CHOICE UNCIRCULATED**—*No trace of wear. Barely noticeable blemishes.*

Mint mark on reverse 1946-1964.

| | Quan. Minted | VF-20 | EF-40 | MS-63 | Proof-65 |
|---|---|---|---|---|---|
| 1946 . . . . . . . . . . . . . . . . . . . . . . . . . . . . . . | 255,250,000 | *$.50* | *$.50* | *$.60* | |
| 1946D. . . . . . . . . . . . . . . . . . . . . . . . . . . . . . | 61,043,500 | *.50* | *.50* | *.80* | |
| 1946S . . . . . . . . . . . . . . . . . . . . . . . . . . . . . . | 27,900,000 | *.50* | *.50* | 1.60 | |

*Italic prices indicate unsettled values due to fluctuating bullion market. See Bullion Chart.*

| | | Quan. Minted | VF-20 | EF-40 | MS-63 | Proof-65 |
|---|---|---|---|---|---|---|
| 1947 | | 121,520,000 | *$.50* | *$.50* | $1.25 | |
| 1947D | | 46,835,000 | *.50* | *.50* | 2.15 | |
| 1947S | | 34,840,000 | *.50* | *.50* | 1.60 | |
| 1948 | | 74,950,000 | *.50* | *.50* | 1.65 | |
| 1948D | | 52,841,000 | *.50* | *.50* | 2.50 | |
| 1948S | | 35,520,000 | *.50* | *.50* | 2.20 | |
| 1949 | | 30,940,000 | *.50* | *.50* | 7.50 | |
| 1949D | | 26,034,000 | *.50* | *.50* | 3.75 | |
| 1949S | | 13,510,000 | *.50* | *.50* | 18.00 | |
| 1950 | (51,386) | 50,181,500 | *.50* | *.50* | 1.45 | $30.00 |
| 1950D | | 46,803,000 | *.50* | *.50* | 1.25 | |
| 1950S | | 20,440,000 | *.50* | *.50* | 8.25 | |
| 1951 | (57,500) | 103,937,602 | *.50* | *.50* | *.85* | 20.00 |
| 1951D | | 56,529,000 | *.50* | *.50* | *.80* | |
| 1951S | | 31,630,000 | *.50* | *.50* | 6.00 | |
| 1952 | (81,980) | 99,122,073 | *.50* | *.50* | *.85* | 12.00 |
| 1952D | | 122,100,000 | *.50* | *.50* | 1.00 | |
| 1952S | | 44,419,500 | *.50* | *.50* | 2.20 | |
| 1953 | (128,800) | 53,618,920 | *.50* | *.50* | *.90* | 9.00 |
| 1953D | | 136,433,000 | *.50* | *.50* | *.65* | |
| 1953S | | 39,180,000 | *.50* | *.50* | *.60* | |
| 1954 | (233,300) | 114,243,503 | *.50* | *.50* | *.55* | 5.00 |
| 1954D | | 106,397,000 | *.50* | *.50* | *.55* | |
| 1954S | | 22,860,000 | *.50* | *.50* | *.60* | |
| 1955 | (378,200) | 12,828,381 | *.50* | *.50* | *.65* | 5.00 |
| 1955D | | 13,959,000 | *.50* | *.50* | *.60* | |
| 1955S | | 18,510,000 | *.50* | *.50* | *.55* | |
| 1956 | (669,384) | 109,309,384 | *.50* | *.50* | *.55* | 2.00 |
| 1956D | | 108,015,100 | *.50* | *.50* | *.55* | |
| 1957 | (1,247,952) | 161,407,952 | *.50* | *.50* | *.50* | 2.00 |
| 1957D | | 113,354,330 | *.50* | *.50* | *.50* | |
| 1958 | (875,652) | 32,785,652 | *.50* | *.50* | *.55* | 2.00 |
| 1958D | | 136,564,600 | *.50* | *.50* | *.50* | |
| 1959 | (1,149,291) | 86,929,291 | *.50* | *.50* | *.50* | 1.00 |
| 1959D | | 164,919,790 | *.50* | *.50* | *.50* | |
| 1960 | (1,691,602) | 72,081,602 | *.50* | *.50* | *.50* | 1.00 |
| 1960D | | 200,160,400 | *.50* | *.50* | *.50* | |
| 1961 | (3,028,244) | 96,758,244 | *.50* | *.50* | *.50* | .75 |
| 1961D | | 209,146,550 | *.50* | *.50* | *.50* | |
| 1962 | (3,218,019) | 75,668,019 | *.50* | *.50* | *.50* | .75 |
| 1962D | | 334,948,380 | *.50* | *.50* | *.50* | |
| 1963 | (3,075,645) | 126,725,645 | *.50* | *.50* | *.50* | .75 |
| 1963D | | 421,476,530 | *.50* | *.50* | *.50* | |
| 1964 | (3,950,762) | 933,310,762 | *.50* | *.50* | *.50* | .75 |
| 1964D | | 1,357,517,180 | *.50* | *.50* | *.50* | |

## Clad Coinage

Mint mark on obverse starting 1968

| | Quan. Minted | MS-65 | Proof-65 |
|---|---|---|---|
| 1965 | 1,652,140,570 | .10 | |
| 1966 | 1,382,734,540 | .10 | |

*Italic prices indicate unsettled values due to fluctuating bullion market. See Bullion Chart.*

## DIMES

| | Quan. Minted | MS-65 | Proof-65 |
|---|---|---|---|
| 1967 | 2,244,007,320 | $.10 | |
| 1968 | 424,470,400 | .10 | |
| 1968D | 480,748,280 | .10 | |
| 1968S Proof | (3,041,506) | | $.25 |
| 1969 | 145,790,000 | .18 | |
| 1969D | 563,323,870 | .10 | |
| 1969S Proof | (2,934,631) | | .25 |
| 1970 | 345,570,000 | .10 | |
| 1970D | 754,942,100 | .10 | |
| 1970S Proof | (2,632,810) | | .35 |
| 1971 | 162,690,000 | .10 | |
| 1971D | 377,914,240 | .10 | |
| 1971S Proof | (3,220,733) | | .35 |
| 1972 | 431,540,000 | .10 | |
| 1972D | 330,290,000 | .10 | |
| 1972S Proof | (3,260,996) | | .35 |
| 1973 | 315,670,000 | .10 | |
| 1973D | 455,032,426 | .10 | |
| 1973S Proof | (2,760,339) | | .25 |
| 1974 | 470,248,000 | .10 | |
| 1974D | 571,083,000 | .10 | |
| 1974S Proof | (2,612,568) | | .35 |
| 1975 | 585,673,900 | .10 | |
| 1975D | 313,705,300 | .10 | |
| 1975S Proof | (2,845,450) | | $.35 |
| 1976 | 568,760,000 | $.10 | |
| 1976D | 695,222,774 | .10 | |
| 1976S Proof | (4,149,730) | | .25 |
| 1977 | 796,930,000 | .10 | |
| 1977D | 376,607,228 | .10 | |
| 1977S Proof | (3,251,152) | | .25 |
| 1978 | 663,980,000 | .10 | |
| 1978D | 282,847,540 | .10 | |
| 1978S Proof | (3,127,781) | | .35 |
| 1979 | 315,440,000 | .10 | |
| 1979D | 390,921,184 | .10 | |
| 1979S Proof | (3,677,175) | | |
| Filled S | | | .45 |
| Clear S | | | 2.00 |
| 1980P | 735,170,000 | .10 | |
| 1980D | 719,354,321 | .10 | |
| 1980S Proof | (3,554,806) | | .35 |
| 1981P | 676,650,000 | .10 | |
| 1981D | 712,284,143 | .10 | |
| 1981S Proof | (4,063,083) | | .35 |
| 1982P | | .10 | |
| 1982D | | .10 | |
| 1982S Proof | | | .35 |

## TWENTY-CENT PIECES — 1875-1878

This short-lived coin was authorized by the Act of March 3, 1875. The edge of the coin is plain. Most of the 1876CC coins were melted at the mint and never released. Mint mark is on the reverse below the eagle.

**G-4 GOOD**—*LIBERTY on shield obliterated. Letters and date legible.*
**VG-8 VERY GOOD**—*One or two letters in LIBERTY may show. Other details will be bold.*
**F-12 FINE**—*At least 3 letters of LIBERTY show.*
**VF-20 VERY FINE**—*LIBERTY completely readable, but partly weak.*
**EF-40 EXTREMELY FINE**—*LIBERTY sharp. Only slight wear on high points of coin.*
**MS-60 UNCIRCULATED**—*No trace of wear. Light blemishes.*

| | Quan. Minted | G-4 | VG-8 | F-12 | VF-20 | EF-40 | MS-60 | Proof-60 |
|---|---|---|---|---|---|---|---|---|
| 1875 (2,790) | 39,700 | $25.00 | $30.00 | $40.00 | $60.00 | $120.00 | $750.00 | $800.00 |
| 1875CC | 133,290 | 25.00 | 30.00 | 40.00 | 60.00 | 110.00 | 700.00 | |
| 1875S | 1,155,000 | 20.00 | 25.00 | 35.00 | 55.00 | 100.00 | 650.00 | — |
| 1876 (1,260) | 15,900 | 35.00 | 45.00 | 60.00 | 75.00 | 150.00 | 800.00 | 1,000 |
| 1876CC | 10,000 | | | | | | — | |
| 1877 (350) | 350 | | | | | | | 1,650 |
| 1878 (600) | 600 | | | | | | | 1,500 |

# QUARTER DOLLARS — 1796 to Date

Authorized in 1792, this denomination was not issued until four years later. The first type weighed 104 grains which remained standard until modified to 103⅛ grains by the Act of January 18, 1837. As with the dime and half dime, the weight was reduced and arrows placed at the date in 1853. Rays were placed in the field of the reverse during that year only.

## DRAPED BUST TYPE, SMALL EAGLE REVERSE 1796

**AG-3 ABOUT GOOD**—*Details clear enough to identify.*

**G-4 GOOD**—*Date readable. Bust outlined, but no detail.*

**VG-8 VERY GOOD**—*All but deepest drapery folds worn smooth. Hairlines nearly gone and curls lack detail.*

**F-12 FINE**—*All drapery lines visible. Hair partly worn.*

**VF-20 VERY FINE**—*Only left side of drapery is indistinct.*

**EF-40 EXTREMELY FINE**—*Hair well outlined and detailed.*

**MS-60 UNCIRCULATED**—*No trace of wear. Light blemishes.*

| | *Quan. Minted* | *AG-3* | *G-4* | *VG-8* | *F-12* | *VF-20* | *EF-40* | *MS-60* |
|---|---|---|---|---|---|---|---|---|
| 1796 | 6,146 | $900.00 | $1,700 | $2,300 | $3,200 | $4,700 | $7,000 | $14,000 |

## DRAPED BUST TYPE, HERALDIC EAGLE REVERSE 1804-1807

| | | | | | | | | |
|---|---|---|---|---|---|---|---|---|
| 1804 | 6,738 | 200.00 | 350.00 | 500.00 | 1,100 | 1,900 | 4,500 | —— |
| 1805 | 121,395 | 70.00 | 125.00 | 150.00 | 275.00 | 600.00 | 1,300 | 4,500 |
| 1806 6 over 5 | 206,124 | 70.00 | 125.00 | 150.00 | 275.00 | 600.00 | 1,300 | 4,500 |
| 1806 | | 70.00 | 125.00 | 150.00 | 275.00 | 600.00 | 1,300 | 4,500 |
| 1807 | 220,643 | 70.00 | 125.00 | 150.00 | 275.00 | 600.00 | 1,300 | 4,500 |

## CAPPED BUST TYPE 1815-1838

### Large Size 1815-1828

**AG-3 ABOUT GOOD**—*Details clear enough to identify.*

**G-4 GOOD**—*Date, letters and stars readable. Hair under headband smooth. Cap lines worn smooth.*

**VG-8 VERY GOOD**—*Rim well defined. Main details visible. Full LIBERTY on cap. Hair above eye nearly smooth.*

**F-12 FINE**—*All hairlines show but drapery has only part details. Shoulder clasp distinct.*

**VF-20 VERY FINE**—*All details show, but some wear. Clasp and ear sharp.*

**EF-40 EXTREMELY FINE**—*All details show distinctly. Hair well outlined.*

**MS-60 UNCIRCULATED**—*No trace of wear. Light blemishes.*

# QUARTER DOLLARS

| | Quan. Minted | AG-3 | G-4 | VG-8 | F-12 | VF-20 | EF-40 | MS-60 |
|---|---|---|---|---|---|---|---|---|
| 1815 | 89,235 | $13.00 | $25.00 | $35.00 | $60.00 | $150.00 | $425.00 | $1,800 |
| 1818 8 over 5 | 361,174 | 13.00 | 25.00 | 35.00 | 55.00 | 150.00 | 425.00 | 1,800 |
| 1818 Normal | | 13.00 | 25.00 | 35.00 | 55.00 | 135.00 | 375.00 | 1,700 |
| 1819 | 144,000 | 13.00 | 25.00 | 35.00 | 55.00 | 135.00 | 375.00 | 1,700 |
| 1820 | 127,444 | 13.00 | 25.00 | 35.00 | 55.00 | 135.00 | 375.00 | 1,700 |
| 1821 | 216,851 | 13.00 | 25.00 | 35.00 | 55.00 | 135.00 | 375.00 | 1,700 |
| 1822 All kinds | 64,080 | 13.00 | 25.00 | 35.00 | 55.00 | 135.00 | 375.00 | 1,800 |
| 1822, 25 over 50c | | 70.00 | 100.00 | 150.00 | 250.00 | 475.00 | 800.00 | 3,000 |
| 1823, 3 over 2 | 17,800 | 550.00 | 1,000 | 2,500 | 4,500 | 6,000 | 12,000 | — |
| 1824 | 168,000 | 15.00 | 30.00 | 37.00 | 65.00 | 160.00 | 385.00 | 2,200 |
| 1825 | | 12.00 | 23.00 | 30.00 | 50.00 | 125.00 | 350.00 | 1,800 |
| 1827 Original (Curled base 2 in 25c) | 4,000 Minted | | | | | | | — |
| 1827 Restrike (Square base 2 in 25c) | | | | | | | | — |
| 1828 All kds | 102,000 | 12.00 | 23.00 | 30.00 | 50.00 | 125.00 | 350.00 | 2,000 |
| 1828, 25 over 50c | | 22.00 | 40.00 | 60.00 | 110.00 | 250.00 | 400.00 | 2,800 |

## Reduced Size, No Motto on Reverse 1831-1838

**G-4 GOOD**—*Bust well defined. Hair under headband smooth. Date, letters, stars readable. Scant rims.*
**VG-8 VERY GOOD**—*Details apparent but worn on high spots. Rims strong. Full LIBERTY.*
**F-12 FINE**—*All hairlines visible. Drapery partly worn. Shoulder clasp distinct.*
**VF-20 VERY FINE**—*Only top spots worn. Clasp sharp. Ear distinct.*
**EF-40 EXTREMELY FINE**—*Hair details and clasp are bold and clear.*
**MS-60 UNCIRCULATED**—*No trace of wear. Light blemishes.*

| | Quan. Minted | G-4 | VG-8 | F-12 | VF-20 | EF-40 | MS-60 |
|---|---|---|---|---|---|---|---|
| 1831 | 398,000 | $20.00 | $24.00 | $30.00 | $60.00 | $150.00 | $1,100 |
| 1832 | 320,000 | 20.00 | 24.00 | 30.00 | 60.00 | 150.00 | 1,100 |
| 1833 | 156,000 | 21.00 | 25.00 | 35.00 | 70.00 | 165.00 | 1,200 |
| 1834 | 286,000 | 20.00 | 24.00 | 30.00 | 60.00 | 150.00 | 1,100 |
| 1835 | 1,952,000 | 20.00 | 24.00 | 30.00 | 60.00 | 150.00 | 1,100 |
| 1836 | 472,000 | 20.00 | 24.00 | 30.00 | 60.00 | 150.00 | 1,100 |
| 1837 | 252,400 | 20.00 | 24.00 | 30.00 | 60.00 | 150.00 | 1,100 |
| 1838 | 366,000 | 20.00 | 24.00 | 30.00 | 60.00 | 150.00 | 1,100 |

# QUARTER DOLLARS
## LIBERTY SEATED TYPE 1838-1891
## No Motto Above Eagle 1838-1853

**G-4 GOOD**—*Scant rim. LIBERTY on shield worn off. Date and letters readable.*
**VG-8 VERY GOOD**—*Rim fairly defined, at least 3 letters in LIBERTY evident.*
**F-12 FINE**—*LIBERTY complete, but partly weak.*
**VF-20 VERY FINE**—*LIBERTY strong.*
**EF-40 EXTREMELY FINE**—*Complete LIBERTY and edges of scroll. Clasp shows plainly.*
**MS-60 UNCIRCULATED**—*No trace of wear. Light blemishes.*

Mint mark location is on the reverse below the eagle.

| | Quan. Minted | G-4 | VG-8 | F-12 | VF-20 | EF-40 | MS-60 |
|---|---|---|---|---|---|---|---|
| 1838 | 466,000 | $4.00 | $6.00 | $11.00 | $21.00 | $60.00 | $1,500 |
| 1839 | 491,146 | 4.00 | 6.00 | 11.00 | 21.00 | 70.00 | 1,500 |
| 1840O | 425,200 | 4.00 | 6.00 | 11.00 | 21.00 | 70.00 | 1,500 |
| 1840 | 188,127 | 7.00 | 9.00 | 15.00 | 30.00 | 60.00 | 1,100 |
| 1841 | 120,000 | 11.00 | 14.00 | 30.00 | 50.00 | 90.00 | 450.00 |
| 1841O | 452,000 | 4.00 | 6.00 | 11.00 | 24.00 | 70.00 | 450.00 |

Small Date

Large Date

| | Quan. Minted | G-4 | VG-8 | F-12 | VF-20 | EF-40 | MS-60 |
|---|---|---|---|---|---|---|---|
| 1842 | 88,000 | 30.00 | 40.00 | 70.00 | 130.00 | 225.00 | 1,100 |
| 1842O Small date | 769,000 (both) | 60.00 | 125.00 | 185.00 | 300.00 | 600.00 | — |
| 1842O Large date | | 5.00 | 7.00 | 11.00 | 18.00 | 40.00 | 500.00 |
| 1843 | 645,600 | 4.50 | 6.00 | 9.00 | 18.00 | 40.00 | 300.00 |
| 1843O | 968,000 | 7.00 | 12.00 | 20.00 | 35.00 | 100.00 | 500.00 |
| 1844 | 421,200 | 4.50 | 6.00 | 11.00 | 19.00 | 40.00 | 300.00 |
| 1844O | 740,000 | 4.50 | 6.00 | 11.00 | 21.00 | 50.00 | 500.00 |
| 1845 | 922,000 | 4.50 | 6.00 | 9.00 | 18.00 | 40.00 | 300.00 |
| 1846 | 510,000 | 4.50 | 6.00 | 11.00 | 19.00 | 40.00 | 300.00 |
| 1847 | 734,000 | 4.50 | 6.00 | 11.00 | 18.00 | 40.00 | 300.00 |
| 1847O | 368,000 | 9.00 | 14.00 | 24.00 | 40.00 | 90.00 | 500.00 |
| 1848 | 146,000 | 8.00 | 12.00 | 24.00 | 40.00 | 70.00 | 450.00 |
| 1849 | 340,000 | 7.00 | 9.00 | 15.00 | 21.00 | 65.00 | 300.00 |
| 1849O | †incl. below | 125.00 | 200.00 | 300.00 | 500.00 | 1,500 | — |
| 1850 | 190,800 | 4.50 | 9.00 | 14.00 | 21.00 | 40.00 | 450.00 |
| 1850O | 412,000 | 12.00 | 16.00 | 22.00 | 35.00 | 65.00 | 450.00 |
| 1851 | 160,000 | 4.50 | 9.00 | 14.00 | 21.00 | 60.00 | 400.00 |
| 1851O | 88,000 | 60.00 | 85.00 | 150.00 | 225.00 | 600.00 | 1,100 |
| 1852 | 177,060 | 9.00 | 14.00 | 21.00 | 30.00 | 60.00 | 450.00 |
| 1852O | 96,000 | 100.00 | 140.00 | 185.00 | 325.00 | 650.00 | 1,900 |
| 1853 No arrows or rays | 44,200 | 70.00 | 90.00 | 125.00 | 225.00 | 275.00 | 1,100 |

†Coinage for 1849O included with 1850O.

## Arrows at Date, Rays Around Eagle 1853 Only

1853, 3 over 4

# QUARTER DOLLARS

| | Quan. Minted | G-4 | VG-8 | F-12 | VF-20 | EF-40 | MS-60 |
|---|---|---|---|---|---|---|---|
| 1853 | 15,210,000 | $5.00 | $7.00 | $9.00 | $16.00 | $50.00 | $525.00 |
| 1853, 3 over 4 | | 25.00 | 60.00 | 150.00 | 200.00 | 450.00 | —— |
| 1853O | 1,332,000 | 5.00 | 7.00 | 11.00 | 22.00 | 70.00 | 550.00 |

## Arrows at Date, No Rays 1854-1855

| | Quan. Minted | G-4 | VG-8 | F-12 | VF-20 | EF-40 | MS-60 |
|---|---|---|---|---|---|---|---|
| 1854 | 12,380,000 | 4.00 | 5.00 | 7.00 | 15.00 | 35.00 | 500.00 |
| 1854O | 1,484,000 | 4.00 | 5.00 | 7.00 | 15.00 | 35.00 | 525.00 |
| 1855 | 2,857,000 | 4.00 | 5.00 | 7.00 | 15.00 | 35.00 | 525.00 |
| 1855O | 176,000 | 22.00 | 35.00 | 50.00 | 100.00 | 170.00 | 900.00 |
| 1855S | 396,400 | 22.00 | 35.00 | 50.00 | 90.00 | 150.00 | 900.00 |

## No Motto Above Eagle 1856-1865

| | Quan. Minted | G-4 | VG-8 | F-12 | VF-20 | EF-40 | MS-60 | Proof-60 |
|---|---|---|---|---|---|---|---|---|
| 1856 | 7,264,000 | $4.00 | $5.00 | $7.00 | $10.00 | $21.00 | $300.00 | $750.00 |
| 1856O | 968,000 | 5.00 | 7.00 | 11.00 | 16.00 | 30.00 | 310.00 | |
| 1856S | 286,000 | 10.00 | 14.00 | 21.00 | 50.00 | 100.00 | 1,100 | |
| 1857 | 9,644,000 | 4.00 | 5.00 | 7.00 | 10.00 | 21.00 | 300.00 | 600.00 |
| 1857O | 1,180,000 | 4.00 | 6.00 | 8.00 | 11.00 | 21.00 | 310.00 | |
| 1857S | 82,000 | 20.00 | 32.00 | 45.00 | 120.00 | 225.00 | 1,250 | |
| 1858 | 7,368,000 | 4.00 | 5.00 | 7.00 | 10.00 | 20.00 | 300.00 | 500.00 |
| 1858O | 520,000 | 4.00 | 6.00 | 8.00 | 11.00 | 22.00 | 325.00 | |
| 1858S | 121,000 | 16.00 | 18.00 | 30.00 | 75.00 | 115.00 | 600.00 | |
| 1859 .... (800) | 1,344,000 | 4.00 | 5.00 | 7.00 | 10.00 | 21.00 | 300.00 | 350.00 |
| 1859O | 260,000 | 6.00 | 10.00 | 16.00 | 25.00 | 40.00 | 500.00 | |
| 1859S | 80,000 | 25.00 | 40.00 | 75.00 | 125.00 | 250.00 | 1,000 | |
| 1860 .. (1,000) | 805,400 | 4.00 | 5.00 | 7.00 | 10.00 | 21.00 | 300.00 | 350.00 |
| 1860O | 388,000 | 5.00 | 7.00 | 10.00 | 14.00 | 30.00 | 310.00 | |
| 1860S | 56,000 | 40.00 | 65.00 | 120.00 | 210.00 | 450.00 | 1,250 | |
| 1861 .. (1,000) | 4,854,600 | 4.00 | 5.00 | 7.00 | 10.00 | 21.00 | 300.00 | 350.00 |
| 1861S | 96,000 | 10.00 | 14.00 | 21.00 | 45.00 | 150.00 | 1,100 | |
| 1862 .... (550) | 932,550 | 4.00 | 5.00 | 7.00 | 10.00 | 21.00 | 300.00 | 350.00 |
| 1862S | 67,000 | 11.00 | 15.00 | 22.00 | 50.00 | 150.00 | 1,100 | |
| 1863 .... (460) | 192,060 | 7.00 | 9.00 | 14.00 | 20.00 | 40.00 | 400.00 | 375.00 |
| 1864 .... (470) | 94,070 | 11.00 | 15.00 | 22.00 | 40.00 | 80.00 | 500.00 | 375.00 |
| 1864S | 20,000 | 50.00 | 85.00 | 150.00 | 225.00 | 500.00 | —— | |
| 1865 .... (500) | 59,300 | 16.00 | 21.00 | 35.00 | 50.00 | 90.00 | 475.00 | 375.00 |
| 1865S | 41,000 | 15.00 | 20.00 | 30.00 | 60.00 | 135.00 | 1,700 | |

## Motto Above Eagle 1866-1873

| | Quan. Minted | G-4 | VG-8 | F-12 | VF-20 | EF-40 | MS-60 | Proof-60 |
|---|---|---|---|---|---|---|---|---|
| 1866 .... (725) | 17,525 | 45.00 | 75.00 | 90.00 | 130.00 | 200.00 | 600.00 | 300.00 |
| 1866S | 28,000 | 20.00 | 30.00 | 60.00 | 100.00 | 200.00 | 1,200 | |
| 1867 .... (625) | 20,625 | 20.00 | 30.00 | 70.00 | 110.00 | 200.00 | 500.00 | 300.00 |
| 1867S | 48,000 | 18.00 | 25.00 | 40.00 | 65.00 | 90.00 | 1,200 | |
| 1868 .... (600) | 30,000 | 19.00 | 27.00 | 45.00 | 70.00 | 125.00 | 400.00 | 300.00 |

| | Quan. Minted | G-4 | VG-8 | F-12 | VF-20 | EF-40 | MS-60 | Proof-60 |
|---|---|---|---|---|---|---|---|---|
| 1868S | 96,000 | $11.00 | $17.00 | $30.00 | $40.00 | $80.00 | $600.00 | |
| 1869 .... (600) | 16,600 | 20.00 | 30.00 | 75.00 | 110.00 | 185.00 | 550.00 | $300.00 |
| 1869S | 76,000 | 11.00 | 17.00 | 28.00 | 35.00 | 80.00 | 550.00 | |
| 1870 .. (1,000) | 87,400 | 11.00 | 15.00 | 22.00 | 37.00 | 60.00 | 300.00 | 300.00 |
| 1870CC | 8,340 | 225.00 | 325.00 | 550.00 | 850.00 | 2,100 | 2,750 | |
| 1871 .... (960) | 119,160 | 4.00 | 6.00 | 10.00 | 18.00 | 30.00 | 285.00 | 300.00 |
| 1871CC | 10,890 | 175.00 | 250.00 | 400.00 | 650.00 | 1,100 | —— | |
| 1871S | 30,900 | 35.00 | 65.00 | 125.00 | 175.00 | 270.00 | 1,300 | |
| 1872 .... (950) | 182,950 | 4.00 | 6.00 | 9.00 | 14.00 | 30.00 | 300.00 | 300.00 |
| 1872CC | 22,850 | 90.00 | 125.00 | 190.00 | 350.00 | 500.00 | 1,900 | |
| 1872S | 83,000 | 35.00 | 65.00 | 120.00 | 175.00 | 275.00 | 1,700 | |
| 1873 .... (600) | 212,600 | 4.00 | 9.00 | 14.00 | 21.00 | 150.00 | 300.00 | 300.00 |
| 1873CC | 4,000 | | | | | | —— | |

## Arrows at Date 1873-1874

| | Quan. Minted | G-4 | VG-8 | F-12 | VF-20 | EF-40 | MS-60 | Proof-60 |
|---|---|---|---|---|---|---|---|---|
| 1873 .... (540) | 1,271,700 | 6.00 | 8.00 | 14.00 | 35.00 | 100.00 | 700.00 | 675.00 |
| 1873CC | 12,462 | 200.00 | 250.00 | 350.00 | 550.00 | 825.00 | 3,000 | |
| 1873S | 156,000 | 9.00 | 10.00 | 18.00 | 40.00 | 115.00 | 800.00 | |
| 1874 .... (700) | 471,900 | 6.00 | 8.00 | 14.00 | 35.00 | 100.00 | 700.00 | 675.00 |
| 1874S | 392,000 | 9.00 | 10.00 | 18.00 | 40.00 | 115.00 | 800.00 | |

## No Arrows at Date 1875-1891

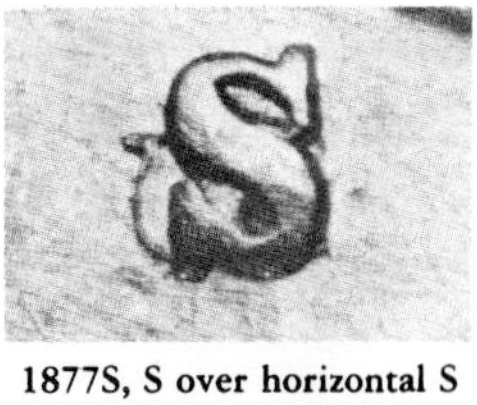

1877S, S over horizontal S

| | Quan. Minted | G-4 | VG-8 | F-12 | VF-20 | EF-40 | MS-60 | Proof-60 |
|---|---|---|---|---|---|---|---|---|
| 1875 .... (700) | 4,293,500 | 3.00 | 4.00 | 5.00 | 10.00 | 20.00 | 275.00 | 275.00 |
| 1875CC | 140,000 | 15.00 | 20.00 | 50.00 | 75.00 | 160.00 | 600.00 | |
| 1875S | 680,000 | 4.00 | 6.00 | 10.00 | 18.00 | 30.00 | 300.00 | |
| 1876 .. (1,150) | 17,817,150 | 3.00 | 4.00 | 5.00 | 10.00 | 20.00 | 275.00 | 275.00 |
| 1876CC | 4,944,000 | 4.00 | 5.00 | 7.00 | 14.00 | 30.00 | 300.00 | |
| 1876S | 8,596,000 | 3.00 | 4.00 | 5.00 | 10.00 | 20.00 | 275.00 | |
| 1877 .... (510) | 10,911,710 | 3.00 | 4.00 | 5.00 | 10.00 | 20.00 | 250.00 | 275.00 |
| 1877CC | 4,192,000 | 4.00 | 5.00 | 7.00 | 14.00 | 30.00 | 300.00 | |
| 1877S | 8,996,000 (both) | 3.00 | 4.00 | 5.00 | 10.00 | 20.00 | 250.00 | |
| 1877S over horizontal S | | 4.00 | 6.00 | 40.00 | 50.00 | 90.00 | 350.00 | |
| 1878 .... (800) | 2,260,800 | 3.00 | 4.00 | 5.00 | 10.00 | 20.00 | 250.00 | 275.00 |
| 1878CC | 996,000 | 4.00 | 5.00 | 7.00 | 11.00 | 25.00 | 350.00 | |
| 1878S | 140,000 | 27.00 | 37.00 | 65.00 | 90.00 | 125.00 | 1,200 | |
| 1879 .. *(1,100)* | 14,700 | 35.00 | 40.00 | 55.00 | 75.00 | 100.00 | 350.00 | 300.00 |

# QUARTER DOLLARS

| | Quan. Minted | G-4 | VG-8 | F-12 | VF-20 | EF-40 | MS-60 | Proof-60 |
|---|---|---|---|---|---|---|---|---|
| 1880 .. (1,355) | 14,955 | $35.00 | $40.00 | $55.00 | $75.00 | $100.00 | $350.00 | $285.00 |
| 1881 .... (975) | 12,975 | 35.00 | 40.00 | 55.00 | 75.00 | 100.00 | 325.00 | 300.00 |
| 1882 .. (1,100) | 16,300 | 35.00 | 40.00 | 55.00 | 75.00 | 100.00 | 325.00 | 300.00 |
| 1883 .. (1,039) | 15,439 | 35.00 | 40.00 | 55.00 | 75.00 | 100.00 | 325.00 | 300.00 |
| 1884 .... (875) | 8,875 | 40.00 | 50.00 | 65.00 | 90.00 | 125.00 | 375.00 | 300.00 |
| 1885 .... (930) | 14,530 | 35.00 | 40.00 | 55.00 | 75.00 | 110.00 | 350.00 | 300.00 |
| 1886 .... (886) | 5,886 | 45.00 | 60.00 | 70.00 | 100.00 | 150.00 | 375.00 | 300.00 |
| 1887 .... (710) | 10,710 | 35.00 | 40.00 | 55.00 | 75.00 | 110.00 | 350.00 | 300.00 |
| 1888 .... (832) | 10,833 | 35.00 | 40.00 | 55.00 | 75.00 | 110.00 | 350.00 | 300.00 |
| 1888S ............ | 1,216,000 | 4.00 | 5.00 | 6.00 | 11.00 | 20.00 | 250.00 | |
| 1889 .... (711) | 12,711 | 33.00 | 37.00 | 50.00 | 65.00 | 90.00 | 350.00 | 300.00 |
| 1890 .... (590) | 80,590 | 20.00 | 25.00 | 33.00 | 45.00 | 70.00 | 300.00 | 285.00 |
| 1891 .... (600) | 3,920,600 | 3.00 | 4.00 | 5.00 | 10.00 | 20.00 | 275.00 | 275.00 |
| 1891O ............... | 68,000 | 50.00 | 65.00 | 100.00 | 150.00 | 275.00 | 1,500 | |
| 1891S ............ | 2,216,000 | 3.00 | 5.00 | 7.00 | 12.00 | 23.00 | 250.00 | |

## BARBER or LIBERTY HEAD TYPE 1892-1916

Like other silver coins of this type the quarter dollars minted from 1892 to 1916 were designed by Charles E. Barber. His initial B is found at the truncation of the neck of Liberty.

**G-4 GOOD**—*Date and legends readable. LIBERTY worn off headband.*

**VG-8 VERY GOOD**—*Minimum of 3 letters in LIBERTY readable.*

**F-12 FINE**—*LIBERTY completely readable but not sharp.*

**VF-20 VERY FINE**—*All letters in LIBERTY evenly plain.*

**EF-40 EXTREMELY FINE**—*LIBERTY bold, and its ribbon distinct.*

**MS-60 UNCIRCULATED**—*No trace of wear. Light blemishes.*

Mint mark location is on the reverse below the eagle.

| | Quan. Minted | G-4 | VG-8 | F-12 | VF-20 | EF-40 | MS-60 | Proof-63 |
|---|---|---|---|---|---|---|---|---|
| 1892 .. (1,245) | 8,237,245 | *1.25* | *1.25* | 3.50 | 7.50 | 26.00 | 200.00 | 500.00 |
| 1892O ............ | 2,640,000 | *2.00* | 3.00 | 4.50 | 9.00 | 30.00 | 225.00 | |
| 1892S .............. | 964,079 | 7.00 | 8.00 | 12.00 | 20.00 | 50.00 | 300.00 | |
| 1893 .... (792) | 5,444,815 | *1.25* | *1.25* | 3.50 | 8.00 | 27.00 | 225.00 | 500.00 |
| 1893O ............ | 3,396,000 | *1.25* | *1.75* | 6.00 | 12.00 | 28.00 | 260.00 | |
| 1893S ............ | 1,454,535 | *2.00* | 3.50 | 8.00 | 14.00 | 35.00 | 260.00 | |
| 1894 .... (972) | 3,432,972 | *1.25* | *1.25* | 3.50 | 11.00 | 27.00 | 225.00 | 500.00 |
| 1894O ............ | 2,852,000 | *1.25* | *1.75* | 6.00 | 9.00 | 30.00 | 270.00 | |
| 1894S ............ | 2,648,821 | *1.25* | *1.75* | 6.00 | 9.00 | 30.00 | 270.00 | |
| 1895 .... (880) | 4,440,880 | *1.25* | *1.25* | 3.50 | 7.00 | 25.00 | 225.00 | 500.00 |
| 1895O ............ | 2,816,000 | *1.25* | *1.75* | 6.00 | 9.00 | 28.00 | 280.00 | |
| 1895S ............ | 1,764,681 | *1.25* | *2.00* | 7.00 | 12.00 | 25.00 | 275.00 | |
| 1896 .... (762) | 3,874,762 | *1.25* | *1.25* | 3.50 | 9.00 | 28.00 | 225.00 | 500.00 |
| 1896O ............ | 1,484,000 | *1.25* | 3.00 | 7.00 | 20.00 | 60.00 | 700.00 | |
| 1896S .............. | 188,039 | 140.00 | 175.00 | 400.00 | 550.00 | 1,000 | 2,750 | |
| 1897 .... (731) | 8,140,731 | *1.25* | *1.25* | 3.50 | 7.00 | 24.00 | 150.00 | 500.00 |
| 1897O ............ | 1,414,800 | *2.50* | 3.50 | 8.00 | 24.00 | 65.00 | 700.00 | |
| 1897S .............. | 542,229 | 5.00 | 7.00 | 14.00 | 28.00 | 60.00 | 315.00 | |
| 1898 .... (735) | 11,100,735 | *1.25* | *1.25* | 3.50 | 7.00 | 24.00 | 150.00 | 500.00 |

*Italic prices indicate unsettled values due to fluctuating bullion market. See Bullion Chart.*

# QUARTER DOLLARS

| | Quan. Minted | G-4 | VG-8 | F-12 | VF-20 | EF-40 | MS-60 | Proof-63 |
|---|---|---|---|---|---|---|---|---|
| 1898O | 1,868,000 | *$1.75* | *$2.50* | $6.00 | $14.00 | $40.00 | $450.00 | |
| 1898S | 1,020,592 | *1.50* | *2.50* | 5.00 | 9.00 | 30.00 | 300.00 | |
| 1899 .... (846) | 12,624,846 | *1.25* | *1.25* | 3.50 | 7.00 | 24.00 | 150.00 | $500.00 |
| 1899O | 2,644,000 | *1.25* | *2.00* | 5.00 | 12.00 | 25.00 | 400.00 | |
| 1899S | 708,000 | 4.50 | 6.00 | 9.00 | 18.00 | 35.00 | 300.00 | |
| 1900 .... (912) | 10,016,912 | *1.25* | *1.25* | 3.50 | 7.00 | 24.00 | 150.00 | 500.00 |
| 1900O | 3,416,000 | *2.00* | 3.50 | 8.00 | 18.00 | 35.00 | 425.00 | |
| 1900S | 1,858,585 | *1.50* | *2.00* | 5.00 | 11.00 | 25.00 | 275.00 | |
| 1901 .... (813) | 8,892,813 | *1.25* | *1.25* | 3.50 | 7.00 | 24.00 | 150.00 | 500.00 |
| 1901O | 1,612,000 | 5.00 | 8.00 | 18.00 | 35.00 | 75.00 | 700.00 | |
| 1901S | 72,664 | 650.00 | 750.00 | 1,000 | 1,500 | 2,200 | 8,000 | |
| 1902 .... (777) | 12,197,744 | *1.25* | *1.25* | 3.50 | 7.00 | 24.00 | 150.00 | 500.00 |
| 1902O | 4,748,000 | *1.50* | *2.00* | 5.00 | 10.00 | 25.00 | 375.00 | |
| 1902S | 1,524,612 | *1.50* | 4.00 | 6.00 | 16.00 | 38.00 | 350.00 | |
| 1903 .... (755) | 9,670,064 | *1.25* | *1.25* | 3.50 | 7.00 | 24.00 | 150.00 | 500.00 |
| 1903O | 3,500,000 | *1.25* | *2.00* | 7.00 | 12.00 | 27.00 | 275.00 | |
| 1903S | 1,036,000 | *2.00* | *2.50* | 8.00 | 14.00 | 30.00 | 325.00 | |
| 1904 .... (670) | 9,588,813 | *1.25* | *1.25* | 3.50 | 7.00 | 24.00 | 150.00 | 500.00 |
| 1904O | 2,456,000 | *1.50* | *2.50* | 8.00 | 12.00 | 35.00 | 650.00 | |
| 1905 .... (727) | 4,968,250 | *1.25* | *1.25* | 3.50 | 7.00 | 24.00 | 150.00 | 500.00 |
| 1905O | 1,230,000 | *2.00* | *2.50* | 8.00 | 12.00 | 30.00 | 275.00 | |
| 1905S | 1,884,000 | *1.50* | *2.00* | 5.00 | 11.00 | 25.00 | 275.00 | |
| 1906 .... (675) | 3,656,435 | *1.25* | *1.25* | 3.50 | 7.00 | 24.00 | 150.00 | 500.00 |
| 1906D | 3,280,000 | *1.25* | *1.25* | 3.50 | 7.00 | 24.00 | 225.00 | |
| 1906O | 2,056,000 | *1.25* | *1.25* | 3.50 | 7.00 | 24.00 | 250.00 | |
| 1907 .... (575) | 7,192,575 | *1.25* | *1.25* | 3.50 | 7.00 | 24.00 | 150.00 | 500.00 |
| 1907D | 2,484,000 | *1.25* | *1.25* | 3.50 | 7.00 | 24.00 | 250.00 | |
| 1907O | 4,560,000 | *1.25* | *1.25* | 3.50 | 7.00 | 24.00 | 235.00 | |
| 1907S | 1,360,000 | *1.25* | *1.25* | 3.50 | 7.00 | 24.00 | 285.00 | |
| 1908 .... (545) | 4,232,545 | *1.25* | *1.25* | 3.50 | 7.00 | 24.00 | 150.00 | 500.00 |
| 1908D | 5,788,000 | *1.25* | *1.25* | 3.50 | 7.00 | 24.00 | 225.00 | |
| 1908O | 6,244,000 | *1.25* | *1.25* | 3.50 | 7.00 | 24.00 | 225.00 | |
| 1908S | 784,000 | *2.00* | 4.00 | 8.00 | 16.00 | 45.00 | 375.00 | |
| 1909 .... (650) | 9,268,650 | *1.25* | *1.25* | 3.50 | 7.00 | 24.00 | 150.00 | 500.00 |
| 1909D | 5,114,000 | *1.25* | *1.25* | 3.50 | 7.00 | 24.00 | 225.00 | |
| 1909O | 712,000 | 4.00 | 6.00 | 18.00 | 25.00 | 75.00 | 575.00 | |
| 1909S | 1,348,000 | *1.25* | *1.25* | 3.50 | 7.00 | 24.00 | 300.00 | |
| 1910 .... (551) | 2,244,551 | *1.25* | *1.25* | 3.50 | 7.00 | 24.00 | 150.00 | 500.00 |
| 1910D | 1,500,000 | *1.25* | *1.25* | 3.50 | 7.00 | 24.00 | 275.00 | |
| 1911 .... (543) | 3,720,543 | *1.25* | *1.25* | 3.50 | 7.00 | 24.00 | 150.00 | 500.00 |
| 1911D | 933,600 | *1.25* | *1.25* | 5.00 | 10.00 | 30.00 | 200.00 | |
| 1911S | 988,000 | *1.25* | *1.25* | 5.00 | 10.00 | 30.00 | 250.00 | |
| 1912 .... (700) | 4,400,700 | *1.25* | *1.25* | 3.50 | 7.00 | 24.00 | 150.00 | 500.00 |
| 1912S | 708,000 | *1.25* | *1.25* | 5.00 | 10.00 | 30.00 | 260.00 | |
| 1913 .... (613) | 484,613 | 5.00 | 8.00 | 25.00 | 65.00 | 200.00 | 900.00 | 800.00 |
| 1913D | 1,450,800 | *1.25* | *1.25* | 3.50 | 7.00 | 24.00 | 250.00 | |
| 1913S | 40,000 | 210.00 | 275.00 | 425.00 | 700.00 | 1,000 | 2,500 | |
| 1914 .... (380) | 6,244,610 | *1.25* | *1.25* | 3.50 | 7.00 | 24.00 | 150.00 | 550.00 |
| 1914D | 3,046,000 | *1.25* | *1.25* | 3.50 | 7.00 | 24.00 | 200.00 | |
| 1914S | 264,000 | 7.00 | 11.00 | 20.00 | 50.00 | 135.00 | 750.00 | |
| 1915 .... (450) | 3,480,450 | *1.25* | *1.25* | 3.50 | 7.00 | 24.00 | 150.00 | 550.00 |
| 1915D | 3,694,000 | *1.25* | *1.25* | 3.50 | 7.00 | 24.00 | 150.00 | |
| 1915S | 704,000 | *1.25* | *1.25* | 5.00 | 10.00 | 30.00 | 210.00 | |
| 1916 | 1,788,000 | *1.25* | *1.25* | 3.50 | 7.00 | 24.00 | 150.00 | |
| 1916D | 6,540,888 | *1.25* | *1.25* | 3.50 | 7.00 | 24.00 | 150.00 | |

*Italic prices indicate unsettled values due to fluctuating bullion market. See Bullion Chart.*

# QUARTER DOLLARS

## STANDING LIBERTY TYPE 1916-1930

This design is by Hermon A. MacNeil, whose initial M is above and to the right of the date. Liberty bears a shield of protection in her left arm, while the right hand holds the olive branch of peace. There was a modification in 1917. The reverse has a new arrangement of stars and the eagle is higher. After 1924 the date was "recessed," thereby giving it greater protection from the effects of circulation.

**G-4 GOOD**—*Date and lettering readable. Top of date worn. Liberty's right leg and toes worn off. Left leg and drapery lines show much wear.*

**VG-8 VERY GOOD**—*Distinct date. Toes show faintly. Drapery lines visible above her left leg.*

**F-12 FINE**—*High curve of right leg flat from thigh to ankle. Left leg shows only slight wear. Drapery lines over right thigh seen only at sides of leg.*

**VF-20 VERY FINE**—*Garment line across right leg will be worn but show at sides.*

**EF-40 EXTREMELY FINE**—*Flattened only at high spots. Her toes are sharp. Drapery lines across right leg are evident.*

**MS-60 UNCIRCULATED**—*No trace of wear. Light blemishes.*

### No stars below eagle 1916-1917

| | *Quan. Minted* | *G-4* | *VG-8* | *F-12* | *VF-20* | *EF-40* | *MS-60* |
|---|---|---|---|---|---|---|---|
| 1916 | 52,000 | $650.00 | $800.00 | $1,400 | $1,750 | $2,000 | $2,500 |
| 1917 | 8,740,000 | 3.00 | 6.00 | 7.50 | 15.00 | 25.00 | 110.00 |
| 1917D | 1,509,200 | 6.00 | 9.00 | 13.00 | 30.00 | 65.00 | 160.00 |
| 1917S | 1,952,000 | 5.00 | 8.00 | 12.00 | 30.00 | 65.00 | 130.00 |

### Stars below eagle 1917-1930

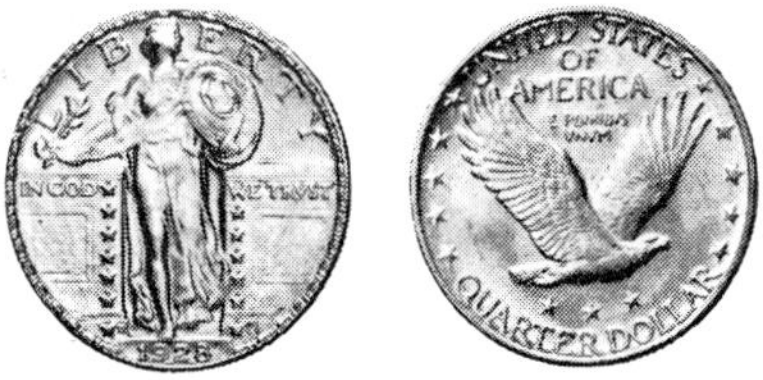

1918S, 8 over 7

Mint mark position is on obverse at left of date.

| | Quan. Minted | G-4 | VG-8 | F-12 | VF-20 | EF-40 | MS-60 |
|---|---|---|---|---|---|---|---|
| 1917 | 13,880,000 | 5.00 | 7.00 | 9.00 | 12.00 | 20.00 | 100.00 |
| 1917D | 6,224,400 | 9.00 | 11.00 | 20.00 | 30.00 | 60.00 | 125.00 |
| 1917S | 5,552,000 | 9.00 | 11.00 | 14.00 | 22.00 | 40.00 | 125.00 |
| 1918 | 14,240,000 | 5.00 | 7.00 | 10.00 | 18.00 | 30.00 | 110.00 |
| 1918D | 7,380,000 | 13.00 | 15.00 | 22.00 | 30.00 | 60.00 | 160.00 |
| 1918S Norm. date | 11,072,000 | 7.00 | 11.00 | 12.00 | 14.00 | 30.00 | 100.00 |
| 1918S 8 over 7 | | 600.00 | 800.00 | 1,200 | 1,800 | 3,200 | 5,000 |
| 1919 | 11,324,000 | 15.00 | 18.00 | 20.00 | 25.00 | 35.00 | 125.00 |
| 1919D | 1,944,000 | 25.00 | 35.00 | 60.00 | 80.00 | 150.00 | 450.00 |
| 1919S | 1,836,000 | 25.00 | 35.00 | 50.00 | 65.00 | 135.00 | 350.00 |
| 1920 | 27,860,000 | 3.00 | 4.00 | 5.00 | 10.00 | 18.00 | 95.00 |
| 1920D | 3,586,400 | 15.00 | 20.00 | 30.00 | 50.00 | 65.00 | 150.00 |
| 1920S | 6,380,000 | 6.00 | 8.00 | 12.00 | 15.00 | 20.00 | 100.00 |

# QUARTER DOLLARS

| | Quan. Minted | G-4 | VG-8 | F-12 | VF-20 | EF-40 | MS-60 |
|---|---|---|---|---|---|---|---|
| 1921 | 1,916,000 | $35.00 | $45.00 | $65.00 | $85.00 | $130.00 | $275.00 |
| 1923 | 9,716,000 | 3.00 | 4.00 | 5.00 | 10.00 | 18.00 | 95.00 |
| 1923S | 1,360,000 | 60.00 | 90.00 | 120.00 | 175.00 | 285.00 | 500.00 |
| 1924 | 10,920,000 | 3.00 | 4.00 | 5.00 | 10.00 | 18.00 | 95.00 |
| 1924D | 3,112,000 | 10.00 | 15.00 | 25.00 | 35.00 | 60.00 | 110.00 |
| 1924S | 2,860,000 | 8.00 | 10.00 | 12.00 | 15.00 | 28.00 | 150.00 |

### Recessed Date 1925-1930

| | Quan. Minted | G-4 | VG-8 | F-12 | VF-20 | EF-40 | MS-60 |
|---|---|---|---|---|---|---|---|
| 1925 | 12,280,000 | *1.25* | *1.25* | 3.00 | 5.00 | 10.00 | 55.00 |
| 1926 | 11,316,000 | *1.25* | *1.25* | 3.00 | 5.00 | 10.00 | 55.00 |
| 1926D | 1,716,000 | *1.50* | *2.00* | 6.00 | 10.00 | 15.00 | 55.00 |
| 1926S | 2,700,000 | *1.25* | *1.25* | 4.00 | 8.00 | 20.00 | 100.00 |
| 1927 | 11,912,000 | *1.25* | *1.25* | 3.00 | 5.00 | 10.00 | 55.00 |
| 1927D | 976,000 | *1.50* | *2.00* | 6.00 | 12.00 | 18.00 | 75.00 |
| 1927S | 396,000 | 3.00 | 5.00 | 20.00 | 50.00 | 200.00 | 1,000 |
| 1928 | 6,336,000 | *1.25* | *1.25* | 3.00 | 5.00 | 10.00 | 55.00 |
| 1928D | 1,627,600 | *1.25* | *1.25* | 3.00 | 5.00 | 10.00 | 55.00 |
| 1928S | 2,644,000 | *1.25* | *1.25* | 3.00 | 5.00 | 10.00 | 55.00 |
| 1929 | 11,140,000 | *1.25* | *1.25* | 3.00 | 5.00 | 10.00 | 55.00 |
| 1929D | 1,358,000 | *1.25* | *1.25* | 3.00 | 5.00 | 10.00 | 55.00 |
| 1929S | 1,764,000 | *1.25* | *1.25* | 3.00 | 5.00 | 10.00 | 55.00 |
| 1930 | 5,632,000 | *1.25* | *1.25* | 3.00 | 5.00 | 10.00 | 55.00 |
| 1930S | 1,556,000 | *1.25* | *1.25* | 3.00 | 5.00 | 10.00 | 55.00 |

## WASHINGTON TYPE 1932 to Date

This type was intended to be a commemorative issue marking the two-hundredth anniversary of Washington's birth. John Flannagan, a New York sculptor, was the designer. The initials JF are found at the base of the neck. Mint mark is on reverse below wreath, 1932 to 1964. Starting in 1968 mint mark is on obverse at right of ribbon.

**VG-8 VERY GOOD**—*Wing tips outlined. Rims are fine and even. Tops of letters at rim are flattened.*

**F-12 FINE**—*Hairlines about ear are visible. Tiny feathers on eagle's breast are faintly visible.*

**VF-20 VERY FINE**—*Hair details worn but plain. Feathers at sides of eagle's breast are plain.*

**EF-40 EXTREMELY FINE**—*Hairlines sharp. Wear spots confined to top of eagle's legs and center of breast.*

**MS-60 UNCIRCULATED**—*No trace of wear. Light blemishes.*

**MS-65 CHOICE UNCIRCULATED**—*No trace of wear. Barely noticeable blemishes.*

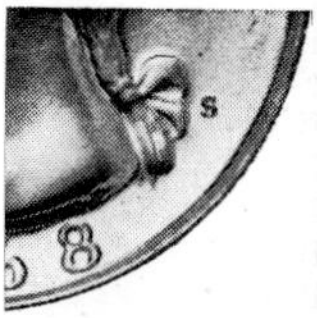

1976 Bicentennial reverse design

| | Quan. Minted | VG-8 | F-12 | VF-20 | EF-40 | MS-60 | MS-65 |
|---|---|---|---|---|---|---|---|
| 1932 | 5,404,000 | *$1.25* | *$1.25* | *$2.00* | $3.00 | $12.00 | $65.00 |
| 1932D | 436,800 | 20.00 | 25.00 | 35.00 | 50.00 | 200.00 | 950.00 |
| 1932S | 408,000 | 18.00 | 23.00 | 30.00 | 35.00 | 100.00 | 450.00 |
| 1934 | 31,912,052 | *1.25* | *1.25* | *2.00* | 3.00 | 15.00 | 30.00 |
| 1934D | 3,527,200 | *1.25* | *1.25* | *2.00* | 5.00 | 40.00 | 160.00 |
| 1935 | 32,484,000 | *1.25* | *1.25* | *2.00* | 3.00 | 8.00 | 20.00 |
| 1935D | 5,780,000 | *1.25* | *1.25* | *2.00* | 5.00 | 40.00 | 160.00 |
| 1935S | 5,660,000 | *1.25* | *1.25* | *2.00* | 4.00 | 35.00 | 90.00 |

*Italic prices indicate unsettled values due to fluctuating bullion market. See Bullion Chart.*

# QUARTER DOLLARS

| | Quan. Minted | F-12 | VF-20 | EF-40 | MS-60 | MS-65 | Proof-65 |
|---|---|---|---|---|---|---|---|
| 1936 ........ (3,837) | 41,303,837 | *$1.25* | *$1.25* | *$1.50* | $8.00 | $20.00 | $400.00 |
| 1936D................ | 5,374,000 | *1.25* | 3.00 | 8.00 | 75.00 | 300.00 | |
| 1936S................ | 3,828,000 | *1.25* | *1.25* | 3.00 | 30.00 | 85.00 | |
| 1937 ........ (5,542) | 19,701,542 | *1.25* | *1.25* | *1.50* | 8.00 | 20.00 | 80.00 |
| 1937D................ | 7,189,600 | *1.25* | *1.25* | *1.75* | 12.00 | 37.50 | |
| 1937S................ | 1,652,000 | *1.25* | *2.00* | 5.00 | 35.00 | 85.00 | |
| 1938 ........ (8,045) | 9,480,045 | *1.25* | *1.25* | 4.00 | 20.00 | 45.00 | 100.00 |
| 1938S................ | 2,832,000 | *1.25* | *1.50* | 3.00 | 19.00 | 40.00 | |
| 1939 ........ (8,795) | 33,548,795 | *1.25* | *1.25* | *1.25* | 5.00 | 10.00 | 55.00 |
| 1939D................ | 7,092,000 | *1.25* | *1.25* | *1.25* | 10.00 | 30.00 | |
| 1939S................ | 2,628,000 | *1.25* | *1.50* | 3.00 | 20.00 | 45.00 | |
| 1940 ....... (11,246) | 35,715,246 | *1.25* | *1.25* | *1.25* | 1.95 | 3.50 | 40.00 |
| 1940D................ | 2,797,600 | *1.25* | *1.25* | 3.50 | 20.00 | 50.00 | |
| 1940S................ | 8,244,000 | *1.25* | *1.25* | *1.25* | 5.00 | 10.00 | |
| 1941 ....... (15,287) | 79,047,287 | *1.25* | *1.25* | *1.25* | *2.00* | 3.75 | 35.00 |
| 1941D.............. | 16,714,800 | *1.25* | *1.25* | *1.25* | 7.00 | 13.00 | |
| 1941S.............. | 16,080,000 | *1.25* | *1.25* | *1.25* | 6.50 | 12.50 | |
| 1942 ....... (21,123) | 102,117,123 | *1.25* | *1.25* | *1.25* | *2.00* | 3.75 | 35.00 |
| 1942D.............. | 17,487,200 | *1.25* | *1.25* | *1.25* | 3.50 | 7.00 | |
| 1942S.............. | 19,384,000 | *1.25* | *1.25* | *1.25* | 18.00 | 35.00 | |
| 1943 ............... | 99,700,000 | *1.25* | *1.25* | *1.25* | *2.00* | 3.75 | |
| 1943D.............. | 16,095,600 | *1.25* | *1.25* | *1.25* | 5.00 | 10.00 | |
| 1943S.............. | 21,700,000 | *1.25* | *1.25* | *1.25* | 12.00 | 25.00 | |
| 1944 ............... | 104,956,000 | *1.25* | *1.25* | *1.25* | *2.00* | 3.00 | |
| 1944D.............. | 14,600,800 | *1.25* | *1.25* | *1.25* | 3.00 | 7.00 | |
| 1944S.............. | 12,560,000 | *1.25* | *1.25* | *1.25* | *2.50* | 6.00 | |
| 1945 ............... | 74,372,000 | *1.25* | *1.25* | *1.25* | *2.00* | *2.50* | |
| 1945D.............. | 12,341,600 | *1.25* | *1.25* | *1.25* | *2.00* | 5.00 | |
| 1945S.............. | 17,004,001 | *1.25* | *1.25* | *1.25* | *2.00* | 4.00 | |
| 1946 ............... | 53,436,000 | *1.25* | *1.25* | *1.25* | *2.00* | *2.25* | |
| 1946D................ | 9,072,800 | *1.25* | *1.25* | *1.25* | *2.00* | *2.50* | |
| 1946S................ | 4,204,000 | *1.25* | *1.25* | *1.25* | *2.00* | *2.50* | |
| 1947 ............... | 22,556,000 | *1.25* | *1.25* | *1.25* | *2.00* | 3.00 | |
| 1947D.............. | 15,338,400 | *1.25* | *1.25* | *1.25* | *2.00* | 4.00 | |
| 1947S................ | 5,532,000 | *1.25* | *1.25* | *1.25* | *2.00* | 3.00 | |
| 1948 ............... | 35,196,000 | *1.25* | *1.25* | *1.25* | *2.00* | *2.25* | |
| 1948D.............. | 16,766,800 | *1.25* | *1.25* | *1.25* | *2.00* | 3.00 | |
| 1948S.............. | 15,960,000 | *1.25* | *1.25* | *1.25* | *2.00* | 3.00 | |
| 1949 ................ | 9,312,000 | *1.25* | *1.25* | *1.25* | 7.00 | 15.00 | |
| 1949D.............. | 10,068,400 | *1.25* | *1.25* | *1.25* | *2.25* | 5.00 | |
| 1950 ....... (51,386) | 24,971,512 | *1.25* | *1.25* | *1.25* | *2.00* | *2.50* | 40.00 |
| 1950D............ | | *1.25* | *1.25* | *1.25* | *2.00* | *2.50* | |
| 1950D, D over S | 21,075,600 | | 15.00 | 40.00 | 80.00 | 125.00 | |
| 1950S............ | | *1.25* | *1.25* | *1.25* | *2.50* | 5.00 | |
| 1950S, S over D | 10,284,004 | | 15.00 | 45.00 | 120.00 | 200.00 | |
| 1951 ....... (57,500) | 43,505,602 | *1.25* | *1.25* | *1.25* | *1.75* | *2.00* | 25.00 |
| 1951D.............. | 35,354,800 | *1.25* | *1.25* | *1.25* | *1.75* | *2.00* | |
| 1951S................ | 9,048,000 | *1.25* | *1.25* | *1.25* | 3.00 | 6.00 | |
| 1952 ...... (81,980) | 38,862,073 | *1.25* | *1.25* | *1.25* | *1.75* | *2.00* | 15.00 |
| 1952D.............. | 49,795,200 | *1.25* | *1.25* | *1.25* | *1.75* | *2.00* | |
| 1952S.............. | 13,707,800 | *1.25* | *1.25* | *1.25* | *2.00* | 4.00 | |
| 1953 ...... (122,800) | 18,664,920 | *1.25* | *1.25* | *1.25* | *1.75* | *2.00* | 7.50 |
| 1953D.............. | 56,112,400 | *1.25* | *1.25* | *1.25* | *1.50* | *1.75* | |
| 1953S.............. | 14,016,000 | *1.25* | *1.25* | *1.25* | *1.75* | *2.25* | |

*Italic prices indicate unsettled values due to fluctuating bullion market. See Bullion Chart.*

# QUARTER DOLLARS

| | | *Quan. Minted* | *F-12* | *EF-40* | *MS-65* | *Proof-65* |
|---|---|---|---|---|---|---|
| 1954 | (233,300) | 54,645,503 | *$1.25* | *$1.25* | *$1.50* | $6.00 |
| 1954D | | 46,305,500 | *1.25* | *1.25* | *1.50* | |
| 1954S | | 11,834,722 | *1.25* | *1.25* | *1.75* | |
| 1955 | (378,200) | 18,558,381 | *1.25* | *1.25* | *1.50* | 5.00 |
| 1955D | | 3,182,400 | *1.25* | *1.25* | *1.75* | |
| 1956 | (669,384) | 44,813,384 | *1.25* | *1.25* | *1.25* | 3.00 |
| 1956D | | 32,334,500 | *1.25* | *1.25* | *1.25* | |
| 1957 | (1,247,952) | 47,779,952 | *1.25* | *1.25* | *1.25* | *2.50* |
| 1957D | | 77,924,160 | *1.25* | *1.25* | *1.25* | |
| 1958 | (875,652) | 7,235,652 | *1.25* | *1.25* | *1.50* | *2.50* |
| 1958D | | 78,124,900 | *1.25* | *1.25* | *1.25* | |
| 1959 | (1,149,291) | 25,533,291 | *1.25* | *1.25* | *1.25* | *2.00* |
| 1959D | | 62,054,232 | *1.25* | *1.25* | *1.25* | |
| 1960 | (1,691,602) | 30,855,602 | *1.25* | *1.25* | *1.25* | *1.75* |
| 1960D | | 63,000,324 | *1.25* | *1.25* | *1.25* | |
| 1961 | (3,028,244) | 40,064,244 | *1.25* | *1.25* | *1.25* | *1.50* |
| 1961D | | 83,656,928 | *1.25* | *1.25* | *1.25* | |
| 1962 | (3,218,019) | 39,374,019 | *1.25* | *1.25* | *1.25* | *1.50* |
| 1962D | | 127,554,756 | *1.25* | *1.25* | *1.25* | |
| 1963 | (3,075,645) | 77,391,645 | *1.25* | *1.25* | *1.25* | *1.50* |
| 1963D | | 135,288,184 | *1.25* | *1.25* | *1.25* | |
| 1964 | (3,950,762) | 564,341,347 | *1.25* | *1.25* | *1.25* | *1.50* |
| 1964D | | 704,135,528 | *1.25* | *1.25* | *1.25* | |

## Clad Coinage—1965 to Date

| | *Quan. Minted* | *MS-65* | *Proof-65* |
|---|---|---|---|
| 1965 | 1,819,717,540 | $.25 | |
| 1966 | 821,101,500 | .25 | |
| 1967 | 1,524,031,848 | .25 | |
| 1968 | 220,731,500 | .25 | |
| 1968D | 101,534,000 | .25 | |
| 1968S Proof | (3,041,506) | | $.35 |
| 1969 | 176,212,000 | .25 | |
| 1969D | 114,372,000 | .25 | |
| 1969S Proof | (2,934,631) | | .35 |
| 1970 | 136,420,000 | .25 | |
| 1970D | 417,341,364 | .25 | |
| 1970S Proof | (2,632,810) | | .40 |
| 1971 | 109,284,000 | .25 | |
| 1971D | 258,634,428 | .25 | |
| 1971S Proof | (3,220,733) | | .35 |
| 1972 | 215,048,000 | .25 | |
| 1972D | 311,067,732 | .25 | |
| 1972S Proof | (3,260,996) | | .35 |
| 1973 | 346,924,000 | .25 | |
| 1973D | 232,977,400 | .25 | |
| 1973S Proof | (2,760,339) | | .35 |
| 1974 | 801,456,000 | .25 | |
| 1974D | 353,160,300 | .25 | |
| 1974S Proof | (2,612,568) | | .40 |
| **Eagle Reverse Resumed (Dies slightly modified to lower relief)** | | | |
| 1977 | 468,556,000 | .25 | |
| 1977D | 256,524,978 | .25 | |
| 1977S Proof | (3,251,152) | | .30 |

| | *Quan. Minted* | *MS-65* | *Proof-65* |
|---|---|---|---|
| 1978 | 521,452,000 | $.25 | |
| 1978D | 287,373,152 | .25 | |
| 1978S Proof | (3,127,781) | | $.30 |
| 1979 | 515,708,000 | .25 | |
| 1979D | 489,789,780 | .25 | |
| 1979S Proof | (3,677,175) | | |
| Filled S | | | .40 |
| Clear S | | | 3.00 |
| 1980P | 635,832,000 | .25 | |
| 1980D | 518,327,487 | .25 | |
| 1980S Proof | (3,554,806) | | .30 |
| 1981P | 601,716,000 | .25 | |
| 1981D | 575,722,833 | .25 | |
| 1981S Proof | (4,063,083) | | .35 |
| 1982P | | | .25 |
| 1982D | | .25 | |
| 1982S Proof | | | .50 |

*Italic prices indicate unsettled values due to fluctuating bullion market. See Bullion Chart.*

# QUARTER DOLLARS

## BICENTENNIAL COINAGE DATED 1776-1976

| | *Quan. Minted* | *MS-65* | *Proof-65* |
|---|---|---|---|
| 1976 Copper-nickel clad | 809,784,016 | $.25 | |
| 1976D Copper-nickel clad | 860,118,839 | .25 | |
| 1976S Copper-nickel clad | (7,059,099) | | $.30 |
| 1976S Silver clad | **11,000,000* | .60 | |
| 1976S Silver clad | *(*4,000,000)* | | 1.50 |

*Approximate mintage. Not all released.

# HALF DOLLARS — 1794 to Date

The half dollar, authorized by the Act of April 2, 1792, was not minted until December, 1794.

The weight of the half dollar was 208 grains and its fineness .8924 when first issued. This standard was not changed until 1837 when the law of January 18, 1837 specified 206¼ grains, .900 fine.

Arrows at the date in 1853 indicate the reduction of weight to 192 grains. During that year only, rays were added to the field on the reverse side. Arrows remained in 1854 and 1855.

In 1873 the weight was raised to 192.9 grains and arrows were again placed at the date.

## FLOWING HAIR TYPE 1794-1795

**AG-3 ABOUT GOOD**—*Clear enough to identify.*

**G-4 GOOD**—*Date and letters sufficient to be readable. Main devices outlined, but lack details.*

**VG-8 VERY GOOD**—*Major details discernible. Letters well formed but worn.*

**F-12 FINE**—*Hair ends distinguishable. Top hairlines show, but otherwise worn smooth.*

**VF-20 VERY FINE**—*Hair in center shows some detail. Other details more bold.*

**EF-40 EXTREMELY FINE**—*Hair above head and down neck detailed with slight wear.*

3 Leaves under Wings

| | *Quan. Minted* | *AG-3* | *G-4* | *VG-8* | *F-12* | *VF-20* | *EF-40* |
|---|---|---|---|---|---|---|---|
| 1794 | 23,464 | $225.00 | $450.00 | $650.00 | $1,000 | $1,750 | $3,000 |
| 1795 All kinds | 299,680 | 175.00 | 400.00 | 500.00 | 650.00 | 1,100 | 2,000 |
| 1795 Recut date | | 175.00 | 400.00 | 550.00 | 700.00 | 1,200 | 2,200 |
| 1795 3 leaves under each wing | | 225.00 | 450.00 | 675.00 | 1,100 | 1,800 | 3,100 |

## DRAPED BUST TYPE, SMALL EAGLE REVERSE 1796-1797

*Grading same as above for About Good to Fine.*

**VF-20 VERY FINE**—*Right side of drapery slightly worn. Left side to curls is smooth.*

**EF-40 EXTREMELY FINE**—*All lines in drapery on bust will show distinctly around to hair curls.*

"1976, 15 Stars

1796, 16 Stars

| | Quan. Minted | AG-3 | G-4 | VG-8 | F-12 | VF-20 | EF-40 |
|---|---|---|---|---|---|---|---|
| 1796, 15 Stars | 3,918 | $3,500 | $6,000 | $8,000 | $12,000 | $15,000 | $22,000 |
| 1796, 16 stars | | 3,500 | 6,000 | 8,000 | 12,000 | 15,000 | 22,000 |
| 1797, 15 stars | | 3,500 | 6,000 | 8,000 | 12,000 | 15,000 | 22,000 |

## DRAPED BUST TYPE, HERALDIC EAGLE REVERSE 1801-1807

| | Quan. Minted | G-4 | VG-8 | F-12 | VF-20 | EF-40 | MS-60 |
|---|---|---|---|---|---|---|---|
| 1801 | 30,289 | $75.00 | $100.00 | $200.00 | $400.00 | $700.00 | $5,750 |
| 1802 | 29,890 | 65.00 | 95.00 | 175.00 | 300.00 | 550.00 | 4,750 |
| 1803 | 188,234 | 40.00 | 55.00 | 125.00 | 250.00 | 450.00 | 4,500 |

1805, 5 over 4

1805, 6 over 5

| | Quan. Minted | G-4 | VG-8 | F-12 | VF-20 | EF-40 | MS-60 |
|---|---|---|---|---|---|---|---|
| 1805, 5 over 4 | 211,722 | 50.00 | 65.00 | 130.00 | 275.00 | 550.00 | 5,000 |
| 1805 Normal date | | 40.00 | 50.00 | 80.00 | 225.00 | 400.00 | 4,250 |
| 1806 | 839,576 | 40.00 | 50.00 | 80.00 | 225.00 | 400.00 | 4,250 |
| 1806, 6 over 5 | | 40.00 | 50.00 | 90.00 | 250.00 | 425.00 | 4,250 |
| 1806, 6 over inverted 6 | | 45.00 | 55.00 | 100.00 | 275.00 | 450.00 | 4,500 |
| 1807 | 301,076 | 35.00 | 45.00 | 75.00 | 200.00 | 400.00 | 4,250 |

## CAPPED BUST TYPE, Lettered Edge 1807-1836

John Reich designed this Capped Head concept of Liberty. The head of Liberty facing left was used on all U.S. coin denominations for the next thirty years.

# HALF DOLLARS

**G-4 GOOD**—*Date and letters readable. Bust worn smooth with outline distinct.*

**VG-8 VERY GOOD**—*LIBERTY visible but faint. Legends distinguishable. Clasp at shoulder visible. Curl above it nearly smooth.*

**F-12 FINE**—*Clasp and adjacent curl clearly outlined with slight details.*

**VF-20 VERY FINE**—*Clasp at shoulder clear. Curl has wear only on highest point. Hair over brow distinguishable.*

**EF-40 EXTREMELY FINE**—*Clasp and adjacent curl fairly sharp. Brow and hair above distinct. Curls well defined.*

**MS-60 UNCIRCULATED**—*No trace of wear. Light blemishes.*

## First style 1807-1808

| | *Quan. Minted* | *G-4* | *VG-8* | *F-12* | *VF-20* | *EF-40* | *MS-60* |
|---|---|---|---|---|---|---|---|
| 1807 . . . . . . . . . . . . . . . . . | 750,500 | $16.00 | $21.00 | $35.00 | $75.00 | $150.00 | $600.00 |
| 1808, 8 over 7 . . . . . . . . | 1,368,600 | 16.00 | 20.00 | 30.00 | 50.00 | 90.00 | 500.00 |
| 1808 . . . . . . . . . . . . . . . . . | | 16.00 | 20.00 | 25.00 | 40.00 | 70.00 | 410.00 |

## Remodeled Portrait and Eagle 1809-1834

| | | | | | | | |
|---|---|---|---|---|---|---|---|
| 1809 . . . . . . . . . . . . . . . . . | 1,405,810 | 14.00 | 17.00 | 20.00 | 30.00 | 65.00 | 350.00 |
| 1810 . . . . . . . . . . . . . . . . . | 1,276,276 | 13.00 | 16.00 | 19.00 | 25.00 | 55.00 | 375.00 |
| 1811 . . . . . . . . . . . . . . . . . | 1,203,644 | 13.00 | 15.00 | 18.00 | 25.00 | 55.00 | 350.00 |

1812, 2 over 1

1813, 50 C. over UNI

1814, 4 over 3

| | | | | | | | |
|---|---|---|---|---|---|---|---|
| 1812, 2 over 1 . . . . . . . . | 1,628,059 | 14.00 | 16.00 | 25.00 | 50.00 | 100.00 | 400.00 |
| 1812 Normal . . . . . . . . . | | 13.00 | 15.00 | 18.00 | 25.00 | 55.00 | 350.00 |
| 1813 . . . . . . . . . . . . . . . . . | 1,241,903 | 13.00 | 15.00 | 18.00 | 25.00 | 55.00 | 335.00 |
| 1813, 50C over UNI . . . | | 15.00 | 18.00 | 32.00 | 50.00 | 90.00 | 410.00 |
| 1814, 4 over 3 . . . . . . . . | 1,039,075 | 13.00 | 16.00 | 21.00 | 30.00 | 65.00 | 335.00 |
| 1814 Normal . . . . . . . . . | | 13.00 | 15.00 | 18.00 | 25.00 | 55.00 | 335.00 |

# HALF DOLLARS

1817, 7 over 3

1817, 7 over 4

1817 Punctuated Date

| | *Quan. Minted* | *G-4* | *VG-8* | *F-12* | *VF-20* | *EF-40* | *MS-60* |
|---|---|---|---|---|---|---|---|
| 1815, 5 over 2 | 47,150 | $150.00 | $200.00 | $275.00 | $400.00 | $600.00 | $1,800 |
| 1817, 7 over 3 | 1,215,567 | 14.00 | 25.00 | 75.00 | 125.00 | 210.00 | 600.00 |
| 1817, 7 over 4 | | | | 1,500 | —— | —— | |
| 1817 dated 181.7 | | 13.00 | 16.00 | 22.00 | 40.00 | 80.00 | 375.00 |
| 1817 Normal | | 13.00 | 15.00 | 18.00 | 25.00 | 55.00 | 335.00 |

1818, 2nd 8 over 7

1819, 9 over 8

1820, 20 over 19

| | | | | | | | |
|---|---|---|---|---|---|---|---|
| 1818, 8 over 7 | 1,960,322 | 13.00 | 15.00 | 18.00 | 25.00 | 55.00 | 375.00 |
| 1818 Normal | | 13.00 | 15.00 | 18.00 | 25.00 | 55.00 | 335.00 |
| 1819 9 over 8 | 2,208,00 | 13.00 | 15.00 | 18.00 | 25.00 | 55.00 | 350.00 |
| 1819 Normal | | 13.00 | 15.00 | 18.00 | 25.00 | 55.00 | 350.00 |
| 1820, 20 over 19 | 751,122 | 13.00 | 15.00 | 18.00 | 25.00 | 55.00 | 375.00 |
| 1820 Normal | | 12.00 | 14.00 | 17.00 | 24.00 | 50.00 | 375.00 |
| 1821 | 1,305,797 | 12.00 | 14.00 | 17.00 | 24.00 | 50.00 | 350.00 |
| 1822, 2 over 1 | 1,559,573 | 18.00 | 25.00 | 40.00 | 50.00 | 90.00 | 400.00 |
| 1822 Normal | | 12.00 | 14.00 | 17.00 | 24.00 | 50.00 | 350.00 |
| 1823 Normal | 1,694,200 | 12.00 | 14.00 | 17.00 | 24.00 | 50.00 | 335.00 |

"Various Dates"
1828 Square Base 2
(probably 4 over
2 over 0)

1824, 4 over 1

1828 Curl Base, Knob 2

1828 Square Base 2

| | | | | | | | |
|---|---|---|---|---|---|---|---|
| 1824 over various dates | 3,504,954 | 12.00 | 14.00 | 17.00 | 24.00 | 50.00 | 335.00 |
| 1824, 4 over 1 | | 12.00 | 14.00 | 17.00 | 24.00 | 50.00 | 335.00 |
| 1824 Normal | | 12.00 | 14.00 | 17.00 | 24.00 | 50.00 | 350.00 |
| 1825 | 2,943,166 | 12.00 | 14.00 | 17.00 | 24.00 | 50.00 | 335.00 |
| 1826 | 4,004,180 | 12.00 | 14.00 | 17.00 | 24.00 | 50.00 | 335.00 |
| 1827, 7 over 6 | 5,493,400 | 12.00 | 14.00 | 17.00 | 24.00 | 50.00 | 350.00 |
| 1827 Normal | | 12.00 | 14.00 | 17.00 | 24.00 | 50.00 | 335.00 |
| 1828 All kinds | 3,075,200 | | | | | | |
| 1828 Curl base no knob 2 | | 12.00 | 14.00 | 17.00 | 24.00 | 50.00 | 335.00 |
| 1828 Curl base knob 2 | | 16.00 | 20.00 | 27.00 | 40.00 | 60.00 | 400.00 |
| 1828 Sq. base | | 12.00 | 14.00 | 17.00 | 24.00 | 50.00 | 350.00 |

# HALF DOLLARS

| | Quan. Minted | G-4 | VG-8 | F-12 | VF-20 | EF-40 | MS-60 |
|---|---|---|---|---|---|---|---|
| 1829, 9 over 7 | 3,712,156 | $12.00 | $14.00 | $17.00 | $24.00 | $50.00 | $350.00 |
| 1829 Normal | | 12.00 | 14.00 | 17.00 | 24.00 | 50.00 | 350.00 |
| 1830 | 4,764,800 | 12.00 | 14.00 | 17.00 | 24.00 | 50.00 | 335.00 |
| 1831 | 5,873,660 | 12.00 | 14.00 | 17.00 | 24.00 | 50.00 | 335.00 |
| 1832 | 4,797,000 | 12.00 | 14.00 | 17.00 | 24.00 | 50.00 | 335.00 |
| 1833 | 5,206,000 | 12.00 | 14.00 | 17.00 | 24.00 | 50.00 | 335.00 |
| 1834 | 6,412,004 | 12.00 | 14.00 | 17.00 | 24.00 | 50.00 | 350.00 |
| 1835 | 5,352,006 | 12.00 | 14.00 | 17.00 | 24.00 | 50.00 | 335.00 |
| 1836 | 6,545,000 | 12.00 | 14.00 | 17.00 | 24.00 | 50.00 | 335.00 |
| 1836, 50 over 00 | | 15.00 | 20.00 | 25.00 | 40.00 | 70.00 | 425.00 |

## Reeded Edge, Reverse "50 CENTS" 1836-1837

**G-4 GOOD**—*LIBERTY discernible on headband.*

**VG-8 VERY GOOD**—*Minimum of 3 letters in LIBERTY must be clear.*

**F-12 FINE**—*LIBERTY complete.*

**VF-20 VERY FINE**—*LIBERTY is sharp. Shoulder clasp is clear.*

**EF-40 EXTREMELY FINE**—*LIBERTY sharp and strong. Hair details show.*

**MS-60 UNCIRCULATED**—*No trace of wear. Light blemishes.*

| | Quan. Minted | G-4 | VG-8 | F-12 | VF-20 | EF-40 | MS-60 |
|---|---|---|---|---|---|---|---|
| 1836 | 1,200 | 175.00 | 225.00 | 300.00 | 500.00 | 900.00 | 2,200 |
| 1837 | 3,629,820 | 18.00 | 20.00 | 25.00 | 45.00 | 100.00 | 650.00 |

## Reeded Edge, Reverse "HALF DOL." 1838-1839

In 1838-39 the mint mark appears on the obverse; thereafter it is on the reverse below the eagle.

| | Quan. Minted | G-4 | VG-8 | F-12 | VF-20 | EF-40 | MS-60 |
|---|---|---|---|---|---|---|---|
| 1838 | 3,546,000 | 18.00 | 20.00 | 25.00 | 45.00 | 100.00 | 750.00 |
| 1838O | (20) | | | | | | 30,000 |
| 1839 | 1,392,976 | 18.00 | 20.00 | 25.00 | 45.00 | 100.00 | 750.00 |
| 1839O | 178,976 | 55.00 | 80.00 | 125.00 | 185.00 | 275.00 | 2,400 |

## LIBERTY SEATED TYPE 1839-1891

## No Motto Above Eagle 1839-1853

**G-4 GOOD**—*Scant rim. LIBERTY on shield worn off. Date and letters readable.*

**VG-8 VERY GOOD**—*Rim fairly defined. At least 3 letters in LIBERTY are evident.*

**F-12 FINE**—*LIBERTY complete, but weak.*

**VF-20 VERY FINE**—*LIBERTY mostly sharp.*

**EF-40 EXTREMELY FINE**—*LIBERTY entirely sharp. Scroll edges and clasp distinct.*

**MS-60 UNCIRCULATED**—*No trace of wear. Light blemishes.*

# HALF DOLLARS

| | Quan. Minted | G-4 | VG-8 | F-12 | VF-20 | EF-40 | MS-60 |
|---|---|---|---|---|---|---|---|
| 1839 No drapery from elbow.......... | | $17.00 | $25.00 | $40.00 | $75.00 | $250.00 | $4,000 |

Drapery from Elbow starting 1839

1842 Small Date

| | | | | | | | |
|---|---|---|---|---|---|---|---|
| 1839 | 1,972,400 | 9.00 | 11.00 | 16.00 | 22.00 | 40.00 | 375.00 |
| 1840 | 1,435,008 | 8.00 | 10.00 | 15.00 | 20.00 | 37.00 | 375.00 |
| 1840O | 855,100 | 8.00 | 10.00 | 15.00 | 20.00 | 37.00 | 375.00 |
| 1841 | 310,000 | 8.00 | 10.00 | 15.00 | 20.00 | 45.00 | 400.00 |
| 1841O | 401,000 | 8.00 | 10.00 | 15.00 | 20.00 | 37.00 | 375.00 |
| 1842 Sm. date } 1842 Med. date | 2,012,764 | 8.00 | 10.00 | 15.00 | 21.00 | 37.00 | 375.00 |
| 1842 Med. date | | 8.00 | 10.00 | 15.00 | 21.00 | 37.00 | 375.00 |
| 1842O Small date | 203,000 | 55.00 | 100.00 | 150.00 | 250.00 | 500.00 | — |
| 1842O Med. date | 754,000 | 8.00 | 9.00 | 13.00 | 20.00 | 35.00 | 375.00 |
| 1843 | 3,844,000 | 8.00 | 9.00 | 13.00 | 20.00 | 35.00 | 375.00 |
| 1843O | 2,268,000 | 8.00 | 9.00 | 13.00 | 20.00 | 35.00 | 375.00 |
| 1844 | 1,766,000 | 8.00 | 9.00 | 13.00 | 20.00 | 35.00 | 375.00 |
| 1844O | 2,005,000 | 8.00 | 9.00 | 13.00 | 20.00 | 35.00 | 375.00 |
| 1845 | 589,000 | 8.00 | 9.00 | 13.00 | 20.00 | 35.00 | 375.00 |
| 1845O | 2,094,000 | 8.00 | 9.00 | 13.00 | 20.00 | 35.00 | 375.00 |
| 1846 All kinds | 2,210,000 | 8.00 | 9.00 | 13.00 | 18.00 | 35.00 | 375.00 |
| 1846 over horizontal 6 (error) | | 15.00 | 30.00 | 45.00 | 75.00 | 100.00 | 550.00 |
| 1846O | 2,304,000 | 8.00 | 9.00 | 13.00 | 18.00 | 35.00 | 375.00 |
| 1847 | 1,156,000 | 8.00 | 9.00 | 13.00 | 18.00 | 35.00 | 375.00 |
| 1847O | 2,584,000 | 8.00 | 9.00 | 13.00 | 18.00 | 35.00 | 375.00 |
| 1848 | 580,000 | 12.00 | 17.00 | 25.00 | 35.00 | 60.00 | 450.00 |
| 1848O | 3,180,000 | 8.00 | 9.00 | 13.00 | 18.00 | 35.00 | 375.00 |
| 1849 | 1,252,000 | 8.00 | 9.00 | 13.00 | 18.00 | 35.00 | 375.00 |
| 1849O | 2,310,000 | 8.00 | 9.00 | 13.00 | 18.00 | 35.00 | 375.00 |
| 1850 | 227,000 | 15.00 | 21.00 | 35.00 | 45.00 | 80.00 | 450.00 |
| 1850O | 2,456,000 | 8.00 | 9.00 | 13.00 | 18.00 | 35.00 | 375.00 |
| 1851 | 200,750 | 15.00 | 21.00 | 35.00 | 45.00 | 80.00 | 450.00 |
| 1851O | 402,000 | 8.00 | 9.00 | 13.00 | 18.00 | 35.00 | 375.00 |
| 1852 | 77,130 | 25.00 | 35.00 | 60.00 | 110.00 | 200.00 | 600.00 |
| 1852O | 144,000 | 15.00 | 21.00 | 35.00 | 45.00 | 80.00 | 450.00 |
| 1853O | | 2,000 | 4,000 | 10,000 | 15,000 | | |

# HALF DOLLARS

## Arrows at Date, Rays Around Eagle 1853 Only

| | Quan. Minted | G-4 | VG-8 | F-12 | VF-20 | EF-40 | MS-60 |
|---|---|---|---|---|---|---|---|
| 1853 | 3,532,708 | $7.00 | $9.00 | $15.00 | $45.00 | $135.00 | $1,600 |
| 1853O All kinds | 1,328,000 | 7.00 | 9.00 | 15.00 | 45.00 | 135.00 | 1,800 |

## Arrows at Date, No Rays 1854-1855

| | | | | | | | |
|---|---|---|---|---|---|---|---|
| 1854 | 2,982,000 | 6.00 | 7.00 | 12.00 | 21.00 | 45.00 | 675.00 |
| 1854O | 5,240,000 | 6.00 | 7.00 | 12.00 | 21.00 | 45.00 | 675.00 |
| 1855 over 1854 | } 759,500 | | 25.00 | 50.00 | 100.00 | 200.00 | 900.00 |
| 1855 Normal date | } | 6.00 | 7.00 | 12.00 | 21.00 | 45.00 | 675.00 |
| 1855O | 3,688,000 | 6.00 | 7.00 | 12.00 | 21.00 | 45.00 | 675.00 |
| 1855S | 129,950 | 50.00 | 70.00 | 120.00 | 250.00 | 350.00 | 1,900 |

## No Arrows at Date 1856-1866

| | | | | | | | |
|---|---|---|---|---|---|---|---|
| 1856 | 938,000 | 7.00 | 8.00 | 12.00 | 17.00 | 35.00 | 350.00 |
| 1856O | 2,658,000 | 7.00 | 8.00 | 12.00 | 17.00 | 35.00 | 350.00 |
| 1856S | 211,000 | 9.00 | 11.00 | 17.00 | 40.00 | 80.00 | 500.00 |
| 1857 | 1,988,000 | 7.00 | 8.00 | 12.00 | 17.00 | 35.00 | 350.00 |
| 1857O | 818,000 | 7.00 | 8.00 | 12.00 | 17.00 | 35.00 | 350.00 |
| 1857S | 158,000 | 11.00 | 16.00 | 20.00 | 45.00 | 90.00 | 525.00 |

| | Quan. Minted | G-4 | VG-8 | F-12 | VF-20 | EF-40 | MS-60 | Proof-60 |
|---|---|---|---|---|---|---|---|---|
| 1858 | 4,226,000 | $7.00 | $8.00 | $12.00 | $17.00 | $35.00 | $350.00 | $600.00 |
| 1858O | 7,294,000 | 7.00 | 8.00 | 12.00 | 17.00 | 35.00 | 350.00 | |
| 1858S | 476,000 | 9.00 | 11.00 | 15.00 | 24.00 | 45.00 | 550.00 | |
| 1859 (800) | 748,000 | 7.00 | 8.00 | 12.00 | 17.00 | 35.00 | 350.00 | 450.00 |
| 1859O | 2,834,000 | 7.00 | 8.00 | 12.00 | 17.00 | 35.00 | 350.00 | |
| 1859S | 566,000 | 9.00 | 11.00 | 15.00 | 25.00 | 70.00 | 500.00 | |
| 1860 (1,000) | 303,700 | 9.00 | 11.00 | 14.00 | 22.00 | 40.00 | 400.00 | 375.00 |
| 1860O | 1,290,000 | 7.00 | 8.00 | 12.00 | 17.00 | 35.00 | 350.00 | |
| 1860S | 472,000 | 9.00 | 11.00 | 14.00 | 20.00 | 35.00 | 375.00 | |
| 1861 (1,000) | 2,888,400 | 7.00 | 8.00 | 12.00 | 17.00 | 35.00 | 350.00 | 375.00 |
| 1861O | 2,532,633 | 7.00 | 8.00 | 12.00 | 17.00 | 35.00 | 350.00 | |
| 1861S | 939,500 | 7.00 | 8.00 | 12.00 | 17.00 | 35.00 | 350.00 | |
| 1862 (550) | 253,550 | 10.00 | 14.00 | 18.00 | 35.00 | 50.00 | 450.00 | 375.00 |
| 1862S | 1,352,000 | 7.00 | 8.00 | 12.00 | 17.00 | 35.00 | 350.00 | |
| 1863 (460) | 503,660 | 9.00 | 11.00 | 14.00 | 22.00 | 40.00 | 400.00 | 375.00 |
| 1863S | 916,000 | 7.00 | 8.00 | 12.00 | 17.00 | 35.00 | 350.00 | |
| 1864 (470) | 379,570 | 9.00 | 11.00 | 14.00 | 22.00 | 40.00 | 400.00 | 375.00 |
| 1864S | 658,000 | 7.00 | 8.00 | 12.00 | 17.00 | 35.00 | 350.00 | |
| 1865 (500) | 511,900 | 9.00 | 11.00 | 14.00 | 22.00 | 40.00 | 400.00 | 375.00 |
| 1865S | 675,000 | 7.00 | 8.00 | 12.00 | 17.00 | 35.00 | 350.00 | |
| 1866S No motto | 60,000 | 23.00 | 39.00 | 70.00 | 120.00 | 175.00 | 2,000 | |

# HALF DOLLARS

## Motto "In God We Trust" Added Above Eagle 1866-1873

| | *Quan. Minted* | *G-4* | *VG-8* | *F-12* | *VF-20* | *EF-40* | *MS-60* | *Proof-60* |
|---|---|---|---|---|---|---|---|---|
| 1866 . . . . . . (725) | 745,625 | $5.00 | $6.00 | $10.00 | $15.00 | $30.00 | $350.00 | $350.00 |
| 1866S . . . . . . . . . . . . | 994,000 | 5.00 | 6.00 | 10.00 | 15.00 | 30.00 | 375.00 | |
| 1867 . . . . . . (625) | 449,925 | 6.00 | 7.00 | 11.00 | 16.00 | 35.00 | 400.00 | 350.00 |
| 1867S . . . . . . . . . . | 1,196,000 | 5.00 | 6.00 | 10.00 | 15.00 | 30.00 | 375.00 | |
| 1868 . . . . . . (600) | 418,200 | 5.00 | 6.00 | 10.00 | 15.00 | 30.00 | 350.00 | 350.00 |
| 1868S . . . . . . . . . . | 1,160,000 | 5.00 | 6.00 | 10.00 | 15.00 | 30.00 | 375.00 | |
| 1869 . . . . . . (600) | 795,900 | 5.00 | 6.00 | 10.00 | 15.00 | 30.00 | 350.00 | 350.00 |
| 1869S . . . . . . . . . . . . | 656,000 | 5.00 | 6.00 | 10.00 | 15.00 | 30.00 | 375.00 | |
| 1870 . . . . . (1,000) | 634,900 | 5.00 | 6.00 | 10.00 | 15.00 | 30.00 | 350.00 | 350.00 |
| 1870CC . . . . . . . . . . . . | 54,617 | 70.00 | 125.00 | 275.00 | 450.00 | 850.00 | —— | |
| 1870S . . . . . . . . . . | 1,004,000 | 5.00 | 6.00 | 10.00 | 15.00 | 30.00 | 375.00 | |
| 1871 . . . . . . (960) | 1,204,560 | 5.00 | 6.00 | 10.00 | 15.00 | 30.00 | 350.00 | 350.00 |
| 1871CC . . . . . . . . . . . | 153,950 | 24.00 | 35.00 | 65.00 | 120.00 | 250.00 | 1,700 | |
| 1871S . . . . . . . . . . | 2,178,000 | 5.00 | 6.00 | 10.00 | 15.00 | 30.00 | 375.00 | |
| 1872 . . . . . . (950) | 881,550 | 5.00 | 6.00 | 10.00 | 15.00 | 30.00 | 325.00 | 350.00 |
| 1872CC . . . . . . . . . . . | 257,000 | 15.00 | 25.00 | 40.00 | 90.00 | 150.00 | 1,100 | |
| 1872S . . . . . . . . . . . . | 580,000 | 6.00 | 7.00 | 11.00 | 15.00 | 30.00 | 400.00 | |
| 1873 . . . . . . (600) | 801,800 | 5.00 | 6.00 | 10.00 | 15.00 | 30.00 | 400.00 | 350.00 |
| 1873CC . . . . . . . . . . . | 122,500 | 23.00 | 37.00 | 80.00 | 135.00 | 200.00 | 1,500 | |

## Arrows at Date 1873-1874

| | *Quan. Minted* | *G-4* | *VG-8* | *F-12* | *VF-20* | *EF-40* | *MS-60* | *Proof-60* |
|---|---|---|---|---|---|---|---|---|
| 1873 . . . . . . (550) | 1,815,700 | 10.00 | 14.00 | 18.00 | 45.00 | 125.00 | 700.00 | 600.00 |
| 1873CC . . . . . . . . . . . | 214,560 | 16.00 | 25.00 | 50.00 | 90.00 | 150.00 | 2,250 | |
| 1873S . . . . . . . . . . . . | 228,000 | 14.00 | 20.00 | 30.00 | 50.00 | 125.00 | 700.00 | |
| 1874 . . . . . . (700) | 2,360,300 | 10.00 | 14.00 | 18.00 | 45.00 | 125.00 | 700.00 | 600.00 |
| 1874CC . . . . . . . . . . . | 59,000 | 21.00 | 38.00 | 100.00 | 150.00 | 300.00 | 1,400 | |
| 1874S . . . . . . . . . . . . | 394,000 | 14.00 | 20.00 | 35.00 | 60.00 | 125.00 | 1,300 | |

## No Arrows at Date 1875-1891

| | *Quan. Minted* | *G-4* | *VG-8* | *F-12* | *VF-20* | *EF-40* | *MS-60* | *Proof-60* |
|---|---|---|---|---|---|---|---|---|
| 1875 . . . . . . (700) | 6,027,500 | 5.00 | 6.00 | 10.00 | 15.00 | 27.00 | 325.00 | 350.00 |
| 1875CC . . . . . . . . . | 1,008,000 | 5.00 | 7.00 | 11.00 | 20.00 | 35.00 | 375.00 | |

| | Quan. Minted | G-4 | VG-8 | F-12 | VF-20 | EF-40 | MS-60 | Proof-60 |
|---|---|---|---|---|---|---|---|---|
| 1875S | 3,200,000 | $5.00 | $6.00 | $10.00 | $15.00 | $27.00 | $325.00 | |
| 1876 . . . . . (1,150) | 8,419,150 | 5.00 | 6.00 | 10.00 | 15.00 | 27.00 | 325.00 | $350.00 |
| 1876CC | 1,956,000 | 5.00 | 6.00 | 10.00 | 16.00 | 30.00 | 400.00 | |
| 1876S | 4,528,000 | 5.00 | 6.00 | 10.00 | 15.00 | 27.00 | 325.00 | |
| 1877 . . . . . . (510) | 8,304,510 | 5.00 | 6.00 | 10.00 | 15.00 | 27.00 | 325.00 | 350.00 |
| 1877CC | 1,420,000 | 5.00 | 6.00 | 10.00 | 16.00 | 32.00 | 375.00 | |
| 1877S | 5,356,000 | 5.00 | 6.00 | 10.00 | 15.00 | 27.00 | 325.00 | |
| 1878 . . . . . . (800) | 1,378,400 | 5.00 | 6.00 | 10.00 | 15.00 | 27.00 | 325.00 | 350.00 |
| 1878CC | 62,000 | 60.00 | 120.00 | 175.00 | 270.00 | 450.00 | 1,800 | |
| 1878S | 12,000 | 750.00 | 1,000 | 1,800 | 2,500 | 3,500 | 6,000 | |
| 1879 . . . . . (1,100) | 5,900 | 60.00 | 75.00 | 100.00 | 125.00 | 180.00 | 550.00 | 450.00 |
| 1880 . . . . . (1,355) | 9,755 | 50.00 | 65.00 | 90.00 | 110.00 | 150.00 | 500.00 | 450.00 |
| 1881 . . . . . . (975) | 10,975 | 50.00 | 65.00 | 90.00 | 110.00 | 150.00 | 500.00 | 450.00 |
| 1882 . . . . . (1,100) | 5,500 | 60.00 | 75.00 | 100.00 | 125.00 | 180.00 | 550.00 | 450.00 |
| 1883 . . . . . (1,039) | 9,039 | 50.00 | 65.00 | 90.00 | 110.00 | 150.00 | 500.00 | 450.00 |
| 1884 . . . . . . (875) | 5,275 | 60.00 | 75.00 | 100.00 | 125.00 | 180.00 | 600.00 | 450.00 |
| 1885 . . . . . . (930) | 6,130 | 50.00 | 65.00 | 90.00 | 110.00 | 150.00 | 600.00 | 450.00 |
| 1886 . . . . . . (886) | 5,886 | 50.00 | 65.00 | 90.00 | 110.00 | 150.00 | 600.00 | 450.00 |
| 1887 . . . . . . (710) | 5,710 | 50.00 | 65.00 | 90.00 | 110.00 | 150.00 | 600.00 | 450.00 |
| 1888 . . . . . . (832) | 12,833 | 45.00 | 60.00 | 75.00 | 100.00 | 140.00 | 500.00 | 450.00 |
| 1889 . . . . . . (711) | 12,711 | 45.00 | 60.00 | 75.00 | 100.00 | 140.00 | 500.00 | 450.00 |
| 1890 . . . . . . (590) | 12,590 | 45.00 | 60.00 | 75.00 | 100.00 | 140.00 | 500.00 | 450.00 |
| 1891 . . . . . . (600) | 200,600 | 5.00 | 6.00 | 10.00 | 16.00 | 30.00 | 325.00 | 450.00 |

## BARBER or LIBERTY HEAD TYPE 1892-1915

Like the dime and quarter dollar, this type was designed by Charles E. Barber, whose initial B is on the truncation of the neck.

**G-4 GOOD**—*Date and legends readable. LIBERTY worn off headband.*
**VG-8 VERY GOOD**—*Minimum of 3 letters readable in LIBERTY.*
**F-12 FINE**—*LIBERTY completely readable, but not sharp.*
**VF-20 VERY FINE**—*All letters in LIBERTY evenly plain.*
**EF-40 EXTREMELY FINE**—*LIBERTY bold, and its ribbon distinct.*
**MS-60 UNCIRCULATED**—*No trace of wear. Light blemishes.*

Mint mark location on reverse below eagle.

| | Quan. Minted | G-4 | VG-8 | F-12 | VF-20 | EF-40 | MS-60 | Proof-63 |
|---|---|---|---|---|---|---|---|---|
| 1892 . . . . . (1,245) | 935,245 | $4.00 | $5.00 | $9.00 | $20.00 | $75.00 | $275.00 | $500.00 |
| 1892O | 390,000 | 40.00 | 45.00 | 65.00 | 125.00 | 180.00 | 450.00 | |
| 1892S | 1,029,028 | 40.00 | 45.00 | 65.00 | 125.00 | 180.00 | 450.00 | |
| 1893 . . . . . . (792) | 1,826,792 | *3.50* | 4.00 | 9.00 | 20.00 | 75.00 | 275.00 | 500.00 |
| 1893O | 1,389,000 | 5.00 | 8.00 | 15.00 | 35.00 | 100.00 | 375.00 | |
| 1893S | 740,000 | 20.00 | 25.00 | 35.00 | 80.00 | 135.00 | 400.00 | |
| 1894 . . . . . . (972) | 1,148,972 | *3.00* | *3.50* | 9.00 | 20.00 | 75.00 | 275.00 | 500.00 |
| 1894O | 2,138,000 | *3.00* | *3.50* | 9.00 | 20.00 | 80.00 | 325.00 | |
| 1894S | 4,048,690 | *3.00* | *3.50* | 9.00 | 20.00 | 75.00 | 300.00 | |

*Italic prices indicate unsettled values due to fluctuating bullion market. See Bullion Chart.*

# HALF DOLLARS

| | *Quan. Minted* | *G-4* | *VG-8* | *F-12* | *VF-20* | *EF-40* | *MS-60* | *Proof-63* |
|---|---|---|---|---|---|---|---|---|
| 1895 ...... | (880) 1,835,218 | *$3.00* | *$3.50* | $9.00 | $20.00 | $75.00 | $300.00 | $500.00 |
| 1895O ........... | 1,766,000 | *3.00* | *3.50* | 9.00 | 20.00 | 75.00 | 375.00 | |
| 1895S ........... | 1,108,086 | 5.00 | 7.00 | 12.00 | 30.00 | 80.00 | 300.00 | |
| 1896 ...... | (762) 950,762 | *3.00* | *3.50* | 9.00 | 20.00 | 75.00 | 275.00 | 500.00 |
| 1896O ............. | 924,000 | 5.00 | 8.00 | 15.00 | 35.00 | 115.00 | 500.00 | |
| 1896S ........... | 1,140,948 | 20.00 | 25.00 | 35.00 | 75.00 | 125.00 | 550.00 | |
| 1897 ...... | (731) 2,480,731 | *2.50* | *2.50* | 7.00 | 15.00 | 60.00 | 265.00 | 500.00 |
| 1897O ............. | 632,000 | 20.00 | 25.00 | 35.00 | 85.00 | 225.00 | 650.00 | |
| 1897S ............. | 933,900 | 40.00 | 45.00 | 60.00 | 90.00 | 150.00 | 550.00 | |
| 1898 ...... | (735) 2,956,735 | *2.50* | *2.50* | 7.00 | 15.00 | 60.00 | 265.00 | 500.00 |
| 1898O ............. | 874,000 | 5.00 | 7.00 | 12.00 | 35.00 | 100.00 | 375.00 | |
| 1898S ........... | 2,358,550 | *3.00* | *3.50* | 9.00 | 20.00 | 75.00 | 325.00 | |
| 1899 ...... | (846) 5,538,846 | *2.50* | *2.50* | 7.00 | 15.00 | 60.00 | 265.00 | 500.00 |
| 1899O ........... | 1,724,000 | *3.00* | *3.50* | 9.00 | 20.00 | 75.00 | 375.00 | |
| 1899S ........... | 1,686,411 | *3.00* | *3.50* | 9.00 | 20.00 | 75.00 | 300.00 | |
| 1900 ...... | (912) 4,762,912 | *2.50* | *2.50* | 7.00 | 15.00 | 60.00 | 265.00 | 500.00 |
| 1900O ........... | 2,744,000 | *3.00* | *3.50* | 9.00 | 20.00 | 75.00 | 400.00 | |
| 1900S ........... | 2,560,322 | *3.00* | *3.50* | 9.00 | 20.00 | 75.00 | 300.00 | |
| 1901 ...... | (813) 4,268,813 | *2.50* | *2.50* | 7.00 | 15.00 | 60.00 | 265.00 | 500.00 |
| 1901O ........... | 1,124,000 | *3.00* | 4.00 | 12.00 | 22.00 | 110.00 | 450.00 | |
| 1901S ............. | 847,044 | 5.00 | 7.00 | 15.00 | 50.00 | 175.00 | 650.00 | |
| 1902 ...... | (777) 4,922,777 | *2.50* | *2.50* | 7.00 | 15.00 | 60.00 | 265.00 | 500.00 |
| 1902O ........... | 2,526,000 | *3.00* | *3.50* | 9.00 | 20.00 | 75.00 | 375.00 | |
| 1902S ........... | 1,460,670 | *3.00* | *3.50* | 9.00 | 20.00 | 75.00 | 325.00 | |
| 1903 ...... | (755) 2,278,755 | *2.50* | *2.50* | 7.00 | 15.00 | 60.00 | 265.00 | 500.00 |
| 1903O ........... | 2,100,000 | *3.00* | *3.50* | 9.00 | 20.00 | 75.00 | 365.00 | |
| 1903S ........... | 1,920,772 | *3.00* | *3.50* | 9.00 | 20.00 | 75.00 | 325.00 | |
| 1904 ...... | (670) 2,992,670 | *2.50* | *2.50* | 7.00 | 15.00 | 60.00 | 265.00 | 500.00 |
| 1904O ........... | 1,117,600 | 4.00 | 5.00 | 11.00 | 25.00 | 110.00 | 450.00 | |
| 1904S ............. | 553,038 | 5.00 | 6.00 | 15.00 | 45.00 | 130.00 | 400.00 | |
| 1905 ...... | (727) 662,727 | 4.00 | 5.00 | 11.00 | 27.00 | 90.00 | 375.00 | 600.00 |
| 1905O ............. | 505,000 | 4.00 | 5.00 | 12.00 | 35.00 | 100.00 | 400.00 | |
| 1905S ........... | 2,494,000 | *2.75* | *3.00* | 9.00 | 18.00 | 70.00 | 325.00 | |
| 1906 ...... | (675) 2,638,675 | *2.50* | *2.50* | 7.00 | 15.00 | 60.00 | 265.00 | 500.00 |
| 1906D ........... | 4,028,000 | *2.75* | *3.00* | 9.00 | 15.00 | 60.00 | 265.00 | |
| 1906O ........... | 2,446,000 | *2.75* | *3.00* | 9.00 | 15.00 | 65.00 | 300.00 | |
| 1906S ........... | 1,740,154 | *2.75* | *3.00* | 9.00 | 18.00 | 70.00 | 325.00 | |
| 1907 ...... | (575) 2,598,575 | *2.50* | *2.50* | 7.00 | 15.00 | 60.00 | 265.00 | 500.00 |
| 1907D ........... | 3,856,000 | *2.75* | *3.00* | 9.00 | 15.00 | 60.00 | 265.00 | |
| 1907O ........... | 3,946,600 | *2.75* | *3.00* | 9.00 | 15.00 | 60.00 | 265.00 | |
| 1907S ........... | 1,250,000 | *2.75* | *3.00* | 9.00 | 18.00 | 70.00 | 365.00 | |
| 1908 ...... | (545) 1,354,545 | *2.50* | *2.50* | 7.00 | 15.00 | 60.00 | 265.00 | 500.00 |
| 1908D ........... | 3,280,000 | *2.50* | *2.50* | 7.00 | 15.00 | 60.00 | 265.00 | |
| 1908O ........... | 5,360,000 | *2.50* | *2.50* | 7.00 | 15.00 | 60.00 | 265.00 | |
| 1908S ........... | 1,644,828 | *2.75* | *3.00* | 9.00 | 18.00 | 65.00 | 300.00 | |
| 1909 ...... | (650) 2,368,650 | *2.50* | *2.50* | 7.00 | 15.00 | 60.00 | 265.00 | 500.00 |
| 1909O ............. | 925,400 | *2.75* | *3.00* | 9.00 | 25.00 | 95.00 | 375.00 | |
| 1909S ........... | 1,764,000 | *2.50* | *2.50* | 7.00 | 15.00 | 60.00 | 300.00 | |
| 1910 ...... | (551) 418,551 | *3.50* | 4.00 | 10.00 | 25.00 | 95.00 | 325.00 | 600.00 |
| 1910S ........... | 1,948,000 | *2.50* | *2.50* | 7.00 | 15.00 | 60.00 | 300.00 | |
| 1911 ...... | (543) 1,406,543 | *2.50* | *2.50* | 7.00 | 15.00 | 60.00 | 265.00 | 500.00 |
| 1911D ............. | 695,080 | *2.50* | *2.50* | 7.00 | 15.00 | 60.00 | 265.00 | |
| 1911S ........... | 1,272,000 | *2.50* | *2.50* | 7.00 | 15.00 | 60.00 | 285.00 | |

*Italic prices indicate unsettled values due to fluctuating bullion market. See Bullion Chart.*

# HALF DOLLARS

| | Quan. Minted | G-4 | VG-8 | F-12 | VF-20 | EF-40 | MS-60 | Proof-63 |
|---|---|---|---|---|---|---|---|---|
| 1912 ...... (700) | 1,550,700 | *$2.50* | *$2.50* | $7.00 | $15.00 | $60.00 | $265.00 | $500.00 |
| 1912D........... | 2,300,800 | *2.50* | *2.50* | 7.00 | 15.00 | 60.00 | 265.00 | |
| 1912S........... | 1,370,000 | *2.50* | *2.50* | 7.00 | 15.00 | 60.00 | 285.00 | |
| 1913 ...... (627) | 188,627 | 7.00 | 8.00 | 15.00 | 35.00 | 90.00 | 375.00 | 650.00 |
| 1913D............. | 534,000 | *2.75* | *3.00* | 9.00 | 18.00 | 60.00 | 285.00 | |
| 1913S............. | 604,000 | *2.75* | *3.00* | 9.00 | 25.00 | 75.00 | 325.00 | |
| 1914 ...... (380) | 124,610 | 8.00 | 10.00 | 20.00 | 60.00 | 120.00 | 400.00 | 700.00 |
| 1914S............. | 992,000 | *2.75* | *3.00* | 9.00 | 18.00 | 65.00 | 300.00 | |
| 1915 ...... (450) | 138,450 | 7.00 | 9.00 | 16.00 | 38.00 | 100.00 | 385.00 | 700.00 |
| 1915D........... | 1,170,400 | *2.50* | *2.50* | 7.00 | 15.00 | 60.00 | 265.00 | |
| 1915S........... | 1,604,000 | *2.50* | *2.50* | 7.00 | 15.00 | 60.00 | 265.00 | |

## LIBERTY WALKING TYPE 1916-1947

This type was designed by A. A. Weinman. The designer's monogram AAW appears under the tip of the wing feathers. On the 1916 coins and some of the 1917 coins the mint mark is located on the obverse below the motto.

**G-4 GOOD**—*Rims are defined. Motto IN GOD WE TRUST readable.*

**VG-8 VERY GOOD**—*Motto is distinct. About half of skirt lines at left are clear.*

**F-12 FINE**—*All skirt lines evident, but worn in spots. Details in sandal below motto are clear.*

**VF-20 VERY FINE**—*Skirt lines sharp including leg area. Little wear on breast and right arm.*

**EF-40 EXTREMELY FINE**—*All skirt lines bold.*

**MS-60 UNCIRCULATED**—*No trace of wear. Light blemishes.*

**MS-65 CHOICE UNCIRCULATED**—*No trace of wear. Barely noticeable blemishes.*

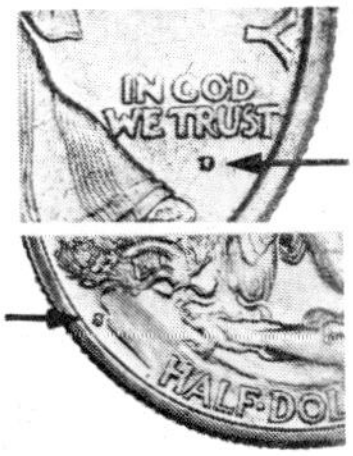


*Choice uncirculated well struck specimens are worth more than values listed.*

| | Quan. Minted | G-4 | VG-8 | F-12 | VF-20 | EF-40 | MS-60 | Proof-65 |
|---|---|---|---|---|---|---|---|---|
| 1916 .............. | 608,000 | $8.00 | $10.00 | $20.00 | $45.00 | $75.00 | $225.00 | |
| 1916D.... (Obv.) | 1,014,400 | 6.00 | 8.00 | 10.00 | 22.00 | 50.00 | 225.00 | |
| 1916S.... (Obv.) | 508,000 | 11.00 | 17.00 | 40.00 | 85.00 | 140.00 | 500.00 | |
| 1917 ........... | 12,292,000 | *2.50* | *2.50* | *2.75* | 7.00 | 12.00 | 90.00 | |
| 1917D.... (Obv.) | 765,400 | 4.00 | 6.00 | 12.00 | 30.00 | 65.00 | 260.00 | |
| 1917D.... (Rev.) | 1,940,000 | *2.75* | *3.00* | 6.00 | 18.00 | 45.00 | 300.00 | |
| 1917S.... (Obv.) | 952,000 | 4.00 | 6.00 | 14.00 | 50.00 | 135.00 | 600.00 | |
| 1917S.... (Rev.) | 5,554,000 | *2.50* | *2.50* | *2.75* | 9.00 | 16.00 | 175.00 | |
| 1918 .............. | 6,634,00 | *2.50* | *2.50* | *2.75* | 15.00 | 50.00 | 225.00 | |
| 1918D........... | 3,853,040 | *2.50* | *2.50* | *2.75* | 16.00 | 55.00 | 500.00 | |
| 1918S.......... | 10,282,000 | *2.50* | *2.50* | *2.75* | 9.00 | 15.00 | 185.00 | |
| 1919 .............. | 962,000 | 4.00 | 5.50 | 10.00 | 40.00 | 135.00 | 700.00 | |

*Italic prices indicate unsettled values due to fluctuating bullion market. See Bullion Chart.*

# HALF DOLLARS

| | Quan. Minted | G-4 | VG-8 | F-12 | VF-20 | EF-40 | MS-60 | Proof-65 |
|---|---|---|---|---|---|---|---|---|
| 1919D | 1,165,000 | *$3.00* | $4.00 | $10.00 | $50.00 | $160.00 | $1,500 | |
| 1919S | 1,552,000 | *2.75* | *3.00* | 7.00 | 35.00 | 140.00 | 1,400 | |
| 1920 | 6,372,000 | *2.50* | *2.50* | *2.75* | 7.00 | 16.00 | 135.00 | |
| 1920D | 1,551,000 | *2.50* | *2.50* | 8.00 | 30.00 | 90.00 | 800.00 | |
| 1920S | 4,624,000 | *2.50* | *2.50* | 5.00 | 13.00 | 35.00 | 600.00 | |
| 1921 | 246,000 | 27.50 | 45.00 | 90.00 | 250.00 | 600.00 | 1,600 | |
| 1921D | 208,000 | 45.00 | 60.00 | 140.00 | 300.00 | 700.00 | 1,800 | |
| 1921S | 548,000 | 5.00 | 8.00 | 14.00 | 90.00 | 750.00 | 5,000 | |
| 1923S | 2,178,000 | *2.50* | *2.50* | *2.50* | 15.00 | 40.00 | 700.00 | |
| 1927S | 2,392,000 | *2.50* | *2.50* | *2.50* | 8.00 | 25.00 | 550.00 | |
| 1928S | 1,940,000 | *2.50* | *2.50* | *2.50* | 10.00 | 30.00 | 600.00 | |
| 1929D | 1,001,200 | *2.50* | *2.50* | *2.50* | 7.00 | 18.00 | 200.00 | |
| 1929S | 1,902,000 | *2.50* | *2.50* | *2.50* | 5.00 | 18.00 | 200.00 | |
| 1933S | 1,786,000 | *2.50* | *2.50* | *2.50* | *3.00* | 10.00 | 200.00 | |
| 1934 | 6,964,000 | *2.50* | *2.50* | *2.50* | *2.50* | 5.00 | 50.00 | |
| 1934D | 2,361,400 | *2.50* | *2.50* | *2.50* | *2.50* | 8.00 | 120.00 | |
| 1934S | 3,652,000 | *2.50* | *2.50* | *2.50* | *2.50* | 6.00 | 175.00 | |
| 1935 | 9,162,000 | *2.50* | *2.50* | *2.50* | *2.50* | *3.00* | 30.00 | |
| 1935D | 3,003,800 | *2.50* | *2.50* | *2.50* | *2.50* | 8.00 | 120.00 | |
| 1935S | 3,854,000 | *2.50* | *2.50* | *2.50* | *2.50* | 7.00 | 150.00 | |
| 1936 (3,901) | 12,617,901 | *2.50* | *2.50* | *2.50* | *2.50* | *3.00* | 30.00 | $700.00 |
| 1936D | 4,252,400 | *2.50* | *2.50* | *2.50* | *2.50* | 6.00 | 80.00 | |
| 1936S | 3,884,000 | *2.50* | *2.50* | *2.50* | *2.50* | 6.00 | 90.00 | |
| 1937 (5,728) | 9,527,728 | *2.50* | *2.50* | *2.50* | *2.50* | *3.00* | 30.00 | 475.00 |
| 1937D | 1,676,000 | *2.50* | *2.50* | *2.50* | *2.50* | 8.00 | 150.00 | |
| 1937S | 2,090,000 | *2.50* | *2.50* | *2.50* | *2.50* | 6.00 | 120.00 | |
| 1938 (8,152) | 4,118,152 | *2.50* | *2.50* | *2.50* | *2.50* | *3.00* | 60.00 | 400.00 |
| 1938D | 491,600 | 10.00 | 11.00 | 12.00 | 15.00 | 35.00 | 300.00 | |
| 1939 (8,808) | 6,820,808 | *2.50* | *2.50* | *2.50* | *2.50* | *3.00* | 35.00 | 350.00 |
| 1939D | 4,267,800 | *2.50* | *2.50* | *2.50* | *2.50* | *3.00* | 40.00 | |
| 1939S | 2,552,000 | *2.50* | *2.50* | *2.50* | *2.50* | 4.00 | 60.00 | |

| | Quan. Minted | VG-8 | F-12 | VF-20 | EF-40 | MS-60 | MS-65 | Proof-65 |
|---|---|---|---|---|---|---|---|---|
| 1940 (11,279) | 9,167,279 | $2.50 | *$2.50* | *$2.50* | *$2.75* | $20.00 | $70.00 | $300.00 |
| 1940S | 4,550,000 | 2.50 | *2.50* | *2.50* | *3.00* | 50.00 | 175.00 | |
| 1941 (15,412) | 24,207,412 | 2.50 | *2.50* | *2.50* | *2.50* | 15.00 | 30.00 | 250.00 |
| 1941D | 11,248,400 | 2.50 | *2.50* | *2.50* | *2.50* | 20.00 | 65.00 | |
| 1941S | 8,098,000 | 2.50 | *2.50* | *2.50* | *2.50* | 60.00 | 185.00 | |
| 1942 (21,120) | 47,839,120 | 2.50 | *2.50* | *2.50* | *2.50* | 15.00 | 35.00 | 250.00 |
| 1942D | 10,973,800 | 2.50 | *2.50* | *2.50* | *2.50* | 25.00 | 90.00 | |
| 1942S | 12,708,000 | 2.50 | *2.50* | *2.50* | *2.50* | 50.00 | 145.00 | |
| 1943 | 53,190,000 | 2.50 | *2.50* | *2.50* | *2.50* | 15.00 | 30.00 | |
| 1943D | 11,346,000 | 2.50 | *2.50* | *2.50* | *2.50* | 30.00 | 125.00 | |
| 1943S | 13,450,000 | 2.50 | *2.50* | *2.50* | *2.50* | 50.00 | 140.00 | |
| 1944 | 28,206,000 | 2.50 | *2.50* | *2.50* | *2.50* | 15.00 | 30.00 | |
| 1944D | 9,769,000 | 2.50 | *2.50* | *2.50* | *2.50* | 25.00 | 75.00 | |
| 1944S | 8,904,000 | 2.50 | *2.50* | *2.50* | *2.50* | 35.00 | 125.00 | |
| 1945 | 31,502,000 | 2.50 | *2.50* | *2.50* | *2.50* | 15.00 | 25.00 | |
| 1945D | 9,966,800 | 2.50 | *2.50* | *2.50* | *2.50* | 20.00 | 65.00 | |
| 1945S | 10,156,000 | 2.50 | *2.50* | *2.50* | *2.50* | 30.00 | 100.00 | |
| 1946 | 12,118,000 | 2.50 | *2.50* | *2.50* | *2.50* | 15.00 | 30.00 | |
| 1946D | 2,151,000 | 2.50 | *2.50* | *2.50* | *2.50* | 20.00 | 30.00 | |
| 1946S | 3,724,000 | 2.50 | *2.50* | *2.50* | *2.50* | 25.00 | 80.00 | |
| 1947 | 4,094,000 | 2.50 | *2.50* | *2.50* | *2.50* | 25.00 | 80.00 | |
| 1947D | 3,900,600 | 2.50 | *2.50* | *2.50* | *2.50* | 20.00 | 70.00 | |

*Italic prices indicate unsettled values due to* ***fluctuating bullion*** *market. See Bullion Chart.*

# HALF DOLLARS

## FRANKLIN-LIBERTY BELL TYPE 1948-1963

The Benjamin Franklin half dollar and the Roosevelt dime were both designed by John R. Sinnock. His initials appear below the shoulder.

**VF-20 VERY FINE**—*At least half of the lower and upper incused lines on the rim of the bell must show.*

**EF-40 EXTREMELY FINE**—*Wear spots appear at top of end curls and hair back of ears. On reverse, Liberty Bell will show wear at top and on lettering.*

**MS-60 UNCIRCULATED**—*No trace of wear. Light blemishes.*

**MS-65 CHOICE UNCIRCULATED**—*No trace of wear. Barely noticeable blemishes.*

Mint mark location

*Choice, well struck uncirculated halves command higher prices.*

| | *Quan. Minted* | *VF-20* | *EF-40* | *MS-60* | *MS-65* | *Proof-65* |
|---|---|---|---|---|---|---|
| 1948 | 3,006,814 | *$2.50* | *$2.50* | *$3.00* | $9.00 | |
| 1948D | 4,028,600 | *2.50* | *2.50* | *3.00* | 5.75 | |
| 1949 | 5,614,000 | *2.50* | *2.50* | 12.00 | 42.50 | |
| 1949D | 4,120,600 | *2.50* | *2.50* | 14.00 | 38.50 | |
| 1949S | 3,744,000 | *2.50* | *2.50* | 40.00 | 100.00 | |
| 1950 | (51,386) 7,793,509 | *2.50* | *2.50* | 5.00 | 20.00 | $135.00 |
| 1950D | 8,031,600 | *2.50* | *2.50* | 4.00 | 13.00 | |
| 1951 | (57,500) 16,859,602 | *2.50* | *2.50* | *3.00* | 6.50 | 100.00 |
| 1951D | 9,475,200 | *2.50* | *2.50* | 12.00 | 28.00 | |
| 1951S | 13,696,000 | *2.50* | *2.50* | 6.00 | 15.00 | |
| 1952 | (81,980) 21,274,073 | *2.50* | *2.50* | *3.00* | 6.00 | 40.00 |
| 1952D | 25,395,600 | *2.50* | *2.50* | *3.00* | 5.00 | |
| 1952S | 5,526,000 | *2.50* | *2.50* | 6.00 | 16.00 | |
| 1953 | (128,800) 2,796,920 | *2.50* | *2.50* | 5.00 | 11.00 | 30.00 |
| 1953D | 20,900,400 | *2.50* | *2.50* | *2.75* | *3.75* | |
| 1953S | 4,148,000 | *2.50* | *2.50* | *3.25* | 7.00 | |
| 1954 | (233,300) 13,421,503 | *2.50* | *2.50* | *2.50* | *2.75* | 18.00 |
| 1954D | 25,445,580 | *2.50* | *2.50* | *2.50* | *2.75* | |
| 1954S | 4,993,400 | *2.50* | *2.50* | *2.75* | *3.75* | |
| 1955 | (378,200) 2,876,381 | *2.50* | *2.50* | *3.00* | 4.00 | 16.00 |
| 1956 | (669,384) 4,701,384 | *2.50* | *2.50* | *2.50* | *3.50* | 7.00 |
| 1957 | (1,247,952) 6,361,952 | *2.50* | *2.50* | *2.50* | *3.50* | 5.00 |
| 1957D | 19,966,850 | *2.50* | *2.50* | *2.50* | *2.75* | |
| 1958 | (875,652) 4,917,652 | *2.50* | *2.50* | *2.50* | *2.75* | 6.00 |
| 1958D | 23,962,412 | *2.50* | *2.50* | *2.50* | *2.50* | |
| 1959 | (1,149,291) 7,349,291 | *2.50* | *2.50* | *2.50* | *2.50* | 5.00 |
| 1959D | 13,053,750 | *2.50* | *2.50* | *2.50* | *2.50* | |
| 1960 | (1,691,602) 7,715,602 | *2.50* | *2.50* | *2.50* | *2.50* | 4.00 |
| 1960D | 18,215,812 | *2.50* | *2.50* | *2.50* | *2.50* | |

*Italic prices indicate unsettled values due to fluctuating bullion market. See Bullion Chart.*

# HALF DOLLARS

| | | Quan. Minted | VF-20 | EF-40 | MS-60 | MS-65 | Proof-65 |
|---|---|---|---|---|---|---|---|
| 1961 | (3,028,244) | 11,318,244 | *$2.50* | *$2.50* | *$2.50* | *$2.50* | $4.00 |
| 1961D | | 20,276,442 | *2.50* | *2.50* | *2.50* | *2.50* | |
| 1962 | (3,218,019) | 12,932,019 | *2.50* | *2.50* | *2.50* | *2.50* | 4.00 |
| 1962D | | 35,473,281 | *2.50* | *2.50* | *2.50* | *2.50* | |
| 1963 | (3,075,645) | 25,239,645 | *2.50* | *2.50* | *2.50* | *2.50* | 4.00 |
| 1963D | | 67,069,292 | *2.50* | *2.50* | *2.50* | *2.50* | |

## KENNEDY TYPE 1964 to Date

Gilroy Roberts, former Chief Engraver of the Mint, designed the obverse of this coin. His stylized initials are on the truncation of the forceful bust of President John F. Kennedy. The reverse, which uses the presidential coat of arms for the motif, is the work of Chief Engraver Frank Gasparro.

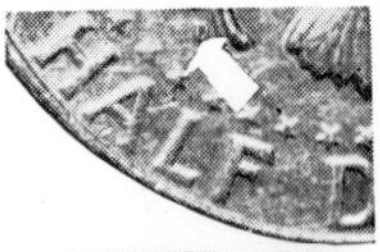
1964 Mint mark location

1968 Mint mark location

### Silver Coinage 1964

| | | Quan. Minted | MS-65 | Proof-65 |
|---|---|---|---|---|
| 1964 | (3,950,762) | 277,254,766 | *$2.50* | *$3.00* |
| 1964D | | 156,205,446 | *2.50* | |

### Silver Clad Coinage 1965-1970

| | Quan. Minted | MS-65 | Proof-65 |
|---|---|---|---|
| 1965 | 65,879,366 | *.75* | |
| 1966 | 108,984,932 | *.75* | |
| 1967 | 295,046,978 | *.75* | |
| 1968D | 246,951,930 | *.75* | |
| 1968S Proof | (3,041,506) | | 2.00 |
| 1969D | 129,881,800 | *.75* | |
| 1969S Proof | (2,934,631) | | 2.00 |
| 1970D (Issued only in mint sets) | 2,150,000 | 16.00 | |
| 1970S Proof | (2,632,810) | | 4.00 |

### Copper-Nickel Clad Coinage 1971-

| | Quan. Minted | MS-65 | Proof-65 |
|---|---|---|---|
| 1971 | 155,164,000 | $.50 | |
| 1971D | 302,097,424 | .50 | |
| 1971S Proof | (3,220,733) | | $1.00 |
| 1972 | 153,180,000 | .50 | |
| 1972D | 141,890,000 | .50 | |
| 1972S Proof | (3,260,996) | | 1.00 |
| 1973 | 64,964,000 | .50 | |
| 1973D | 83,171,400 | .50 | |
| 1973S Proof | (2,760,339) | | $1.00 |
| 1974 | 201,596,000 | $.50 | |
| 1974D | 79,066,300 | .50 | |
| 1974S Proof | (2,612,568) | | 1.00 |
| 1977 | 43,598,000 | .50 | |
| 1977D | 31,449,106 | .50 | |
| 1977S Proof | (3,251,152) | | .90 |
| 1978 | 14,350,000 | .70 | |

*Italic prices indicate unsettled values due to fluctuating bullion market. See Bullion Chart.*

## HALF DOLLARS

| | Quan. Minted | MS-65 | Proof-65 |
|---|---|---|---|
| 1978D | 13,765,799 | $.70 | |
| 1978S Proof | (3,127,781) | | $1.25 |
| 1979 | 68,312,000 | .50 | |
| 1979D | 15,815,422 | .50 | |
| 1979S Proof | (3,677,175) | | |
| Filled S | | | 1.00 |
| Clear S | | | 20.00 |
| 1980P | 44,134,000 | .50 | |
| 1980D | 33,456,449 | $.50 | |
| 1980S Proof | (3,554,806) | | $.85 |
| 1981P | 29,544,000 | .50 | |
| 1981D | 27,839,533 | .50 | |
| 1981S Proof | (4,063,083) | | 1.00 |
| 1982P | | .50 | |
| 1982D | | .50 | |
| 1982S Proof | | | 4.00 |

### BICENTENNIAL COINAGE DATED 1776—1976

| | Quan. Minted | MS-65 | Proof-65 |
|---|---|---|---|
| 1976 Copper-nickel clad | 234,308,000 | $.50 | |
| 1976D Copper-nickel clad | 287,565,248 | .50 | |
| 1976S Copper-nickel clad | (7,059,099) | | $.75 |
| 1976S Silver clad | *11,000,000 | 2.00 | |
| 1976S Silver clad | *(4,000,000) | | 3.50 |

*Approximate mintage. Not all released.

## SILVER DOLLARS — 1794 to Date

The silver dollar was authorized by Congress April 2, 1792. Weight and fineness were specified at 416 grains and 892.4 fine. The first issues appeared in 1794 and until 1804 all silver dollars had the value stamped on the edge: HUNDRED CENTS, ONE DOLLAR OR UNIT. After a lapse in coinage of the silver dollar during the period 1804 to 1839, these coins had reeded edges and the value was placed on the reverse side.

The weight was changed by the law of January 18, 1837 to 412½ grains, fineness .900. The coinage was discontinued by the Act of February 12, 1873 and reauthorized by the Act of February 28, 1878. The dollar was again discontinued after 1935, and since then only the copper-nickel pieces first authorized in 1971 have been coined for circulation.

### FLOWING HAIR TYPE 1794-1795

**AG-3 ABOUT GOOD**—*Clear enough to identify.*
**G-4 GOOD**—*Date and letters readable. Main devices outlined, but lack details.*
**VG-8 VERY GOOD**—*Major details discernible. Letters well formed but worn.*
**F-12 FINE**—*Hair ends distinguishable. Top hairlines show, but otherwise worn smooth.*
**VF-20 VERY FINE**—*Hair in center shows some detail. Other details more bold.*
**EF-40 EXTREMELY FINE**—*Hair well defined but will show some wear.*
**MS-60 UNCIRCULATED**—*No trace of wear. Light blemishes.*

# SILVER DOLLARS

| | Quan. Minted | AG-3 | G-4 | VG-8 | F-12 | VF-20 | EF-40 | MS-60 |
|---|---|---|---|---|---|---|---|---|
| 1794 | 1,758 | $1,750 | $3,500 | $5,500 | $8,000 | $14,000 | $25,000 | —— |
| 1795 | 160,295 | 350.00 | 850.00 | 1,200 | 1,650 | 2,300 | 4,000 | $15,000 |

## DRAPED BUST TYPE, SMALL EAGLE REVERSE 1795-1798

**AG-3 ABOUT GOOD**—*Clear enough to identify.*
**G-4 GOOD**—*Bust outlined, no detail. Date readable, some leaves evident.*
**VG-8 VERY GOOD**—*Drapery worn except deepest folds. Hairlines smooth.*
**F-12 FINE**—*All drapery lines distinguishable. Hairlines near cheek and neck show some detail.*
**VF-20 VERY FINE**—*Left side of drapery worn smooth.*
**EF-40 EXTREMELY FINE**—*Drapery shows distinctly. Hair well outlined and detailed.*
**MS-60 UNCIRCULATED**—*No trace of wear. Light blemishes.*

| | | | | | | | | |
|---|---|---|---|---|---|---|---|---|
| 1975 Bust Type | 42,738 | $400.00 | $850.00 | $1,200 | $1,700 | $2,300 | $3,750 | $14,000 |
| 1796 | 72,920 | 200.00 | 500.00 | 850.00 | 1,000 | 1,400 | 2,500 | 10,000 |
| 1797 | 7,776 | 200.00 | 500.00 | 850.00 | 1,000 | 1,400 | 2,500 | 10,000 |
| 1798 All kinds | 327,536 | 200.00 | 500.00 | 850.00 | 1,000 | 1,400 | 2,500 | 10,000 |

## HERALDIC EAGLE REVERSE 1798-1804

**G-4 GOOD**—*Letters and date readable. E PLURIBUS UNUM obliterated.*
**VG-8 VERY GOOD**—*Motto partially readable. Only deepest drapery details visible. All other lines smooth.*
**F-12 FINE**—*All drapery lines distinguishable. Hairlines near cheek and neck show some detail.*
**VF-20 VERY FINE**—*Left side of drapery worn smooth.*
**EF-40 EXTREMELY FINE**—*Drapery is distinct. Hair well detailed.*
**MS-60 UNCIRCULATED**—*No trace of wear. Light blemishes.*

# SILVER DOLLARS

| | Quan. Minted | G-4 | VG-8 | F-12 | VF-20 | EF-40 | MS-60 |
|---|---|---|---|---|---|---|---|
| 1798 Heraldic eagle |  | $215.00 | $285.00 | $305.00 | $475.00 | $775.00 | $5,500 |
| 1799 | 423,515 | 215.00 | 285.00 | 365.00 | 475.00 | 775.00 | 5,500 |
| 1800 | 220,920 | 215.00 | 285.00 | 365.00 | 475.00 | 775.00 | 5,500 |
| 1801 | 54,454 | 215.00 | 285.00 | 365.00 | 475.00 | 775.00 | 5,500 |
| 1802 | 41,650 | 215.00 | 285.00 | 365.00 | 475.00 | 775.00 | 5,500 |
| 1803 | 85,634 | 215.00 | 285.00 | 365.00 | 475.00 | 775.00 | 5,500 |
| 1804 Variety 1, letter O in "OF" above cloud |  |  |  |  |  |  | Proof $125,000 |
| 1804 Variety 2, letter O above space between clouds |  |  |  |  |  |  | Proof $100,000 |

## GOBRECHT SILVER DOLLARS

Silver dollars of 1836, 1838 and 1839 were mostly made as trial pieces, but some were made in quantities for general circulation. There was no regular issue of dollars 1805 to 1835 inclusive.

| | VF-20 | EF-40 | Proof-60 |
|---|---|---|---|
| 1836 C. GOBRECHT F. on base. Rev. Eagle flying left amid stars. Plain edge. Although scarce, this is the most common variety and was issued for circulation as regular coinage | $1,000 | $1,500 | $3,500 |
| 1838 Similar obv., designer's name omitted, stars added around border. Rev. Eagle flying left in plain field. Reeded edge | 1,500 | 2,500 | 4,500 |
| 1839 Obv. as above. Rev. Eagle in plain field. Reeded edge. Issued for circulation as regular coinage | 1,500 | 2,500 | 4,500 |

# SILVER DOLLARS

## LIBERTY SEATED TYPE — REGULAR ISSUES 1840-1873

In 1840 silver dollars were again issued for general circulation, and the seated figure of Liberty device was adopted for the obverse.

**VG-8 VERY GOOD**—*Any 3 letters of LIBERTY at least two-thirds complete.*
**F-12 FINE**—*All 7 letters of LIBERTY visible though weak.*
**VF-20 VERY FINE**—*LIBERTY is strong but its ribbon shows slight wear.*
**EF-40 EXTREMELY FINE**—*Horizontal lines of shield complete. Eagle's eye plain.*
**MS-60 UNCIRCULATED**—*No trace of wear. Light marks or blemishes.*

Mint mark location is on the reverse below eagle.

| | *Quan. Minted* | *VG-8* | *F-12* | *VF-20* | *EF-40* | *MS-60* | *Proof-60* |
|---|---|---|---|---|---|---|---|
| 1840 | 61,005 | $55.00 | $85.00 | $125.00 | $185.00 | $500.00 | $1,500 |
| 1841 | 173,000 | 55.00 | 80.00 | 120.00 | 175.00 | 450.00 | 1,500 |
| 1842 | 184,618 | 55.00 | 80.00 | 120.00 | 175.00 | 450.00 | 1,500 |
| 1843 | 165,100 | 55.00 | 80.00 | 120.00 | 175.00 | 450.00 | 1,500 |
| 1844 | 20,000 | 65.00 | 90.00 | 135.00 | 200.00 | 600.00 | 1,500 |
| 1845 | 24,500 | 65.00 | 90.00 | 135.00 | 200.00 | 600.00 | 1,500 |
| 1846 | 110,600 | 55.00 | 80.00 | 120.00 | 175.00 | 450.00 | 1,500 |
| 1846O | 59,000 | 70.00 | 100.00 | 135.00 | 225.00 | 1,000 | |
| 1847 | 140,750 | 55.00 | 80.00 | 120.00 | 175.00 | 450.00 | 1,500 |
| 1848 | 15,000 | 65.00 | 90.00 | 135.00 | 225.00 | 600.00 | 1,500 |
| 1849 | 62,600 | 55.00 | 80.00 | 120.00 | 175.00 | 450.00 | 1,500 |
| 1850 | 7,500 | 65.00 | 90.00 | 135.00 | 200.00 | 1,000 | 2,500 |
| 1850O | 40,000 | 70.00 | 100.00 | 160.00 | 270.00 | 1,200 | |
| 1851 | 1,300 | 450.00 | 600.00 | 1,000 | 2,000 | 5,500 | 6,000 |
| 1852 | 1,100 | | | | | 4,500 | 4,500 |
| 1853 | 46,110 | 55.00 | 80.00 | 120.00 | 175.00 | 550.00 | 2,500 |
| 1854 | 33,140 | 60.00 | 100.00 | 150.00 | 250.00 | 625.00 | 1,700 |
| 1855 | 26,000 | 100.00 | 125.00 | 175.00 | 300.00 | 625.00 | 2,750 |
| 1856 | 63,500 | 65.00 | 100.00 | 140.00 | 200.00 | 550.00 | 2,600 |
| 1857 | 94,000 | 60.00 | 90.00 | 135.00 | 185.00 | 550.00 | 1,500 |
| 1858 Est. (80) | 80 | | | | | | 2,000 |
| 1859 (800) | 256,500 | 55.00 | 80.00 | 120.00 | 175.00 | 500.00 | 650.00 |
| 1859O | 360,000 | 55.00 | 80.00 | 120.00 | 175.00 | 500.00 | |
| 1859S | 20,000 | 60.00 | 90.00 | 135.00 | 225.00 | 850.00 | |
| 1860 (1,330) | 218,930 | 55.00 | 80.00 | 120.00 | 175.00 | 450.00 | 650.00 |
| 1860O | 515,000 | 55.00 | 80.00 | 120.00 | 175.00 | 450.00 | |
| 1861 (1,000) | 78,500 | 57.50 | 85.00 | 125.00 | 185.00 | 550.00 | 650.00 |
| 1862 (550) | 12,090 | 100.00 | 125.00 | 225.00 | 325.00 | 900.00 | 650.00 |
| 1863 (460) | 27,660 | 65.00 | 100.00 | 140.00 | 235.00 | 650.00 | 650.00 |
| 1864 (470) | 31,170 | 65.00 | 100.00 | 140.00 | 235.00 | 650.00 | 650.00 |
| 1865 (500) | 47,000 | 65.00 | 100.00 | 140.00 | 235.00 | 650.00 | 650.00 |

# SILVER DOLLARS

## Motto "In God We Trust" Added to Reverse

| | Quan. Minted | VG-8 | F-12 | VF-20 | EF-40 | MS-60 | Proof-60 |
|---|---|---|---|---|---|---|---|
| 1866 ....... (725) | 49,625 | $55.00 | $80.00 | $120.00 | $175.00 | $475.00 | $650.00 |
| 1867 ....... (625) | 47,525 | 55.00 | 80.00 | 120.00 | 175.00 | 475.00 | 650.00 |
| 1868 ....... (600) | 162,700 | 55.00 | 80.00 | 120.00 | 175.00 | 475.00 | 650.00 |
| 1869 ....... (600) | 424,300 | 55.00 | 80.00 | 120.00 | 175.00 | 475.00 | 650.00 |
| 1870 ...... (1,000) | 416,000 | 55.00 | 80.00 | 120.00 | 175.00 | 475.00 | 650.00 |
| 1870CC ............. | 12,462 | 70.00 | 100.00 | 150.00 | 275.00 | 1,100 | |
| 1870S ..................... | | | | | 17,500 | 30,000 | |
| 1871 ....... (960) | 1,074,760 | 55.00 | 80.00 | 120.00 | 175.00 | 475.00 | 650.00 |
| 1871CC ............. | 1,376 | 350.00 | 500.00 | 750.00 | 1,200 | 4,200 | |
| 1872 ....... (950) | 1,106,450 | 55.00 | 80.00 | 120.00 | 175.00 | 475.00 | 650.00 |
| 1872CC ............. | 3,150 | 200.00 | 300.00 | 400.00 | 600.00 | 1,900 | |
| 1872S ............... | 9,000 | 65.00 | 100.00 | 150.00 | 375.00 | 1,400 | |
| 1873 ....... (600) | 293,600 | 55.00 | 80.00 | 120.00 | 175.00 | 475.00 | 650.00 |
| 1873CC ............. | 2,300 | 400.00 | 600.00 | 900.00 | 1,600 | 6,500 | |

## TRADE DOLLARS 1873-1885

This coin was issued for circulation in the Orient to compete with dollar-size coins of other countries. It weighed 420 grains compared to 412½ grains, the weight of the regular silver dollar.

**VG-8 VERY GOOD**—*About half of mottoes IN GOD WE TRUST and E PLURIBUS UNUM will show. Rim on both sides well defined.*

**F-12 FINE**—*Mottoes and LIBERTY readable but worn.*

**EF-40 EXTREMELY FINE**—*Mottoes and LIBERTY are sharp. Only slight wear on rims.*

**MS-60 UNCIRCULATED**—*No trace of wear. Light blemishes.*

1875S
S over CC

# TRADE DOLLARS 1873 - 1885

| | Quan. Minted | VG-8 | F-12 | EF-40 | MS-60 | Proof-63 |
|---|---|---|---|---|---|---|
| 1873 (865) | 397,500 | $30.00 | $40.00 | $80.00 | $400.00 | $1,000 |
| 1873CC | 124,500 | 35.00 | 45.00 | 85.00 | 600.00 | |
| 1873S | 703,000 | 30.00 | 40.00 | 80.00 | 400.00 | |
| 1874 (700) | 987,800 | 30.00 | 40.00 | 80.00 | 335.00 | 1,000 |
| 1874CC | 1,373,200 | 35.00 | 45.00 | 85.00 | 500.00 | |
| 1874S | 2,549,000 | 30.00 | 40.00 | 80.00 | 335.00 | |
| 1875 (700) | 218,900 | 40.00 | 60.00 | 125.00 | 600.00 | 1,000 |
| 1875CC | 1,573,700 | 35.00 | 45.00 | 85.00 | 425.00 | |
| 1875S | 4,487,000 | 30.00 | 40.00 | 80.00 | 335.00 | |
| 1875S, S over CC | | 40.00 | 70.00 | 150.00 | 700.00 | |
| 1876 (1,150) | 456,150 | 30.00 | 40.00 | 80.00 | 335.00 | 1,000 |
| 1876CC | 509,000 | 35.00 | 45.00 | 85.00 | 425.00 | |
| 1876S | 5,227,000 | 30.00 | 40.00 | 80.00 | 335.00 | |
| 1877 (510) | 3,039,710 | 30.00 | 40.00 | 80.00 | 335.00 | 1,000 |
| 1877CC | 534,000 | 35.00 | 50.00 | 100.00 | 600.00 | |
| 1877S | 9,519,000 | 30.00 | 40.00 | 80.00 | 335.00 | |
| 1878 (900) | 900 | | | | 1,200 | |
| 1878CC | 97,000 | 65.00 | 100.00 | 275.00 | 1,500 | |
| 1878S | 4,162,000 | 30.00 | 40.00 | 80.00 | 335.00 | |
| 1879 (1,541) | 1,541 | | | | 1,000 | |
| 1880 (1,987) | 1,987 | | | | 1,000 | |
| 1881 (960) | 960 | | | | 1,000 | |
| 1882 (1,097) | 1,097 | | | | 1,000 | |
| 1883 (979) | 979 | | | | 1,000 | |

## LIBERTY HEAD OR MORGAN TYPE 1878-1921

George T. Morgan, formerly a pupil of Wyon in the Royal Mint in London, designed the new dollar. His initial M is found at the truncation of the neck, at the last tress. It also appears on the reverse on the left-hand loop of the ribbon.

Sharply struck "proof-like" coins have a highly reflective surface and usually command substantial premiums.

**VF-20 VERY FINE**—*Two-thirds of hairlines from top of forehead to ear must show. Ear well defined. Feathers on eagle's breast worn.*

**EF-40 EXTREMELY FINE**—*All hairlines strong and ear bold. Eagle's feathers all plain but slight wear on breast and wing tips.*

**AU-50 ABOUT UNCIRCULATED**—*Slight trace of wear. Most of mint luster is present although marred by bag marks.*

**MS-60 UNCIRCULATED**—*No trace of wear. Has full mint luster, but may be noticeably marred by scuff marks or bag abrasions.*

**MS-63 SELECT UNCIRCULATED**—*No trace of wear, full mint luster, few noticeable surface marks.*

*Most uncirculated silver dollars have scratches or nicks because of handling of mint bags. Choice sharply struck coins with full brilliance and without blemishes are worth more than listed values.*

8 Tail Feathers, 1878 Philadelphia Only

# SILVER DOLLARS

Mint mark location on the reverse below wreath

| | *Quan. Minted* | *VF-20* | *EF-40* | *AU-50* | *MS-60* | *MS-63* |
|---|---|---|---|---|---|---|
| 1878, 8 tail feathers. (500) | 750,000 | *$9.00* | *$11.00* | $15.00 | $30.00 | $45.00 |
| 1878, 7 tail feathers. (500) | 9,759,550 | *7.00* | *7.50* | *8.00* | 20.00 | 25.00 |
| 1878, 7 over 8 feathers.. | | 10.00 | 12.00 | 16.00 | 35.00 | 45.00 |
| 1878CC | 2,212,000 | 12.00 | 14.00 | 30.00 | 45.00 | 60.00 |
| 1878S | 9,774,000 | *7.00* | *7.50* | *8.00* | 15.00 | 20.00 |
| 1879 (1,100) | 14,807,100 | *7.00* | *7.50* | *8.00* | 15.00 | 22.00 |
| 1879CC | 756,000 | 40.00 | 125.00 | 225.00 | 400.00 | 600.00 |
| 1879O | 2,887,000 | *7.00* | *7.50* | *8.00* | 25.00 | 50.00 |
| 1879S | 9,110,000 | *7.00* | *7.50* | *8.00* | 15.00 | 20.00 |
| 1880, 8 over 7 | 12,601,355 | 20.00 | 30.00 | 40.00 | — | — |
| 1880 (1,355) | | *7.00* | *7.50* | *8.00* | 15.00 | 20.00 |
| 1880CC | 591,000 | 35.00 | 50.00 | 75.00 | 105.00 | 130.00 |
| 1880O | 5,305,000 | *7.00* | *7.50* | *8.00* | 35.00 | 55.00 |
| 1880S | 8,900,000 | *7.00* | *7.50* | *8.00* | 14.00 | 18.00 |
| 1881 (975) | 9,163,975 | *7.00* | *7.50* | *8.00* | 17.00 | 22.00 |
| 1881CC | 296,000 | 45.00 | 60.00 | 65.00 | 85.00 | 100.00 |
| 1881O | 5,708,000 | *7.00* | *7.50* | *8.00* | 17.00 | 20.00 |
| 1881S | 12,760,000 | *7.00* | *7.50* | *8.00* | 14.00 | 18.00 |
| 1882 (1,100) | 11,101,100 | *7.00* | *7.50* | *8.00* | 16.00 | 18.00 |
| 1882CC | 1,133,000 | 20.00 | 23.00 | 27.00 | 32.00 | 38.00 |
| 1882O | 6,090,000 | *7.00* | *7.50* | *8.00* | 16.00 | 18.00 |
| 1882S | 9,250,000 | *7.00* | *7.50* | *8.00* | 15.00 | 20.00 |
| 1883 (1,039) | 12,291,039 | *7.00* | *7.50* | *8.00* | 16.00 | 18.00 |
| 1883CC | 1,204,000 | 20.00 | 23.00 | 27.00 | 32.00 | 38.00 |
| 1883O | 8,725,000 | *7.00* | *7.50* | *8.00* | 12.00 | 14.00 |
| 1883S | 6,250,000 | 12.00 | 12.00 | 70.00 | 200.00 | 350.00 |
| 1884 (875) | 14,070,875 | *7.00* | *7.50* | *8.00* | 20.00 | 30.00 |
| 1884CC | 1,136,000 | 20.00 | 23.00 | 27.00 | 32.00 | 38.00 |
| 1884O | 9,730,000 | *7.00* | *7.50* | *8.00* | 12.00 | 14.00 |
| 1884S | 3,200,000 | 10.00 | 15.00 | 125.00 | 400.00 | 1,000 |
| 1885 (930) | 17,787,767 | *7.00* | *7.50* | *8.00* | 12.00 | 14.00 |
| 1885CC | 228,000 | 75.00 | 80.00 | 85.00 | 90.00 | 100.00 |
| 1885O | 9,185,000 | *7.00* | *7.50* | *8.00* | 12.00 | 14.00 |
| 1885S | 1,497,000 | *7.00* | *7.50* | 25.00 | 65.00 | 85.00 |
| 1886 (886) | 19,963,886 | *7.00* | *7.50* | *8.00* | 12.00 | 14.00 |
| 1886O | 10,710,000 | *7.00* | *7.50* | 20.00 | 160.00 | 240.00 |
| 1886S | 750,000 | 15.00 | 20.00 | 24.00 | 60.00 | 85.00 |
| 1887 (710) | 20,290,710 | *7.00* | *7.50* | *8.00* | 12.00 | 14.00 |
| 1887O | 11,550,000 | *7.00* | *7.50* | *8.00* | 18.00 | 30.00 |
| 1887S | 1,771,000 | *7.00* | *7.50* | *8.00* | 40.00 | 55.00 |
| 1888 (832) | 19,183,333 | *7.00* | *7.50* | *8.00* | 15.00 | 18.00 |
| 1888O | 12,150,000 | *7.00* | *7.50* | *8.00* | 16.00 | 19.00 |
| 1888S | 657,000 | 15.00 | 22.00 | 30.00 | 65.00 | 85.00 |
| 1889 (811) | 21,726,811 | *7.00* | *7.50* | *8.00* | 15.00 | 18.00 |
| 1889CC | 350,000 | 175.00 | 400.00 | 900.00 | 2,000 | 3,000 |
| 1889O | 11,875,000 | *7.00* | *7.50* | *8.00* | 30.00 | 80.00 |
| 1889S | 700,000 | 12.00 | 15.00 | 20.00 | 30.00 | 60.00 |
| 1890 (590) | 16,802,590 | *7.00* | *7.50* | *8.00* | 15.00 | 19.00 |
| 1890CC | 2,309,041 | 18.00 | 22.00 | 38.00 | 85.00 | 125.00 |
| 1890O | 10,701,000 | *7.00* | *7.50* | *8.00* | 22.00 | 40.00 |

Proof Morgan Dollars where indicated in mintage record (quantity shown in parenthesis) are valued approximately as follows:
Proof-60 $250.00 Proof-63 $600.00 Proof-65 $1,600

*Italic prices indicate unsettled values due to fluctuating bullion market. See Bullion Chart.*

# SILVER DOLLARS

| | Quan. Minted | VF-20 | EF-40 | AU-50 | MS-60 | MS-63 |
|---|---|---|---|---|---|---|
| 1890S | 8,230,373 | *$7.00* | *$7.50* | *$8.00* | $20.00 | $30.00 |
| 1891 (650) | 8,694,206 | *7.00* | *7.50* | 12.00 | 35.00 | 75.00 |
| 1891CC | 1,618,000 | 20.00 | 25.00 | 30.00 | 60.00 | 95.00 |
| 1891O | 7,954,529 | *7.00* | *7.50* | 15.00 | 40.00 | 75.00 |
| 1891S | 5,296,000 | *7.00* | *7.50* | 11.00 | 22.00 | 35.00 |
| 1892 (1,245) | 1,037,245 | 10.00 | 12.00 | 18.00 | 75.00 | 150.00 |
| 1892CC | 1,352,000 | 30.00 | 45.00 | 110.00 | 125.00 | 175.00 |
| 1892O | 2,744,000 | 10.00 | 12.00 | 15.00 | 75.00 | 120.00 |
| 1892S | 1,200,000 | 20.00 | 70.00 | 350.00 | 2,000 | 3,500 |
| 1893 (792) | 389,792 | 35.00 | 60.00 | 80.00 | 200.00 | 300.00 |
| 1893CC | 677,000 | 100.00 | 250.00 | 300.00 | 400.00 | 600.00 |
| 1893O | 300,000 | 60.00 | 120.00 | 160.00 | 500.00 | 850.00 |
| 1893S | 100,000 | 1,200 | 2,000 | 5,000 | 8,000 | 12,000 |
| 1894 (972) | 110,972 | 200.00 | 300.00 | 400.00 | 500.00 | 750.00 |
| 1894O | 1,723,000 | 10.00 | 12.00 | 30.00 | 250.00 | 400.00 |
| 1894S | 1,260,000 | 25.00 | 40.00 | 75.00 | 200.00 | 350.00 |
| 1895 (880) | 12,880 | | | | 4,000 | 7,000 |
| 1895O | 450,000 | 80.00 | 150.00 | 350.00 | 1,000 | 2,700 |
| 1895S | 400,000 | 90.00 | 250.00 | 400.00 | 600.00 | 775.00 |
| 1896 (762) | 9,976,762 | *7.00* | *7.50* | *8.00* | 16.00 | 20.00 |
| 1896O | 4,900,000 | *7.00* | *7.50* | 30.00 | 300.00 | 550.00 |
| 1896S | 5,000,000 | 20.00 | 25.00 | 85.00 | 200.00 | 350.00 |
| 1897 (731) | 2,822,731 | *7.00* | *7.50* | *8.00* | 16.00 | 22.00 |
| 1897O | 4,004,000 | *7.00* | *7.50* | 15.00 | 200.00 | 400.00 |
| 1897S | 5,825,000 | *7.00* | *7.50* | 10.00 | 20.00 | 35.00 |
| 1898 (735) | 5,884,735 | *7.00* | *7.50* | *8.00* | 16.00 | 20.00 |
| 1898O | 4,440,000 | *7.00* | *7.50* | *8.00* | 14.00 | 18.00 |
| 1898S | 4,102,000 | *7.00* | *7.50* | 20.00 | 75.00 | 110.00 |
| 1899 (846) | 330,846 | 20.00 | 35.00 | 40.00 | 50.00 | 70.00 |
| 1899O | 12,290,000 | *7.00* | *7.50* | *8.00* | 14.00 | 18.00 |
| 1899S | 2,562,000 | *7.00* | *7.50* | 10.00 | 75.00 | 110.00 |
| 1900 (912) | 8,830,912 | *7.00* | *7.50* | *8.00* | 14.00 | 18.00 |
| 1900O | 12,590,000 | *7.00* | *7.50* | *8.00* | 14.00 | 18.00 |
| 1900S | 3,540,000 | *7.00* | *7.50* | 10.00 | 65.00 | 95.00 |
| 1901 (813) | 6,962,813 | 18.00 | 30.00 | 90.00 | 350.00 | 800.00 |
| 1901O | 13,320,000 | *7.00* | *7.50* | *8.00* | 14.00 | 18.00 |
| 1901S | 2,284,000 | 10.00 | 14.00 | 30.00 | 165.00 | 225.00 |
| 1902 (777) | 7,994,777 | *7.00* | *7.50* | 14.00 | 28.00 | 45.00 |
| 1902O | 8,636,000 | *7.00* | *7.50* | *8.00* | 12.00 | 14.00 |
| 1902S | 1,530,000 | 30.00 | 45.00 | 70.00 | 125.00 | 200.00 |
| 1903 (755) | 4,652,755 | *7.00* | *7.50* | 14.00 | 30.00 | 40.00 |
| 1903O | 4,450,000 | 80.00 | 130.00 | 90.00 | 100.00 | 125.00 |
| 1903S | 1,241,000 | 20.00 | 90.00 | 300.00 | 850.00 | 1,200 |
| 1904 (650) | 2,788,650 | *7.00* | *7.50* | 20.00 | 50.00 | 85.00 |
| 1904O | 3,720,000 | *7.00* | *7.50* | *8.00* | 12.00 | 14.00 |
| 1904S | 2,304,000 | 25.00 | 60.00 | 220.00 | 400.00 | 800.00 |
| 1921 | 44,690,000 | *7.00* | *7.50* | *8.00* | 10.00 | 12.00 |
| 1921D | 20,345,000 | *7.00* | *7.50* | *8.00* | 12.00 | 14.00 |
| 1921S | 21,695,000 | *7.00* | *7.50* | *8.00* | 14.00 | 19.00 |

**Proof Morgan Dollars where indicated in mintage record (quantity shown in parenthesis) are valued approximately as follows:**

**Proof-60 $250.00 Proof-63 $600.00 Proof-65 $1,600**

*Italic prices indicate unsettled values due to fluctuating bullion market. See Bullion Chart.*

# SILVER DOLLARS

## PEACE TYPE 1921-1935

Anthony De Francisci, a medalist, designed this dollar. His monogram is located in the field of the coin under the neck of Liberty.

**VF-20 VERY FINE**—*Hair over eye well worn. Some strands over ear well defined. Some eagle feathers on top and outside edge of right wing will show.*

**EF-40 EXTREMELY FINE**—*Hairlines over brow and ear are strong though slightly worn. Outside wing feathers at right and those at top are visible but faint.*

**AU-50 ABOUT UNCIRCULATED**—*Slight trace of wear. Most of mint luster is present although marred by bag marks.*

**MS-60 UNCIRCULATED**—*No trace of wear. Has full mint luster but may be noticeably marred by stains, skuff marks or bag abrasions.*

**MS-63 SELECT UNCIRCULATED**—*No trace of wear, full mint luster, few noticeable surface marks.*

*Most uncirculated silver dollars have scratches or nicks because of handling of mint bags. Choice sharply struck coins with full brilliance and without blemishes are worth more than listed values.*

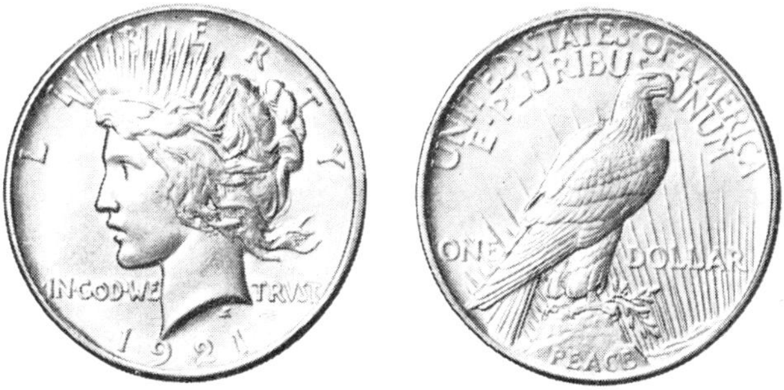


| | *Quan. Minted* | *VF-20* | *EF-40* | *AU-50* | *MS-60* | *MS-63* |
|---|---|---|---|---|---|---|
| 1921 | 1,006,473 | $18.00 | $20.00 | $30.00 | $75.00 | $150.00 |
| 1922 | 51,737,000 | *7.00* | *7.50* | *8.00* | 10.00 | 12.00 |
| 1922D | 15,063,000 | *7.00* | *7.50* | *8.00* | 12.00 | 20.00 |
| 1922S | 17,475,000 | *7.00* | *7.50* | *8.00* | 14.00 | 30.00 |
| 1923 | 30,800,000 | *7.00* | *7.50* | *8.00* | 10.00 | 12.00 |
| 1923D | 6,811,000 | *7.00* | *7.50* | *8.00* | 14.00 | 22.00 |
| 1923S | 19,020,000 | *7.00* | *7.50* | *8.00* | 14.00 | 30.00 |
| 1924 | 11,811,000 | *7.00* | *7.50* | *8.00* | 12.00 | 18.00 |
| 1924S | 1,728,000 | *7.00* | *8.00* | 10.00 | 60.00 | 120.00 |
| 1925 | 10,198,000 | *7.00* | *7.50* | *8.00* | 11.00 | 15.00 |
| 1925S | 1,610,000 | *7.50* | *8.00* | 9.00 | 40.00 | 85.00 |
| 1926 | 1,939,000 | *7.00* | *8.00* | 9.00 | 20.00 | 30.00 |
| 1926D | 2,348,700 | *7.00* | *8.00* | 10.00 | 30.00 | 50.00 |
| 1926S | 6,980,000 | *7.00* | *8.00* | 9.00 | 20.00 | 30.00 |
| 1927 | 848,000 | *8.00* | 9.00 | 12.00 | 60.00 | 85.00 |
| 1927D | 1,268,900 | *7.50* | 9.00 | 20.00 | 110.00 | 200.00 |
| 1927S | 866,000 | *7.50* | 9.00 | 12.00 | 85.00 | 125.00 |
| 1928 | 360,649 | 50.00 | 60.00 | 75.00 | 100.00 | 200.00 |
| 1928S | 1,632,000 | *8.00* | 9.00 | 12.00 | 65.00 | 120.00 |
| 1934 | 954,057 | 9.00 | 11.00 | 20.00 | 45.00 | 75.00 |
| 1934D | 1,569,500 | *7.50* | 9.00 | 12.00 | 50.00 | 100.00 |
| 1934S | 1,011,000 | 12.00 | 50.00 | 175.00 | 650.00 | 850.00 |
| 1935 | 1,576,000 | *7.00* | *8.00* | 10.00 | 25.00 | 50.00 |
| 1935S | 1,964,000 | *7.50* | *8.00* | 16.00 | 75.00 | 125.00 |

*Italic prices indicate unsettled values due to fluctuating bullion market. See Bullion Chart.*

# EISENHOWER DOLLARS 1971-1978

Honoring both President Dwight D. Eisenhower and the first landing of man on the moon, this design is the work of Chief Engraver Frank Gasparro, whose initials are on the truncation and below the eagle. The reverse is an adaptation of the official Apollo 11 insignia.

Mint mark location is above the date.

| | Quan. Minted Proof | Regular | MS-65 | Proof-65 |
|---|---|---|---|---|
| 1971 Copper-nickel clad | | 47,799,000 | $1.00 | |
| 1971D Copper-nickel clad | | 68,587,424 | 1.00 | |
| 1971S Silver clad | (4,265,234) | 6,868,530 | 2.00 | $4.00 |
| 1972 Copper-nickel clad | | 75,890,000 | 1.00 | |
| 1972D Copper-nickel clad | | 92,548,511 | 1.00 | |
| 1972S Silver clad | (1,811,631) | 2,193,056 | 5.00 | 8.00 |
| 1973 Copper-nickel clad | | *2,000,056 | 5.00 | |
| 1973D Copper-nickel clad | | *2,000,000 | 5.00 | |
| 1973S Copper-nickel clad | (2,760,339) | | | 3.00 |
| 1973S Silver clad | (1,013,646) | 1,883,140 | 7.00 | 40.00 |
| 1974 Copper-nickel clad | | 27,366,000 | 1.00 | |
| 1974D Copper-nickel clad | | 45,517,000 | 1.00 | |
| 1974S Copper-nickel clad | (2,612,568) | | | 2.50 |
| 1974S Silver clad | (1,306,579) | 1,900,000 | 4.00 | 8.00 |

*1,769,258 of each sold only in sets and not released for circulation. Unissued coins destroyed at mint.

## BICENTENNIAL COINAGE DATED 1776-1976

Obverse and Reverse Variety II Reverse Var. I

Variety I: Design in low relief, bold lettering on reverse. Variety II: Sharp design, delicate lettering on reverse.

# BICENTENNIAL DOLLARS

| | Quan. Minted | MS-65 | Proof-65 |
|---|---|---|---|
| 1976 Copper-nickel clad, variety I | 4,019,000 | $1.00 | |
| 1976 Copper-nickel clad, variety II | 113,318,000 | 1.00 | |
| 1976D Copper-nickel clad, variety I | 21,048,710 | 1.00 | |
| 1976D Copper-nickel clad, variety II | 82,179,564 | 1.00 | |
| 1976S Copper-nickel clad, variety I | (2,845,450) | | $2.25 |
| 1976S Copper-nickel clad, variety II | (4,149,730) | | 1.95 |
| 1976S Silver clad, variety I | * 11,000,000 | 5.00 | |
| 1976S Silver clad, variety I | *(4,000,000) | | 6.00 |

*Approximate mintage. Not all released.

## EAGLE REVERSE RESUMED

| | Quan. Minted | MS-65 | Proof-65 |
|---|---|---|---|
| 1977 Copper-nickel clad | 12,596,000 | 1.00 | |
| 1977D Copper-nickel clad | 32,983,006 | 1.00 | |
| 1977S Copper-nickel clad | (3,251,152) | | 1.95 |
| 1978 Copper-nickel clad | 25,702,000 | 1.00 | |
| 1978D Copper-nickel clad | 23,012,890 | 1.00 | |
| 1978S Copper-nickel clad | (3,127,781) | | 3.50 |

# SUSAN B. ANTHONY DOLLARS 1979-1981

Clear S

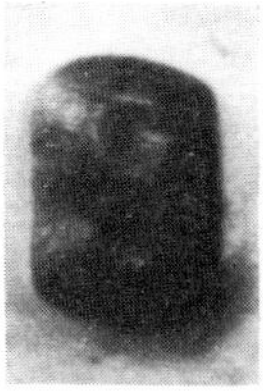
Filled S

| | Quan. minted | MS-65 | Proof-65 |
|---|---|---|---|
| 1979P | 360,222,000 | $1.00 | |
| 1979D | 288,015,744 | 1.00 | |
| 1979S | 109,576,000 | 1.00 | |
| 1979S Proof | (3,677,175) | | |
| Filled S | | | $5.00 |
| Clear S | | | 40.00 |
| 1980P | 27,610,000 | 1.00 | |

| | Quan. minted | MS-65 | Proof-65 |
|---|---|---|---|
| 1980D | 41,628,708 | $1.00 | |
| 1980S | 20,422,000 | 1.00 | |
| 1980S Proof | (3,554,806) | | $3.00 |
| 1981P | 3,000,000 | 2.25 | |
| 1981D | 3,250,000 | 2.25 | |
| 1981S | 3,492,000 | 2.25 | |
| 1981S Proof | (4,063,083) | | 3.00 |

# GOLD

## GOLD DOLLARS 1849-1889

Coinage of the gold dollar was authorized by the Act of March 3, 1849. The weight was 25.8 grains, fineness .900. The first type, struck until 1854, is known as the Liberty Head or small-sized type.

In 1854 the piece was made larger in diameter and thinner. The design was changed to a feather headdress on a female, generally referred to as the Indian Head or large-sized type. In 1856 the type was changed slightly by enlarging the size of the head.

### LIBERTY HEAD TYPE 1849-1854

**VF-20 VERY FINE**—*LIBERTY on headband complete and readable. Knobs on coronet are defined.*

**EF-40 EXTREMELY FINE**—*Slight wear on Liberty's hair. Knobs on coronet sharp.*

**AU-50 ABOUT UNCIRCULATED**—*Trace of wear over eye and on coronet.*

**MS-60 UNCIRCULATED**—*No trace of wear. Light marks and blemishes.*

Mint mark is below wreath.

| | *Quan. Minted* | *VF-20* | *EF-40* | *AU-50* | *MS-60* |
|---|---|---|---|---|---|
| 1849 | 688,567 | $75.00 | $85.00 | $100.00 | $325.00 |
| 1849C | 11,634 | 125.00 | 225.00 | 325.00 | 1,000 |
| 1849D | 21,588 | 125.00 | 225.00 | 325.00 | 1,000 |
| 1849O | 215,000 | 75.00 | 85.00 | 100.00 | 350.00 |
| 1850 | 481,953 | 75.00 | 85.00 | 100.00 | 325.00 |
| 1850C | 6,966 | 125.00 | 225.00 | 325.00 | 1,000 |
| 1850D | 8,382 | 125.00 | 225.00 | 325.00 | 800.00 |
| 1850O | 14,000 | 110.00 | 140.00 | 185.00 | 700.00 |
| 1851 | 3,317,671 | 75.00 | 85.00 | 100.00 | 325.00 |
| 1851C | 41,267 | 125.00 | 225.00 | 325.00 | 800.00 |
| 1851D | 9,882 | 125.00 | 225.00 | 325.00 | 800.00 |
| 1851O | 290,000 | 75.00 | 85.00 | 100.00 | 350.00 |
| 1852 | 2,045,351 | 75.00 | 85.00 | 100.00 | 325.00 |
| 1852C | 9,434 | 125.00 | 225.00 | 325.00 | 850.00 |
| 1852D | 6,360 | 125.00 | 225.00 | 325.00 | 850.00 |
| 1852O | 140,000 | 75.00 | 85.00 | 100.00 | 350.00 |
| 1853 | 4,076,051 | 75.00 | 85.00 | 100.00 | 325.00 |
| 1853C | 11,515 | 125.00 | 225.00 | 325.00 | 1,000 |
| 1853D | 6,583 | 125.00 | 225.00 | 325.00 | 1,000 |
| 1853O | 290,000 | 75.00 | 85.00 | 100.00 | 350.00 |
| 1854 | 855,502 | 75.00 | 85.00 | 100.00 | 325.00 |
| 1854D | 2,935 | 200.00 | 275.00 | 600.00 | 1,500 |
| 1854S | 14,632 | 125.00 | 225.00 | 325.00 | 850.00 |

### INDIAN HEAD TYPE, Small Head 1854-1856

**VF-20 VERY FINE**—*Feather curl tips outlined but details worn.*

**EF-40 EXTREMELY FINE**—*Slight wear on tips of feather curls on headdress.*

**AU-50 ABOUT UNCIRCULATED**—*Trace of wear on headdress.*

**MS-60 UNCIRCULATED**—*No trace of wear. Light marks and blemishes.*

| | *Quan. Minted* | *VF-20* | *EF-40* | *AU-50* | *MS-60* | *Proof-63* |
|---|---|---|---|---|---|---|
| 1854 | 783,943 | $160.00 | $225.00 | $450.00 | $1,000 | —— |
| 1855 | 758,269 | 160.00 | 225.00 | 450.00 | 1,000 | —— |
| 1855C | 9,803 | 275.00 | 400.00 | 800.00 | 3,000 | |
| 1855D | 1,811 | 1,400 | 1,900 | 2,750 | 7,500 | |
| 1855O | 55,000 | 175.00 | 250.00 | 600.00 | 2,000 | |
| 1856S | 24,600 | 175.00 | 250.00 | 600.00 | 1,800 | |

# GOLD DOLLARS

## INDIAN HEAD TYPE, Large Head 1856-1889

**VF-20 VERY FINE**—*Curled feathers have slight detail. Details worn smooth at eyebrow, hair below headdress and behind ear and bottom curl.*

**EF-40 EXTREMELY FINE**—*Slight wear above and to right of eye and on top of curled feathers.*

**AU-50 ABOUT UNCIRCULATED**—*Trace of wear on headdress.*

**MS-60 UNCIRCULATED**—*No trace of wear. Light marks and blemishes.*

| | | *Quan. Minted* | *VF-20* | *EF-40* | *AU-50* | *MS-60* | *Proof-63* |
|---|---|---|---|---|---|---|---|
| 1856 | | 1,762,936 | $75.00 | $85.00 | $100.00 | $300.00 | $3,000 |
| 1856D | | 1,460 | 1,200 | 2,200 | 3,000 | 7,500 | |
| 1857 | | 774,789 | 75.00 | 85.00 | 100.00 | 300.00 | 3,000 |
| 1857C | | 13,280 | 170.00 | 230.00 | 350.00 | 800.00 | |
| 1857D | | 3,533 | 250.00 | 350.00 | 600.00 | 2,000 | |
| 1857S | | 10,000 | 100.00 | 150.00 | 225.00 | 700.00 | |
| 1858 | | 117,995 | 75.00 | 85.00 | 100.00 | 300.00 | 3,000 |
| 1858D | | 3,477 | 300.00 | 400.00 | 650.00 | 1,800 | |
| 1858S | | 10,000 | 100.00 | 150.00 | 225.00 | 700.00 | |
| 1859 | (80) | 168,244 | 75.00 | 85.00 | 100.00 | 300.00 | 2,900 |
| 1859C | | 5,235 | 160.00 | 250.00 | 350.00 | 1,300 | |
| 1859D | | 4,952 | 200.00 | 300.00 | 450.00 | 1,500 | |
| 1859S | | 15,000 | 100.00 | 150.00 | 225.00 | 700.00 | |
| 1860 | (154) | 36,668 | 75.00 | 85.00 | 100.00 | 300.00 | 2,500 |
| 1860D | | 1,566 | 1,000 | 2,200 | 4,000 | 6,500 | |
| 1860S | | 13,000 | 100.00 | 150.00 | 225.00 | 700.00 | |
| 1861 | (349) | 527,499 | 75.00 | 85.00 | 100.00 | 300.00 | 2,500 |
| 1861D | | | 3,000 | 5,000 | 7,000 | 14,000 | |
| 1862 | (35) | 1,361,390 | 75.00 | 85.00 | 100.00 | 300.00 | 2,500 |
| 1863 | (50) | 6,250 | 150.00 | 200.00 | 375.00 | 1,600 | 4,000 |
| 1864 | (50) | 5,950 | 140.00 | 175.00 | 350.00 | 1,500 | 4,000 |
| 1865 | (25) | 3,725 | 140.00 | 175.00 | 350.00 | 1,500 | 4,000 |
| 1866 | (30) | 7,130 | 100.00 | 175.00 | 325.00 | 700.00 | 3,000 |
| 1867 | (50) | 5,250 | 130.00 | 180.00 | 300.00 | 850.00 | 3,000 |
| 1868 | (25) | 10,525 | 90.00 | 170.00 | 250.00 | 600.00 | 3,000 |
| 1869 | (25) | 5,925 | 100.00 | 175.00 | 325.00 | 700.00 | 3,000 |
| 1870 | (35) | 6,335 | 100.00 | 175.00 | 325.00 | 700.00 | 3,000 |
| 1870S | | 3,000 | 250.00 | 375.00 | 600.00 | 1,800 | |
| 1871 | (30) | 3,930 | 100.00 | 170.00 | 250.00 | 700.00 | 3,000 |
| 1872 | (30) | 3,530 | 100.00 | 170.00 | 250.00 | 700.00 | 3,000 |
| 1873 Closed 3 | (25) | 1,825 | 120.00 | 180.00 | 300.00 | 800.00 | 4,000 |
| 1873 Open 3 | | 123,300 | 75.00 | 85.00 | 100.00 | 300.00 | |
| 1874 | (20) | 198,820 | 75.00 | 85.00 | 100.00 | 300.00 | 3,000 |
| 1875 | (20) | 420 | 1,000 | 1,500 | 2,500 | 5,000 | 12,000 |
| 1876 | (45) | 3,245 | 100.00 | 150.00 | 200.00 | 750.00 | 2,500 |
| 1877 | (20) | 3,920 | 100.00 | 150.00 | 200.00 | 750.00 | 2,500 |
| 1878 | (20) | 3,020 | 100.00 | 150.00 | 200.00 | 750.00 | 2,500 |
| 1879 | (30) | 3,030 | 100.00 | 150.00 | 200.00 | 750.00 | 2,500 |
| 1880 | (36) | 1,636 | 100.00 | 150.00 | 200.00 | 750.00 | 2,500 |
| 1881 | (87) | 7,707 | 75.00 | 85.00 | 100.00 | 300.00 | 2,400 |
| 1882 | (125) | 5,125 | 75.00 | 85.00 | 100.00 | 300.00 | 2,400 |
| 1883 | (207) | 11,007 | 75.00 | 85.00 | 100.00 | 300.00 | 2,400 |
| 1884 | (1,006) | 6,236 | 75.00 | 85.00 | 100.00 | 300.00 | 1,800 |
| 1885 | (1,105) | 12,261 | 75.00 | 85.00 | 100.00 | 300.00 | 1,800 |
| 1886 | (1,016) | 6,016 | 75.00 | 85.00 | 100.00 | 300.00 | 1,800 |
| 1887 | (1,043) | 8,543 | 75.00 | 85.00 | 100.00 | 300.00 | 1,800 |
| 1888 | (1,079) | 16,580 | 75.00 | 85.00 | 100.00 | 300.00 | 1,800 |
| 1889 | (1,779) | 30,729 | 75.00 | 85.00 | 100.00 | 300.00 | 1,800 |

# QUARTER EAGLES—1796-1929
## ($2.50 GOLD PIECES)

Although authorized by the Act of April 2, 1792, coinage of quarter eagles was not begun until 1796.

### CAPPED BUST TO RIGHT 1796-1807

#### No Stars on Obverse 1796 Only

**F-12 FINE**—*Hair worn smooth on high spots. E PLURIBUS UNUM weak but readable.*

**VF-20 VERY FINE**—*Some wear on high spots.*

**EF-40 EXTREMELY FINE**—*Only slight wear on hair and cheek.*

**MS-60 UNCIRCULATED**—*No trace of wear. Light blemishes.*

#### Stars on Obverse 1796-1807

| | *Quan. Minted* | *F-12* | *VF-20* | *EF-40* | *MS-60* |
|---|---|---|---|---|---|
| 1796 No stars on obverse | 963 | $5,000 | $7,000 | $12,000 | $22,000 |
| 1796 Stars on obverse | 432 | 3,500 | 6,000 | 8,000 | 17,500 |
| 1797 | 427 | 2,500 | 4,000 | 7,000 | 12,000 |
| 1798 | 1,094 | 1,800 | 2,600 | 3,600 | 8,000 |
| 1802, 2 over 1 | 3,035 | 1,000 | 1,600 | 2,750 | 7,500 |
| 1804, 13-Star reverse | 3,327 | 2,000 | 4,000 | 6,000 | 10,000 |
| 1804, 14-Star reverse | | 1,000 | 1,600 | 2,750 | 7,500 |
| 1805 | 1,781 | 1,000 | 1,600 | 2,750 | 7,500 |
| 1806, 6 over 4, stars 8+5 | 1,136 | 1,000 | 1,600 | 2,750 | 7,500 |
| 1806, 6 over 5, stars 7+6 | 480 | 1,500 | 3,000 | 4,500 | 10,000 |
| 1807 | 6,812 | 1,000 | 1,600 | 2,750 | 7,500 |

### CAPPED BUST TO LEFT, Large Size 1808

**F-12 FINE**—*E PLURIBUS UNUM and LIBERTY on headband readable but weak.*

**VF-20 VERY FINE**—*Motto and LIBERTY clear.*

**EF-40 EXTREMELY FINE**—*All details of hair are plain.*

**MS-60 UNCIRCULATED**—*No trace of wear. Light blemishes.*

| | | | | | |
|---|---|---|---|---|---|
| 1808 | 2,710 | 4,500 | 7,000 | 10,000 | 27,500 |

### CAPPED HEAD TO LEFT 1821-1834

Those dated 1829 - 1834 are smaller in diameter than the 1821-1827 pieces.

| | | | | | |
|---|---|---|---|---|---|
| 1821 | 6,448 | 1,200 | 2,000 | 3,000 | 8,500 |
| 1824, 4 over 1 | 2,600 | 1,200 | 2,000 | 3,000 | 8,500 |
| 1825 | 4,434 | 1,200 | 2,000 | 3,000 | 8,500 |
| 1826, 6 over 5 | 760 | 2,200 | 3,300 | 5,000 | 16,000 |

# QUARTER EAGLES

| | Quan. Minted | F-12 | VF-20 | EF-40 | MS-60 |
|---|---|---|---|---|---|
| 1827 | 2,800 | $1,200 | $2,000 | $3,000 | $8,500 |
| 1829 | 3,403 | 1,200 | 2,000 | 3,000 | 7,500 |
| 1830 | 4,540 | 1,000 | 1,500 | 2,500 | 7,500 |
| 1831 | 4,520 | 1,000 | 1,500 | 2,500 | 7,500 |
| 1832 | 4,400 | 1,000 | 1,500 | 2,500 | 7,500 |
| 1833 | 4,160 | 1,000 | 1,500 | 2,500 | 7,500 |
| 1834 (Motto) | 4,000 | 2,600 | 4,300 | 6,750 | 14,000 |

## CLASSIC HEAD TYPE, No Motto on Reverse 1834-1839

In 1834 the quarter eagle was redesigned. A ribbon binding the hair, bearing the word LIBERTY, replaces the Liberty cap. The motto was omitted from the reverse.

**F-12 FINE**—*LIBERTY readable and complete. Curl under ear oulined but no detail.*

**VF-20 VERY FINE**—*LIBERTY plain. Hair curl has detail.*

**EF-40 EXTREMELY FINE**—*Small amount of wear on top of hair and below L in LIBERTY. Wear evident on wing.*

**AU-50 ABOUT UNCIRCULATED**—*Trace of wear on coronet and hair above ear.*

**MS-60 UNCIRCULATED**—*No trace of wear. Light blemishes.*

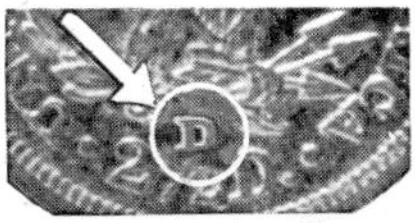

Mint mark location.

| | Quan. Minted | F-12 | VF-20 | EF-40 | AU-50 | MS-60 |
|---|---|---|---|---|---|---|
| 1834 No motto | 112,234 | $125.00 | $150.00 | $225.00 | $400.00 | $1,200 |
| 1835 | 131,402 | 125.00 | 150.00 | 225.00 | 400.00 | 1,200 |
| 1836 | 547,986 | 125.00 | 150.00 | 225.00 | 400.00 | 1,200 |
| 1837 | 45,080 | 125.00 | 160.00 | 250.00 | 450.00 | 1,750 |
| 1838 | 47,030 | 125.00 | 160.00 | 250.00 | 450.00 | 1,750 |
| 1838C | 7,880 | 175.00 | 250.00 | 500.00 | 600.00 | 2,500 |
| 1839 | 27,021 | 125.00 | 160.00 | 250.00 | 450.00 | 1,750 |
| 1839C | 18,140 | 175.00 | 250.00 | 500.00 | 600.00 | 2,400 |
| 1839D | 13,674 | 175.00 | 250.00 | 500.00 | 650.00 | 2,500 |
| 1839O | 17,781 | 150.00 | 200.00 | 300.00 | 500.00 | 2,300 |

## CORONET TYPE 1840-1907

Mint mark location.

**4** Plain 4

**4** Crosslet 4

| | Quan. Minted | VF-20 | EF-40 | AU-50 | MS-60 |
|---|---|---|---|---|---|
| 1840 | 18,859 | $100.00 | $125.00 | $140.00 | $350.00 |
| 1840C | 12,822 | 180.00 | 275.00 | 400.00 | 1,000 |
| 1840D | 3,532 | 250.00 | 425.00 | 600.00 | 1,500 |
| 1840O | 33,580 | 100.00 | 125.00 | 140.00 | 350.00 |
| 1841 Proof only | | 5,000 | 10,000 | 15,000 | 30,000 |
| 1841C | 10,281 | 200.00 | 300.00 | 400.00 | 750.00 |
| 1841D | 4,164 | 225.00 | 375.00 | 500.00 | 1,400 |
| 1842 | 2,823 | 200.00 | 300.00 | 400.00 | 1,000 |
| 1842C | 6,729 | 200.00 | 300.00 | 400.00 | 750.00 |
| 1842D | 4,643 | 225.00 | 375.00 | 500.00 | 1,100 |
| 1842O | 19,800 | 100.00 | 125.00 | 140.00 | 350.00 |
| 1843 | 100,546 | 100.00 | 125.00 | 140.00 | 300.00 |

| | Quan. Minted | VF-20 | EF-40 | AU-50 | MS-60 |
|---|---|---|---|---|---|
| 1843D | 36,209 | $200.00 | $300.00 | $400.00 | $700.00 |
| 1843O | 364,002 | 100.00 | 125.00 | 140.00 | 350.00 |
| 1844 | 6,784 | 130.00 | 170.00 | 300.00 | 650.00 |
| 1844C | 11,622 | 150.00 | 225.00 | 350.00 | 850.00 |
| 1844D | 17,332 | 150.00 | 225.00 | 400.00 | 1,000 |
| 1845 | 91,051 | 75.00 | 100.00 | 125.00 | 300.00 |
| 1845D | 19,460 | 150.00 | 225.00 | 375.00 | 900.00 |
| 1845O | 4,000 | 200.00 | 300.00 | 500.00 | —— |
| 1846 | 21,598 | 75.00 | 100.00 | 125.00 | 300.00 |
| 1846C | 4,808 | 200.00 | 350.00 | 475.00 | 1,000 |
| 1846D | 19,303 | 150.00 | 225.00 | 375.00 | 900.00 |
| 1846O | 62,000 | 75.00 | 100.00 | 125.00 | 300.00 |
| 1847 | 29,814 | 75.00 | 100.00 | 125.00 | 300.00 |
| 1847C | 23,226 | 150.00 | 200.00 | 325.00 | 700.00 |
| 1847D | 15,784 | 150.00 | 200.00 | 325.00 | 800.00 |
| 1847O | 124,000 | 75.00 | 100.00 | 125.00 | 300.00 |
| 1848 | 7,497 | 225.00 | 350.00 | 500.00 | 1,000 |

CAL. Above Eagle on Reverse

### California Gold Quarter Eagle

In 1848 about two hundred and thirty ounces of gold were sent to Secretary of War Marcy by Col. R. B. Mason, Military Governor of California. The gold was turned over to the mint and made into quarter eagles. The distinguishing mark "CAL." was punched above the eagle on the reverse side, while the coins were in the die.

| | Quan. Minted | VF-20 | EF-40 | AU-50 | MS-60 |
|---|---|---|---|---|---|
| 1848 CAL. above eagle | 1,389 | 3,000 | 5,000 | 6,500 | 12,500 |
| 1848C | 16,788 | 175.00 | 250.00 | 350.00 | 900.00 |
| 1848D | 13,771 | 200.00 | 300.00 | 450.00 | 1,100 |
| 1849 | 23,294 | 90.00 | 125.00 | 150.00 | 325.00 |
| 1849C | 10,220 | 150.00 | 225.00 | 375.00 | 900.00 |
| 1849D | 10,945 | 175.00 | 275.00 | 400.00 | 1,000 |
| 1850 | 252,923 | 75.00 | 100.00 | 125.00 | 300.00 |
| 1850C | 9,148 | 150.00 | 225.00 | 375.00 | 900.00 |
| 1850D | 12,148 | 150.00 | 225.00 | 375.00 | 900.00 |
| 1850O | 84,000 | 75.00 | 100.00 | 125.00 | 300.00 |
| 1851 | 1,372,748 | 75.00 | 100.00 | 125.00 | 250.00 |
| 1851C | 14,923 | 150.00 | 200.00 | 325.00 | 800.00 |
| 1851D | 11,264 | 150.00 | 225.00 | 375.00 | 900.00 |
| 1851O | 148,000 | 75.00 | 100.00 | 125.00 | 300.00 |
| 1852 | 1,159,681 | 75.00 | 100.00 | 125.00 | 250.00 |
| 1852C | 9,772 | 150.00 | 225.00 | 375.00 | 850.00 |
| 1852D | 4,078 | 225.00 | 400.00 | 600.00 | 1,500 |
| 1852O | 140,000 | 75.00 | 100.00 | 125.00 | 300.00 |
| 1853 | 1,404,668 | 75.00 | 100.00 | 125.00 | 250.00 |
| 1853D | 3,178 | 300.00 | 550.00 | 700.00 | 2,000 |
| 1854 | 596,258 | 75.00 | 100.00 | 125.00 | 250.00 |
| 1854C | 7,295 | 150.00 | 225.00 | 375.00 | 850.00 |
| 1854D | 1,760 | 1,000 | 1,600 | 2,000 | 3,500 |
| 1854O | 153,000 | 75.00 | 100.00 | 125.00 | 325.00 |
| 1854S | 246 | | 9,000 | 15,000 | —— |
| 1855 | 235,480 | 75.00 | 100.00 | 125.00 | 250.00 |
| 1855C | 3,677 | 300.00 | 550.00 | 700.00 | 2,000 |

# QUARTER EAGLES

| | | Quan. Minted | VF-20 | EF-40 | AU-50 | MS-60 | Proof-63 |
|---|---|---|---|---|---|---|---|
| 1855D | | 1,123 | $750.00 | $1,400 | $2,000 | $5,000 | |
| 1856 | | 384,240 | 75.00 | 100.00 | 125.00 | 225.00 | |
| 1856C | | 7,913 | 150.00 | 225.00 | 375.00 | 1,100 | |
| 1856D | | 874 | 1,100 | 2,500 | 4,000 | 7,500 | |
| 1856O | | 21,100 | 90.00 | 125.00 | 150.00 | 400.00 | |
| 1856S | | 72,120 | 90.00 | 125.00 | 150.00 | 400.00 | |
| 1857 | | 214,130 | 75.00 | 100.00 | 125.00 | 225.00 | |
| 1857D | | 2,364 | 200.00 | 400.00 | 700.00 | 1,800 | |
| 1857O | | 34,000 | 75.00 | 100.00 | 135.00 | 325.00 | |
| 1857S | | 69,200 | 75.00 | 100.00 | 125.00 | 400.00 | |
| 1858 | | 47,377 | 75.00 | 100.00 | 125.00 | 250.00 | |
| 1858C | | 9,056 | 150.00 | 225.00 | 375.00 | 800.00 | |
| 1859 | (80) | 39,444 | 75.00 | 100.00 | 125.00 | 225.00 | $4,000 |
| 1859D | | 2,244 | 200.00 | 400.00 | 700.00 | 1,800 | |
| 1859S | | 15,200 | 90.00 | 125.00 | 150.00 | 400.00 | |
| 1860 | (112) | 22,675 | 75.00 | 100.00 | 125.00 | 225.00 | 3,000 |
| 1860C | | 7,469 | 150.00 | 300.00 | 400.00 | 1,000 | |
| 1860S | | 35,600 | 75.00 | 100.00 | 125.00 | 400.00 | |
| 1861 | (90) | 1,283,878 | 75.00 | 100.00 | 125.00 | 225.00 | 3,000 |
| 1861S | | 24,000 | 75.00 | 100.00 | 150.00 | 350.00 | |
| 1862, 2 over 1 | (35) | 98,543 | | 700.00 | 1,000 | —— | |
| 1862 | | | 75.00 | 100.00 | 125.00 | 225.00 | 3,500 |
| 1862S | | 8,000 | 85.00 | 120.00 | 175.00 | 600.00 | |
| 1863 Proofs only | (30) | 30 | | | | | —— |
| 1863S | | 10,800 | 75.00 | 110.00 | 150.00 | 500.00 | |
| 1864 | (50) | 2,874 | 250.00 | 400.00 | 850.00 | 1,500 | 5,000 |
| 1865 | (25) | 1,545 | 250.00 | 400.00 | 850.00 | 1,500 | 5,000 |
| 1865S | | 23,376 | 75.00 | 100.00 | 135.00 | 350.00 | |
| 1866 | (30) | 3,110 | 125.00 | 175.00 | 300.00 | 700.00 | 4,000 |
| 1866S | | 38,960 | 75.00 | 100.00 | 125.00 | 400.00 | |
| 1867 | (50) | 3,250 | 125.00 | 175.00 | 300.00 | 600.00 | 3,200 |
| 1867S | | 28,000 | 75.00 | 100.00 | 125.00 | 375.00 | |
| 1868 | (25) | 3,625 | 100.00 | 150.00 | 275.00 | 600.00 | 3,200 |
| 1868S | | 34,000 | 75.00 | 100.00 | 125.00 | 350.00 | |
| 1869 | (25) | 4,345 | 85.00 | 120.00 | 225.00 | 375.00 | 3,200 |
| 1869S | | 29,500 | 75.00 | 100.00 | 125.00 | 350.00 | |
| 1870 | (35) | 4,555 | 85.00 | 110.00 | 200.00 | 500.00 | 3,200 |
| 1870S | | 16,000 | 75.00 | 100.00 | 125.00 | 350.00 | |
| 1871 | (30) | 5,350 | 85.00 | 110.00 | 200.00 | 450.00 | 3,200 |
| 1871S | | 22,000 | 75.00 | 100.00 | 125.00 | 275.00 | |
| 1872 | (30) | 3,030 | 100.00 | 150.00 | 250.00 | 500.00 | 3,200 |
| 1872S | | 18,000 | 75.00 | 100.00 | 125.00 | 250.00 | |
| 1873 | (25) | 178,025 | 75.00 | 100.00 | 125.00 | 225.00 | 3,200 |
| 1873S | | 27,000 | 75.00 | 100.00 | 125.00 | 250.00 | |
| 1874 | (20) | 3,940 | 90.00 | 120.00 | 200.00 | 375.00 | 4,000 |
| 1875 | (20) | 420 | 800.00 | 1,500 | 2,500 | 5,000 | 12,000 |
| 1875S | | 11,600 | 75.00 | 100.00 | 125.00 | 250.00 | |
| 1876 | (45) | 4,221 | 85.00 | 120.00 | 225.00 | 500.00 | 3,000 |
| 1876S | | 5,000 | 75.00 | 110.00 | 150.00 | 400.00 | |
| 1877 | (20) | 1,652 | 175.00 | 250.00 | 325.00 | 900.00 | 4,000 |
| 1877S | | 35,400 | 75.00 | 100.00 | 125.00 | 225.00 | |
| 1878 | (20) | 286,260 | 75.00 | 100.00 | 125.00 | 225.00 | 3,000 |
| 1878S | | 178,000 | 75.00 | 100.00 | 125.00 | 225.00 | |
| 1879 | (30) | 88,990 | 75.00 | 100.00 | 125.00 | 225.00 | 3,000 |
| 1879S | | 43,500 | 75.00 | 100.00 | 125.00 | 225.00 | |
| 1880 | (36) | 2,996 | 75.00 | 110.00 | 135.00 | 400.00 | 3,000 |
| 1881 | (51) | 691 | 250.00 | 400.00 | 800.00 | 1,400 | 4,500 |
| 1882 | (67) | 4,067 | 85.00 | 110.00 | 135.00 | 400.00 | 3,000 |

# QUARTER EAGLES

| | *Quan. Minted* | *VF-20* | *EF-40* | *AU-50* | *MS-60* | *Proof-63* |
|---|---|---|---|---|---|---|
| 1883 | (82) 2,002 | $100.00 | $120.00 | $175.00 | $400.00 | $3,000 |
| 1884 | (73) 2,023 | 100.00 | 120.00 | 175.00 | 400.00 | 3,000 |
| 1885 | (87) 887 | 250.00 | 400.00 | 800.00 | 1,400 | 4,000 |
| 1886 | (88) 4,088 | 85.00 | 110.00 | 135.00 | 400.00 | 2,750 |
| 1887 | (122) 6,282 | 75.00 | 100.00 | 125.00 | 325.00 | 2,500 |
| 1888 | (97) 16,098 | 75.00 | 100.00 | 125.00 | 225.00 | 2,500 |
| 1889 | (48) 17,648 | 75.00 | 100.00 | 125.00 | 225.00 | 2,500 |
| 1890 | (93) 8,813 | 75.00 | 100.00 | 125.00 | 250.00 | 2,500 |
| 1891 | (80) 11,040 | 75.00 | 100.00 | 125.00 | 250.00 | 2,500 |
| 1892 | (105) 2,545 | 90.00 | 120.00 | 200.00 | 450.00 | 2,400 |
| 1893 | (106) 30,106 | 75.00 | 100.00 | 125.00 | 200.00 | 2,400 |
| 1894 | (122) 4,122 | 85.00 | 110.00 | 135.00 | 375.00 | 2,200 |
| 1895 | (119) 6,119 | 75.00 | 100.00 | 125.00 | 275.00 | 2,200 |
| 1896 | (132) 19,202 | 75.00 | 100.00 | 125.00 | 200.00 | 2,200 |
| 1897 | (136) 29,904 | 75.00 | 100.00 | 125.00 | 200.00 | 2,200 |
| 1898 | (165) 24,165 | 75.00 | 100.00 | 125.00 | 200.00 | 2,000 |
| 1899 | (150) 27,350 | 75.00 | 100.00 | 125.00 | 200.00 | 2,000 |
| 1900 | (205) 67,205 | 75.00 | 100.00 | 125.00 | 200.00 | 2,000 |
| 1901 | (223) 91,323 | 75.00 | 100.00 | 125.00 | 200.00 | 2,000 |
| 1902 | (193) 133,733 | 75.00 | 100.00 | 125.00 | 200.00 | 2,000 |
| 1903 | (197) 201,257 | 75.00 | 100.00 | 125.00 | 200.00 | 2,000 |
| 1904 | (170) 160,960 | 75.00 | 100.00 | 125.00 | 200.00 | 2,000 |
| 1905 | (144) 217,944 | 75.00 | 100.00 | 125.00 | 200.00 | 2,000 |
| 1906 | (160) 176,490 | 75.00 | 100.00 | 125.00 | 200.00 | 2,000 |
| 1907 | (154) 336,448 | 75.00 | 100.00 | 125.00 | 200.00 | 2,000 |

## INDIAN HEAD TYPE 1908-1929

Bela Lyon Pratt was the designer of this and the half eagle piece. The coin has no raised milling and the main devices and legends are incuse.

**VF-20 VERY FINE**—*Hair cord knot distinct. Feathers at top of head clear. Cheekbone worn.*

**EF-40 EXTREMELY FINE**—*Cheekbone, war bonnet and headband feathers slightly worn.*

**AU-50 ABOUT UNCIRCULATED**—*Trace of wear on cheekbone and headdress.*

**MS-60 UNCIRCULATED**—*No trace of wear. Light blemishes.*

Mint mark location is on reverse left of fasces.

| | *Quan. Minted* | *VF-20* | *EF-40* | *AU-50* | *MS-60* | *Matte Proof-63* |
|---|---|---|---|---|---|---|
| 1908 | (236) 565,057 | $70.00 | $80.00 | $90.00 | $135.00 | $2,500 |
| 1909 | (139) 441,899 | 70.00 | 80.00 | 90.00 | 135.00 | 2,500 |
| 1910 | (682) 492,682 | 70.00 | 80.00 | 90.00 | 135.00 | 2,500 |
| 1911 | (191) 704,191 | 70.00 | 80.00 | 90.00 | 135.00 | 2,500 |
| 1911D | 55,680 | 500.00 | 750.00 | 900.00 | 2,400 | |
| 1912 | (197) 616,197 | 70.00 | 80.00 | 90.00 | 135.00 | 2,500 |
| 1913 | (165) 722,165 | 70.00 | 80.00 | 90.00 | 135.00 | 2,500 |
| 1914 | (117) 240,117 | 70.00 | 80.00 | 90.00 | 135.00 | 2,500 |
| 1914D | 448,000 | 70.00 | 80.00 | 90.00 | 135.00 | |
| 1915 | (100) 606,100 | 70.00 | 80.00 | 90.00 | 135.00 | 2,500 |
| 1925D | 578,000 | 70.00 | 80.00 | 90.00 | 135.00 | |
| 1926 | 446,000 | 70.00 | 80.00 | 90.00 | 135.00 | |
| 1927 | 388,000 | 70.00 | 80.00 | 90.00 | 135.00 | |
| 1928 | 416,000 | 70.00 | 80.00 | 90.00 | 135.00 | |
| 1929 | 532,000 | 70.00 | 80.00 | 90.00 | 135.00 | |

# THREE-DOLLAR GOLD PIECES

## THREE-DOLLAR GOLD PIECES — 1854-1889

The three-dollar gold piece was authorized by the Act of February 21, 1853. The coin was first struck in 1854. It was never popular and saw very little circulation.

Mint mark location is on reverse below wreath

**VF-20 VERY FINE**—*Eyebrow, hair about forehead and ear and bottom curl are worn smooth. Curled feather-ends have faint details showing.*

**EF-40 EXTREMELY FINE**—*Light wear above and to right of eye and on top of curled feathers.*

**AU-50 ABOUT UNCIRCULATED**—*Trace of wear on top of curled feathers and in hair above and to right of eye.*

**MS-60 UNCIRCULATED**—*No trace of wear. Light blemishes.*

| | *Quan. Minted* | *VF-20* | *EF-40* | *AU-50* | *MS-60* | *Proof-63* |
|---|---|---|---|---|---|---|
| 1854 | 138,618 | $300.00 | $450.00 | $600.00 | $1,250 | $12,000 |
| 1854D | 1,120 | 2,500 | 5,000 | 7,500 | 12,000 | |
| 1854O | 24,000 | 300.00 | 450.00 | 600.00 | 1,300 | |
| 1855 | 50,555 | 300.00 | 450.00 | 600.00 | 1,250 | 15,000 |
| 1855S | 6,600 | 300.00 | 450.00 | 600.00 | 2,350 | |
| 1856 | 26,010 | 300.00 | 450.00 | 600.00 | 1,300 | 9,000 |
| 1856S | 34,500 | 300.00 | 450.00 | 600.00 | 1,500 | |
| 1857 | 20,891 | 300.00 | 450.00 | 600.00 | 1,300 | 7,500 |
| 1857S | 14,000 | 300.00 | 450.00 | 600.00 | 1,500 | |
| 1858 | 2,133 | 375.00 | 500.00 | 700.00 | 2,200 | 7,000 |
| 1859 (80) | 15,638 | 300.00 | 450.00 | 600.00 | 1,300 | 6,000 |
| 1860 (119) | 7,155 | 300.00 | 450.00 | 600.00 | 1,400 | 4,000 |
| 1860S (2,592 melted at Mint) | 7,000 | 400.00 | 550.00 | 700.00 | 1,800 | |
| 1861 (113) | 6,072 | 300.00 | 450.00 | 600.00 | 1,400 | 4,000 |
| 1862 (35) | 5,785 | 300.00 | 450.00 | 600.00 | 1,400 | 4,000 |
| 1863 (39) | 5,039 | 300 | 450.00 | 600.00 | 1,400 | 4,000 |
| 1864 (50) | 2,680 | 300.00 | 450.00 | 600.00 | 1,400 | 4,000 |
| 1865 (25) | 1,165 | 450.00 | 575.00 | 800.00 | 3,000 | 6,500 |
| 1866 (30) | 4,030 | 300.00 | 450.00 | 600.00 | 1,400 | 4,000 |
| 1867 (50) | 2,650 | 300.00 | 450.00 | 600.00 | 1,400 | 4,000 |
| 1868 (25) | 4,875 | 300.00 | 450.00 | 600.00 | 1,400 | 4,000 |
| 1869 (25) | 2,525 | 300.00 | 450.00 | 600.00 | 1,400 | 4,000 |
| 1870 (35) | 3,535 | 300.00 | 450.00 | 600.00 | 1,400 | 4,000 |
| 1871 (30) | 1,330 | 375.00 | 500.00 | 700.00 | 1,700 | 4,000 |
| 1872 (30) | 2,030 | 300.00 | 450.00 | 600.00 | 1,400 | 4,000 |
| 1873 Open 3 (original) (25) | 25 | | | | | 16,000 |
| 1873 Closed 3 | | 1,200 | 1,800 | 2,300 | 4,000 | 8,000 |
| 1874 (20) | 41,820 | 300.00 | 450.00 | 600.00 | 1,200 | 5,000 |
| 1875 Proofs only (20) | 20 | | | | | —— |
| 1876 Proofs only (45) | 45 | | | | | —— |
| 1877 (20) | 1,488 | 450.00 | 700.00 | 1,100 | 2,500 | 6,000 |
| 1878 (20) | 82,324 | 300.00 | 450.00 | 600.00 | 1,250 | 5,000 |
| 1879 (30) | 3,030 | 300.00 | 450.00 | 600.00 | 1,400 | 4,000 |
| 1880 (36) | 1,036 | 400.00 | 500.00 | 700.00 | 1,500 | 4,000 |
| 1881 (54) | 554 | 500.00 | 750.00 | 1,100 | 2,000 | 5,000 |
| 1882 (76) | 1,576 | 300.00 | 450.00 | 600.00 | 1,400 | 3,500 |
| 1883 (89) | 989 | 400.00 | 500.00 | 700.00 | 1,500 | 3,500 |
| 1884 (106) | 1,106 | 400.00 | 500.00 | 700.00 | 1,500 | 3,000 |
| 1885 (109) | 910 | 400.00 | 500.00 | 700.00 | 1,500 | 3,000 |
| 1886 (142) | 1,142 | 400.00 | 500.00 | 650.00 | 1,700 | 3,000 |
| 1887 (160) | 6,160 | 400.00 | 450.00 | 600.00 | 1,300 | 3,000 |
| 1888 (291) | 5,291 | 400.00 | 450.00 | 600.00 | 1,300 | 3,000 |
| 1889 (129) | 2,429 | 400.00 | 450.00 | 600.00 | 1,300 | 3,000 |

# FOUR-DOLLAR GOLD OR "STELLA"

These pattern coins were first suggested by the Hon. John A. Kasson, then U.S. Minister to Austria; and it was through the efforts of Dr. W. W. Hubbell, who patented the goloid metal used in making the goloid metric dollars, that we have these beautiful and interesting pieces. Only those struck in gold are listed.

| | *Quan. Minted* | *VF-20* | *EF-40* | *Proof-60* |
|---|---|---|---|---|
| 1879 Flowing hair | 415 | $7,000 | $10,000 | $15,000 |
| 1879 Coiled hair | 10 | 15,000 | 20,000 | 35,000 |
| 1880 Flowing hair | 15 | 10,000 | 12,000 | 20,000 |
| 1880 Coiled hair | 10 | 15,000 | 20,000 | 35,000 |

# HALF EAGLES — 1795-1929

## ($5.00 GOLD PIECES)

The half eagle was the first gold coin struck for the United States. The $5.00 piece was authorized to be coined by the Act of April 2, 1792, and the first type weighed 135 grains, 916 2/3 fine. The weight was changed by the Act of June 28, 1834 to 129 grains, 899.225 fine. Fineness became .900 by the Act of January 18, 1837.

## CAPPED BUST TO RIGHT, SMALL EAGLE 1795-1798

**F-12 FINE**—*Hair worn smooth but with distinct outline. For heraldic type, E PLURIBUS UNUM is faint but readable.*
**VF-20 VERY FINE**—*Slight to noticeable wear on high spots such as hair, turban, eagle's head and wings.*
**EF-40 EXTREMELY FINE**—*Slight wear on hair and highest part of cheek.*
**MS-60 UNCIRCULATED**—*No trace of wear. Light blemishes.*

| | *Quan. Minted* | *F-12* | *VF-20* | *EF-40* | *MS-60* |
|---|---|---|---|---|---|
| 1795 Small eagle | 8,707 | $2,500 | $3,500 | $4,750 | $13,000 |

1796, 6 over 5

1797, 15 Stars

1797, 16 Stars

| | | | | | |
|---|---|---|---|---|---|
| 1796, 6 over 5 | 6,196 | 2,500 | 3,500 | 5,000 | 15,000 |
| 1797, 15 stars | | 3,500 | 4,500 | 7,500 | 16,500 |

# HALF EAGLES

| | Quan. Minted | F-12 | VF-20 | EF-40 | MS-60 |
|---|---|---|---|---|---|
| 1797, 16 stars All kinds | 3,609 | $3,500 | $4,500 | $7,500 | $16,500 |
| 1798 Small eagle (7 known) | | — | — | — | — |

## CAPPED BUST TO RIGHT, HERALDIC EAGLE 1795-1807

| | | | | | |
|---|---|---|---|---|---|
| 1795 Heraldic eagle | | 3,500 | 4,000 | 8,000 | 17,000 |
| 1797, 7 over 5 | | 3,000 | 3,500 | 7,000 | 15,000 |
| 1798 13 star reverse | 24,867 | 650.00 | 900.00 | 1,500 | 4,250 |
| 1798 14 star reverse | | 800.00 | 1,500 | 2,000 | 6,000 |
| 1799 | 7,451 | 650.00 | 900.00 | 1,500 | 4,000 |
| 1800 | 37,628 | 650.00 | 900.00 | 1,500 | 4,000 |
| 1802, 2 over 1 | 53,176 | 650.00 | 900.00 | 1,500 | 4,000 |
| 1803, 3 over 2 | 33,506 | 650.00 | 900.00 | 1,500 | 4,000 |
| 1804 | 30,475 | 650.00 | 900.00 | 1,500 | 4,000 |
| 1805 | 33,183 | 650.00 | 900.00 | 1,500 | 4,000 |
| 1806 | 64,093 | 650.00 | 900.00 | 1,500 | 4,000 |
| 1807 | 32,488 | 650.00 | 900.00 | 1,500 | 4,000 |

## CAPPED DRAPED BUST TO LEFT 1807-1812

**F-12 FINE**—*LIBERTY readable but partly weak.*

**VF-20 VERY FINE**—*Headband edges slightly worn. LIBERTY is bold.*

**EF-40 EXTREMELY FINE**—*Slight wear on highest portions of hair. 80% of major curls are plain.*

**MS-60 UNCIRCULATED**—*No trace of wear. Light blemishes.*

| | | | | | |
|---|---|---|---|---|---|
| 1807 | 51,605 | $650.00 | $900.00 | $1,500 | $3,750 |
| 1808, 8 over 7 | 55,578 | 600.00 | 800.00 | 1,250 | 3,500 |
| 1808 | | 600.00 | 800.00 | 1,250 | 3,500 |
| 1809, 9 over 8 | 33,875 | 600.00 | 800.00 | 1,250 | 3,500 |
| 1810 | 100,287 | 600.00 | 800.00 | 1,250 | 3,500 |
| 1811 | 99,581 | 600.00 | 800.00 | 1,250 | 3,500 |
| 1812 | 58,087 | 600.00 | 800.00 | 1,250 | 3,500 |

## CAPPED HEAD TO LEFT 1813-1829

| | | | | | |
|---|---|---|---|---|---|
| 1813 | 95,428 | 650.00 | 1,000 | 1,500 | 4,000 |
| 1814, 4 over 3 | 15,454 | 750.00 | 1,300 | 1,800 | 5,000 |
| 1815 | 635 | | | | 70,000 |
| 1818 | 48,588 | 700.00 | 1,100 | 1,600 | 4,500 |
| 1819 | 51,723 | | | 20,000 | 45,000 |
| 1820 | 263,806 | 700.00 | 1,100 | 1,750 | 5,000 |
| 1821 | 34,641 | 1,600 | 3,250 | 4,250 | 13,000 |
| 1822 | 17,796 | — | — | — | — |

# HALF EAGLES

| | Quan. Minted | F-12 | VF-20 | EF-40 | MS-60 |
|---|---|---|---|---|---|
| 1823 | 14,485 | $1,000 | $1,700 | $2,300 | $8,000 |
| 1824 | 17,340 | 3,000 | 4,500 | 9,000 | 18,000 |
| 1825, 5 over 1 | 29,060 | 1,500 | 2,500 | 4,000 | 12,000 |
| 1825, 5 over 4 | | | | —— | |
| 1826 | 18,069 | 1,800 | 3,100 | 4,500 | 13,500 |
| 1827 | 24,913 | 3,000 | 5,000 | 13,000 | |
| 1828, 8 over 7 | 28,029 | 2,400 | 3,500 | 7,500 | 12,000 |
| 1828 | | 3,000 | 4,500 | 9,000 | —— |
| 1829 Large date | 57,442 | —— | —— | —— | —— |

## CAPPED HEAD TO LEFT (reduced diameter) 1829-1834

| | Quan. Minted | F-12 | VF-20 | EF-40 | MS-60 |
|---|---|---|---|---|---|
| 1829 Small date | inc. above | | | | 30,000 |
| 1830 | 126,351 | 1,200 | 2,000 | 3,000 | 7,500 |
| 1831 | 140,594 | 1,200 | 2,000 | 3,000 | 7,500 |
| 1832 Curved-base 2, 12 stars | 157,487 | —— | —— | —— | —— |
| 1832 Square-base 2, 13 stars | | 2,000 | 3,500 | 5,000 | 10,000 |
| 1833 | 193,630 | 1,200 | 2,000 | 3,000 | 7,000 |
| 1834 | 50,141 | 1,200 | 2,000 | 3,000 | 7,000 |

## CLASSIC HEAD TYPE 1834-1838

| | Quan. Minted | F-12 | VF-20 | EF-40 | MS-60 |
|---|---|---|---|---|---|
| 1834 | 657,460 | 150.00 | 185.00 | 300.00 | 1,800 |
| 1835 | 371,534 | 150.00 | 185.00 | 300.00 | 1,800 |
| 1836 | 553,147 | 150.00 | 185.00 | 300.00 | 1,800 |
| 1837 | 207,121 | 150.00 | 185.00 | 300.00 | 1,800 |
| 1838 | 286,588 | 150.00 | 185.00 | 300.00 | 1,800 |
| 1838C | 17,179 | 400.00 | 500.00 | 1,000 | 4,200 |
| 1838D | 20,583 | 400.00 | 500.00 | 1,000 | 4,200 |

## CORONET TYPE, No Motto Above Eagle 1839-1866

**VF-20 VERY FINE**—*LIBERTY bold. Major lines show in neck hair.*

**EF-40 EXTREMELY FINE**—*Neck hair details clear. Slight wear on top and lower part of coronet, and hair.*

**AU-50 ABOUT UNCIRCULATED**—*Trace of wear on coronet and hair above eye.*

**MS-60 UNCIRCULATED**—*No trace of wear. Light blemishes.*

**Mint mark above date 1839 only, below eagle 1840-1908.**

# HALF EAGLES

| | Quan. Minted | VF-20 | EF-40 | AU-50 | MS-60 |
|---|---|---|---|---|---|
| 1839 | 118,143 | $100.00 | $125.00 | $275.00 | $500.00 |
| 1839C | 17,205 | 150.00 | 300.00 | 500.00 | 1,200 |
| 1839D | 18,939 | 150.00 | 300.00 | 500.00 | 1,200 |
| 1840 | 137,382 | 100.00 | 120.00 | 225.00 | 500.00 |
| 1840C | 18,992 | 150.00 | 300.00 | 500.00 | 1,200 |
| 1840D | 22,896 | 150.00 | 300.00 | 500.00 | 1,200 |
| 1840O | 40,120 | 125.00 | 200.00 | 400.00 | 700.00 |
| 1841 | 15,833 | 125.00 | 200.00 | 400.00 | 700.00 |
| 1841C | 21,467 | 150.00 | 300.00 | 500.00 | 1,200 |
| 1841D | 29,392 | 150.00 | 300.00 | 500.00 | 1,200 |

1842 Large Date

Large letters

Small Letters

| | Quan. Minted | VF-20 | EF-40 | AU-50 | MS-60 |
|---|---|---|---|---|---|
| 1842 Small Letters | 27,578 | 100.00 | 120.00 | 185.00 | 500.00 |
| 1842 Large letters | | 100.00 | 120.00 | 185.00 | 500.00 |
| 1842C Small date | 27,432 | 350.00 | 500.00 | 900.00 | 1,750 |
| 1842C Large date | | 125.00 | 200.00 | 400.00 | 1,000 |
| 1842D Small date | 59,608 | 125.00 | 200.00 | 400.00 | 1,200 |
| 1842D Large date | | 150.00 | 300.00 | 500.00 | 1,400 |
| 1842O | 16,400 | 100.00 | 150.00 | 300.00 | 600.00 |
| 1843 | 611,205 | 100.00 | 120.00 | 175.00 | 400.00 |
| 1843C | 44,277 | 125.00 | 200.00 | 400.00 | 1,000 |
| 1843D | 98,452 | 125.00 | 200.00 | 400.00 | 1,000 |
| 1843O Small letters | 19,075 | 100.00 | 150.00 | 300.00 | 600.00 |
| 1843O Large letters | 82,000 | 100.00 | 120.00 | 200.00 | 900.00 |
| 1844 | 340,330 | 100.00 | 120.00 | 175.00 | 400.00 |
| 1844C | 23,631 | 125.00 | 250.00 | 500.00 | 1,400 |
| 1844D | 88,982 | 125.00 | 200.00 | 400.00 | 1,000 |
| 1844O | 364,600 | 100.00 | 120.00 | 200.00 | 500.00 |
| 1845 | 417,099 | 100.00 | 120.00 | 175.00 | 400.00 |
| 1845D | 90,629 | 125.00 | 200.00 | 250.00 | 900.00 |
| 1845O | 41,000 | 100.00 | 120.00 | 200.00 | 500.00 |
| 1846 | 395,942 | 100.00 | 120.00 | 175.00 | 400.00 |
| 1846C | 12,995 | 150.00 | 300.00 | 500.00 | 1,200 |
| 1846D | 80,294 | 125.00 | 200.00 | 400.00 | 900.00 |
| 1846O | 58,000 | 100.00 | 120.00 | 200.00 | 500.00 |
| 1847 | 915,981 | 100.00 | 120.00 | 175.00 | 400.00 |
| 1847C | 84,151 | 125.00 | 200.00 | 400.00 | 1,000 |
| 1847D | 64,405 | 125.00 | 200.00 | 400.00 | 1,000 |
| 1847O | 12,000 | 125.00 | 225.00 | 450.00 | 1,000 |
| 1848 | 260,775 | 100.00 | 120.00 | 175.00 | 400.00 |
| 1848C | 64,472 | 125.00 | 200.00 | 400.00 | 900.00 |
| 1848D | 47,465 | 125.00 | 200.00 | 400.00 | 1,000 |
| 1849 | 133,070 | 100.00 | 120.00 | 175.00 | 400.00 |
| 1849C | 64,823 | 125.00 | 200.00 | 400.00 | 1,000 |
| 1849D | 39,036 | 125.00 | 200.00 | 400.00 | 1,000 |
| 1850 | 64,491 | 100.00 | 120.00 | 175.00 | 400.00 |

*Values of common gold coins are based on the prevailing price of gold bullion, and will vary according to current market price. See Bullion Chart.*

## HALF EAGLES

| | Quan. Minted | VF-20 | EF-40 | AU-50 | MS-60 | Proof-60 |
|---|---|---|---|---|---|---|
| 1850C | 63,591 | $125.00 | $200.00 | $400.00 | $1,000 | |
| 1850D | 43,984 | 125.00 | 200.00 | 400.00 | 1,000 | |
| 1851 | 377,505 | 100.00 | 120.00 | 175.00 | 400.00 | |
| 1851C | 49,176 | 125.00 | 200.00 | 400.00 | 1,000 | |
| 1851D | 62,710 | 125.00 | 200.00 | 400.00 | 1,000 | |
| 1851O | 41,000 | 100.00 | 125.00 | 250.00 | 500.00 | |
| 1852 | 573,901 | 100.00 | 120.00 | 175.00 | 400.00 | |
| 1852C | 72,574 | 125.00 | 200.00 | 400.00 | 1,000 | |
| 1852D | 91,584 | 125.00 | 200.00 | 400.00 | 1,000 | |
| 1853 | 305,770 | 100.00 | 120.00 | 175.00 | 400.00 | |
| 1853C | 65,571 | 125.00 | 200.00 | 400.00 | 1,000 | |
| 1853D | 89,678 | 125.00 | 200.00 | 400.00 | 1,000 | |
| 1854 | 160,675 | 100.00 | 120.00 | 175.00 | 400.00 | |
| 1854C | 39,283 | 125.00 | 200.00 | 400.00 | 1,000 | |
| 1854D | 56,413 | 125.00 | 200.00 | 400.00 | 1,000 | |
| 1854O | 46,000 | 100.00 | 125.00 | 250.00 | 500.00 | |
| 1854S | 268 | | — | — | — | |
| 1855 | 117,098 | 100.00 | 120.00 | 175.00 | 400.00 | |
| 1855C | 39,788 | 125.00 | 200.00 | 400.00 | 1,000 | |
| 1855D | 22,432 | 125.00 | 200.00 | 400.00 | 1,000 | |
| 1855O | 11,100 | 125.00 | 200.00 | 400.00 | 1,000 | |
| 1855S | 61,000 | 100.00 | 120.00 | 175.00 | 500.00 | |
| 1856 | 197,990 | 100.00 | 120.00 | 175.00 | 400.00 | |
| 1856C | 28,457 | 125.00 | 200.00 | 400.00 | 1,000 | |
| 1856D | 19,786 | 125.00 | 200.00 | 400.00 | 1,000 | |
| 1856O | 10,000 | 150.00 | 300.00 | 500.00 | 1,200 | |
| 1856S | 105,100 | 100.00 | 120.00 | 175.00 | 400.00 | |
| 1857 | 98,188 | 100.00 | 120.00 | 175.00 | 400.00 | |
| 1857C | 31,360 | 125.00 | 200.00 | 400.00 | 1,000 | |
| 1857D | 17,046 | 125.00 | 200.00 | 400.00 | 1,000 | |
| 1857O | 13,000 | 125.00 | 200.00 | 400.00 | 1,000 | |
| 1857S | 87,000 | 100.00 | 120.00 | 175.00 | 400.00 | |
| 1858 | 15,136 | 100.00 | 125.00 | 250.00 | 500.00 | |
| 1858C | 38,856 | 125.00 | 200.00 | 400.00 | 1,000 | |
| 1858D | 15,362 | 125.00 | 200.00 | 400.00 | 1,000 | |
| 1858S | 18,600 | 100.00 | 125.00 | 275.00 | 450.00 | |
| 1859 (80) | 16,814 | 100.00 | 125.00 | 250.00 | 450.00 | $4,000 |
| 1859C | 31,847 | 125.00 | 200.00 | 400.00 | 1,000 | |
| 1859D | 10,366 | 150.00 | 250.00 | 500.00 | 1,250 | |
| 1859S | 13,220 | 100.00 | 125.00 | 275.00 | 450.00 | |
| 1860 (62) | 19,825 | 100.00 | 125.00 | 250.00 | 450.00 | 3,000 |
| 1860C | 14,813 | 125.00 | 200.00 | 400.00 | 1,000 | |
| 1860D | 14,635 | 125.00 | 200.00 | 400.00 | 1,200 | |
| 1860S | 21,200 | 100.00 | 125.00 | 250.00 | — | |
| 1861 (66) | 688,150 | 100.00 | 120.00 | 175.00 | 400.00 | 3,000 |
| 1861C | 6,879 | 700.00 | 1,000 | 1,700 | 3,250 | |
| 1861D | 1,597 | 1,750 | 2,500 | 4,000 | 10,000 | |
| 1861S | 18,000 | 100.00 | 125.00 | 185.00 | — | |
| 1862 (35) | 4,465 | 100.00 | 150.00 | 275.00 | — | 3,000 |
| 1862S | 9,500 | 125.00 | 225.00 | 350.00 | — | |
| 1863 (30) | 2,472 | 150.00 | 350.00 | 500.00 | 1,250 | 3,000 |
| 1863S | 17,000 | 100.00 | 150.00 | 275.00 | 600.00 | |
| 1864 (50) | 4,220 | 125.00 | 200.00 | 400.00 | 1,400 | 3,000 |

*Values of common gold coins are based on the prevailing price of gold bullion, and will vary according to current market price. See Bullion Chart.*

# HALF EAGLES

| | Quan. Minted | VF-20 | EF-40 | AU-50 | MS-60 | Proof-63 |
|---|---|---|---|---|---|---|
| 1864S | 3,888 | $350.00 | $700.00 | $1,200 | —— | |
| 1865 (25) | 1,295 | 300.00 | 400.00 | 600.00 | $1,500 | $3,000 |
| 1865S | 27,612 | 100.00 | 125.00 | 185.00 | —— | |
| 1866S | 9,000 | 125.00 | 200.00 | 400.00 | —— | |

## Motto Above Eagle 1866-1908

**VF-20 VERY FINE**—*Half of hairlines above coronet missing. Hair curls under ear evident, but worn. Motto and its ribbon sharp.*

**EF-40 EXTREMELY FINE**—*Small amount of wear on top of hair and below L in LIBERTY. Wear evident on wing tips and neck of eagle.*

**AU-50 ABOUT UNCIRCULATED**—*Trace of wear on tip of coronet and hair above eye.*

**MS-60 UNCIRCULATED**—*No trace of wear. Light blemishes.*

| | Quan. Minted | VF-20 | EF-40 | AU-50 | MS-60 | Proof-63 |
|---|---|---|---|---|---|---|
| 1866 (30) | 6,730 | 120.00 | 170.00 | 300.00 | 750.00 | 4,500 |
| 1866S | 34,920 | 100.00 | 150.00 | 275.00 | 500.00 | |
| 1867 (50) | 6,920 | 120.00 | 170.00 | 300.00 | 700.00 | 4,500 |
| 1867S | 29,000 | 100.00 | 150.00 | 250.00 | —— | |
| 1868 (25) | 5,725 | 120.00 | 170.00 | 300.00 | 700.00 | 4,500 |
| 1868S | 52,000 | 100.00 | 150.00 | 250.00 | —— | |
| 1869 (25) | 1,785 | 150.00 | 275.00 | 400.00 | 1,000 | 4,500 |
| 1869S | 31,000 | 100.00 | 120.00 | 175.00 | 400.00 | |
| 1870 (35) | 4,035 | 100.00 | 150.00 | 275.00 | 500.00 | 4,500 |
| 1870CC | 7,675 | 650.00 | 1,200 | 2,000 | | |
| 1870S | 17,000 | 100.00 | 120.00 | 200.00 | —— | |
| 1871 (30) | 3,230 | 120.00 | 170.00 | 300.00 | —— | 4,500 |
| 1871CC | 20,770 | 150.00 | 275.00 | 500.00 | 1,100 | |
| 1871S | 25,000 | 100.00 | 120.00 | 200.00 | 600.00 | |
| 1872 (30) | 1,690 | 200.00 | 275.00 | 500.00 | 1,100 | 4,500 |
| 1872CC | 16,980 | 200.00 | 275.00 | 500.00 | 1,100 | |
| 1872S | 36,400 | 100.00 | 120.00 | 175.00 | 350.00 | |
| 1873 (25) | 112,505 | 90.00 | 100.00 | 110.00 | 175.00 | |
| 1873CC | 7,416 | 200.00 | 400.00 | 700.00 | 1,500 | |
| 1873S | 31,000 | 100.00 | 120.00 | 200.00 | 500.00 | |
| 1874 (20) | 3,508 | 120.00 | 170.00 | 300.00 | 750.00 | 4,500 |
| 1874CC | 21,198 | 120.00 | 170.00 | 300.00 | 850.00 | |
| 1874S | 16,000 | 100.00 | 120.00 | 175.00 | —— | |
| 1875 (20) | 220 | | —— | —— | —— | —— |
| 1875CC | 11,828 | 150.00 | 350.00 | 550.00 | 1,000 | |
| 1875S | 9,000 | 125.00 | 275.00 | 400.00 | 850.00 | |
| 1876 (45) | 1,477 | 200.00 | 350.00 | 600.00 | 1,250 | 4,000 |
| 1876CC | 6,887 | 150.00 | 275.00 | 500.00 | 1,100 | |
| 1876S | 4,000 | 150.00 | 275.00 | 500.00 | 1,000 | |
| 1877 (20) | 1,152 | 175.00 | 325.00 | 600.00 | 1,500 | 4,500 |
| 1877CC | 8,680 | 150.00 | 275.00 | 500.00 | 1,100 | |
| 1877S | 26,700 | 90.00 | 100.00 | 125.00 | 200.00 | |
| 1878 (20) | 131,740 | 90.00 | 100.00 | 110.00 | 135.00 | 4,500 |
| 1878CC | 9,054 | 400.00 | 900.00 | 1,250 | | |
| 1878S | 144,700 | 90.00 | 100.00 | 110.00 | 135.00 | |
| 1879 (30) | 301,950 | 90.00 | 100.00 | 110.00 | 135.00 | 4,000 |
| 1879CC | 17,281 | 125.00 | 150.00 | 300.00 | 650.00 | |

*Values of common gold coins are based on the prevailing price of gold bullion, and will vary according to current market price. See Bullion Chart.*

# HALF EAGLES

| | | Quan. Minted | VF-20 | EF-40 | AU-50 | MS-60 | Proof-63 |
|---|---|---|---|---|---|---|---|
| 1879S | | 426,200 | $90.00 | $100.00 | $110.00 | $135.00 | |
| 1880 | (36) | 3,166,436 | 90.00 | 100.00 | 110.00 | 125.00 | $3,500 |
| 1880CC | | 51,017 | 120.00 | 170.00 | 225.00 | 450.00 | |
| 1880S | | 1,348,900 | 90.00 | 100.00 | 110.00 | 125.00 | |
| 1881 | (42) | 5,708,802 | 90.00 | 100.00 | 110.00 | 125.00 | 3,000 |
| 1881CC | | 13,886 | 125.00 | 150.00 | 300.00 | 600.00 | |
| 1881S | | 969,000 | 90.00 | 100.00 | 110.00 | 125.00 | |
| 1882 | (48) | 2,514,568 | 90.00 | 100.00 | 110.00 | 125.00 | 3,000 |
| 1882CC | | 82,817 | 100.00 | 120.00 | 175.00 | 350.00 | |
| 1882S | | 969,000 | 90.00 | 100.00 | 110.00 | 125.00 | |
| 1883 | (61) | 233,461 | 90.00 | 100.00 | 110.00 | 125.00 | 3,000 |
| 1883CC | | 12,958 | 125.00 | 150.00 | 300.00 | 450.00 | |
| 1883S | | 83,200 | 90.00 | 100.00 | 110.00 | 125.00 | |
| 1884 | (48) | 191,078 | 90.00 | 100.00 | 110.00 | 125.00 | 3,000 |
| 1884CC | | 16,402 | 125.00 | 150.00 | 300.00 | 450.00 | |
| 1884S | | 177,000 | 90.00 | 100.00 | 110.00 | 125.00 | |
| 1885 | (66) | 601,506 | 90.00 | 100.00 | 110.00 | 125.00 | 3,000 |
| 1885S | | 1,211,500 | 90.00 | 100.00 | 110.00 | 125.00 | |
| 1886 | (72) | 388,432 | 90.00 | 100.00 | 110.00 | 125.00 | 3,000 |
| 1886S | | 3,268,000 | 90.00 | 100.00 | 110.00 | 125.00 | |
| 1887 Proofs only | (87) | 87 | | | | | 10,000 |
| 1887S | | 1,912,000 | 90.00 | 100.00 | 110.00 | 125.00 | |
| 1888 | (95) | 18,296 | 100.00 | 120.00 | 125.00 | 175.00 | 2,000 |
| 1888S | | 293,900 | 90.00 | 100.00 | 110.00 | 125.00 | |
| 1889 | (45) | 7,565 | 100.00 | 125.00 | 200.00 | 500.00 | 2,000 |
| 1890 | (88) | 4,328 | 100.00 | 200.00 | 300.00 | 600.00 | 2,000 |
| 1890CC | | 53,800 | 100.00 | 120.00 | 175.00 | 250.00 | |
| 1891 | (53) | 61,413 | 90.00 | 100.00 | 110.00 | 125.00 | 2,000 |
| 1891CC | | 208,000 | 100.00 | 120.00 | 150.00 | 200.00 | |
| 1892 | (92) | 753,572 | 90.00 | 100.00 | 110.00 | 125.00 | 2,000 |
| 1892CC | | 82,968 | 100.00 | 120.00 | 150.00 | 200.00 | |
| 1892O | | 10,000 | 225.00 | 350.00 | 600.00 | 1,100 | |
| 1892S | | 298,400 | 90.00 | 100.00 | 110.00 | 125.00 | |
| 1893 | (77) | 1,528,197 | 90.00 | 100.00 | 110.00 | 125.00 | 2,000 |
| 1893CC | | 60,000 | 100.00 | 120.00 | 150.00 | 300.00 | |
| 1893O | | 110,000 | 100.00 | 120.00 | 175.00 | 350.00 | |
| 1893S | | 224,000 | 90.00 | 100.00 | 110.00 | 125.00 | |
| 1894 | (75) | 957,955 | 90.00 | 100.00 | 110.00 | 125.00 | 2,000 |
| 1894O | | 16,600 | 100.00 | 120.00 | 175.00 | 375.00 | |
| 1894S | | 55,900 | 90.00 | 100.00 | 110.00 | 150.00 | |
| 1895 | (81) | 1,345,936 | 90.00 | 100.00 | 110.00 | 125.00 | 2,000 |
| 1895S | | 112,000 | 90.00 | 100.00 | 110.00 | 125.00 | |
| 1896 | (103) | 59,063 | 90.00 | 100.00 | 110.00 | 125.00 | 2,000 |
| 1896S | | 155,400 | 90.00 | 100.00 | 110.00 | 125.00 | |
| 1897 | (83) | 867,883 | 90.00 | 100.00 | 110.00 | 125.00 | 2,000 |
| 1897S | | 354,000 | 90.00 | 100.00 | 110.00 | 125.00 | |
| 1898 | (75) | 633,495 | 90.00 | 100.00 | 110.00 | 125.00 | 2,000 |
| 1898S | | 1,397,400 | 90.00 | 100.00 | 110.00 | 125.00 | |
| 1899 | (99) | 1,710,729 | 90.00 | 100.00 | 110.00 | 125.00 | 2,000 |
| 1899S | | 1,545,000 | 90.00 | 100.00 | 110.00 | 125.00 | |
| 1900 | (230) | 1,405,730 | 90.00 | 100.00 | 110.00 | 125.00 | 2,000 |
| 1900S | | 329,000 | 90.00 | 100.00 | 110.00 | 125.00 | |
| 1901 | (140) | 616,040 | 90.00 | 100.00 | 110.00 | 125.00 | 2,000 |

*Values of common gold coins are based on the prevailing price of gold bullion, and will vary according to current market price. See Bullion Chart.*

# HALF EAGLES

| | Quan. Minted | VF-20 | EF-40 | AU-50 | MS-60 | Proof-63 |
|---|---|---|---|---|---|---|
| 1901S, 1 over 0 | 3,648,000 | $90.00 | $100.00 | $125.00 | $150.00 | |
| 1901S | | 90.00 | 100.00 | 110.00 | 125.00 | |
| 1902 (162) | 172,562 | 90.00 | 100.00 | 110.00 | 125.00 | $2,000 |
| 1902S | 939,000 | 90.00 | 100.00 | 110.00 | 125.00 | |
| 1903 (154) | 227,024 | 90.00 | 100.00 | 110.00 | 125.00 | 2,000 |
| 1903S | 1,855,000 | 90.00 | 100.00 | 110.00 | 125.00 | |
| 1904 (136) | 392,136 | 90.00 | 100.00 | 110.00 | 125.00 | 2,000 |
| 1904S | 97,000 | 90.00 | 100.00 | 110.00 | 125.00 | |
| 1905 (108) | 302,308 | 90.00 | 100.00 | 110.00 | 125.00 | 2,000 |
| 1905S | 880,700 | 90.00 | 100.00 | 110.00 | 125.00 | |
| 1906 (85) | 348,820 | 90.00 | 100.00 | 110.00 | 125.00 | 2,000 |
| 1906D | 320,000 | 90.00 | 100.00 | 110.00 | 125.00 | |
| 1906S | 598,000 | 90.00 | 100.00 | 110.00 | 125.00 | |
| 1907 (92) | 626,192 | 90.00 | 100.00 | 110.00 | 125.00 | 2,000 |
| 1907D | 888,000 | 90.00 | 100.00 | 110.00 | 125.00 | |
| 1908 | 421,874 | 90.00 | 100.00 | 110.00 | 125.00 | |

## INDIAN HEAD TYPE 1908-1929

This type conforms to the quarter eagle of the same date. The incuse designs and lettering make this a unique series, along with the quarter eagle, in United States coinage.

**VF-20 VERY FINE**—*Noticeable wear on large middle feathers and tip of eagle's wing.*

**EF-40 EXTREMELY FINE**—*Cheekbone, war bonnet and headband feathers slightly worn. Feathers on eagle's upper wing show considerable wear.*

**AU-50 ABOUT UNCIRCULATED**—*Trace of wear on cheekbone and headdress.*

**MS-60 UNCIRCULATED**—*No trace of wear. Light blemishes.*

*Scarcer coins with well struck mint marks command higher prices.*

Mint mark location

| | | | | | | Matte Proof-63 |
|---|---|---|---|---|---|---|
| 1908 (167) | 578,012 | 100.00 | 110.00 | 125.00 | 350.00 | 3,000 |
| 1908D | 148,000 | 100.00 | 110.00 | 125.00 | 350.00 | |
| 1908S | 82,000 | 135.00 | 160.00 | 280.00 | 1,500 | |
| 1909 (78) | 627,138 | 100.00 | 110.00 | 125.00 | 350.00 | 3,000 |
| 1909D | 3,423,560 | 100.00 | 110.00 | 125.00 | 350.00 | |
| 1909O | 34,200 | 225.00 | 400.00 | 600.00 | 3,500 | |
| 1909S | 297,200 | 100.00 | 110.00 | 160.00 | 1,000 | |
| 1910 (250) | 604,250 | 100.00 | 110.00 | 125.00 | 350.00 | 3,000 |
| 1910D | 193,600 | 100.00 | 110.00 | 125.00 | 500.00 | |
| 1910S | 770,200 | 100.00 | 110.00 | 160.00 | 1,100 | |
| 1911 (139) | 915,139 | 100.00 | 110.00 | 125.00 | 350.00 | 3,000 |
| 1911D | 72,500 | 130.00 | 175.00 | 350.00 | 2,000 | |
| 1911S | 1,416,000 | 100.00 | 110.00 | 160.00 | 650.00 | |
| 1912 (144) | 790,144 | 100.00 | 110.00 | 125.00 | 350.00 | 3,000 |
| 1912S | 392,000 | 100.00 | 110.00 | 160.00 | 800.00 | |
| 1913 (99) | 916,000 | 100.00 | 110.00 | 125.00 | 350.00 | 3,000 |

*Values of common gold coins are based on the prevailing price of gold bullion, and will vary according to current market price. See Bullion Chart.*

# HALF EAGLES

| | Quan. Minted | VF-20 | EF-40 | AU-50 | MS-60 | Matte Proof-63 |
|---|---|---|---|---|---|---|
| 1913S | 408,000 | $100.00 | $110.00 | $200.00 | $1,600 | |
| 1914 (125) | 247,125 | 100.00 | 110.00 | 125.00 | 350.00 | $3,000 |
| 1914D | 247,000 | 100.00 | 110.00 | 125.00 | 350.00 | |
| 1914S | 263,000 | 100.00 | 110.00 | 160.00 | 650.00 | |
| 1915 (75) | 588,075 | 100.00 | 110.00 | 125.00 | 350.00 | 3,000 |
| 1915S | 164,000 | 100.00 | 110.00 | 175.00 | 1,200 | |
| 1916S | 240,000 | 100.00 | 110.00 | 160.00 | 800.00 | |
| 1929 | 662,000 | 1,200 | 1,800 | 2,200 | 3,500 | |

# EAGLES ($10.00 Gold Pieces) — 1795-1933

Coinage authority including specified weights and fineness of the eagle conforms to that of the half eagle. The small eagle reverse was used until 1797 when the large, heraldic eagle replaced it.

## CAPPED BUST TO RIGHT, SMALL EAGLE 1795-1797

**F-12 FINE**—*Details on turban and head obliterated.*

**VF-20 VERY FINE**—*Neck hairlines and details under turban and over forehead are worn but distinguishable.*

**EF-40 EXTREMELY FINE**—*Definite wear on hair to left of eye and strand of hair across and around turban, also on eagle's wing tips.*

**MS-60 UNCIRCULATED**—*No trace of wear. Light blemishes.*

| | Quan. Minted | F-12 | VF-20 | EF-40 | MS-60 |
|---|---|---|---|---|---|
| 1795 | 5,583 | 3,000 | 4,500 | 7,000 | 20,000 |
| 1796 | 4,146 | 3,000 | 4,500 | 7,000 | 20,000 |
| 1797 Small eagle | 3,615 | 3,000 | 4,500 | 7,500 | 21,500 |

## CAPPED BUST TO RIGHT, HERALDIC EAGLE 1797-1804

| | Quan. Minted | F-12 | VF-20 | EF-40 | MS-60 |
|---|---|---|---|---|---|
| 1797 Large eagle | 10,940 | 1,000 | 1,800 | 3,000 | 9,000 |
| 1798, 8 over 7, 9 stars left, 4 right | 900 | 2,500 | 4,000 | 7,000 | 14,000 |
| 1798, 8 over 7, 7 stars left, 6 right | 842 | 7,000 | 14,000 | — | — |
| 1799 | 37,449 | 1,000 | 1,500 | 2,500 | 7,000 |
| 1800 | 5,999 | 1,100 | 1,600 | 2,600 | 7,500 |

# EAGLES

| | *Quan. Minted* | *F-12* | *VF-20* | *EF-40* | *MS-60* |
|---|---|---|---|---|---|
| 1801 | 44,344 | $1,000 | $1,500 | $2,500 | $7,000 |
| 1803 | 15,017 | 1,100 | 1,600 | 2,600 | 7,500 |
| 1804 | 3,757 | 1,500 | 2,200 | 3,000 | 12,000 |

## CORONET TYPE, No Motto Above Eagle 1838-1866

In 1838 the weight and diameter of the eagle were reduced and the obverse and reverse were redesigned. Liberty now faces left and the word LIBERTY is placed on the coronet.

**VF-20 VERY FINE**—*Hairlines above coronet partly worn. Curls under ear worn but defined.*

**EF-40 EXTREMELY FINE**—*Small amount of wear on top of hair and below L in LIBERTY. Wear evident on wing tips and neck of eagle.*

**AU-50 ABOUT UNCIRCULATED**—*Trace of wear on tip of coronet and hair above eye.*

**MS-60 UNCIRCULATED**—*No trace of wear. Light blemishes.*

Mint mark location on reverse below eagle

| | *Quan. Minted* | *VF-20* | *EF-40* | *AU-50* | *MS-60* |
|---|---|---|---|---|---|
| 1838 | 7,200 | $300.00 | $600.00 | $1,000 | $4,000 |
| 1839 Large letters | 25,801 | 225.00 | 400.00 | 750.00 | 2,500 |
| 1839 Small letters | 12,447 | 275.00 | 500.00 | 1,000 | 3,000 |
| 1840 | 47,338 | 200.00 | 225.00 | 350.00 | 1,700 |
| 1841 | 63,131 | 200.00 | 225.00 | 350.00 | 1,500 |
| 1841O | 2,500 | 250.00 | 550.00 | 700.00 | 3,000 |
| 1842 | 81,507 | 200.00 | 225.00 | 325.00 | 1,100 |
| 1842O | 27,400 | 200.00 | 225.00 | 350.00 | 1,900 |
| 1843 | 75,462 | 200.00 | 225.00 | 325.00 | 1,100 |
| 1843O | 175,162 | 200.00 | 225.00 | 300.00 | 1,200 |
| 1844 | 6,361 | 225.00 | 400.00 | 550.00 | 2,000 |
| 1844O | 118,700 | 200.00 | 225.00 | 300.00 | 1,200 |
| 1845 | 26,153 | 200.00 | 225.00 | 325.00 | 1,400 |
| 1845O | 47,500 | 200.00 | 225.00 | 300.00 | 1,200 |
| 1846 | 20,095 | 200.00 | 225.00 | 325.00 | 1,500 |
| 1846O | 81,780 | 200.00 | 225.00 | 300.00 | 1,200 |
| 1847 | 862,258 | 180.00 | 200.00 | 280.00 | 750.00 |
| 1847O | 571,500 | 180.00 | 200.00 | 280.00 | 750.00 |
| 1848 | 145,484 | 180.00 | 200.00 | 280.00 | 750.00 |
| 1848O | 35,850 | 200.00 | 225.00 | 300.00 | 1,200 |
| 1849 | 653,618 | 180.00 | 200.00 | 280.00 | 750.00 |
| 1849O | 23,900 | 200.00 | 225.00 | 300.00 | 1,200 |
| 1850 | 291,451 | 180.00 | 200.00 | 280.00 | 750.00 |
| 1850O | 57,500 | 190.00 | 210.00 | 290.00 | 1,100 |

# EAGLES

| | Quan. Minted | VF-20 | EF-40 | AU-50 | MS-60 | Proof-60 |
|---|---|---|---|---|---|---|
| 1851 | 176,328 | $180.00 | $200.00 | $280.00 | $750.00 | |
| 1851O | 263,000 | 180.00 | 200.00 | 280.00 | 750.00 | |
| 1852 | 263,106 | 180.00 | 200.00 | 280.00 | 750.00 | |
| 1852O | 18,000 | 220.00 | 250.00 | 350.00 | 1,400 | |
| 1853, 3 over 2 | 201,253 | 225.00 | 400.00 | | | |
| 1853 | | 180.00 | 200.00 | 280.00 | 750.00 | |
| 1853O | 51,000 | 180.00 | 200.00 | 280.00 | 1,000 | |
| 1854 | 54,250 | 180.00 | 200.00 | 280.00 | 850.00 | |
| 1854O | 52,500 | 180.00 | 200.00 | 280.00 | 1,000 | |
| 1854S | 123,826 | 180.00 | 200.00 | 280.00 | 750.00 | |
| 1855 | 121,701 | 180.00 | 200.00 | 280.00 | 750.00 | — |
| 1855O | 18,000 | 220.00 | 250.00 | 350.00 | 1,400 | |
| 1855S | 9,000 | 250.00 | 400.00 | 600.00 | 2,500 | — |
| 1856 | 60,490 | 180.00 | 200.00 | 280.00 | 750.00 | |
| 1856O | 14,500 | 200.00 | 250.00 | 300.00 | 1,400 | |
| 1856S | 68,000 | 180.00 | 200.00 | 280.00 | 750.00 | |
| 1857 | 16,606 | 180.00 | 200.00 | 280.00 | 1,000 | — |
| 1857O | 5,500 | 300.00 | 600.00 | 800.00 | 2,500 | |
| 1857S | 26,000 | 180.00 | 200.00 | 280.00 | 875.00 | |
| 1858 | 2,521 | 2,000 | 3,000 | 4,500 | 12,000 | — |
| 1858O | 20,000 | 190.00 | 210.00 | 290.00 | 1,400 | |
| 1858S | 11,800 | 200.00 | 250.00 | 350.00 | 1,600 | |
| 1859 (80) | 16,093 | 180.00 | 200.00 | 280.00 | 1,300 | $4,000 |
| 1859O | 2,300 | 550.00 | 900.00 | 1,500 | 3,000 | |
| 1859S | 7,000 | 300.00 | 550.00 | 700.00 | 2,000 | |
| 1860 (50) | 15,105 | 180.00 | 200.00 | 280.00 | 1,300 | 4,000 |
| 1860O | 11,100 | 200.00 | 250.00 | 300.00 | 1,500 | |
| 1860S | 5,000 | 300.00 | 600.00 | 750.00 | 2,500 | |
| 1861 (69) | 113,233 | 180.00 | 200.00 | 280.00 | 1,000 | 4,000 |
| 1861S | 15,500 | 180.00 | 215.00 | 300.00 | 1,000 | |
| 1862 (35) | 10,995 | 190.00 | 210.00 | 290.00 | 1,200 | 4,000 |
| 1862S | 12,500 | 190.00 | 210.00 | 290.00 | 1,000 | |
| 1863 (30) | 1,248 | 1,000 | 2,200 | 2,800 | 3,500 | 7,500 |
| 1863S | 10,000 | 275.00 | 400.00 | 550.00 | 1,400 | |
| 1864 (50) | 3,580 | 400.00 | 650.00 | 850.00 | 2,000 | 6,000 |
| 1864S | 2,500 | 900.00 | 1,600 | | | |
| 1865 (25) | 4,005 | 340.00 | 550.00 | 675.00 | 2,000 | 5,000 |
| 1865S | 16,700 | 340.00 | 550.00 | 675.00 | 2,000 | |
| 1866S | 8,500 | 400.00 | 750.00 | 1,100 | 2,400 | |

## Motto Above Eagle 1866-1907

**Mint mark location on the reverse below eagle.**

*Values of common gold coins are based on the prevailing price of gold bullion, and will vary according to current market price. See Bullion Chart.*

# EAGLES

**VF-20 VERY FINE**—*Half of hairlines over coronet visible. Curls under ear worn but defined. IN GOD WE TRUST and its ribbon are sharp.*

**EF-40 EXTREMELY FINE**—*Small amount of wear on top of hair and below L in LIBERTY. Wear evident on wing tips and neck of eagle.*

**AU-50 ABOUT UNCIRCULATED**—*Trace of wear on hair above eye and on coronet.*

**MS-60 UNCIRCULATED**—*No trace of wear. Light blemishes.*

| | | *Quan. Minted* | *VF-20* | *EF-40* | *AU-50* | *MS-60* | *Proof-63* |
|---|---|---|---|---|---|---|---|
| 1866 | (30) | 3,780 | $225.00 | $275.00 | $450.00 | $1,000 | $7,500 |
| 1866S | | 11,500 | 200.00 | 250.00 | 300.00 | 700.00 | |
| 1867 | (50) | 3,140 | 225.00 | 275.00 | 450.00 | 1,000 | 6,000 |
| 1867S | | 9,000 | 200.00 | 250.00 | 300.00 | 700.00 | |
| 1868 | (25) | 10,655 | 200.00 | 250.00 | 300.00 | 600.00 | 6,000 |
| 1868S | | 13,500 | 200.00 | 250.00 | 300.00 | 600.00 | |
| 1869 | (25) | 1,855 | 300.00 | 500.00 | 800.00 | 1,200 | 6,000 |
| 1869S | | 6,430 | 200.00 | 250.00 | 300.00 | 700.00 | |
| 1870 | (35) | 4,025 | 225.00 | 300.00 | 450.00 | 750.00 | 6,000 |
| 1870CC | | 5,908 | 500.00 | 1,200 | 2,200 | | |
| 1870S | | 8,000 | 200.00 | 250.00 | 300.00 | 700.00 | |
| 1871 | (30) | 1,820 | 300.00 | 500.00 | 800.00 | 2,000 | 6,000 |
| 1871CC | | 8,085 | 300.00 | 500.00 | 800.00 | | |
| 1871S | | 16,500 | 200.00 | 250.00 | 300.00 | 600.00 | |
| 1872 | (30) | 1,650 | 400.00 | 700.00 | 1,100 | 1,800 | 6,000 |
| 1872CC | | 4,600 | 275.00 | 475.00 | 600.00 | 1,800 | |
| 1872S | | 17,300 | 200.00 | 250.00 | 300.00 | 550.00 | |
| 1873 | (25) | 825 | 650.00 | 1,200 | 2,000 | 4,000 | 13,000 |
| 1873CC | | 4,543 | 425.00 | 800.00 | 1,500 | 3,000 | |
| 1873S | | 12,000 | 200.00 | 250.00 | 300.00 | 550.00 | |
| 1874 | (20) | 53,160 | 150.00 | 150.00 | 175.00 | 200.00 | 6,500 |
| 1874CC | | 16,767 | 200.00 | 225.00 | 250.00 | 700.00 | |
| 1874S | | 10,000 | 200.00 | 225.00 | 250.00 | 550.00 | |
| 1875 | (20) | 120 | | — | — | | — |
| 1875CC | | 7,715 | 250.00 | 275.00 | 550.00 | 1,200 | |
| 1876 | (45) | 732 | 500.00 | 1,100 | 1,800 | 4,000 | 8,000 |
| 1876CC | | 4,696 | 300.00 | 600.00 | 725.00 | 1,600 | |
| 1876S | | 5,000 | 200.00 | 250.00 | 425.00 | 900.00 | |
| 1877 | (20) | 817 | 600.00 | 1,100 | 1,800 | 4,500 | 10,000 |
| 1877CC | | 3,332 | 300.00 | 550.00 | 800.00 | 2,000 | |
| 1877S | | 17,000 | 190.00 | 200.00 | 215.00 | 315.00 | |
| 1878 | (20) | 73,800 | 150.00 | 150.00 | 175.00 | 200.00 | 5,000 |
| 1878CC | | 3,244 | 300.00 | 550.00 | 1,000 | 2,000 | |
| 1878S | | 26,100 | 150.00 | 150.00 | 175.00 | 200.00 | |
| 1879 | (30) | 384,770 | 150.00 | 150.00 | 175.00 | 200.00 | 4,000 |
| 1879CC | | 1,762 | 1,100 | 2,500 | 3,500 | 6,000 | |
| 1879O | | 1,500 | 500.00 | 900.00 | 1,500 | 4,000 | |
| 1879S | | 224,000 | 150.00 | 150.00 | 175.00 | 200.00 | |
| 1880 | | 1,644,876 | 150.00 | 150.00 | 115.00 | 200.00 | 4,000 |
| 1880CC | | 11,190 | 175.00 | 225.00 | 275.00 | 5,000 | |
| 1880O | | 9,200 | 175.00 | 225.00 | 225.00 | 400.00 | |
| 1880S | | 506,250 | 150.00 | 150.00 | 175.00 | 200.00 | |
| 1881 | (40) | 3,877,260 | 150.00 | 150.00 | 175.00 | 200.00 | 4,000 |
| 1881CC | | 24,015 | 175.00 | 225.00 | 275.00 | 375.00 | |
| 1881O | | 8,350 | 200.00 | 250.00 | 300.00 | 550.00 | |
| 1881S | | 970,000 | 150.00 | 150.00 | 175.00 | 200.00 | |
| 1882 | (40) | 2,324,480 | 150.00 | 150.00 | 175.00 | 200.00 | 4,000 |
| 1882CC | | 6,764 | 200.00 | 250.00 | 300.00 | 600.00 | |
| 1882O | | 10,820 | 175.00 | 225.00 | 250.00 | 350.00 | |

*Values of common gold coins are based on the prevailing price of gold bullion, and will vary according to current market price. See Bullion Chart.*

# EAGLES

| | | Quan. Minted | VF-20 | EF-40 | AU-50 | MS-60 | Proof-63 |
|---|---|---|---|---|---|---|---|
| 1882S | | 132,000 | $150.00 | $150.00 | $175.00 | $200.00 | |
| 1883 | (40) | 208,740 | 150.00 | 150.00 | 175.00 | 200.00 | $4,000 |
| 1883CC | | 12,000 | 200.00 | 250.00 | 300.00 | 600.00 | |
| 1883O | | 800 | 800.00 | 1,800 | 2,500 | 5,000 | |
| 1883S | | 38,000 | 150.00 | 150.00 | 175.00 | 200.00 | |
| 1884 | (15) | 76,905 | 150.00 | 150.00 | 175.00 | 200.00 | 8,000 |
| 1884CC | | 9,925 | 200.00 | 250.00 | 300.00 | 600.00 | |
| 1884S | | 124,250 | 150.00 | 150.00 | 175.00 | 200.00 | |
| 1885 | (65) | 253,527 | 150.00 | 150.00 | 175.00 | 200.00 | 4,000 |
| 1885S | | 228,000 | 150.00 | 150.00 | 175.00 | 200.00 | |
| 1886 | (60) | 236,160 | 150.00 | 150.00 | 175.00 | 200.00 | 4,000 |
| 1886S | | 826,000 | 150.00 | 150.00 | 175.00 | 200.00 | |
| 1887 | (80) | 53,680 | 150.00 | 150.00 | 175.00 | 200.00 | 4,000 |
| 1887S | | 817,000 | 150.00 | 150.00 | 175.00 | 200.00 | |
| 1888 | (75) | 132,996 | 150.00 | 150.00 | 175.00 | 200.00 | 4,000 |
| 1888O | | 21,335 | 150.00 | 150.00 | 175.00 | 250.00 | |
| 1888S | | 648,700 | 150.00 | 150.00 | 175.00 | 200.00 | |
| 1889 | (45) | 4,485 | 200.00 | 250.00 | 300.00 | 550.00 | 4,000 |
| 1889S | | 425,400 | 150.00 | 150.00 | 175.00 | 200.00 | |
| 1890 | (63) | 58,043 | 150.00 | 150.00 | 175.00 | 375.00 | 4,000 |
| 1890CC | | 17,500 | 150.00 | 150.00 | 175.00 | 250.00 | |
| 1891 | (48) | 91,868 | 150.00 | 150.00 | 175.00 | 200.00 | 4,000 |
| 1891CC | | 103,732 | 150.00 | 150.00 | 175.00 | 250.00 | |
| 1892 | (72) | 797,552 | 150.00 | 150.00 | 175.00 | 200.00 | 4,000 |
| 1892CC | | 40,000 | 150.00 | 150.00 | 240.00 | 400.00 | |
| 1892O | | 28,688 | 150.00 | 150.00 | 175.00 | 225.00 | |
| 1892S | | 115,500 | 150.00 | 150.00 | 175.00 | 200.00 | |
| 1893 | (55) | 1,840,895 | 150.00 | 150.00 | 175.00 | 200.00 | 3,500 |
| 1893CC | | 14,000 | 200.00 | 250.00 | 300.00 | 450.00 | |
| 1893O | | 17,000 | 150.00 | 150.00 | 250.00 | 350.00 | |
| 1893S | | 141,350 | 150.00 | 150.00 | 175.00 | 200.00 | |
| 1894 | (43) | 2,470,778 | 150.00 | 150.00 | 175.00 | 200.00 | 3,500 |
| 1894O | | 107,500 | 150.00 | 150.00 | 175.00 | 200.00 | |
| 1894S | | 25,000 | 150.00 | 150.00 | 175.00 | 200.00 | |
| 1895 | (56) | 567,826 | 150.00 | 150.00 | 175.00 | 200.00 | 3,500 |
| 1895O | | 98,000 | 150.00 | 150.00 | 175.00 | 200.00 | |
| 1895S | | 49,000 | 150.00 | 150.00 | 175.00 | 200.00 | |
| 1896 | (78) | 76,348 | 150.00 | 150.00 | 175.00 | 200.00 | 3,500 |
| 1896S | | 123,750 | 150.00 | 150.00 | 175.00 | 200.00 | |
| 1897 | (69) | 1,000,159 | 150.00 | 150.00 | 175.00 | 200.00 | 3,500 |
| 1897O | | 42,500 | 150.00 | 150.00 | 175.00 | 200.00 | |
| 1897S | | 234,750 | 150.00 | 150.00 | 175.00 | 200.00 | |
| 1898 | (67) | 812,197 | 150.00 | 150.00 | 175.00 | 200.00 | 3,500 |
| 1898S | | 473,600 | 150.00 | 150.00 | 175.00 | 200.00 | |
| 1899 | (86) | 1,262,305 | 150.00 | 150.00 | 175.00 | 200.00 | 3,000 |
| 1899O | | 37,047 | 150.00 | 150.00 | 175.00 | 200.00 | |
| 1899S | | 841,000 | 150.00 | 150.00 | 175.00 | 200.00 | |
| 1900 | (120) | 293,960 | 150.00 | 150.00 | 175.00 | 200.00 | 3,000 |
| 1900S | | 81,000 | 150.00 | 150.00 | 175.00 | 200.00 | |
| 1901 | (85) | 1,718,825 | 150.00 | 150.00 | 175.00 | 200.00 | 3,000 |
| 1901O | | 72,041 | 150.00 | 150.00 | 175.00 | 200.00 | |
| 1901S | | 2,812,750 | 150.00 | 150.00 | 175.00 | 200.00 | |
| 1902 | (113) | 82,513 | 150.00 | 150.00 | 175.00 | 200.00 | 3,000 |
| 1902S | | 469,500 | 150.00 | 150.00 | 175.00 | 200.00 | |

*Values of common gold coins are vased on the prevailing price of gold bullion, and will vary according to current market price. See Bullion Chart.*

# EAGLES

| | Quan. Minted | VF-20 | EF-40 | AU-50 | MS-60 | Proof-63 |
|---|---|---|---|---|---|---|
| 1903 . . . . . . . . . (96) | 125,926 | $150.00 | $150.00 | $175.00 | $200.00 | $3,000 |
| 1903O | 112,771 | 150.00 | 150.00 | 175.00 | 200.00 | |
| 1903S | 538,000 | 150.00 | 150.00 | 175.00 | 200.00 | |
| 1904 . . . . . . . . . (108) | 162,038 | 150.00 | 150.00 | 175.00 | 200.00 | 3,000 |
| 1904O | 108,950 | 150.00 | 150.00 | 175.00 | 200.00 | |
| 1905 . . . . . . . . . (86) | 201,078 | 150.00 | 150.00 | 175.00 | 200.00 | 3,000 |
| 1905S | 369,250 | 150.00 | 150.00 | 175.00 | 200.00 | |
| 1906 . . . . . . . . . (77) | 165,497 | 150.00 | 150.00 | 175.00 | 200.00 | 3,000 |
| 1906D | 981,000 | 150.00 | 150.00 | 175.00 | 200.00 | |
| 1906O | 86,895 | 150.00 | 150.00 | 175.00 | 200.00 | |
| 1906S | 457,000 | 150.00 | 150.00 | 175.00 | 200.00 | |
| 1907 . . . . . . . . . (74) | 1,203,973 | 150.00 | 150.00 | 175.00 | 200.00 | 3,000 |
| 1907D | 1,030,000 | 150.00 | 150.00 | 175.00 | 200.00 | |
| 1907S | 210,500 | 150.00 | 150.00 | 175.00 | 200.00 | |

## INDIAN HEAD TYPE 1907-1933

### No Motto on Reverse 1907-1908

With Motto
IN GOD WE TRUST

**Mint mark location is on the reverse at left of fasces**

**VF-20 VERY FINE**—*Bonnet feathers worn near band. Hair high points show wear.*
**EF-40 EXTREMELY FINE**—*Slight wear on cheekbone and headdress feathers. Eagle's eye and left wing will show slight wear.*
**AU-50 ABOUT UNCIRCULATED**—*Trace of wear on hair above eye and on forehead.*
**MS-60 UNCIRCULATED**—*No trace of wear. Light blemishes.*

*Choice uncirculated (MS-65) coins are worth substantial premiums.*

| | Quan. Minted | VF-20 | EF-40 | AU-50 | MS-60 | Proof-63 |
|---|---|---|---|---|---|---|
| 1907 Rounded edge, periods before and after •E•PLURIBUS•UNUM• | 42 | | | | | $20,000 |
| 1907 "Wire edge" (rim), periods | 500 | | | $2,000 | $5,500 | 7,500 |
| 1907 No periods | 239,406 | $200.00 | $250.00 | 300.00 | 375.00 | |
| 1908 No motto | 33,500 | 200.00 | 275.00 | 325.00 | 750.00 | |
| 1908D No motto | 210,000 | 200.00 | 225.00 | 250.00 | 500.00 | |

### Motto on Reverse 1908-1933

| | | | | | | Matte Proof-63 |
|---|---|---|---|---|---|---|
| 1908 . . . . . . . . . (116) | 341,486 | 200.00 | 225.00 | 250.00 | 300.00 | 5,500 |
| 1908D | 836,500 | 200.00 | 225.00 | 250.00 | 400.00 | |
| 1908S | 59,850 | 200.00 | 225.00 | 350.00 | 1,500 | |
| 1909 . . . . . . . . . (74) | 184,863 | 200.00 | 225.00 | 250.00 | 300.00 | 5,500 |
| 1909D | 121,540 | 200.00 | 225.00 | 250.00 | 350.00 | |

*Values of common gold coins are based on the prevailing price of gold bullion, and will vary according to current market price. See Bullion Chart.*

# EAGLES

| | | Quan. Minted | VF-20 | EF-40 | AU-50 | MS-60 | Matte Proof-63 |
|---|---|---|---|---|---|---|---|
| 1909S | | 292,350 | $200.00 | $225.00 | $250.00 | $700.00 | |
| 1910 | (204) | 318,704 | 200.00 | 225.00 | 250.00 | 300.00 | $5,500 |
| 1910D | | 2,356,640 | 200.00 | 225.00 | 250.00 | 300.00 | |
| 1910S | | 811,000 | 200.00 | 225.00 | 250.00 | 700.00 | |
| 1911 | (95) | 505,595 | 200.00 | 225.00 | 250.00 | 300.00 | 5,500 |
| 1911D | | 30,100 | 225.00 | 300.00 | 400.00 | 2,000 | |
| 1911S | | 51,000 | 200.00 | 225.00 | 275.00 | 1,200 | |
| 1912 | (83) | 405,083 | 200.00 | 225.00 | 250.00 | 300.00 | 5,500 |
| 1912S | | 300,000 | 200.00 | 225.00 | 250.00 | 950.00 | |
| 1913 | (71) | 442,071 | 200.00 | 225.00 | 250.00 | 300.00 | 5,500 |
| 1913S | | 66,000 | 225.00 | 275.00 | 375.00 | 6,500 | |
| 1914 | (50) | 151,050 | 200.00 | 225.00 | 250.00 | 300.00 | 5,500 |
| 1914D | | 343,500 | 200.00 | 225.00 | 250.00 | 300.00 | |
| 1914S | | 208,000 | 200.00 | 225.00 | 250.00 | 850.00 | |
| 1915 | (75) | 351,075 | 200.00 | 225.00 | 250.00 | 300.00 | 5,500 |
| 1915S | | 59,000 | 200.00 | 225.00 | 275.00 | 1,200 | |
| 1916S | | 138,500 | 200.00 | 225.00 | 250.00 | 800.00 | |
| 1920S | | 126,500 | 2,200 | 3,500 | 6,000 | 15,000 | |
| 1926 | | 1,014,000 | 200.00 | 225.00 | 250.00 | 300.00 | |
| 1930S | | 96,000 | 1,300 | 1,800 | 2,700 | 6,000 | |
| 1932 | | 4,463,000 | 200.00 | 225.00 | 250.00 | 300.00 | |
| 1933 | | 312,500 | | | | | — |

## DOUBLE EAGLES ($20.00 Gold Pieces) — 1849-1933

This largest denomination of all regular United States issues was authorized to be coined by the Act of March 3, 1849. Its weight was 516 grains, .900 fine.

**Mint mark location is below the eagle**

**VF-20 VERY FINE**—*LIBERTY is bold. Jewels on crown defined. Lower half worn flat. Hair worn about ear.*
**EF-40 EXTREMELY FINE**—*Trace of wear on rounded prongs of crown and down hair curls. Minor bag marks.*
**AU-50 ABOUT UNCIRCULATED**—*Trace of wear on hair over eye and on coronet.*
**MS-60 UNCIRCULATED**—*No trace of wear. Light blemishes.*

### Without Motto on Reverse 1849-1866

| | Quan. Minted | VF-20 | EF-40 | AU-50 | MS-60 | Proof-63 |
|---|---|---|---|---|---|---|
| 1850 | 1,170,261 | $325.00 | $350.00 | $375.00 | $1,200 | |
| 1850O | 141,000 | 325.00 | 375.00 | 450.00 | 1,500 | |
| 1851 | 2,087,155 | 325.00 | 350.00 | 375.00 | 900.00 | |
| 1851O | 315,000 | 325.00 | 375.00 | 450.00 | 1,500 | |
| 1852 | 2,053,026 | 325.00 | 350.00 | 375.00 | 900.00 | |
| 1852O | 190,000 | 325.00 | 375.00 | 450.00 | 1,500 | |

*Values of common gold coins are based on the prevailing price of gold bullion, and will vary according to current market price. See Bullion Chart.*

# DOUBLE EAGLES

| | | Quan. Minted | VF-20 | EF-40 | AU-50 | MS-60 | Proof-63 |
|---|---|---|---|---|---|---|---|
| 1853 | | 1,261,326 | $325.00 | $350.00 | $375.00 | $900.00 | |
| 1853O | | 71,000 | 325.00 | 375.00 | 450.00 | 1,500 | |
| 1854 | | 757,899 | 325.00 | 350.00 | 375.00 | 900.00 | |
| 1854O | | 3,250 | | | 20,000 | | |
| 1854S | | 141,468 | 325.00 | 350.00 | 375.00 | 1,900 | |
| 1855 | | 364,666 | 325.00 | 350.00 | 375.00 | 750.00 | |
| 1855O | | 8,000 | 600.00 | 900.00 | 1,500 | 4,000 | |
| 1855S | | 879,675 | 325.00 | 350.00 | 375.00 | 750.00 | |
| 1856 | | 329,878 | 325.00 | 350.00 | 375.00 | 750.00 | |
| 1856O | | 2,250 | 10,000 | 15,000 | 20,000 | | |
| 1856S | | 1,189,750 | 325.00 | 350.00 | 375.00 | 750.00 | |
| 1857 | | 439,375 | 325.00 | 350.00 | 375.00 | 750.00 | |
| 1857O | | 30,000 | 325.00 | 375.00 | 450.00 | 1,500 | |
| 1857S | | 970,500 | 325.00 | 350.00 | 375.00 | 750.00 | |
| 1858 | | 211,714 | 325.00 | 350.00 | 375.00 | 750.00 | |
| 1858O | | 35,250 | 325.00 | 400.00 | 700.00 | 2,500 | |
| 1858S | | 846,710 | 325.00 | 350.00 | 375.00 | 750.00 | |
| 1859 | (80) | 43,597 | 325.00 | 350.00 | 375.00 | 1,250 | |
| 1859O | | 9,100 | 800.00 | 1,200 | 2,000 | 3,500 | |
| 1859S | | 636,445 | 325.00 | 350.00 | 375.00 | 750.00 | |
| 1860 | (59) | 577,670 | 325.00 | 350.00 | 375.00 | 750.00 | |
| 1860O | | 6,600 | 800.00 | 1,500 | 2,000 | 3,500 | |
| 1860S | | 544,950 | 325.00 | 350.00 | 375.00 | 750.00 | |
| 1861 | (66) | 2,976,453 | 325.00 | 350.00 | 375.00 | 750.00 | |
| 1861O | | 17,741 | 500.00 | 900.00 | 1,400 | 3,000 | |
| 1861S | | 768,000 | 325.00 | 350.00 | 375.00 | 750.00 | |
| 1862 | (35) | 92,133 | 325.00 | 350.00 | 375.00 | 1,500 | $10,000 |
| 1862S | | 854,173 | 325.00 | 350.00 | 375.00 | 750.00 | |
| 1863 | (30) | 142,790 | 325.00 | 350.00 | 375.00 | 1,200 | 10,000 |
| 1863S | | 966,570 | 325.00 | 350.00 | 375.00 | 750.00 | |
| 1864 | (50) | 204,285 | 325.00 | 350.00 | 375.00 | 1,000 | 10,000 |
| 1864S | | 793,660 | 325.00 | 350.00 | 375.00 | 750.00 | |
| 1865 | (25) | 351,200 | 325.00 | 350.00 | 375.00 | 750.00 | 10,000 |
| 1865S | | 1,042,500 | 325.00 | 350.00 | 375.00 | 750.00 | |
| 1866S | | | 325.00 | 350.00 | 450.00 | 1,200 | |

## Motto Above Eagle, Value TWENTY D. 1866-1876

| | | Quan. Minted | VF-20 | EF-40 | AU-50 | MS-60 | Proof-63 |
|---|---|---|---|---|---|---|---|
| 1866 | (30) | 698,775 | 300.00 | 310.00 | 350.00 | 700.00 | 8,000 |
| 1866S | | 842,250 | 300.00 | 310.00 | 350.00 | 650.00 | |
| 1867 | (50) | 251,065 | 300.00 | 310.00 | 350.00 | 650.00 | 8,000 |
| 1867S | | 920,750 | 300.00 | 310.00 | 350.00 | 650.00 | |

*Values of common gold coins are based on the prevailing price of gold bullion, and will vary according to current market price. See Bullion Chart.*

# DOUBLE EAGLES

| | | Quan. Minted | VF-20 | EF-40 | AU-50 | MS-60 | Proof-63 |
|---|---|---|---|---|---|---|---|
| 1868 | (25) | 98,600 | $300.00 | $310.00 | $350.00 | $700.00 | $8,000 |
| 1868S | | 837,500 | 300.00 | 310.00 | 350.00 | 650.00 | |
| 1869 | (25) | 175,155 | 300.00 | 310.00 | 350.00 | 650.00 | 8,000 |
| 1869S | | 686,750 | 300.00 | 310.00 | 350.00 | 650.00 | |
| 1870 | (35) | 155,185 | 300.00 | 310.00 | 350.00 | 650.00 | 8,000 |
| 1870CC | | 3,789 | 6,000 | 12,000 | — | — | |
| 1870S | | 982,000 | 300.00 | 310.00 | 350.00 | 600.00 | |
| 1871 | (30) | 80,150 | 300.00 | 310.00 | 350.00 | 650.00 | 8,000 |
| 1871CC | | 17,387 | 750.00 | 1,200 | 1,600 | | |
| 1871S | | 928,000 | 300.00 | 310.00 | 350.00 | 550.00 | |
| 1872 | (30) | 251,880 | 300.00 | 310.00 | 350.00 | 550.00 | 8,000 |
| 1872CC | | 26,900 | 375.00 | 450.00 | 650.00 | 1,200 | |
| 1872S | | 780,000 | 300.00 | 310.00 | 350.00 | 550.00 | |
| 1873 | (25) | 1,709,825 | 300.00 | 310.00 | 350.00 | 550.00 | 8,000 |
| 1873CC | | 22,410 | 350.00 | 400.00 | 600.00 | 1,200 | |
| 1873S | | 1,040,600 | 300.00 | 310.00 | 350.00 | 550.00 | |
| 1874 | (20) | 366,800 | 300.00 | 310.00 | 350.00 | 550.00 | 8,500 |
| 1874CC | | 115,085 | 350.00 | 400.00 | 500.00 | 800.00 | |
| 1874S | | 1,214,000 | 300.00 | 310.00 | 350.00 | 550.00 | |
| 1875 | (20) | 295,740 | 300.00 | 310.00 | 350.00 | 550.00 | — |
| 1875CC | | 111,151 | 300.00 | 350.00 | 400.00 | 650.00 | |
| 1875S | | 1,230,000 | 300.00 | 310.00 | 350.00 | 550.00 | |
| 1876 | (45) | 583,905 | 300.00 | 310.00 | 350.00 | 550.00 | 8,000 |
| 1876CC | | 138,441 | 300.00 | 350.00 | 400.00 | 600.00 | |
| 1876S | | 1,597,000 | 300.00 | 310.00 | 350.00 | 550.00 | |

## TWENTY DOLLARS 1877-1907

| | | Quan. Minted | VF-20 | EF-40 | AU-50 | MS-60 | Proof-63 |
|---|---|---|---|---|---|---|---|
| 1877 | (20) | 397,670 | 300.00 | 300.00 | 325.00 | 350.00 | 8,000 |
| 1877CC | | 42,565 | 400.00 | 475.00 | 500.00 | 650.00 | |
| 1877S | | 1,735,000 | 300.00 | 300.00 | 325.00 | 350.00 | |
| 1878 | (20) | 543,645 | 300.00 | 300.00 | 325.00 | 350.00 | 8,000 |
| 1878CC | | 13,180 | 400.00 | 475.00 | 550.00 | 1,000 | |
| 1878S | | 1,739,000 | 300.00 | 300.00 | 325.00 | 350.00 | |
| 1879 | (30) | 207,630 | 300.00 | 300.00 | 325.00 | 350.00 | 8,000 |
| 1879CC | | 10,708 | 500.00 | 600.00 | 750.00 | 1,700 | |
| 1879O | | 2,325 | 1,000 | 1,400 | 2,200 | 4,500 | |
| 1879S | | 1,223,800 | 300.00 | 300.00 | 325.00 | 350.00 | |
| 1880 | (36) | 51,456 | 300.00 | 300.00 | 325.00 | 400.00 | 8,000 |
| 1880S | | 836,000 | 300.00 | 300.00 | 325.00 | 350.00 | |
| 1881 | (61) | 2,260 | 1,000 | 2,000 | 3,000 | 4,500 | 12,500 |
| 1881S | | 727,000 | 300.00 | 300.00 | 325.00 | 350.00 | |

*Values of common gold coins are based on the prevailing price of gold bullion and will vary according to current market price. See Bullion Chart.*

# DOUBLE EAGLES

| | Quan. Minted | VF-20 | EF-40 | AU-50 | MS-60 | Proof-63 |
|---|---|---|---|---|---|---|
| 1882 (59) | 630 | $1,500 | $3,500 | $6,000 | $11,000 | —— |
| 1882CC | 39,140 | 350.00 | 400.00 | 450.00 | 700.00 | |
| 1882S | 1,125,000 | 300.00 | 300.00 | 325.00 | 350.00 | |
| 1883 Proofs only (92) | 92 | | | | | —— |
| 1883CC | 59,962 | 350.00 | 400.00 | 500.00 | 650.00 | |
| 1883S | 1,189,000 | 300.00 | 300.00 | 325.00 | 350.00 | |
| 1884 Proofs only (71) | 71 | | | | | —— |
| 1884CC | 81,139 | 350.00 | 400.00 | 500.00 | 650.00 | |
| 1884S | 916,000 | 300.00 | 300.00 | 325.00 | 350.00 | |
| 1885 (77) | 828 | 1,200 | 3,000 | 6,000 | 10,000 | —— |
| 1885CC | 9,450 | 400.00 | 500.00 | 650.00 | 1,000 | |
| 1885S | 683,500 | 300.00 | 300.00 | 325.00 | 350.00 | |
| 1886 (106) | 1,106 | 1,500 | 3,500 | 7,000 | 10,000 | $20,000 |
| 1887 Proofs only (121) | 121 | | | | | 25,000 |
| 1887S | 283,000 | 300.00 | 300.00 | 325.00 | 350.00 | |
| 1888 (105) | 226,266 | 300.00 | 300.00 | 325.00 | 350.00 | 7,000 |
| 1888S | 859,600 | 300.00 | 300.00 | 325.00 | 350.00 | |
| 1889 (41) | 44,111 | 300.00 | 300.00 | 325.00 | 350.00 | 7,000 |
| 1889CC | 30,945 | 325.00 | 350.00 | 400.00 | 750.00 | |
| 1889S | 774,700 | 300.00 | 300.00 | 325.00 | 350.00 | |
| 1890 (55) | 75,995 | 300.00 | 300.00 | 325.00 | 350.00 | 7,000 |
| 1890CC | 91,209 | 325.00 | 350.00 | 375.00 | 650.00 | |
| 1890S | 802,750 | 300.00 | 300.00 | 325.00 | 350.00 | |
| 1891 (52) | 1,442 | 500.00 | 1,000 | 1,800 | 3,000 | 8,500 |
| 1891CC | 5,000 | 500.00 | 800.00 | 1,200 | 2,000 | |
| 1891S | 1,288,125 | 300.00 | 300.00 | 325.00 | 350.00 | |
| 1892 (93) | 4,523 | 500.00 | 650.00 | 900.00 | 2,300 | 8,000 |
| 1892CC | 27,265 | 350.00 | 400.00 | 550.00 | 1,000 | |
| 1892S | 930,150 | 300.00 | 300.00 | 325.00 | 350.00 | |
| 1893 (59) | 344,339 | 300.00 | 300.00 | 325.00 | 350.00 | 5,000 |
| 1893CC | 18,402 | 400.00 | 475.00 | 650.00 | 1,200 | |
| 1893S | 996,175 | 300.00 | 300.00 | 325.00 | 350.00 | |
| 1894 (50) | 1,368,990 | 300.00 | 300.00 | 325.00 | 350.00 | 5,000 |
| 1894S | 1,048,550 | 300.00 | 300.00 | 325.00 | 350.00 | |
| 1895 (51) | 1,114,656 | 300.00 | 300.00 | 325.00 | 350.00 | 5,000 |
| 1895S | 1,143,500 | 300.00 | 300.00 | 325.00 | 350.00 | |
| 1896 (128) | 792,663 | 300.00 | 300.00 | 325.00 | 350.00 | 5,000 |
| 1896S | 1,403,925 | 300.00 | 300.00 | 325.00 | 350.00 | |
| 1897 (86) | 1,383,261 | 300.00 | 300.00 | 325.00 | 350.00 | 5,000 |
| 1897S | 1,470,250 | 300.00 | 300.00 | 325.00 | 350.00 | |
| 1898 (75) | 170,470 | 300.00 | 300.00 | 325.00 | 350.00 | 5,000 |
| 1898S | 2,575,175 | 300.00 | 300.00 | 325.00 | 350.00 | |
| 1899 (84) | 1,669,384 | 300.00 | 300.00 | 325.00 | 350.00 | 5,000 |
| 1899S | 2,010,300 | 300.00 | 300.00 | 325.00 | 350.00 | |
| 1900 (124) | 1,874,584 | 300.00 | 300.00 | 325.00 | 350.00 | 5,000 |
| 1900S | 2,459,500 | 300.00 | 300.00 | 325.00 | 350.00 | |
| 1901 (96) | 111,526 | 300.00 | 300.00 | 325.00 | 350.00 | 5,000 |
| 1901S | 1,596,000 | 300.00 | 300.00 | 325.00 | 350.00 | |
| 1902 (114) | 31,254 | 300.00 | 300.00 | 325.00 | 350.00 | 5,000 |
| 1902S | 1,753,625 | 300.00 | 300.00 | 325.00 | 350.00 | |
| 1903 (158) | 287,428 | 300.00 | 300.00 | 325.00 | 350.00 | 5,000 |
| 1903S | 954,000 | 300.00 | 300.00 | 325.00 | 350.00 | |
| 1904 (98) | 6,256,797 | 300.00 | 300.00 | 325.00 | 350.00 | 5,000 |
| 1904S | 5,134,175 | 300.00 | 300.00 | 325.00 | 350.00 | |

*Values of common gold coins are based on the prevailing price of gold bullion, and will vary according to current market price. See Bullion Chart.*

# DOUBLE EAGLES

| | Quan. Minted | VF-20 | EF-20 | AU-50 | MS-60 | Proof-63 |
|---|---|---|---|---|---|---|
| 1905 . . . (92) | 59,011 | $300.00 | $300.00 | $325.00 | $350.00 | $5,000 |
| 1905S | 1,813,000 | 300.00 | 300.00 | 325.00 | 350.00 | |
| 1906 . . . (94) | 69,690 | 300.00 | 300.00 | 325.00 | 350.00 | 5,000 |
| 1906D | 620,250 | 300.00 | 300.00 | 325.00 | 350.00 | |
| 1906S | 2,065,750 | 300.00 | 300.00 | 325.00 | 350.00 | |
| 1907 . . . (78) | 1,451,864 | 300.00 | 300.00 | 325.00 | 350.00 | 5,000 |
| 1907D | 842,250 | 300.00 | 300.00 | 325.00 | 350.00 | |
| 1907S | 2,165,800 | 300.00 | 300.00 | 325.00 | 350.00 | |

## SAINT-GAUDENS TYPE 1907-1933

This design by Augustus Saint-Gaudens is universally acclaimed as one of the most beautiful of all United States coinages.

A few experimental pieces were struck having an extremely high relief. They are easily distinguished from the ones issued later for general circulation.

The field of the rare experimental pieces is excessively concave and connects directly with the edge without any border, giving it a sharp knifelike appearance; Liberty's shows two folds on the side of her right leg; the Capitol building in the background at left is very small; the sun, on the reverse side, has 14 rays, as opposed to the regular high relief coins that have only 13 rays extending from the sun. High relief proofs are trial or experimental pieces.

11,250 high relief pieces were struck for general circulation. The relief is somewhat lower but both have the date 1907 in Roman numerals. A few of these coins were made using the lettered edge collar from the extremely high relief version. These can be distinguished by a pronounced bottom left serif on the N in UNUM, and other minor differences. Flat-relief double eagles were issued later in 1907 with Arabic numerals.

**VF-20 Very Fine**—*Minor wear on legs and toes. Eagle's left wing and breast feathers worn.*

**EF-40 EXTREMELY FINE**—*Drapery lines on chest visible. Wear on left breast, knee and below. Eagle's feathers on breast and right wing are bold.*

**MS-60 UNCIRCULATED**—*No trace of wear. Light marks or blemishes.*

| | Proof |
|---|---|
| 1907 Ex. high relief, plain edge (Unique) | — |
| 1907 Ex. high relief, lettered edge | — |

| | Quan. Minted | VF-20 | EF-40 | MS-60 | Proof |
|---|---|---|---|---|---|
| **1907 high relief, Roman numerals (MCMVII),** | **11,250** | **$1,500** | **$2,200** | **$4,000** | — |

*Values of common gold coins are based on the prevailing price of gold bullion, and will vary according to current market price. See Bullion Chart.*

# DOUBLE EAGLES

## Arabic Numerals, Without Motto

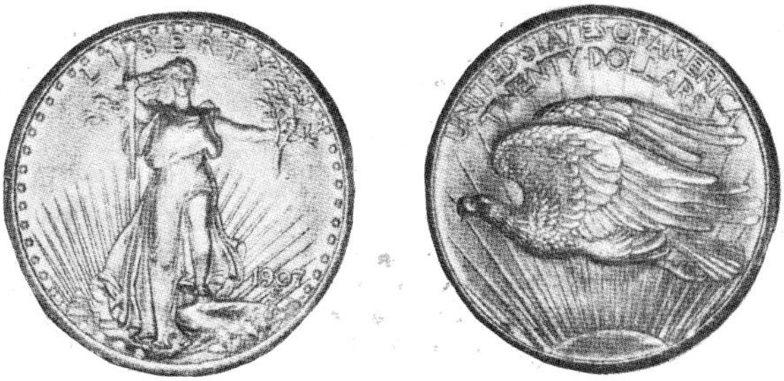


| | *Quan. Minted* | *VF-20* | *EF-40* | *MS-60* |
|---|---|---|---|---|
| 1907 | 361,667 | $325.00 | $335.00 | $375.00 |
| 1908 | 4,271,551 | 325.00 | 335.00 | 375.00 |
| 1908D | 663,750 | 325.00 | 335.00 | 375.00 |

## With Motto IN GOD WE TRUST, 1908-1933

**Mint mark location is on obverse above date.**

| | *Quan. Minted* | *VF-20* | *EF-40* | *MS-60* | *Matte Proof-63* |
|---|---|---|---|---|---|
| 1908 | (101) 156,359 | $325.00 | $335.00 | $375.00 | $9,500 |
| 1908D | 349,500 | 325.00 | 335.00 | 375.00 | |
| 1908S | 22,000 | 325.00 | 450.00 | 2,000 | |

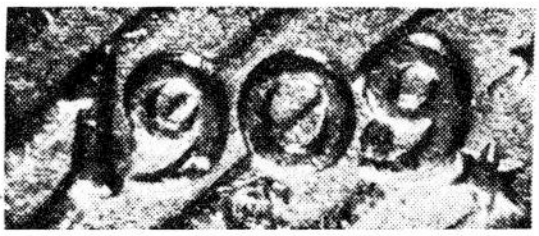

1909, 9 over 8

| | *Quan. Minted* | *VF-20* | *EF-40* | *MS-60* | *Matte Proof-63* |
|---|---|---|---|---|---|
| 1909 | } (67) 161,282 | 325.00 | 335.00 | 450.00 | 7,500 |
| 1909, 9 over 8 | } | 325.00 | 335.00 | 450.00 | |
| 1909D | 52,500 | 400.00 | 500.00 | 1,200 | |
| 1909S | 2,774,925 | 325.00 | 335.00 | 375.00 | |

*Values of common gold coins are based on the prevailing price of gold bullion, and will vary according to current market price. See Bullion Chart.*

# DOUBLE EAGLES

| | Quan. Minted | VF-20 | EF-40 | MS-60 | Matte Proof-63 |
|---|---|---|---|---|---|
| 1910 | (167) 482,167 | $325.00 | $335.00 | $375.00 | $7,500 |
| 1910D | 429,000 | 325.00 | 335.00 | 375.00 | |
| 1910S | 2,128,250 | 325.00 | 335.00 | 375.00 | |
| 1911 | (100) 197,350 | 325.00 | 335.00 | 375.00 | 7,500 |
| 1911D | 846,500 | 325.00 | 335.00 | 375.00 | |
| 1911S | 775,750 | 325.00 | 335.00 | 375.00 | |
| 1912 | (74) 149,824 | 325.00 | 335.00 | 375.00 | 7,500 |
| 1913 | (58) 168,838 | 325.00 | 335.00 | 375.00 | 7,500 |
| 1913D | 393,500 | 325.00 | 335.00 | 375.00 | |
| 1913S | 34,000 | 325.00 | 335.00 | 450.00 | |
| 1914 | (70) 95,320 | 325.00 | 335.00 | 375.00 | 7,500 |
| 1914D | 453,000 | 325.00 | 335.00 | 375.00 | |
| 1914S | 1,498,000 | 325.00 | 335.00 | 375.00 | |
| 1915 | (50) 152,050 | 325.00 | 335.00 | 375.00 | 7,500 |
| 1915S | 567,500 | 325.00 | 335.00 | 375.00 | |
| 1916S | 796,000 | 325.00 | 335.00 | 375.00 | |
| 1920 | 228,250 | 325.00 | 335.00 | 375.00 | |
| 1920S | 558,000 | 3,000 | 5,000 | 9,000 | |
| 1921 | 528,500 | 4,000 | 6,000 | 10,000 | |
| 1922 | 1,375,500 | 325.00 | 335.00 | 375.00 | |
| 1922S | 2,658,000 | 325.00 | 375.00 | 550.00 | |
| 1923 | 566,000 | 325.00 | 335.00 | 375.00 | |
| 1923D | 1,702,250 | 325.00 | 335.00 | 375.00 | |
| 1924 | 4,323,500 | 325.00 | 335.00 | 375.00 | |
| 1924D | 3,049,500 | 375.00 | 425.00 | 900.00 | |
| 1924S | 2,927,500 | 375.00 | 425.00 | 900.00 | |
| 1925 | 2,831,750 | 325.00 | 335.00 | 375.00 | |
| 1925D | 2,938,500 | 400.00 | 550.00 | 1,000 | |
| 1925S | 3,776,500 | 375.00 | 450.00 | 950.00 | |
| 1926 | 816,750 | 325.00 | 335.00 | 375.00 | |
| 1926D | 481,000 | 425.00 | 650.00 | 1,600 | |
| 1926S | 2,041,500 | 375.00 | 450.00 | 800.00 | |
| 1927 | 2,946,750 | 325.00 | 335.00 | 375.00 | |
| 1927D | 180,000 | | | — | |
| 1927S | 3,107,000 | 1,500 | 2,000 | 5,000 | |
| 1928 | 8,816,000 | 325.00 | 335.00 | 375.00 | |
| 1929 | 1,779,750 | 2,000 | 3,000 | 5,000 | |
| 1930S | 74,000 | 3,500 | 6,000 | 12,000 | |
| 1931 | 2,938,250 | 2,500 | 4,500 | 10,000 | |
| 1931D | 106,500 | 3,000 | 5,000 | 10,000 | |
| 1932 | 1,101,750 | 3,000 | 5,000 | 11,000 | |
| 1933 | 445,500 | None placed in circulation | | | |

*Values of common gold coins are based on the prevailing price of gold bullion, and will vary according to current market price. See Bullion Chart.*

# COMMEMORATIVE SILVER COINS

## Isabella, Lafayette, Alabama

In 1892, to commemorate the World's Columbian Exposition in Chicago, Congress authorized the coinage of a special half dollar and quarter dollar, thus starting a long line of United States commemorative coins. All commemorative coins have been distributed by private individuals or commissions; they paid the mint the face value of the coins and in turn sold the pieces at a premium to collectors. There are a few instances in which some of the very large issues were later released to circulation at face value.

| | | Quan. Available | AU-50 | MS-60 |
|---|---|---|---|---|
| 1893 | Isabella Quarter (Columbian Exposition) ........... | 24,214 | $125.00 | $325.00 |

| | | | | |
|---|---|---|---|---|
| 1900 | Lafayette Dollar.................................. | 36,026 | 225.00 | 500.00 |

## HALF DOLLARS
## (Listed alphabetically)

2x2 in Field

| | | | | |
|---|---|---|---|---|
| 1921 | Alabama, "2 × 2" in field.......................... | 6,006 | 80.00 | 300.00 |
| 1921 | Same, no "2 × 2" ................................ | 59,038 | 45.00 | 275.00 |

## Albany, Antietam, Arkansas

| | | Quan. Available | AU-50 | MS-60 |
|---|---|---|---|---|
| 1936 | Albany, New York | 17,671 | $110.00 | $185.00 |

| | | | | |
|---|---|---|---|---|
| 1937 | Battle of Antietam 1862-1937 | 18,028 | 125.00 | 225.00 |

| | | | | |
|---|---|---|---|---|
| 1935 | Arkansas Centennial | 13,012 | | |
| 1935D | Same | 5,505 | Set | 180.00 |
| 1935S | Same | 5,506 | | |
| 1936 | Arkansas Centennial, same as 1935 — date 1936 on reverse | 9,660 | | |
| 1936D | Same | 9,660 | Set | 180.00 |
| 1936S | Same | 9,662 | | |
| 1937 | Arkansas Centennial, same as 1935 | 5,505 | | |
| 1937D | Same | 5,505 | Set | 200.00 |
| 1937S | Same | 5,506 | | |
| 1938 | Arkansas Centennial, same as 1935 | 3,156 | | |
| 1938D | Same | 3,155 | Set | 375.00 |
| 1938S | Same | 3,156 | | |
| 1939 | Arkansas, same as 1935 | 2,104 | | |
| 1939D | Same | 2,104 | Set | 850.00 |
| 1939S | Same | 2,105 | | |
| | Single type coin | | 25.00 | 60.00 |

# COMMEMORATIVE SILVER

## Bay Bridge, Boone

| | | *Quan. Available* | | *AU-50* | *MS-60* |
|---|---|---|---|---|---|
| 1936S | San Francisco-Oakland Bay Bridge | 71,424 | | $40.00 | $80.00 |

| | | | | | |
|---|---|---|---|---|---|
| 1934 | Daniel Boone Bicentennial | 10,007 | | 35.00 | 95.00 |
| 1935 | Same | 10,010 | Set | | 900.00 |
| 1935D | Same | 5,005 | | | |
| 1935S | Same | 5,005 | | | |

| | | | | | |
|---|---|---|---|---|---|
| 1935 | Daniel Boone Bicentennial, same as 1934 but small 1934 added on reverse | 10,008 | Set | | 240.00 |
| 1935D | Same | 2,003 | | | |
| 1935S | Same | 2,004 | | | |
| 1936 | D. Boone Bicentennial, same as 1934 | 12,012 | Set | | 240.00 |
| 1936D | Same | 5,005 | | | |
| 1936S | Same | 5,006 | | | |
| 1937 | D. Boone Bicentennial, same as 1934 | 9,810 | Set | | 500.00 |
| 1937D | Same | 2,506 | | | |
| 1937S | Same | 2,506 | | | |
| 1938 | Daniel Boone, same as 1934 | 2,100 | Set | | 825.00 |
| 1938D | Same | 2,100 | | | |
| 1938S | Same | 2,100 | | | |
| | Single type coin | | | 30.00 | 80.00 |

## Bridgeport, California, Cincinnati, Cleveland

| | | Quan. Available | AU-50 | MS-60 |
|---|---|---|---|---|
| 1936 | Bridgeport, Conn., Centennial | 25,015 | $45.00 | $100.00 |

| | | | | |
|---|---|---|---|---|
| 1925S | California Diamond Jubilee | 86,594 | 40.00 | 80.00 |

| | | | | |
|---|---|---|---|---|
| 1936 | Cincinnati Music Center | 5,005 } Set | | 700.00 |
| 1936D | Same | 5,005 } Set | | |
| 1936S | Same | 5,006 } Set | | |
| | Single type coin | | 135.00 | 225.00 |

| | | | | |
|---|---|---|---|---|
| 1936 | Cleveland, Great Lakes Exposition | 50,030 | 20.00 | 50.00 |

# COMMEMORATIVE SILVER

## Columbia, S.C., Columbian, Connecticut, Delaware

| | | *Quan. Available* | | *AU-50* | *MS-60* |
|---|---|---|---|---|---|
| 1936 | Columbia, S.C., Sesquicentennial | 9,007 | Set | | $575.00 |
| 1936D | Same | 8,009 | | | |
| 1936S | Same | 8,007 | | | |
| | Single type coin | | | $100.00 | 190.00 |

| | | | | |
|---|---|---|---|---|
| 1892 | Columbian Exposition | 950,000 | 6.00 | 16.00 |
| 1893 | Same | 1,550,405 | 6.00 | 15.00 |

| | | | | |
|---|---|---|---|---|
| 1935 | Connecticut Tercentenary | 25,018 | 75.00 | 180.00 |

| | | | | |
|---|---|---|---|---|
| 1936 | Delaware Tercentenary | 20,993 | 80.00 | 150.00 |

# COMMEMORATIVE SILVER

## Elgin, Gettysburg, Grant, Hawaiian

| | | Quan. Available | AU-50 | MS-60 |
|---|---|---|---|---|
| 1936 | Elgin, Illinois, Centennial | 20,015 | $65.00 | $140.00 |

| | | | | |
|---|---|---|---|---|
| 1936 | Battle of Gettysburg 1863-1938 | 26,928 | 75.00 | 175.00 |

| | | | | |
|---|---|---|---|---|
| 1922 | Grant Memorial, small star above word "Grant" in obv. field (Fake stars have flattened spot on reverse.) | 4,256 | 225.00 | 475.00 |
| 1922 | Same, no star in obverse field | 67,405 | 27.50 | 70.00 |

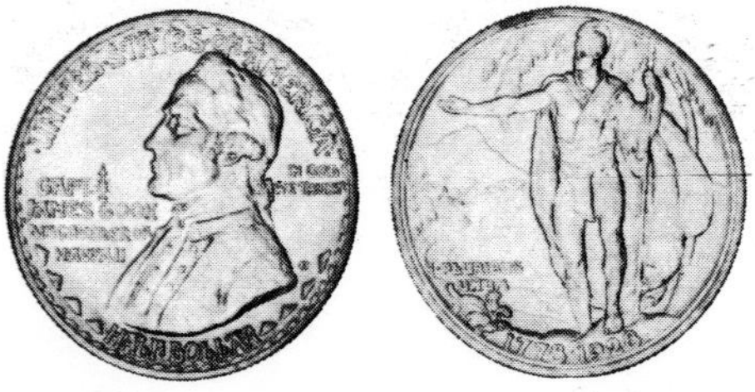


| | | | | |
|---|---|---|---|---|
| 1928 | Hawaiian Sesquicentennial | 10,008 | 375.00 | 700.00 |

# COMMEMORATIVE SILVER
## Hudson, Huguenot, Iowa, Lexington

| | | Quan. Available | AU-50 | MS-60 |
|---|---|---|---|---|
| 1935 | Hudson N. Y. Sesquicentennial | 10,008 | $250.00 | $450.00 |

| | | | | |
|---|---|---|---|---|
| 1924 | Huguenot-Walloon Tercentenary | 142,080 | 32.50 | 70.00 |

| | | | | |
|---|---|---|---|---|
| 1946 | Iowa Centennial | 100,057 | 27.50 | 65.00 |

| | | | | |
|---|---|---|---|---|
| 1925 | Lexington-Concord Sesquicentennial | 162,013 | 20.00 | 40.00 |

# COMMEMORATIVE SILVER

## Lincoln, Long Island, Lynchburg, Maine

| | | *Quan. Available* | *AU-50* | *MS-60* |
|---|---|---|---|---|
| 1918 | Illinois Centennial | 100,058 | $25.00 | $65.00 |

| | | | | |
|---|---|---|---|---|
| 1936 | Long Island Tercentenary | 81,826 | 25.00 | 47.50 |

| | | | | |
|---|---|---|---|---|
| 1936 | Lynchburg, Va., Sesquicentennial | 20,013 | 65.00 | 130.00 |

| | | | | |
|---|---|---|---|---|
| 1920 | Maine Centennial | 50,028 | 37.50 | 75.00 |

## Maryland, Missouri, Monroe, New Rochelle

| | | Quan. Available | AU-50 | MS-60 |
|---|---|---|---|---|
| 1934 | Maryland Tercentenary | 25,015 | $60.00 | $100.00 |

| | | Quan. Available | AU-50 | MS-60 |
|---|---|---|---|---|
| 1921 | Missouri Centennial "2 ★ 4" above "1821" | 5,000 | 150.00 | 400.00 |
| 1921 | Same, no "2 ★ 4" | 15,428 | 140.00 | 375.00 |

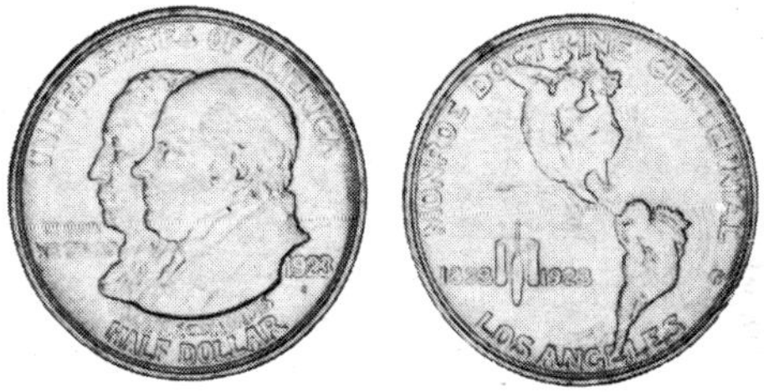


| | | Quan. Available | AU-50 | MS-60 |
|---|---|---|---|---|
| 1923S | Monroe Doctrine Centennial | 274,077 | 15.00 | 40.00 |

| | | Quan. Available | AU-50 | MS-60 |
|---|---|---|---|---|
| 1938 | New Rochelle, N. Y. 1688-1938 | 15,266 | 175.00 | 250.00 |

# COMMEMORATIVE SILVER

## Norfolk, Oregon, Panama-Pacific

| | | *Quan. Available* | *AU-50* | *MS-60* |
|---|---|---|---|---|
| 1936 | Norfolk, Va., Bicentennial | 16,936 | $150.00 | $250.00 |

| | | | | |
|---|---|---|---|---|
| 1926 | Oregon Trail Memorial | 47,955 | 40.00 | 95.00 |
| 1926S | Same | 83,055 | 40.00 | 95.00 |
| 1928 | Oregon Trail Memorial, same as 1926 | 6,028 | 60.00 | 190.00 |
| 1933D | Oregon Trail Memorial, same | 5,008 | 90.00 | 250.00 |
| 1934D | Oregon Trail Memorial, same | 7,006 | 40.00 | 150.00 |
| 1936 | Oregon Trail Memorial, same as 1926 | 10,006 | 40.00 | 100.00 |
| 1936S | Same | 5,006 | 40.00 | 150.00 |
| 1937D | Oregon Trail Mem., D mint, same as 1926 | 12,008 | 40.00 | 100.00 |
| 1938 | Oregon Trail Mem., same as 1926 | 6,006 | | |
| 1938D | Same | 6,005 (Set) | | 450.00 |
| 1938S | Same | 6,006 | | |
| 1939 | Oregon Trail, same as 1926 | 3,004 | | |
| 1939D | Same | 3,004 (Set) | | 600.00 |
| 1939S | Same | 3,005 | | |
| | Single type coin | | 40.00 | 95.00 |

| | | | | |
|---|---|---|---|---|
| 1915S | Panama-Pacific Exposition | 27,134 | 125.00 | 350.00 |

# COMMEMORATIVE SILVER

## Pilgrim, Rhode Island, Roanoke, Robinson

| | | Quan. Available | AU-50 | MS-60 |
|---|---|---|---|---|
| 1920 | Pilgrim Tercentenary | 152,112 | $25.00 | $40.00 |
| 1921 | Same, with 1921 date added in field | 20,053 | 52.00 | 140.00 |

| | | Quan. Available | AU-50 | MS-60 |
|---|---|---|---|---|
| 1936 | Rhode Island Tercentenary | 20,013 } Set | | |
| 1936D | Same | 15,010 } Set | | 300.00 |
| 1936S | Same | 15,011 } Set | | |
| | Single type coin | | 30.00 | 95.00 |

| | | Quan. Available | AU-50 | MS-60 |
|---|---|---|---|---|
| 1937 | Roanoke Island, N. C., 1587-1937 | 29,030 | 50.00 | 125.00 |

| | | Quan. Available | AU-50 | MS-60 |
|---|---|---|---|---|
| 1936 | Arkansas Centennial (Robinson) | 25,265 | 50.00 | 100.00 |

## San Diego, Sesquicentennial, Spanish Trail, Stone Mountain

| | | Quan. Available | AU-50 | MS-60 |
|---|---|---|---|---|
| 1935S | San Diego, California-Pacific Expo. | 70,132 | $22.00 | $60.00 |
| 1936D | Same | 30,092 | 25.00 | 75.00 |

| | | | | |
|---|---|---|---|---|
| 1926 | Sesquicentennial of American Independence | 141,120 | 17.00 | 35.00 |

| | | | | |
|---|---|---|---|---|
| 1935 | Old Spanish Trail 1535-1935 | 10,008 | 375.00 | 525.00 |

| | | | | |
|---|---|---|---|---|
| 1925 | Stone Mountain Memorial | 1,314,709 | 12.00 | 25.00 |

# COMMEMORATIVE SILVER

## Texas, Vancouver, Vermont

| | | Quan. Available | | AU-50 | MS-60 |
|---|---|---|---|---|---|
| 1934 | Texas Centennial | 61,463 | | $40.00 | $75.00 |
| 1935 | Texas Centennial, same as 1934 | 9,996 | Set | | 225.00 |
| 1935D | Same | 10,007 | | | |
| 1935S | Same | 10,008 | | | |
| 1936 | Texas Centennial, same as 1934 | 8,911 | Set | | 225.00 |
| 1936D | Same | 9,039 | | | |
| 1936S | Same | 9,055 | | | |
| 1937 | Texas Centennial, same as 1934 | 6,571 | Set | | 250.00 |
| 1937D | Same | 6,605 | | | |
| 1937S | Same | 6,637 | | | |
| 1938 | Texas Centennial, same as 1934 | 3,780 | Set | | 400.00 |
| 1938D | Same | 3,775 | | | |
| 1938S | Same | 3,814 | | | |
| | Single type coin | | | 40.00 | 75.00 |

| | | | | |
|---|---|---|---|---|
| 1925S | Fort Vancouver Centennial | 14,994 | 140.00 | 400.00 |

| | | | | |
|---|---|---|---|---|
| 1927 | Vermont Sesquicentennial (Bennington) | 28,162 | 65.00 | 165.00 |

# COMMEMORATIVE SILVER

## Washington, B. T., Washington-Carver, Washington, George

| | Quan. Available | | MS-60 |
|---|---|---|---|
| 1946 Booker T. Washington Memorial | 1,000,546 | Set | $30.00 |
| 1946D | 200,113 | | |
| 1946S | 500,279 | | |
| 1947 | 100,017 | Set | 40.00 |
| 1947D | 100,017 | | |
| 1947S | 100,017 | | |
| 1948 | 8,005 | Set | 65.00 |
| 1948D | 8,005 | | |
| 1948S | 8,005 | | |
| 1949 | 6,004 | Set | $120.00 |
| 1949D | 6,004 | | |
| 1949S | 6,004 | | |
| 1950 | 6,004 | Set | 100.00 |
| 1950D | 6,004 | | |
| 1950S | 512,091 | | |
| 1951 | 510,082 | Set | 80.00 |
| 1951D | 7,004 | | |
| 1951S | 7,004 | | |
| Single type coin | | | 10.00 |

| | Quan. Available | | MS-60 |
|---|---|---|---|
| 1951 Washington-Carver | 110,018 | Set | 65.00 |
| 1951D | 10,004 | | |
| 1951S | 10,004 | | |
| 1952 | 2,006,292 | Set | 80.00 |
| 1952D | 8,006 | | |
| 1952S | 8,006 | | |
| 1953 | 8,003 | Set | 100.00 |
| 1953D | 8,003 | | |
| 1953S | 108,020 | | |
| 1954 | 12,006 | Set | 65.00 |
| 1954D | 12,006 | | |
| 1954S | 122,024 | | |
| Single type coin | | | 10.00 |

| | MS-60 | Proof-65 |
|---|---|---|
| 1982D Geo. Washington-250th Anniversary | $8.50* | |
| 1982S Same | | $10.50* |

*Issue Prices

# COMMEMORATIVE SILVER

## Wisconsin, York County

| | | *Quan. Available* | *AU-50* | *MS-60* |
|---|---|---|---|---|
| 1936 | Wisconsin Centennial | 25,015 | $67.00 | $130.00 |

| | | | | |
|---|---|---|---|---|
| 1936 | York County, Maine Centennial | 25,015 | 70.00 | 120.00 |

# COMMEMORATIVE GOLD

## Grant

| | | Quan. Available | | |
|---|---|---|---|---|
| 1922 | Grant Memorial Dollar, star above word "Grant" | 5,016 | $375.00 | $700.00 |
| 1922 | Same, without star | 5,000 | 375.00 | 700.00 |

## Lewis & Clark

| | | | | |
|---|---|---|---|---|
| 1904 | Lewis and Clark Exposition Dollar | 10,025 | 275.00 | 875.00 |
| 1905 | Lewis and Clark Exposition Dollar | 10,041 | 275.00 | 875.00 |

## Louisiana Purchase

| | | | | |
|---|---|---|---|---|
| 1903 | Louisiana Purchase Jefferson Dollar | 17,500 | 210.00 | 450.00 |
| 1903 | Louisiana Purchase McKinley Dollar | 17,500 | 210.00 | 450.00 |

## McKinley

| | | | | |
|---|---|---|---|---|
| 1916 | McKinley Memorial Dollar | 9,977 | 200.00 | 450.00 |
| 1917 | McKinley Memorial Dollar | 10,000 | 200.00 | 500.00 |

## Panama-Pacific

| | | | | |
|---|---|---|---|---|
| 1915S | Panama-Pacific Exposition Dollar | 15,000 | 200.00 | 500.00 |

# COMMEMORATIVE GOLD

## Panama-Pacific

| | | Quan. Available | AU-50 | MS-60 |
|---|---|---|---|---|
| 1915S | Panama-Pacific Exposition $2.50 | 6,749 | $475.00 | $1,000 |

| | | Quan. Available | AU-50 | MS-60 |
|---|---|---|---|---|
| 1915S | Panama-Pacific $50 Round | 483 | 7,000 | 15,000 |
| 1915S | Panama-Pacific $50 Octagonal | 645 | 6,000 | 12,000 |

## Sesquicentennial

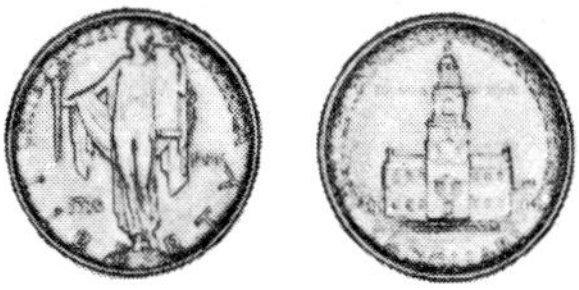

| | | Quan. Available | AU-50 | MS-60 |
|---|---|---|---|---|
| 1926 | Philadelphia Sesquicentennial $2.50 | 46,019 | 200.00 | 300.00 |

# PRIVATE OR TERRITORIAL GOLD COINS

Private coins were circulated in most instances because of a shortage of regular coinage. The words "Private Gold," used with reference to coins struck outside of the United States Mint, are a general term. In the sense that no state or territory had authority to coin money, private gold simply refers to those interesting necessity pieces of various shapes, denominations and degrees of intrinsic worth which were circulated in isolated areas of our country by individuals, assayers, bankers, etc. Some will use the words "Territorial" and "State" to cover certain issues because they were coined and circulated in a territory or state. While the state of California properly sanctioned the ingots stamped by F. D. Kohler as state assayer, in no instance were any of the gold pieces struck by authority of any of the territorial governments.

The stamped ingots put out by Augustus Humbert, the United States assayer of gold, were not recognized at the United States Mint as an official issue of coins, but simply as ingots, though Humbert placed the value and fineness on the pieces as an official agent of the federal government.

## TEMPLETON REID

### Georgia 1830

The first private gold coinage under the Constitution was struck by Templeton Reid, a jeweler and gunsmith, in Milledgeville, Georgia in July, 1830. To be closer to the mines, he moved to Gainesville where most of his coins were made. Although weights were accurate, Reid's assays were not and his coins were slightly short of claimed value. Accordingly, he was severely attacked in the newspapers and soon lost the public's confidence.

| | | |
|---|---|---|
| 1830 $2.50 | E.F. | $25,000 |
| 1830 $5.00 | E.F. | 100,000 |

| | | |
|---|---|---|
| 1830 TEN DOLLARS | V.G. | 20,000 |
| (No date) TEN DOLLARS | V.G. | 15,000 |

# TEMPLETON REID

### "California Gold 1849"

1849 TEN DOLLAR CALIFORNIA GOLD (Smithsonian Collection) ...................... Unique

# THE BECHTLERS

### Rutherford County, N. C. 1830-1852

Two skilled German metallurgists, Christopher Bechtler and his son August, and later Christopher Bechtler, Junior, a nephew of Christopher the elder, operated a "private" mint at Rutherfordton, North Carolina. Rutherford county in which Rutherfordton is located was the principal source of the nation's gold supply from 1790 to 1840.

## CHRISTOPHER BECHTLER

| | V. Fine | E. Fine | Unc. |
|---|---|---|---|
| ONE DOLLAR CAROLINA, 28 gr. N reversed ............... | $500.00 | $700.00 | $1,500 |
| ONE DOLLAR N. CAROLINA, 28 gr. no star ................ | 1,000 | 2,000 | 4,250 |

| | V. Fine | E. Fine | Unc. |
|---|---|---|---|
| ONE DOLLAR N. CAROLINA, 30 gr.. ........................ | 700.00 | 1,000 | 2,000 |
| $2.50 CAROLINA, 67 gr. 21 carats ....................... | 800.00 | 1,100 | 2,750 |

| | V. Fine | E. Fine | Unc. |
|---|---|---|---|
| $2.50 CAROLINA, 70 gr. 20 carats ...................... | 850.00 | 1,200 | 3,000 |
| $2.50 GEORGIA, 64 gr. 22 carats. ....................... | 1,000 | 1,600 | 3,500 |

| | V. Fine | E. Fine | Unc. |
|---|---|---|---|
| $2.50 NORTH CAROLINA, 75 gr. 20 carats. RUTHERFORD in a circle. Border of lg. beads | $2,250 | $3,500 | $5,000 |
| $2.50 NORTH CAROLINA, without 75 G | 2,100 | 3,000 | 4,500 |

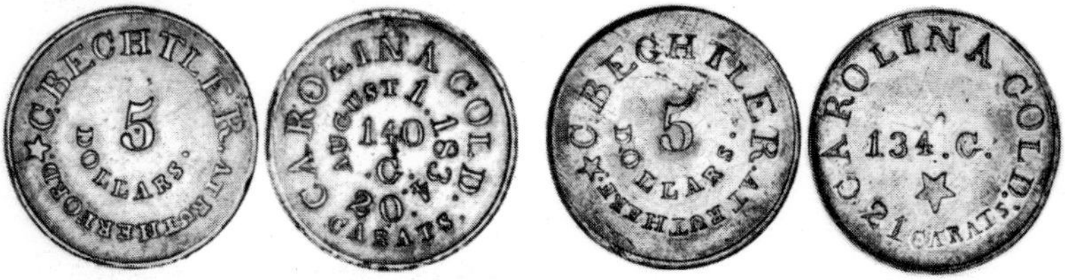

| | | | |
|---|---|---|---|
| 5 DOLLARS CAROLINA, RUTHERFORD, 140 gr. 20 carats. Date August 1, 1834. | | | |
| Plain edge | 1,000 | 1,600 | 3,750 |
| Reeded edge | 1,600 | 2,200 | 4,000 |
| 5 DOLLARS CAROLINA, 134 gr. 21 carats, with star | 900.00 | 1,600 | 3,000 |

| | | | |
|---|---|---|---|
| 5 DOLLARS GEORGIA, RUTHERF. 128 gr. 22 carats | 1,200 | 2,200 | 3,750 |
| 5 DOLLARS GEORGIA, RTHERF. 128 gr. 22 carats | 1,100 | 2,000 | 3,500 |
| 5 DOLLARS CAROLINA, RUTHERF. 140 gr. 20 carats. Date August 1, 1834 (illustrated) | 1,100 | 2,000 | 3,500 |
| Similar. 20 distant from carats | 2,750 | 4,500 | —— |

**Without 150 G**

| | | | |
|---|---|---|---|
| 5 DOLLARS NORTH CAROLINA, 150 gr. 20 carats | 1,600 | 3,000 | 7,000 |
| 5 DOLLARS. Same as last variety without 150 G | 2,100 | 3,500 | 6,500 |

# THE BECHTLERS

## AUGUST BECHTLER
## 1842-1852

| | V. Fine | E. Fine | Unc. |
|---|---|---|---|
| 1 DOLLAR CAROLINA, 27 gr. 21 carats | $450.00 | $600.00 | $1,250 |
| 5 DOLLARS CAROLINA, 134 gr. 21 carats | 1,000 | 1,700 | 3,500 |

| | V. Fine | E. Fine | Unc. |
|---|---|---|---|
| 5 DOLLARS CAROLINA, 128 gr. 22 carats | 1,600 | 2,500 | 5,500 |
| 5 DOLLARS CAROLINA, 141 gr. 20 carats | 1,600 | 2,500 | 5,000 |

# NORRIS, GREGG & NORRIS
## San Francisco 1849

These pieces are considered the first of the California private gold coins. A newspaper account dated May 31, 1849, described a five-dollar gold coin, struck at Benicia City, though with the imprint San Francisco, and the private stamp of Norris, Gregg and Norris.

| | Fine | V. Fine | E. Fine | Unc. |
|---|---|---|---|---|
| 1849 HALF EAGLE — Plain edge | $1,200 | $1,750 | $4,000 | $15,000 |
| 1849 HALF EAGLE — Reeded edge | 1,200 | 1,750 | 4,200 | 16,500 |
| 1850 HALF EAGLE with STOCKTON beneath date | | | | (Unique) |

# MOFFAT & CO.

## San Francisco 1849-1853

The firm of Moffat and Company was perhaps the most important of the California private coiners. The assay office they conducted was semi-official in character, and successors to this firm later established the United States Branch mint of San Francisco.

In June or July, 1849, Moffat & Co. began to issue small rectangular pieces of gold in values from $9.43 to $264. The $9.43, $14.25 and $16.00 varieties are the only types known today.

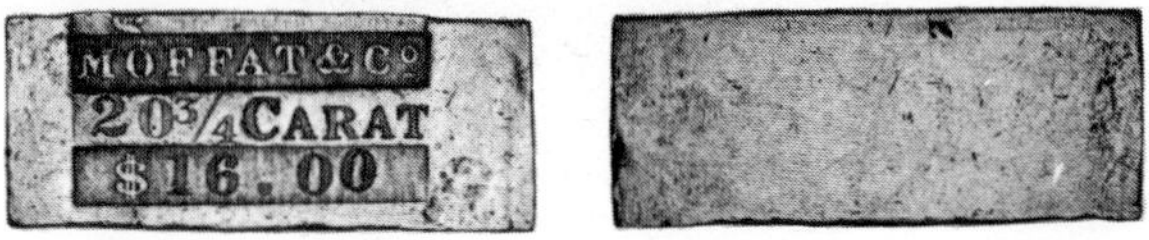


| | | |
|---|---|---|
| $9.43 Ingot (Unique) | | — |
| $14.25 Ingot (Unique) | | — |
| $16.00 Ingot (Beware of spurious specimens cast in base metal) | E.F. | $14,000 |

The dies for the $10 piece were cut by Albert Kuner. The words MOFFAT & CO. appear on the coronet of Liberty instead of the word LIBERTY as in regular United States issues.

| | *Fine* | *V. Fine* | *E. Fine* | *Unc.* |
|---|---|---|---|---|
| 1849 FIVE DOL. | $450.00 | $900.00 | $1,300 | $5,000 |
| 1850 FIVE DOL. | 450.00 | 900.00 | 1,350 | 5,100 |
| 1849 TEN DOL. | 900.00 | 1,300 | 2,600 | 7,200 |
| 1849 TEN D. | 1,300 | 2,100 | 4,000 | |

# United States Assay Office

## AUGUSTUS HUMBERT

## U. S. Assayer 1851

When Augustus Humbert was appointed United States Assayer, he placed his name and the government stamp on the ingots of gold issued by Moffat & Co. The assay office, a Provisional Government Mint, was a temporary expedient to accommodate the Californians until the establishment of a permanent branch mint.

The fifty-dollar gold piece was accepted as legal tender on a par with standard U.S. gold coins.

# MOFFAT — HUMBERT

## LETTERED EDGE VARIETIES

50 on reverse

| | Fine | V. Fine | E. Fine | Unc. |
|---|---|---|---|---|
| 1851 50 D C 880 THOUS., no 50 on Reverse. Sunk in edge: AUGUSTUS HUMBERT UNITED STATES ASSAYER OF GOLD CALIFORNIA 1851 | $3,500 | $5,000 | $10,000 | — |
| 1851 50 D C Similar to last variety, but 50 on Reverse | 4,250 | 5,500 | 12,000 | — |
| 1851 Similar to last variety, but 887 THOUS | 4,000 | 5,250 | 11,000 | — |

## REEDED EDGE VARIETIES

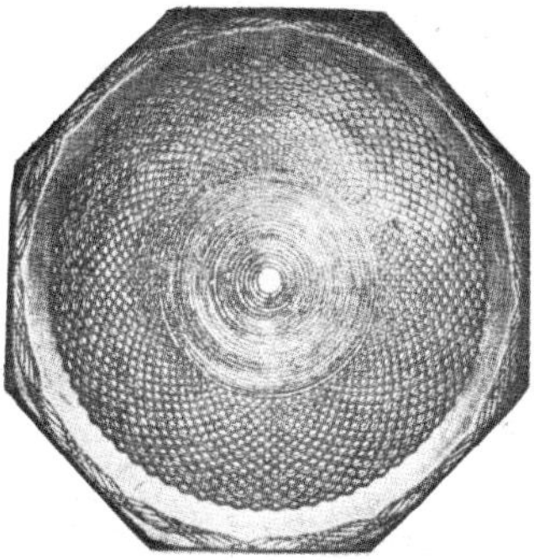

| | Fine | V. Fine | E. Fine | Unc. |
|---|---|---|---|---|
| 1851 FIFTY DOLLS 880 THOUS. "Target" Reverse | 3,500 | 4,500 | 8,000 | 22,000 |
| 1851 FIFTY DOLLS 887 THOUS. "Target" Reverse | 3,500 | 4,500 | 8,000 | 22,000 |
| 1852 FIFTY DOLLS 887 THOUS. | 3,750 | 5,000 | 10,000 | 25,000 |

Moffat & Co. proceeded in January, 1852 to issue a new ten-dollar piece bearing the stamp MOFFAT & CO.

| | Fine | V. Fine | E. Fine | Unc. |
|---|---|---|---|---|
| 1852 TEN D. MOFFAT & CO. | $1,000 | $2,000 | $3,500 | — |

| | Fine | V. Fine | E. Fine | Unc. |
|---|---|---|---|---|
| 1852 TWENTY DOLS. 1852, 2 over 1 | 1,800 | 3,000 | 5,000 | — |

| | Fine | V. Fine | E. Fine | Unc. |
|---|---|---|---|---|
| 1852 TEN DOLS. 1852, 2 over 1 | 700.00 | 1,000 | 2,000 | — |
| 1852 TEN DOLS. | 650.00 | 900.00 | 1,800 | $5,000 |

## UNITED STATES ASSAY OFFICE OF GOLD

### 1852

The firm of Moffat & Co. dissolved and a new reorganized company known as the United States Assay Office of Gold, composed of Curtis, Perry and Ward took over the contract.

# UNITED STATES ASSAY OFFICE

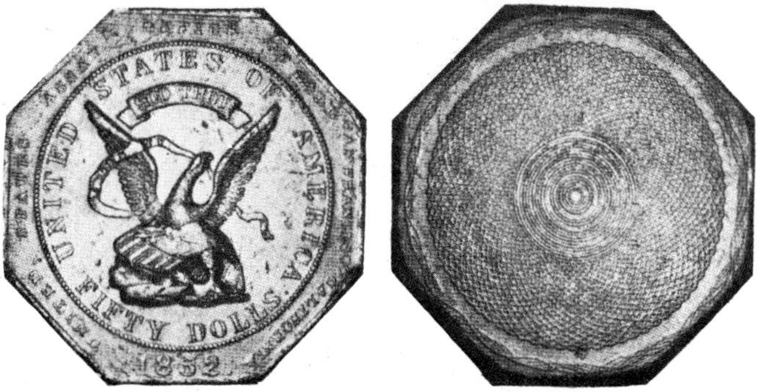


| | Fine | V. Fine | E. Fine | Unc. |
|---|---|---|---|---|
| 1852 FIFTY DOLLS. 887 THOUS. | $3,000 | $5,000 | $9,500 | $25,000 |
| 1852 FIFTY DOLLS. 900 THOUS. | 3,100 | 5,100 | 11,000 | 30,000 |

| | | | | |
|---|---|---|---|---|
| 1852 TEN DOLS 884 THOUS. | 600.00 | 1,100 | 1,600 | 5,500 |
| 1853 TEN D. 884 THOUS. | 2,500 | 3,500 | 7,500 | —— |
| 1853 TEN D. 900 THOUS. | 1,300 | 2,200 | 3,500 | —— |
| 1853 TWENTY D. 884 THOUS. | 3,750 | 6,000 | 11,000 | —— |
| 1853 TWENTY D. 900 THOUS. | 850.00 | 1,500 | 2,500 | 5,500 |

The last Moffat issue was the 1853 twenty dollar piece which is very similar to the U.S. double eagle of that period. It was struck after the retirement of Mr. Moffat from the Assay Office.

| | | | | |
|---|---|---|---|---|
| 1853 TWENTY D. | $1,000 | $2,000 | $3,000 | $6,000 |

## CINCINNATI MINING & TRADING CO.

The origin and location of this company are unknown.

| | E. Fine | Unc. |
|---|---|---|
| 1849 FIVE DOLLARS | —— | —— |
| 1849 TEN DOLLARS | —— | —— |

## MASSACHUSETTS AND CALIFORNIA COMPANY

### San Francisco 1849

This company was believed to have been organized in Northampton, Mass. in May 1849.

| | Fine |
|---|---|
| 1849 FIVE D. | $20,000 |

## MINERS' BANK

### San Francisco 1849

The institution of Wright & Co., exchange brokers located in Portsmouth Square, San Francisco, was known as the Miners' Bank.

A ten dollar piece was issued in the autumn of 1849, but the coins were not readily accepted because they were worth less than face value.

| | V. Fine | E. Fine | Unc. |
|---|---|---|---|
| (1849) TEN. D. | $6,000 | $9,000 | $20,000 |

## J.S. ORMSBY

### Sacramento 1849

The initials J. S. O. which appear on certain issues of California privately coined gold pieces represent the firm of J. S. Ormsby & Co. They struck both five and ten dollar denominations, all undated.

# J.S. ORMSBY

| | V. Fine |
|---|---|
| (1849) 5 DOLLS. (Unique) | —— |
| (1849) 10 DOLLS. | —— |

# PACIFIC COMPANY

## San Francisco 1849

The origin of the Pacific Co. is very uncertain. All data regarding the firm is based on conjecture.

Edgar H. Adams wrote that he believed that the coins bearing the stamp of the Pacific Company were produced by the coining firm of Broderick and Kohler.

| | E. Fine |
|---|---|
| 1849 5 DOLLARS | —— |
| 1849 10 DOLLARS | 14,000 |

# F. D. KOHLER

## California State Assayer 1850

The State Assay Office was authorized April 12, 1850. Governor Burnett appointed F. D. Kohler that year who thereupon sold his assaying business to Baldwin & Co. He served at both San Francisco and Sacramento Offices. The State Assay Offices were discontinued at the time the U. S. Assay Office was established Feb. 1, 1851.

| | | |
|---|---|---|
| $36.55 Sacramento | | —— |
| $37.31 San Francisco | | —— |
| $40.07 San Francisco | | —— |
| $41.68 San Francisco | | —— |
| $45.34 San Francisco | | —— |
| $50.00 San Francisco | E.F. | —— |
| $54.09 San Francisco | | —— |

# DUBOSQ & COMPANY

## San Francisco 1850

Theodore Dubosq, a Philadelphia jeweler who took melting and coining machinery to San Francisco in 1849, produced the following pieces.

| | V. Fine |
|---|---|
| 1850 FIVE D. | $25,000 |
| 1850 TEN D. | 30,000 |

# BALDWIN & COMPANY

## San Francisco 1850

George C. Baldwin and Thomas S. Holman were in the jewelry business in San Francisco and were known as Baldwin & Co. They were the successors to F. D. Kohler & Co., taking over their machinery and other equipment in May, 1850.

| | Fine | V. Fine | E. Fine | Unc. |
|---|---|---|---|---|
| 1850 FIVE DOL. | $1,600 | $3,000 | $5,000 | $10,000 |
| 1850 TEN DOLLARS — Horseman type | 8,000 | 14,000 | 22,500 | — |

# BALDWIN & COMPANY

| | Fine | V. Fine | E. Fine | Unc. |
|---|---|---|---|---|
| 1851 TEN D. | $4,000 | $6,000 | $13,000 | — |

| | | |
|---|---|---|
| 1851 TWENTY D. | $50,000 | — |

## SHULTZ & COMPANY

### San Francisco 1851

The firm located in back of Baldwin's establishment operated a brass foundry beginning in 1851. Judge G. W. Shultz and William T. Garratt were partners in the enterprise.

| | *Fine* | *V. Fine* |
|---|---|---|
| 1851 FIVE D. | $8,000 | $13,000 |

## DUNBAR & COMPANY

### San Francisco 1851

Edward E. Dunbar operated the California Bank in San Francisco. He later returned to New York and organized the famous Continental Bank Note Co.

| | *E. Fine* |
|---|---|
| 1851 FIVE D | $40,000 |

## WASS, MOLITOR & COMPANY

### San Francisco 1852-1855

The gold smelting and assaying plant of Wass, Molitor & Co. was operated by Count S. C. Wass and A. P. Molitor. They maintained an excellent laboratory and complete apparatus for analysis and coinage of gold.

| | *Fine* | *V. Fine* | *E. Fine* | *Unc.* |
|---|---|---|---|---|
| 1852 FIVE DOLLARS | $1,200 | $2,000 | $3,250 | $8,000 |

Large Head

Small Head

| | | | | |
|---|---|---|---|---|
| 1852 TEN D. Large head | 800.00 | 1,500 | 2,500 | — |
| 1852 TEN D. Small head | 1,500 | 2,750 | 4,500 | — |
| 1855 TEN D. | 3,000 | 5,000 | 8,000 | — |

# WASS, MOLITOR & COMPANY

Large Head | Small Head

| | Fine | V. Fine | E. Fine | Unc. |
|---|---|---|---|---|
| 1855 TWENTY DOL. Large head . . . . . . . . . . . . . . | —— | —— | —— | —— |
| 1855 TWENTY DOL. Small head . . . . . . . . . . . . . . | $3,250 | $7,000 | $9,500 | —— |

| | | | | |
|---|---|---|---|---|
| 1855 50 DOLLARS . . . . . . . . . . . . . . . . . . . . . . . . . . | 7,000 | 10,000 | 18,000 | —— |

# KELLOGG & COMPANY

## San Francisco 1854-1855

When the U.S. Assay Office ceased operations a period ensued during which no private firm was striking gold. The new San Francisco branch mint did not produce coins for some months after Curtis & Perry took the contract for the government. The lack of coin was again keenly felt by businessmen who petitioned Kellogg & Richter to "supply the vacuum" by issuing private coin. Their plea was answered on Feb. 9, 1854, when Kellogg & Co. placed their first twenty-dollar piece in circulation.

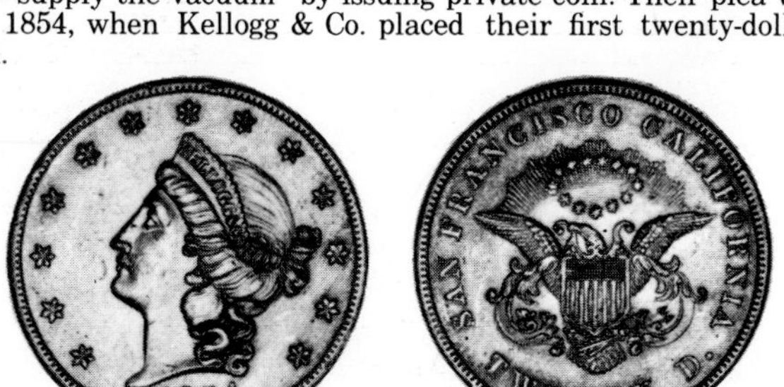


| | | | | |
|---|---|---|---|---|
| 1854 TWENTY D. . . . . . . . . . . . . . . . . . . . . . . . . . . | 900.00 | 1,300 | 2,000 | 6,000 |
| 1855 TWENTY D. . . . . . . . . . . . . . . . . . . . . . . . . . . | 900.00 | 1,300 | 2,100 | 6,500 |

# KELLOGG & COMPANY

| | Proof |
|---|---|
| 1855 FIFTY DOLLS. | —— |

# CALIFORNIA SMALL DENOMINATION GOLD

There was a scarcity of small coins during the California gold rush and starting in 1852, quarter, half and dollar pieces were privately minted from native gold to alleviate the shortage. The need and acceptability of these pieces declined after 1856 and they then became popular as souvenirs. Authentic pieces all have CENTS, DOLLAR, or an abbreviation thereof on the reverse. The tokens are much less valuable. Modern restrikes and replicas have no numismatic value.

*Values are only for genuine coins with the denomination on the reverse expressed as:* CENTS, DOL., DOLL., *or* DOLLAR.

| | | *EF-40* | *AU-50* | *MS-60* |
|---|---|---|---|---|
| 25c Octagonal: | Liberty head | $40.00 | $70.00 | $100.00 |
| | Indian head | 50.00 | 80.00 | 125.00 |
| | Washington head | 250.00 | 300.00 | 500.00 |
| 25c Round: | Liberty head | 40.00 | 70.00 | 100.00 |
| | Indian head | 50.00 | 80.00 | 125.00 |
| | Washington head | 300.00 | 500.00 | 600.00 |
| 50c Octagonal: | Liberty head | 50.00 | 80.00 | 110.00 |
| | Liberty head/Eagle | 300.00 | 500.00 | 600.00 |
| | Indian head | 110.00 | 175.00 | 250.00 |
| 50c Round: | Liberty head | 50.00 | 80.00 | 110.00 |
| | Indian head | 100.00 | 150.00 | 200.00 |
| $1.00 Octagonal: | Liberty head | 110.00 | 175.00 | 250.00 |
| | Liberty head/Eagle | 500.00 | 900.00 | 2,000 |
| | Indian head | 250.00 | 400.00 | 550.00 |
| $1.00 Round: | Liberty head | 550.00 | 800.00 | 1,000 |
| | Indian head | 600.00 | 900.00 | 2,000 |

# OREGON EXCHANGE COMPANY

## Oregon City, 1849

### THE BEAVER COINS OF OREGON

On February 16, 1849, the legislature passed an act providing for a mint and specified five and ten dollar gold coins without alloy. Oregon City, the largest city in the territory with a population of about 1,000, was designated as the location for the mint. At the time this act was passed Oregon had been brought into the United States as a territory by act of Congress. When the new governor arrived March 2, he declared the coinage act unconstitutional.

| | Fine | V. Fine | E. Fine | Unc. |
|---|---|---|---|---|
| 1849 5 D | $4,000 | $8,000 | $12,000 | —— |

| | | | | |
|---|---|---|---|---|
| 1849 TEN D | 15,000 | 20,000 | 27,500 | —— |

# MORMON GOLD PIECES

## Salt Lake City, Utah 1849-1860

Brigham Young was the instigator of this coinage system and personally supervised the mint which was housed in a little adobe building in Salt Lake City. The mint was inaugurated late in 1849 as a public convenience.

| | Fine | V. Fine | E. Fine | Unc. |
|---|---|---|---|---|
| 1849 TWO AND HALF DO | $1,800 | $3,500 | $5,000 | —— |
| 1849 FIVE DOLLARS | 1,200 | 1,900 | 3,000 | $6,000 |

| | Fine |
|---|---|
| 1849 TEN DOLLARS | $45,000 |

# MORMON GOLD PIECES

| | Fine | V. Fine |
|---|---|---|
| 1849 TWENTY DOLLARS | $12,000 | $17,500 |

| 1850 FIVE DOLLARS | |
|---|---|
| Fine | $1,300 |
| V. Fine | 1,800 |
| Ex. Fine | 3,000 |
| Unc. | —— |

| 1860 5D | |
|---|---|
| Fine | $3,000 |
| V. Fine | 4,500 |
| Ex. Fine | 7,000 |
| Unc. | 12,000 |

# COLORADO GOLD PIECES

## Clark, Gruber & Co. — Denver 1860-1861

Clark, Gruber and Co. was a well known private minting firm in Denver, Colo. in the early sixties.

| | Fine | V. Fine | E. Fine | Unc. |
|---|---|---|---|---|
| 1860 2½ D | $400.00 | $700.00 | $1,100 | $4,500 |
| 1860 Five D | 600.00 | 1,100 | 1,800 | 5,750 |

| | Fine | V. Fine | E. Fine | Unc. |
|---|---|---|---|---|
| 1860 TEN D | 1,400 | 1,900 | 3,500 | 8,000 |
| 1860 TWENTY D | 8,000 | 12,000 | 21,000 | —— |

# COLORADO GOLD PIECES

| | Fine | V. Fine | E. Fine | Unc. |
|---|---|---|---|---|
| 1861 2½ D | $400.00 | $600.00 | $1,000 | $4,000 |
| 1861 FIVE D | 600.00 | 900.00 | 1,800 | 5,000 |
| 1861 TEN D | 700.00 | 950.00 | 1,900 | 6,250 |

| | Fine | V. Fine | E. Fine | Unc. |
|---|---|---|---|---|
| 1861 TWENTY D | 2,750 | 5,000 | 10,000 | — |

## JOHN PARSONS & COMPANY

### Tarryall Mines — Colorado 1861

Very little is known about the mint of John Parsons and Co. It probably operated in Colorado, near Tarryall, in the summer of 1861.

### PIKES PEAK GOLD

| | | V. Fine |
|---|---|---|
| (1861) | Undated 2½ D | $30,000 |
| (1861) | Undated FIVE D | 60,000 |

## J. J. CONWAY & COMPANY

### Georgia Gulch, Colorado, 1861

The value of gold dust caused disagreement among the merchants and the miners in all gold mining areas. The firm of J. J. Conway & Co. solved this difficulty by bringing out its gold pieces in August, 1861.

# J. J. CONWAY & COMPANY

| | | *V. Fine* |
|---|---|---|
| (1861) | Undated 2½ DOLL'S | $30,000 |
| (1861) | Undated FIVE DOLLARS | 60,000 |
| (1861) | Undated FIVE DOLLARS, Similar.<br>Variety without numeral 5 on reverse | 20,000 |

| | | |
|---|---|---|
| (1861) | Undated TEN DOLLARS | —— |

# BULLION VALUE OF SILVER COINS

Common date silver coins are valued according to the price of silver bullion. In recent years the price of silver bullion has been subject to extreme fluctuation. Therefore, when you read this it is highly probable that the current bullion price may differ from the prevailing market price used in tabulating valuations of many 19th and 20th century silver coins (priced in italics) listed in this edition. The following chart will help to determine the approximate bullion value of these coins at various price levels. Or, the approximate value may be calculated by multiplying the current spot price of silver times the content for each coin as indicated below. Dealers generally purchase common silver coins at 15% below bullion value, and sell them at 15% above bullion value.

| *Silver Bullion* | *Wartime Nickel .05626 oz.* | *Dime .07234 oz.* | *Quarter .18084 oz.* | *Half Dollar .36169 oz.* | *Silver Clad Half Dollar .14792 oz.* | *Silver Dollar .77344 oz.* |
|---|---|---|---|---|---|---|
| $2.00 | $.11 | $.14 | $.36 | $.72 | $.29 | $1.55 |
| 2.50 | .14 | .18 | .45 | .90 | .37 | 1.93 |
| 3.00 | .17 | .22 | .54 | 1.08 | .44 | 2.32 |
| 3.50 | .20 | .25 | .63 | 1.26 | .52 | 2.71 |
| 4.00 | .23 | .29 | .72 | 1.45 | .59 | 3.09 |
| 4.50 | .25 | .33 | .81 | 1.63 | .67 | 3.48 |
| 5.00 | .28 | .36 | .90 | 1.81 | .74 | 3.87 |
| 5.50 | .31 | .40 | 1.00 | 1.99 | .81 | 4.25 |
| 6.00 | .34 | .44 | 1.09 | 2.17 | .89 | 4.64 |
| 6.50 | .36 | .47 | 1.18 | 2.35 | .96 | 5.03 |
| 7.00 | .40 | .51 | 1.27 | 2.53 | 1.04 | 5.42 |
| 7.50 | .42 | .55 | 1.36 | 2.72 | 1.11 | 5.80 |
| 8.00 | .45 | .58 | 1.45 | 2.90 | 1.19 | 6.19 |
| 8.50 | .48 | .62 | 1.54 | 3.08 | 1.26 | 6.58 |
| 9.00 | .50 | .65 | 1.63 | 3.26 | 1.33 | 6.96 |
| 9.50 | .53 | .69 | 1.72 | 3.44 | 1.42 | 7.35 |
| 10.00 | .56 | .72 | 1.81 | 3.62 | 1.48 | 7.73 |
| 11.00 | .62 | .80 | 1.99 | 3.98 | 1.63 | 8.51 |
| 12.00 | .68 | .87 | 2.17 | 4.34 | 1.78 | 9.28 |
| 13.00 | .73 | .94 | 2.35 | 4.70 | 1.92 | 10.05 |
| 14.00 | .79 | 1.01 | 2.53 | 5.06 | 2.07 | 10.83 |
| 15.00 | .84 | 1.09 | 2.71 | 5.43 | 2.22 | 11.60 |
| 16.00 | .90 | 1.16 | 2.89 | 5.79 | 2.37 | 12.38 |
| 17.00 | .96 | 1.23 | 3.07 | 6.15 | 2.51 | 13.15 |
| 18.00 | 1.01 | 1.30 | 3.26 | 6.51 | 2.66 | 13.92 |
| 19.00 | 1.07 | 1.37 | 3.44 | 6.87 | 2.81 | 14.70 |
| 20.00 | 1.13 | 1.45 | 3.62 | 7.23 | 2.96 | 15.47 |
| 21.00 | 1.18 | 1.52 | 3.80 | 7.60 | 3.11 | 16.24 |
| 22.00 | 1.24 | 1.59 | 3.98 | 7.96 | 3.25 | 17.02 |
| 23.00 | 1.30 | 1.66 | 4.16 | 8.32 | 3.40 | 17.79 |
| 24.00 | 1.35 | 1.74 | 4.34 | 8.68 | 3.55 | 18.56 |
| 25.00 | 1.41 | 1.81 | 4.52 | 9.04 | 3.70 | 19.34 |
| 26.00 | 1.46 | 1.88 | 4.70 | 9.40 | 3.85 | 20.11 |
| 27.00 | 1.52 | 1.95 | 4.88 | 9.77 | 3.99 | 20.88 |
| 28.00 | 1.58 | 2.03 | 5.06 | 10.13 | 4.14 | 21.66 |
| 29.00 | 1.63 | 2.10 | 5.24 | 10.49 | 4.29 | 22.43 |

## BULLION VALUE OF GOLD COINS

The value of common date gold coins listed in this book may be affected by the rise or fall in the price of gold bullion. Nearly all U.S. gold coins have an additional premium value beyond their bullion content, and thus are not subject to the minor variations described for silver coins on the preceding page. The premium amount is not necessarily tied to the bullion price of gold, but is usually determined by supply and demand levels for actual gold coins occurring in the numismatic marketplace. Because these factors can vary significantly, there is no reliable formula for calculating "percentage above bullion" prices that would remain accurate over time. For this reason the chart below lists bullion values based on gold content only. Consult your nearest coin dealer to ascertain current premium prices.

| *Price Per Ounce* | *$5.00 Liberty Head 1839-1908 Indian Head 1908-1929* | *$10.00 Liberty Head 1838-1907 Indian Head 1907-1933* | *$20.00 1849-1933* |
|---|---|---|---|
| $200.00 | $48.37 | $96.75 | $193.50 |
| 225.00 | 54.42 | 108.84 | 217.69 |
| 250.00 | 60.46 | 120.94 | 241.88 |
| 275.00 | 66.51 | 133.03 | 266.06 |
| 300.00 | 72.56 | 145.13 | 290.25 |
| 325.00 | 78.60 | 157.22 | 314.44 |
| 350.00 | 84.65 | 169.31 | 338.63 |
| 375.00 | 90.70 | 181.40 | 362.81 |
| 400.00 | 96.75 | 193.50 | 387.00 |
| 425.00 | 102.80 | 205.60 | 411.19 |
| 450.00 | 108.84 | 217.69 | 435.38 |
| 475.00 | 114.89 | 229.78 | 459.56 |
| 500.00 | 120.94 | 241.87 | 483.75 |
| 525.00 | 126.98 | 253.97 | 507.94 |
| 550.00 | 133.03 | 266.06 | 532.13 |
| 575.00 | 139.08 | 278.16 | 556.31 |
| 600.00 | 145.12 | 290.25 | 580.50 |
| 625.00 | 151.17 | 302.34 | 604.69 |
| 650.00 | 157.22 | 314.44 | 628.88 |
| 675.00 | 163.26 | 326.53 | 653.06 |
| 700.00 | 169.31 | 338.63 | 677.25 |
| 725.00 | 175.36 | 350.72 | 701.44 |
| 750.00 | 181.40 | 362.81 | 725.63 |
| 775.00 | 187.45 | 374.91 | 749.81 |
| 800.00 | 193.50 | 387.00 | 774.00 |

# INDEX

The following numismatic magazines are obtainable by subscription. They are published monthly or as indicated below. Information or sample copies may be obtained by writing to the individual publisher.

The Numismatist
Published by the American
Numismatic Association
P.O. Box 2366
Colorado Springs, Colo. 80901

Hobbies Magazine
1106 S. Michigan Ave.
Chicago, Ill. 60605
(Has a coin section)

Numismatic News Weekly
Iola, Wisconsin 54990

COINage Magazine
17337 Ventura Blvd.
Encino, Calif. 91316

Coins Magazine
Iola, Wisconsin 54990

Coin World (Weekly)
P.O. Box 150
Sidney, Ohio 45367

**ARE YOUR COINS GENUINE . . .**
Coin authentication and certification service is available at a fee through the following associations. Coins must not be submitted without first requesting mailing instructions and a schedule of fees charged for this service. Inquiries about coin authentication should be accompanied by a self-addressed stamped envelope and sent to:

American Numismatic Association
Certification Service
818 N. Cascade
Colorado Springs, Colo. 80903

International Numismatic Society
Authentication Bureau
P.O. Box 19386
Washington, D.C. 20036